MICHAEL J. LEWIS is Professor of A
teaches and lectures on art, architec
and is a regular contributor to the N
He is the author of The Gothic Reviva

C000294190

Thames & Hudson world of art

This famous series provides the widest available
range of illustrated books on art in all its aspects.

If you would like to receive a complete list
of titles in print please write to:

THAMES & HUDSON
181A High Holborn
London WC1V 7QX

In the United States please write to:

THAMES & HUDSON INC.
500 Fifth Avenue
New York, New York 10110

Printed in Singapore

Michael J. Lewis

American Art
and Architecture

280 illustrations, 140 in color

 Thames & Hudson world of art

For Günther Kokkelink,
the humane scholar

© 2006 Thames & Hudson Ltd, London

First published in 2006 in paperback in the United States of America by Thames & Hudson Inc., 500 Fifth Avenue, New York, New York 10110

thamesandhudsonusa.com

Library of Congress Catalog Card Number 2005905560

ISBN-13: 978-0-500-20391-0
ISBN-10: 0-500-20391-1

Printed and bound in Singapore by CS Graphics

Frontispiece:
1 **Matthew Pratt**,
The American School (detail), 1765.

Contents

Chapter 1   Graven Images

American art is provincial—in the narrow and technical sense of the word. It is the product of a parent culture removed to a distant location, where local forces and circumstances transform it into something quite different than the original. To say this is not to belittle it. On the contrary, the traffic of ideas and forms from one place to another, their constant movement and change, is the metabolism of culture. If provincial art is often crude, it is seldom static. The stubborn effort to reproduce the forms of a parent culture under sometimes inhospitable circumstances is a spur to vitality and innovation.

So American art began, and like all provincial or colonial culture, it did not instantly achieve autonomy with political independence. The ingrained habit of deferring to the artistic leadership of Europe persisted well into the twentieth century, and perhaps longer. Under these circumstances, American art forms no simple linear sequence, like one that a museum might offer. It has its own path of growth and change, like a living thing, but it is one that is continually revitalized by injections of genetic matter from its source. In order to do justice to this story, a museum would require a strange shape. It would need a second museum running alongside it, devoted to European art, toward which it sometimes converged, sometimes diverged. For times there would be long stretches of corridor without cross-connections, as American art pursued internal paths of development, and at other times broad and generous passages would pour from the European galleries into the American ones, marking the periodic inundations of European influence, as in 1893, 1913, and 1933. At a certain point the two museums might even merge and become one.

Or perhaps not. This book assumes that there is a distinctive phenomenon called American art, and that it has certain common features and patterns that run across the centuries, which permit us to make generalizations about it in the aggregate. Just as we can

2 **Attrib. Nehemiah Partridge**, *Ariaantje Coeymans Verplanck (Mrs. David Verplanck)*, 1718 or c. 1722–24. Grandeur, dignity, and bemusement distinguish the colonies' first full-length portrait of a woman. In 1723 the fifty-one-year-old woman married David Verplanck, aged twenty-eight. The discrepancy in the couple's ages may account for the unusual format, which shows Ariaantje as both rose-bearing bride and confident, commanding woman of wealth—conflating a wedding portrait with a swagger portrait.

Two houses of seventeenth-century Dutch culture on two different continents: *above*, Ariaantje Coeymans's house near Albany, New York, c. 1700–49 [3]; *opposite*, the manor house of Groot Constantia in Stellenbosch, South Africa [4]. In both instances, the designer adapted a formal prototype according to the demands of climate and the availability of materials. The Albany example represents the Dutch model in a much colder climate, the African one, in a much hotter one.

speak of English literature or French cuisine, and group together things that are separated by centuries and many miles, so we can speak collectively about American art. It is a vast and fluid thing, comprising many discrete points. But these points scatter in a distinct pattern and form a shape on the page, and to attempt the most fitting description of that shape is the goal of this book.

Certain attitudes recur with great regularity in the history of American art, of which the strongest is the notion that the role of art is to do something—either to impart a lesson or to effect a change. A contemporary artist who advocates art as "an instrument of social change" is expressing an instrumental view of art that would have been familiar to the Puritan America of the seventeenth century. American art is also profoundly mercantile in character, the legacy of a prosperous country with no inherited aristocracy. It also has persistent formal hallmarks, including a preference for graphic forms with a schematic clarity of outline and contour, disembodied and purged of any properties that might give tactile pleasure, such as the opulence of color or viscous richness of paint. (In this respect American art is not unlike much American food, such as the modern tomato.)

For all these parochial factors and forces, however, the real context for American art is global. Viewed in isolation, it can seem a pale and dispiriting version of the real thing. But when viewed from a global perspective, it is a manifestation of one of the most fateful events in history, the worldwide spread of European culture in the sixteenth and seventeenth centuries. At the start of that period, the civilizations of Europe, Asia, and the Americas were scarcely aware of one another. By its end, the maritime powers of Europe presided over a global commerce of goods and ideas. The five great powers—Spain, Portugal, France, Holland, and England—had colonies on most of the world's continents. There they built brave renditions of the homeland, which, allowing for differences of climate, materials, and the availability of skilled workmen, could look very different indeed.

The product of hardship and scarcity, the American colonial house was often a homespun and crude affair, like that of Ariaantje Coeymans (1672–1743) near Albany, New York [3]. This was a provincial version of the Dutch vernacular of the early seventeenth century, as found in Amsterdam, Rotterdam, and Delft. There was the same late-medieval character, typically built of brick, informal in its window arrangements, with a tiled roof of steep pitch and smartly dressed gable fronts.

Around the time her house was built, Coeymans had herself painted, and with a very different architectural background, strewn with courtly gardens and proud mansarded pavilions [2]. It was no great paradox that the architecture she built differed from the architecture she imagined. The periphery is but a physical place and mentally Ariaantje was at the center of the Dutch world, projecting herself into a European landscape that she would never see. This division is the essence of the colonial experience.

If Ariaantje's house was humble, the mechanism that made it was not. It was the product of a dynamic and flexible system of worldwide sweep, carried by an international mercantile population that ensured that ideas and innovations moved swiftly from center to periphery and from colony to colony. Compare it to its near contemporary, Groot Constantia, a manor house at Stellenbosch, in the Dutch Cape Colony [4]. While other houses might form a compact mass, huddled against the winter, Groot Constantia formed a breezy H-plan, providing cross-ventilation to each room. Without good building stone or wood, the house was limited to a single story built of mud brick, stuccoed and white-washed; in place of a steep tile roof there was a low one of thatch.

Social and economic factors were just as decisive as the material. In the Cape Colony, a flourishing slave economy sustained a mercantile aristocracy of almost feudal power, who gave their houses a swaggering princely character. Each gable end of the H-planned house was enriched into a stately curvilinear frontispiece, multiplying the gables as an example of authority and fashion. In some houses the stepped gable was a builder's conventional solution for a population of farmers and merchants, but in Groot Constantia it becomes the palatial herald of a colonial lord.

But the principal source for American culture was not Holland but England. When a hundred malnourished English colonists straggled ashore at Jamestown, Virginia in 1607, New Spain was a mighty colonial empire already a century old, its outposts reaching to modern New Mexico and Florida. Other nations were vying for spoils as well. New France had just been founded, a colony thin in population but vast in extent, sweeping from Quebec (1608) and Montreal (1611) deep into the river systems of the interior. Even the Dutch would soon install themselves on the Hudson River, where a string of neat towns culminated in the port of New Amsterdam (1625), the Manhattan of today. In this rush for land and treasure, the English were latecomers.

The English advantage lay in their numbers. Unlike the Spanish, French, and Dutch, whose colonies were mercantile operations, the English had religious motives. The first to come, the separatist Pilgrims who founded the colony of Plymouth, Massachusetts (1620), were relatively few in number and their cultural legacy was limited. Much more important were the Puritans, who founded the Massachusetts Bay Colony (1630) and the New Haven Colony (1638), and who came in considerable numbers. During the period of persecution, from 1629 to 1640, a total of perhaps 21,000 ultimately sailed to New England. They also promptly established universities, founding Harvard in 1636. All this gave them an overwhelming cultural influence. With a strong sense of calling that was annealed by persecution, and a compact, cohesive social structure that gave great force to their ideas, the Puritans formed the intelligentsia of the English colonies.

The Puritans might be called double dissenters, Protestants who had broken first with the Catholic Church and then with the established Church of England. They followed the teachings of the Swiss reformer Calvin and practiced an especially strenuous form of Protestantism. Calvinism proposed five theological points and one of these, the idea of the covenant, took on special resonance in New England. The biblical covenant refers to the pact made between God and Abraham, and celebrated in the Old Testament, establishing the Jews as the chosen people of God; Calvin sought a new covenant. The idea was immensely attractive to the Puritans who, as avid readers of the Bible, could not help but see countless parallels between the wanderings of the Jews in the wilderness and their own tribulations, and their common journey into a promised land. Inevitably they came to interpret America in biblical terms, and to see it as the fulfillment of biblical prophecy.

5 **Edward Hicks**, *Peaceable Kingdom*, c. 1834. In this work America is the fulfillment of biblical prophecy. An itinerant Quaker preacher, Hicks turned to painting after 1820 and based his career almost entirely on the repetition of this one subject, a charmingly naive painted sermon. He depicts the lion laying down peacefully with the lamb, while off in the margins William Penn makes his honorable treaty with the Indians for the purchase of Pennsylvania: Eden is portrayed as a benevolent menagerie, under the stewardship of well-meaning Quakers.

As an artistic sourcebook, the Bible read by the Puritans gives two models of perfect divine order: there was the initial paradise of the Garden of Eden before the Fall, as described in the book of Genesis, and the New Jerusalem, the perfected city that would arise after the second coming of Christ, as described in the book of Revelation. Coming from either end of biblical time, Eden and New Jerusalem offered immensely attractive visions of paradise on Earth, one rural and the other urban. These two mutually exclusive visions would haunt the American consciousness for centuries.

At first, the pristine natural state of the American continent—pristine in comparison with the urbanized landscape of Europe—inevitably suggested the Garden of Eden. Its essential wildness was taken as a sign of goodness, not yet spoiled by the depravity of man (another of Calvin's five points). Of course, this goodness was hypothetical in the early stages of colonization. Sentimentality about untamed nature is not a characteristic of young colonial societies. Governor William Bradford of the Plymouth Plantation saw his colony surrounded by "a hideous and desolate wilderness, full of wild beasts and wild men." But the tendency to see America as Eden, as a surviving shard of innocent paradise, was irresistible, and in the early nineteenth century it became a favorite motif in American folk art [5].

Eden may have been an inspiring symbol but gave no guidance for the building of towns. More useful was New Jerusalem, described as a city of stringent rectilinearity, recalling other gridded settlements in the Bible where divine order was expressed through right angles. This conflation of righteousness and rectilinearity became a mainstay of Protestant thought, especially among Pietist denominations. Among the Shakers it was later taken to an extreme, where the rectilinearity of their settlements and personal habits was carried to the limits of obsessiveness (mandating, for example, that food be cut square and that plates never be passed diagonally).

Of course, regular city plans were a staple of Renaissance thought, and had long since been established in the Spanish New World. In 1573 the "Law of the Indies" was passed to regulate the building of Spanish colonial towns, and to prescribe grids organized about a central plaza. But these Spanish grids lacked the religious theme of the Puritan town plan, which was a diagram of moral order and not merely a convenient system for the equable division of real estate.

New Haven, Connecticut was created by the Puritan minister John Davenport (1597–1670), and was the first of America's great gridded cities. It consisted of a square divided into nine equal smaller squares, the central one reserved for the meeting house [6]. But at the same time, the layout, the disposition of the central square, and even the precise dimensions of the lots, were based on the biblical description of the encampment of the Israelites in the wilderness, as detailed in the book of Numbers. Thus Davenport's town was both utilitarian and Utopian: an uninflected grid of Cartesian coordinates at one level, at another it embodied a communal encampment of pilgrims on a biblical journey, a bold gesture that conjured up biblical time in American space.

New Haven's plan was the first of many gridded Utopias, including Philadelphia (1682), Savannah (1733), and the many Pietist towns of the German Moravians. As later settlements were formed for mercantile rather than religious reasons, they shed the explicitly religious content of the grid, but its rationality and visual clarity became a hallmark of American urbanism. The grid also had the merit of being capable of infinite horizontal extension. In the grid's open-ended geometry, spreading open-handedly and grinning in every direction, it is a diagram of a society without constraint or enemies. This idea was utterly alien to the urbanism of Europe. There the contours of cities were fixed by the stone cinctures of medieval or Baroque fortifications, enforcing density and establishing a strict spatial hierarchy that persisted even after the fortifications were dismantled. This ability to project the city into the country, inherent in American urbanism, has had destructive consequences in the twentieth century.

The Puritan spatial order meant that the entire community was holy, while the physical place of worship itself was not especially sacred. This was called a meeting house, not a church, in order to distinguish it from its Catholic counterparts. In every other respect as well it toppled church forms deliberately. Where a Catholic church was longitudinal in shape, creating a processional hierarchy toward the altar, the meeting house was given a centralized character, like a lecture hall. Where a Catholic church was oriented toward the east, where the rising sun offered a metaphor of spiritual redemption, the meeting house placed its main entrance on the south, like a normal house, which its form resembled. Within was a plain wooden box of a room, stripped bare of all artistic distraction [7].

6 **William Lyon**, *A Plan of the Town of New Haven with all the Buildings in 1748.* This plan fulfills the verse in Psalm 122: "Jerusalem is builded as a city that is compact together." An image of righteousness, enforced through the right angle, and serving both as a diagram of divine order as well as a practical grid for land division, it announced the paradox of idealism and utilitarianism that runs throughout American culture.

This barrenness had the deepest theological justification, and had the authority of the Second Commandment: *thou shalt not make graven images.* This was generally understood as prohibiting idol worship, but reformers such as Calvin and Zwingli interpreted it as a comprehensive ban on all religious imagery. They condemned the visual world of Catholicism—its entire apparatus of carved and gilded altars, statues of saints, stained glass, wall paintings—which they took to be a physical expression of spiritual depravity. In this they were far more extreme than English Anglicans or German Lutherans, who tolerated a discreet amount of religious art. But the iconoclasm of the Puritans was absolute and invincible.

Purged of all sacred ritual and pomp, Puritan worship was an affair of the spoken word. Two sermons, each about two hours in

7 Old Ship Meeting House, Hingham, Massachusetts (1681, with later additions). This is the best preserved of New England's seventeenth-century meeting houses. Austere and sturdy, with no decoration apart from an occasional staring eye painted upon the pulpit, such meeting houses were preaching spaces, in which the spoken and the sung word was intended to reverberate, emphasizing the collective nature of the congregation.

length and delivered in a plain and austere style, constituted the Sunday service; a lengthy prayer, delivered standing, might add another hour or two. The sermons were rather formal in structure, beginning with a biblical text that was unraveled in a lengthy process of explication called "the finding out." In the end, a lesson was extracted and an injunction given to the congregation. This weekly five- or six-hour session—verbal, not visual—was the fundamental aesthetic experience of Puritan America.

Although not visual, a sermon aroused certain psychological expectations that might be asked of the pictorial arts. A successful sermon was legible and followed a lucid narrative line, free of ambiguity; from it, the listener was meant to draw a moral. A culture attuned to these sermons was susceptible to moralizing argumentation, and willing to receive didactic instruction. And when large-scale high art (as opposed to mere portraiture) did eventually assert itself, it did so as a vehicle of public instruction.

Puritan society was also abstemious about sensual delight. Clothing and food, like the visual world, were drained of tactile pleasure. New England food was notorious for its blandness (boiled beans and meat, for instance, unlike the fried foods of Virginia) and lack of spice. Sumptuary laws also restricted clothing, and punished the wearing of too many bright ribbons or too many slits in the sleeves (to permit peeks at the richer colors underneath). The necessity of food and clothing were accepted, but the amount of pleasure to be taken from them was restricted. Under no circumstances was tactile physical pleasure a justification for anything, not in the kitchen nor in any other room of the house.

A culture that justified itself through moral argumentation and that frowned on sensory stimulation would extend these attitudes to art. It would produce a moralizing and realistic art, didactic in purpose and with a strong graphic character. It would also pay more attention to outlines and contours than to the expressive plastic modeling of form. The first paintings known to be produced in the Puritan colonies date from the 1660s. Several dozen survive, nearly all poorly documented and poorly preserved. Without exception these were portraits, which posed no problems for Puritans since there was no danger of idolatry.

It is not clear if these paintings are the work of amateur artisans or immigrants with some artistic training. Quality cannot be used to distinguish them, as there were bad artists in Europe as well. The names of several Boston painters are known, but it has been impossible to assign them to the surviving paintings. John Foster (1648–81) was a Harvard graduate who became a printer and publisher. Although he was called a "cunning artist," his only attested work is a crude woodcut of the Reverend Richard Mather. We know more about the sea captain Thomas Smith (active c. 1650–90), who has left an accomplished self-portrait and from whom Harvard commissioned a portrait in 1680. Foster and Smith were evidently amateurs, however, unlike Augustine Clement (c. 1600–74), an English painter who emigrated to America in 1635. He and his son Samuel Clement (c. 1635–78) were Boston's first professional painters.

These four men, and perhaps several others, worked in two different modes, both of them provincial. There was a distinctly old-fashioned mode, recalling the Elizabethan painting of the late sixteenth century, and a newer Baroque mode, with a decidedly Dutch influence. The Elizabethan paintings comprise a distinct group of ten or so, painted between 1670 and 1674. Several give the age of the sitter under the Latin inscription *aetatis suae* (his/her age). All show a similar technique, particularly in their concentrated linear expression—apparent not only in the meticulous delineation of fabric but also in the conception of the face. In medieval fashion, the light falls on everything evenly and without drama. Light and shade are used descriptively, to model form, rather than expressively; there is no moody chiaroscuro. Nor is there any visual hierarchy of objects; if anything, more attention is lavished on the lace than on the face.

The most haunting of these paintings is *Elizabeth Clarke Freake and Baby Mary* [8], which forms a pair with the portrait of her husband John Freake. Elizabeth Freake (1642–1712/13) was shown as a pious Puritan, although relieved by a glint of humor and a touching pride in her appearance, and the wisp of reddish-yellow hair that strays from under her bonnet; there is a wry alertness in her eyes. The color is strong, with flat areas of bright color, vermilion and terre-verte, and there is a limited but skilled amount of modeling. It is by far the best of seventeenth-century American portraits, because it is free of any stiff masklike quality, and because of the sly enigmatic quality of the expression.

In style, *Elizabeth Clarke Freake and Baby Mary* is utterly unlike anything in contemporary Europe; it shows no awareness of the court style of Rubens and Van Dyck, or of the achievements of Dutch realism. Its technique is archaic. In fact, there is nothing in it that would have been unfamiliar to Holbein a century earlier,

8 **Anonymous**, *Elizabeth Clarke Freake and Baby Mary*, *c.* 1671/74. By the 1670s, the stern Puritan injunctions against worldly display and the wearing of ribbons were breaking down. This painting captures the slackening strictures against pomp. When first painted sometime around 1671, Elizabeth Freake was shown alone; three years later the baby was added, along with the red and black ribbons and jewelry, while her black dress was changed to green.

making it a kind of living fossil of Elizabethan painting. This argues strongly for Samuel Clement, who was taught by his father, whose own artistic education took place in provincial Reading, England, before 1635. The case is circumstantial, but it has the great merit of explaining how the Freake painter was so serenely ignorant of any development in European art since the start of the century.

Thomas Smith, as a mariner, was a more cosmopolitan painter and had presumably seen modern Netherlandish art; he certainly knew that light and shadow could be manipulated dynamically for expressive purposes [9]. His self-portrait of about 16980 treats him as a solid form, a sculptural mass instead of a linear pattern, while the window to the left suggests deep projection into space. And the complex allegory of the painting is Baroque: even as the distant sea battle trumpets Smith's victories, his lengthy handwritten poem chides him for his earthly vanity, a meaning underscored by the skull atop it, a *memento mori* or reminder of

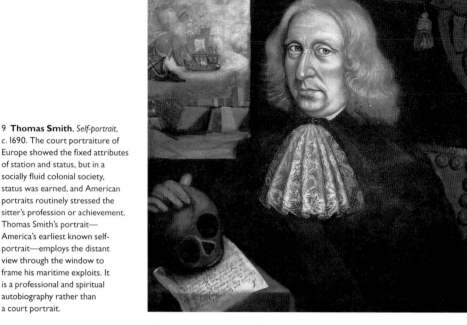

9 **Thomas Smith**, *Self-portrait*, c. 1690. The court portraiture of Europe showed the fixed attributes of station and status, but in a socially fluid colonial society, status was earned, and American portraits routinely stressed the sitter's profession or achievement. Thomas Smith's portrait—America's earliest known self-portrait—employs the distant view through the window to frame his maritime exploits. It is a professional and spiritual autobiography rather than a court portrait.

death. The pessimism and self-questioning is Puritan, as is Smith's "sadd" clothing, but the artistic expression shows a new awareness of a modern world.

Smith's competent provincial realism did not immediately supplant the Elizabethan mode of the Freake painter. Although wildly out of date, its linearity, flatness, and straightforward descriptiveness strongly appealed to the Puritan sensibility. It presented an acceptable alternative to what was otherwise the great preoccupation of Western art since the Renaissance: depicting the tangible corporeality of the human body. In any event, the Elizabethan mode had persisted long enough in New England to form a regional vernacular, in which form it lived on in the folk painting of the eighteenth and nineteenth centuries.

Another painting tradition survived in the prosperous Dutch settlements along the Hudson River basin, with their mercantile burghers or patroons. Although Calvinist as well, they were not averse to the display of luxury, and portraits are known from as early as the 1660s (although they may well have been imported). But in 1664 the English conquered the colony, isolating the culture and cutting it off from regular contact with Holland and with

Dutch art. Portraiture continued, however, probably in the form of an inherited family trade, and displayed a gradual tendency toward simplification and flatness.

In the decades after 1700 the patroon painters flourished. As in New England, we have names and we have paintings, but rarely can we put them together. The known artists include Gerardus Duyckinck, Pieter Vanderlyn, and Nehemiah Partridge, to whom the portrait of Ariaantje Coeymans has been attributed [2]. Coeymans is typical of Partridge's subjects, who are usually stately and poised figures and hold their arms stiffly in emphatic gestures. Although forceful in their expressive outlines, the results are rudimentary in the depiction of volume and in the modeling of form with shadow and color. Foreshortening also seems to have been beyond Partridge, who created depth almost entirely by overlapping. On the other hand, his imaginary architecture is quite realistic, suggesting the hand of a proficient technical draftsman who was nevertheless uncertain with the brush.

In architecture as well, medieval practices persisted until the end of the seventeenth century. The earliest were evidently small framed houses with thatched roofs and consisting of only a room or two. Since most of the Puritans were from East Anglia, they brought with them the highly developed timber architecture of eastern England. The house was constructed as a self-supporting frame, whose members were joined by dovetailed or mortise and tenon joints, which were then pegged into place. (Nails were a luxury well into the eighteenth century.) This supple lattice could then be enclosed according to the demands of climate and economy. The infill could be as massive as brick or as insubstantial as mud and straw, but in New England, where hot damp summers alternated with cold winters, a crisp cladding of oak clapboards proved driest and cheapest.

The best preserved of Puritan houses is that of Parson Joseph Capen (1658–1725), a graduate of Harvard who became the minister of Topsfield, Massachusetts in 1682. According to a carved beam in the parlor, the house was built on "July 8th Ye 1683," presumably the day on which its oak frame was raised and pegged into place. Despite the modern reconstruction of its chimney and diamond-paned windows, the house is remarkably well preserved and testifies to the persistence of medieval features throughout the seventeenth century.

Most conspicuous of these is the bold overhang of the house, or "jetty." This was adorned by pendants ("pendills" in the seventeenth century) that hung beneath it, another vestigial medievalism, the only carved ornament in the entire house [10]. The origin of the overhang is unclear. It has been suggested that it conserved precious street space in the medieval city, a consideration that would not count for much in the American countryside. More likely, it was devised to prevent the upper stories, which were used for storage, from sagging. (By placing weight to either side of the frame, the beam was kept in balanced tension.) Whatever the origin, the form lingered for decades in the New World, only gradually shrinking to vestigial insignificance.

At the core of the Capen House was placed the mighty stone mass of the chimney, which husbanded its warmth, and allowed for an open fire to either side. Around this spine the house was organized, with a hall to one side and a formal parlor to the other.

Although the plan appears symmetrical at first glance, the parlor to the west is distinctly larger than the hall. The absolute lack of interest in architectural formality—or indeed any formality whatsoever—is yet another medievalism of the Capen House.

10 Parson Joseph Capen House, Topsfield, Massachusetts, 1683. The house retains a wealth of late medieval features: the verticality of the roofline, smallness of the windows, and the prominence of the deep overhang. No distinction is made between public and private areas; the visitor enters immediately into a family living hall, as in medieval usage. It would have been painted in earth tones, the ochers that were the most readily available colors (the idea that colonial America was blazing white is a later misconception, derived from the Greek Revival).

11 Parson Joseph Capen House, Topsfield, Massachusetts, 1683. The parlor shows the upper end of Puritan luxury in the seventeenth century: a low-ceilinged room with exposed beams, measuring about 17 by 19 feet (5.3 by 6 meters). The walls are either plastered or paneled, and no effort is made to give them any formal architectural unity, as in the Palladian houses of the next century [31].

12 Harrison-Linsley House, Branford, Connecticut, 1690. Cross-section of lean-to addition. The saltbox house is perhaps the first indigenous creation of American architecture, the first in which the adaptation of English models to local conditions produced a new, authoritative form. Open to the sun in the south and huddling to the ground in the north, its taut efficient contour was shaped entirely by climate and function—the product of impersonal forces rather than conscious invention.

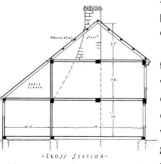

· CROSS SECTION ·
♪ HARRISON-LINSLEY HOUSE -BRANFORD ♪

The stair hall was certainly not a place of formal display, as it would later come to be. It was kept as small as possible, a simple closet with a utilitarian winder stair, the medieval type of stair which spiraled upward around a central newel, into which the treads were fitted.

In the seventeenth century, the word hall had not acquired its modern meaning of a passage between one part of the house and another. That of the Capen House still had its medieval meaning: an all-purpose undifferentiated space that served as kitchen, dining room, living room, and even bedroom. Space was not arranged in a hierarchy of formal and informal spaces. Privacy was not yet a value, nor was modesty, and all aspects of life went on in common space. Whatever formal functions might occur took place in the parlor, which was evidently not heated during the winter except on special occasions [11].

The Capen House is unusual in preserving its compact original form; most seventeenth-century houses expanded as more rooms were needed, growing by accretion. The most sensible way to enlarge a house was to the rear, which preserved the principal entrance. An additional room or two were placed along the north wall, over which the slope of the roof was extended toward the ground [12]. This formal consideration also had practical benefits, and helped shelter the colder northern exposure of the house.

13 Stanley-Whitman House, Farmington, Connecticut, 1720. When saltboxes are the result of an enlargement, as here, they are usually recognizable by the uneven settling of the roof in the main body of the house and the addition; in later houses, in which the rear wing was intended from the beginning, the roof shows a continual slope. The Stanley-Whitman House in Farmington was built in about 1720 (not 1660, as was once believed) and is a very late example of a deeply projecting overhang or jetty.

This peculiar fitness of shape ensured its success, and the form soon came to look normal. Already by the end of the century the form was being built intentionally [13]. Although the saltbox was eclipsed during the course of the next century by the fashionable Palladian mode, it proved durable in the hinterlands where examples were built up to the Revolution.

Outside the orbit of dissenting New England, the American colonies much more closely resembled England, with its established Church and stratified class structure. This was especially true in the South. With no Puritan strictures against pomp and ceremony, painting and architecture permitted a swagger and ostentation not acceptable in Boston or New Haven. Churches here followed the form of Anglican worship, usually a longitudinal vessel oriented to the east and entered from a tower at the west. Most would be simple classical brick boxes but the earliest surviving example, St. Luke's, near Smithfield, Virginia (1632) is Gothic [14]. This is perhaps not as remarkable as it seems. For a century after the Protestant Reformation in 1531, there was little church-building, and well into the next century England continued to build haphazardly in a late Gothic style. St. Luke's is a stray offshoot of that process.

Both society and landscape were marked by great inequality in the South, produced by the plantation economy sustained by slave labor. There was no compact unity of towns and family farms, as in New England. The self-sufficient plantation, rather than the meeting house on the green, was the principal determinant of the spatial order. And where formal towns arose, such as the capitals of Annapolis, Maryland and Williamsburg, Virginia, they were not egalitarian grids but dynamic Baroque creations.

Annapolis and Williamsburg were each the creation of Francis Nicholson (1655–1728), who governed first Maryland and then Virginia (and several other colonies in turn). A professional administrator, Nicholson understood that a capital requires a certain ceremonial dignity, with public buildings commanding formal squares and monumental axes. His Annapolis (1695) was a

14 St. Luke's, Smithfield, Isle of Wight County, Virginia, c. 1632. The church was altered in 1657, when the classical pediment over the entrance was probably added. Apart from this, its forms are strictly medieval features: pointed arches, buttresses, brick tracery of the windows, and the stepped gable at the east end—a baffled Gothic survivor in the New World.

baffling array of converging diagonals and public squares, both circular and square in form. Williamsburg (1699) improved upon this with a simpler but bolder scheme, a grand processional axis that led from the College of William and Mary in the west to the Capitol in the east [15]. Here was all the pomp and ceremony of William and Mary's reign, but compressed and abridged to play in the provinces.

Nicholson regularly sailed between England and America, and his plans show familiarity with the latest English trends. He will have known the English Baroque embodied in the sumptuous churches and palaces of Christopher Wren in London. This dry but vigorous Baroque lacked the voluptuous curvilinearity of the Italian version but compensated in the great animation of its multiple parts and wings. Perhaps he consulted with Wren in 1693 when making his plan for Annapolis, a shrunken version of Wren's proposal for rebuilding London after the fire of 1666. Wren's name is also associated with the original William and Mary building (although any drawings he might have made were drastically simplified in execution).

The spirited gestures of the Baroque influence touched plantation houses as well. Several dozen great manor houses rose, strung out like pearls along the four great rivers of Tidewater Virginia (the James, the York, the Potomac, and the Rappahannock). A full-blown English Baroque, of the order of John Vanbrugh's majestic Blenheim Palace, was out of the question, but some of the larger plantation houses showed a plucky provincial Baroque. Among these were several animated H-plan houses, such as Tuckahoe and Stratford [16]. Stratford shows the limits of American swagger. In England it would have been wrapped with pilasters and cornices, a dandy in court dress, but here it is a nude athlete, asserting its form entirely through the play of vigorous brick masses, which is playfully echoed in the grouped chimneys above. Only in the formal central hall, a room that is nearly 30 feet (9 meters) square, is there a full array of Corinthian columns carrying a rich entablature. As so often will be the case, the opulence and richness is provided by carpentry rather than sculpture.

By the time Stratford was finished, its Baroque play of volumes had fallen from fashion. Its successors abandoned the H-plan, which placed too much attention on the periphery. They preferred the cool formality of the center hall plan, which culminated in an attractive pedimented frontispiece. Westover,

15 The Bodleian plate engraving, showing the principal public buildings of Williamsburg, Virginia. The southern colonies, largely unaffected by religious separatists and Pietists, could indulge in the theatrics and ceremonial hierarchies of the Baroque. In Williamsburg, a monumental axis led from the College of William and Mary at the west to the Capitol in the east; a cross axis led to the governor's palace. Its conception of space was ceremonial, processional, and hierarchical—everything that the Puritan grid loathed and sought to avoid [6].

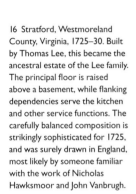

16 Stratford, Westmoreland County, Virginia, 1725–30. Built by Thomas Lee, this became the ancestral estate of the Lee family. The principal floor is raised above a basement, while flanking dependencies serve the kitchen and other service functions. The carefully balanced composition is strikingly sophisticated for 1725, and was surely drawn in England, most likely by someone familiar with the work of Nicholas Hawksmoor and John Vanbrugh.

the Byrd Mansion in Charles City County (c. 1730–34) and Carter's Grove, James City County (1750–53) were simple and stately brick volumes, whose elegance was reserved for the sumptuous stair hall and drawing rooms of the interior.

Other than Stratford, and a few other examples in the southern states, the Baroque was invariably defeated by the essential boxiness of the American building. Where ecstatic curves came in, they were never more than decorative trills on an otherwise foursquare body. A church steeple might erupt into a concave–convex sequence, billowing in and out as it rose; the pediment over a door might break into a pair of rolling scrolls; a Queen Anne high chest might perch on shapely legs, but these were exceptions. Otherwise American architecture was distinguished by its distinct straight-legged stiffness, the legacy certainly of carpentry, but perhaps also of temperament.

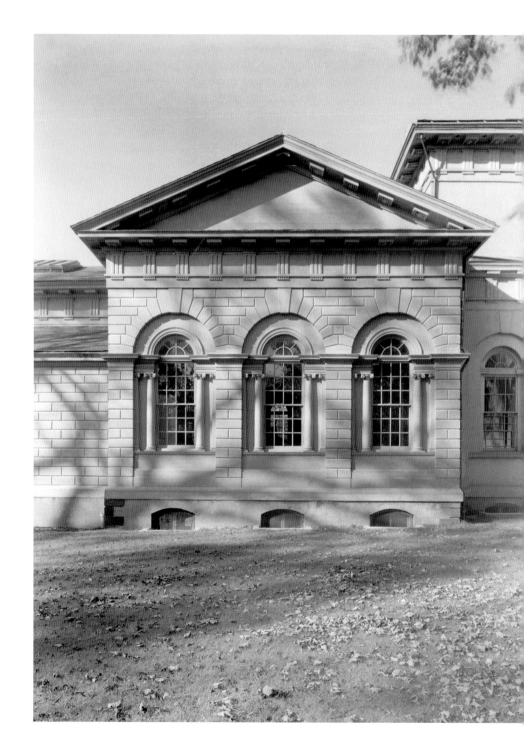

Chapter 2 Flattened Form

The most important development that distinguished the art of the eighteenth century from that of the seventeenth was a new self-consciousness about formality. Originating in the polite culture of Renaissance Italy, this concern about social and artistic etiquette came slowly to the New World, and even to England. The insights and discoveries of the Italian Renaissance filtered through slowly and belatedly, even more slowly after the Protestant Reformation placed a religious barrier between England and Italy. England emerged from the Middle Ages only gradually and late into the seventeenth century; here public and private life were still medieval in essence. Samuel Pepys's diary of the 1660s—that peerless source of private life—records in one jolly entry how he summoned his chambermaid to sit with him and his wife on their bed so that they could sing in three-part harmony. Such a casual intimacy with servants would have been shocking to the mannered society of the eighteenth century, a radically different society with a radically new self-consciousness about formality and artifice. The reasons for this are varied, ranging from the growth of mercantile wealth to the importation of continental etiquette into England, but the consequence was a drastic reordering of taste and fashion. Signs of this are everywhere, from the rejection of Shakespeare as uncouth and obscene to the discovery of table manners and finger bowls (unknown in seventeenth-century England).

The new sense of formality and artifice was carried after 1700 to the mercantile classes of the English colonies, where it quickly made its way into art, architecture, and even body language. Contrast the pose of Elizabeth Clarke Freake [8] with that of Mrs. William Bowdoin, its counterpart of the 1740s [23]: the one is unselfconscious and placid, while the other strikes a contrived and mannered pose, one in vogue in England. And so the new formality came to touch even personal bearing and carriage, on both sides of the Atlantic.

17 **Peter Harrison**, Redwood Library, Newport, Rhode Island, 1748–50.

18 **Gustav Hesselius**, *Lapowinsa*, 1735. One of a pair of portraits of Indian chieftains by Gustav Hesselius, this is a triumph of empirical observation. Because the Indian stood outside the social hierarchy of colonial society, he was outside the rigid conventions of artifice and formality that normally governed the making of a portrait; Hesselius was among the first painters to understand this, and simply to look and record. His portrait anticipates the sympathetic and unaffected realism that would distinguish much American portraiture.

19 **Jeremiah Theus**, *Elizabeth Rothmaler*, 1757. Like most eighteenth-century artists in America, Jeremiah Theus did not use drapery to describe anatomy, as in classical practice, but to conceal it beneath an attractive decorative flourish. He repeated the exact arrangement of dress folds in virtually every one of his female portraits. Occasionally, however, a sense of personal life escaped beyond the rigid format, as in this portrait, where the splash of ribbon and pearls at the sitter's bosom serves as a pendant to the lively poised face above.

These changes were felt in architecture as well. The facade of a building became a matter of decorum, in which correctness of form and propriety counted for everything, the literal act of "putting up a good front." Function now took a back seat to rhetoric and appearance. Even the conception of interior space changed as the separation of public formality and private informality became strictly regulated. Medieval society did not value personal privacy but the eighteenth century did, very much so. The interiors of houses were now segregated into private and public realms, requiring the introduction of corridors—spaces purely for public passage. The word "hall" lost its original meaning and was transferred to the broad passage through the center of the house where the main stair was located. What had been a tiny closet of space in the saltbox now expanded to become a formal space of reception and ceremony, screened from the more private precincts of the house. Even the stair became a formal object, unlike the functional winder of the saltbox, and it boasted lavishly carved balusters and a newel post, serving much the same gratuitous display function as, for example, the hood ornament of a 1950s Cadillac.

The new public demand for emblems of status and formality meant for the first time that professional artists might expect to earn a living in the colonies. After 1700 the first European painters began to trickle in to the larger cities. In 1708 there arrived the German painter Justus Engelhardt Kühn (died 1717), followed in 1711 by the Swedish painter Gustav Hesselius (1682–1755), in 1727 by the English engraver and painter Peter Pelham (1697–1751), and in 1735 by Jeremiah Theus (1716–74), a Swiss-born painter. Quite understandably, these artists distributed themselves across the colonies—Hesselius in Philadelphia, Kühn in Annapolis, Pelham in Boston, and Theus in Charleston—so as not to exhaust the fragile local patronage. Isolated in this way, and at the periphery of the European artistic world, they were too fragmentary to form an artistic community; this required a critical mass that was not in place until the end of the century.

None of these artists was of the first rank, nor would an artist of the first rank have wanted to test his luck in the colonies. The best of the lot was Hesselius, who had been steeped in the late Baroque mode of Europe and was capable of genuine insight and pathos, as in his portraits of the Delaware chiefs Lapowinsa [18] and Tishcohan. Theus's portraits were more formulaic, and more repetitive, which is to be expected from a fashionable society

painter. He specialized in half-length swagger portraits, depicting the Charleston elite in its leisured finery [19]. His paintings are the counterpart to the flourishing architectural culture of South Carolina, where the slave economy and wealth, and perhaps a certain French influence from the Caribbean, encouraged a brasher attitude toward display and pomp.

But none of these artists could make a living solely by painting portraits and the occasional altarpiece. Thus Theus's advertisement in a Charleston newspaper described his versatile studio as a place "where all Gentlemen and Ladies may have their Pictures drawn, likewise Landskips of all Sizes, Crests, and Coats of Arms for Coaches or Chaises." And even the accomplished Hesselius had to resort to painting the walls of buildings, as he did at the Pennsylvania State House.

The first artist of high rank to arrive did so by accident. John Smibert (1688–1751) was a Scotsman who studied in London at the famed academy of Godfrey Kneller, later traveling to Italy where he lived for several years. He returned in the early 1720s to establish himself in London, where he set up a profitable portrait studio. But perhaps not profitable enough: in 1728 he sailed with George Berkeley, Dean of Derry, to found a college in Bermuda for the education and conversion of the local Indians. He had been traveling in Italy when he met Berkeley, who thought he would make a splendid professor of painting and architecture for the Bermuda College.

20 **John Smibert**, *The Bermuda Group: Dean George Berkeley and His Family*, 1729. The painting's composition ingeniously integrates Dean Berkeley with his family and followers, while also setting him apart in a virtually independent portrait as a visionary. The painter himself, wigless and diffident, peers out from the extreme left of the painting, clasping a scroll.

Berkeley made it no farther than Newport, Rhode Island. His expected funding never materialized and he sailed home, later becoming the celebrated Bishop of Cork. The only tangible result of his college was Smibert's group portrait *The Bermuda Group: Dean George Berkeley and His Family* (1729) [20]. The painting, which depicted the entourage on the eve of their departure, would have been startling to American eyes. Not only

was the accomplished drawing of the figures remarkable but so was the animated ease with which they were placed in space. Instead of the usual Colonial formula of a stolid mass at the center, the painting's energy was tossed from figure to figure by a lively play of darting glances and casual gestures. This was a "conversation piece," a genre new to America, in which figures were shown in free and spirited interaction. The sprightly sense of movement was reinforced by the new color sensibility, the rich dark reds, golds, and blues of the Baroque. Smibert's color was not simply a flat thick plane of pigment, but was variously translucent or transparent as it moved from light into shadow.

By the time Berkeley gave up his brave dreams of Bermuda, Smibert had put down roots, marrying a prominent local woman and setting himself up in Boston as a portrait painter and occasional architect (he designed the first part of Faneuil Hall in 1741). Over the next two decades he painted perhaps 250 portraits for Boston's mercantile elite. These were demanding clients: we have a poignant letter from Smibert to his agent in England, requesting a book of ship illustrations so that he might insert them "in a distant view in Portraits of Merchts etc who chuse such … but they must be in the modern construction." Evidently his clients' conception of a painting could be quite maddeningly literal.

Nonetheless, like Hesselius and Theus, he too needed a sideline and in 1734 he opened a "color store," out of which he sold paints, painted fans, frames, and European prints. There he displayed his collection, both his own paintings and those he had purchased or copied in Europe, establishing the first public gallery in America. Smibert's collection remained intact for some time after his death, serving as an inspiration for the next generation of American painters, particularly Copley. A notice in a Boston newspaper offers a window into the activities of Smibert's lively store, a description of a runaway black manservant named Cuffee who wore "a pair of Leather Breeches stain'd with divers sorts of paint."

Of all of Smibert's work, his *Bermuda Group*, by far the most monumental work of pictorial art in the English colonies, exerted the strongest influence. It is easy to see that a prosperous young man, conscious of rank and status, might also wish to be depicted in precisely the same manner. This was Isaac Royall, the Medford rum merchant who was one of the wealthiest citizens of New England. Royall had inherited his father's house, which included quarters for twenty-three slaves, and promptly enlarged it [21]. Just

21 Isaac Royall House, Medford, Massachusetts, 1733–37 and 1747–50. This makes a striking comparison with Parson Capen's House [10]. While Capen felt free to make one side of his house slightly larger than the other, Royall was bound to an inflexible axial symmetry. His house was conceived as a formal frontispiece, precisely composed into five bays and crowned by a classical cornice, each element of which was proportioned according to the rules governing the classical orders. It did not matter that behind this frontispiece the house was still a heavy timber frame like Capen's; what counted was the visible image and not the invisible construction that carried it.

as his house cultivated an air of refinement and decorum, so did his family portrait, which he commissioned in 1741 from the Newport painter Robert Feke [22].

Royall evidently wanted a paraphrase of *The Bermuda Group*, for so faithfully does *Isaac Royall and His Family* quote it that one wonders if Smibert granted the younger artist the run of his studio. The same red tablecloth anchors the composition; the same figure at the far right turns haughtily from his book; and the same blue gown appears, although now worn by Mrs. Royall rather than by "Miss Hancock," the central figure in Smibert's work. But the differences are perhaps more telling. Feke's composition is additive, each figure detached and self-contained; and in place of Smibert's deep Baroque space the figures are crowded here into a thin plane of space. They are patterns and shapes fixed on the page, like stencils, rather than volumes inhabiting a three-dimensional universe. And Feke's handling of paint is less sensitive than Smibert's. Instead of softly rounding shapes in half-light, and giving them translucent shadows, he gives a much narrower range of lights and darks. The result is a composition of hard, strong outlines set in the midst of darkness.

The shadowy Robert Feke (c. 1707–52) was America's first native-born artist of note. Born on Long Island, he is recorded as a "mariner," although by the time he painted Royall, he was already an experienced painter. About his training absolutely nothing is known, and one should take skeptically a contemporary account that reports he acquired his "force of genius, without teaching." Might Smibert have given him some lessons? On the other hand, some of his best paintings have the unaffected bluntness of the self-taught artist, who simply draws what he sees. These include his self-portraits or his haughty head of the Baptist minister Rev. Hiscox, who evidently wanted no portrait of aristocratic vanity.

These were the exceptions, for the vast majority of Feke's work consisted of adaptations of carefully chosen models. The patron first chose from among a small selection of mezzotints, presumably belonging to the artist. These offered a range of formulaic poses: the men invariably stood ramrod straight, with a hand at the waist, while women were seated, wearing a variant of the same low-bodiced dress. After transferring the composition of the mezzotint to the canvas, Feke then added his sitter's face from life, perhaps the hands as well.

22 **Robert Feke**, *Isaac Royall and His Family*, 1741. By the time of Isaac Royall, Puritan New England had traveled far from its seventeenth-century sobriety. In Feke's portrait, Royall is an elegant grandee, comfortably ensconced amid his earthly pomp. As their name foretells, the Royalls were staunchly loyal to the crown and they fled to England during the Revolution.

23 **Robert Feke**, *Portrait of Mrs. William Bowdoin (née Phebe Murdock)*, 1748. As was his custom, Feke modeled this portrait on a mezzotint, which was in turn based on a portrait of Anne Oldfield by the English painter Joseph Richardson. The pale silvers and pastel tones are typical of Feke, and reflect the post-Baroque turn to a lighter palette and a generally more delicate sensibility.

24 Mezzotint of Anne Oldfield, print by Faber after Jonathan Richardson, 1705–40.

Feke's portrait of Mrs. William Bowdoin (Phebe Murdock), one of four Bowdoin portraits he made in 1748, is one of the best [23]. Only the face was based on direct observation; otherwise, the folds and ripples of her silk and satin fabric were improvisations, loosely based on the English original. In the process, the nature of these folds changed, becoming so much decorative patterning, consisting of flat areas of dark and light, without reference to the form of the body beneath. Shapes that in the mezzotint had described the bulge and roundness of the human form now became purely decorative passages, given over to the shimmering play of satin.

If this pirating of print sources strikes us as artificial and false, it is no more so than saying "please" and "thank you": it is the ritualized repetition of formal statements that comprises the world of etiquette. *Mrs. William Bowdoin* should not be judged as an essay in originality or personal creativity, qualities that neither she nor Feke sought. She desired an image of respectability and refinement, which means being correct rather than being novel, and for this she needed a model sanctioned by polite society.

The same practice was followed in architecture, and with similar results. In 1749 the architect Peter Harrison based his design for the Redwood Library and Athenaeum in Newport on the work of Andrea Palladio (1508–80), the Italian Renaissance architect [17, 25 and 26]. One should say, however, that Harrison did not re-create Palladio's architecture but made an image of it. Unlike its masonry prototype, his building was made of wood boards, which were rubbed with a mixture of sand and paint to give them the texture of stone. This was a sham but Americans admired the ingenuity. Even George Washington marveled at Harrison's "rusticated boards," and borrowed the technique for his own house at Mount Vernon; Thomas Jefferson would do the same at Monticello.

Harrison's facade and Feke's *Mrs. William Bowdoin* each show a characteristic American response to European models. In each case, the European prototype was fully plastic in conception: Palladio's voluptuous and sculptural form of classicism and Joseph Richardson's finely modeled portrait. And in each case the American rendition was curiously flattened in expression, and given a quality of schematic abstraction. Of course it is in the nature of wood construction to produce a thin planar object, but

25 **Peter Harrison**, Redwood Library, Newport, Rhode Island, 1748–50. Redwood Library, America's first subscription library, was also America's first fully Palladian building. The career of Peter Harrison (1716–75) shows how connections and sheer luck might elevate the craftsman to a professional. Born to Quaker parents in York, England, Harrison trained as a carpenter and later went to sea. He was captured by a privateer and interned at the French fortress of Louisburg in Nova Scotia, of which he made careful drawings. These he later passed on to the governor of Massachusetts, William Shirley, who promptly captured Louisburg in 1745. Shirley's patronage made Harrison's career.

26 **Edward Hoppus**, plate from Andrea Palladio's *Architecture, Book IV*, 1735.

Harrison's facade is virtually a diagram, and has no integral relationship to what lies behind it. It is a mere billboard of an image, affixed to a building that in construction is essentially the same as Parson Capen's house [10 and 11].

Harrison made his career by replicating the buildings of Palladio in Newport and Boston. He was the primary instigator of the Palladian revival that had swept England after 1715, and which now reached America. The Palladian revival was a curious thing: a Catholic architect of sixteenth-century Italy suddenly became the principal architect of Protestant England in the eighteenth century. In fact, Palladio's native Veneto region was rather similar to England and America, part of a mercantile republic with a landed aristocracy whose estates were working farms. The clear geometric forms of his buildings, their cubes, rectangles, and cylinders, had a visual clarity and sobriety that appealed more to English Protestant taste than recent Italian architecture, then in its florid late Baroque phase. Best of all, Palladio's architecture was infinitely adaptable, since it was based on proportional rules that could be applied to buildings of any size and any material—brick, stone, or stucco—depending on the budget and local circumstances. And his *Four Books of Architecture* (1570), perhaps the most accessible and influential manual of architectural practice ever written, was widely available in cheap, illustrated translation.

After 1715 Palladio's designs began to be revised for modern consumption and there gushed forth a torrent of sumptuous pattern books, which adapted him to modern use, showing how an Italian farmhouse might be reconfigured to serve as an English manor house. Many of these books were sponsored by the dilettante Lord Burlington, who built himself a mock Palladian villa and even managed to acquire Palladio's surviving drawings. But the most influential was surely James Gibbs's *A Book of Architecture* (1728), which brought the Palladian mode to America.

Gibbs's great contribution to America was the steeple, the dominant element of the colonial skyline. As an architectural form, the steeple was unknown to classical antiquity, and was developed only in the Christian churches of the Middle Ages. Palladio gave no guidance for this decidedly unclassical shape. After the London fire of 1666, however, Christopher Wren designed an array of classical steeples, either by placing a classical cupola atop a brick tower or by superimposing a stack of cupolas

27 **William Price**, Old North
Church, Boston, 1723. The tower
is among the first classical spires,
the most conspicuous architectural
element of the eighteenth-century
colonial city. Although built for
Anglican worship, the building
exerted an influence on Boston's
Puritans who, within a few years,
built Old South Meeting House
(1729) with a similar lofty spire.

on top of one another. This form first appeared in Boston on Old
North Church in 1723, a shocking innovation to the Puritan city,
since a spire was the mark of a longitudinally planned church
and not a meeting house [27]. But the finest and most delicately
proportioned of London steeples was designed by Gibbs in the
1720s, St. Martin-in-the-Fields, where it burst forth from the
middle of a classical portico. Gibbs not only illustrated the church
in his *Book of Architecture* but as a show of his virtuosity illustrated
six alternative variants. These variants were the model for spires
throughout the English colonies, from Philadelphia (Christ
Church, 1754) to Charleston (St. Michael's, 1762—which was
gilded by the versatile Theus) to Providence (First Baptist
Church, 1774). At last even the New England Puritans, torn
between Calvinist theology and the temptations of fashion, gave
in to the new classical taste, though sometimes with an amusing
ambivalence [28].

Pattern books like Gibbs's transformed American architectural practice. Previously, almost without exception, American buildings were the work of a craftsman, either a carpenter or a bricklayer. He might provide a serviceable design, invariably in the prevailing vernacular. While he might copy an idea from a book, perhaps for a piece of decorative carving or a doorway, his overall conception of form was not bookish. Harrison represented a new type, the gentleman–amateur, for whom architecture was essentially an affair of graphic imagery and whose knowledge was chiefly derived from books [29]. This was a respectable category, and it included such eminent minds as William Thornton and Thomas Jefferson, but one should not mistake these gentleman–amateurs for the

28 Congregational Meeting House, Farmington, Connecticut, 1771. A simple preaching barn, this odd hybrid might have been built a century earlier than its actual date of construction. But it also boasts an incongruous classical tower, applied only for reasons of fashion and not to mark the actual entrance (which follows the old placement in the middle of the south wall). The building has an odd, awkward vitality, and is a lovely example of how the struggle to maintain purity of tradition while being fashionable can produce new forms.

29 **Peter Harrison**, Brick Market, Newport, Rhode Island, 1761–62.

30 **Richard Munday**, Old Colony House, Newport, Rhode Island, 1739. Eighteenth-century buildings were the work either of the carpenter–builder or the gentleman–amateur. Standing on Washington Square, Newport, Rhode Island, it is possible simultaneously to see splendid examples of both: Richard Munday's Old Colony House and Peter Harrison's Brick Market. Munday's work is a provincial essay in the old-fashioned Baroque of Christopher Wren. Typical of the builder is the contrast between competently handled craftsmanship, such as the handsome frontispiece of the door, and passages of naive paper design, such as the delightfully preposterous pseudo-pediment, a pure paper conception. One can picture the sheet on which Munday first drew the gable, decided it looked too empty, and then filled it with three bull's-eye windows. By contrast, Harrison's design is totally bookish in conception, a paraphrase of Inigo Jones's Somerset House by way of a pattern book. It is splendidly and coolly correct, but lacks Munday's hearty provincial originality.

modern professional architect. The hallmark of the professional is that his role is to design a building, and not to build it, for which he usually received a percentage of the cost of construction, normally five percent. Like other professionals—such as doctors and lawyers—it is his professional advice that the client buys, not his skill with the hammer and saw. Neither of the eighteenth-century types, the carpenter–builder or the gentleman–amateur who drafted plans for his friends, was a professional.

Nonetheless, the exchange of ideas between well-educated clients and increasingly book-oriented builders produced a rich architectural culture. By the middle of the century, the American classical country house was well developed. In its preferred form it displayed a symmetrical five-bay facade, often flanked by outbuildings, called "dependencies." The cubic mass of the house was relieved by an array of carved ornament, which served to accent the all-important center but also to mark the important lines of the building and to dramatize its periphery. Thus the entrance was enlivened with an ornate classical frontispiece, consisting of half columns and a lunette window beneath a pediment. Above this was invariably a Palladian window—a round-headed window set between two smaller flat-headed windows—that gracefully accented the center of a facade. (It is more accurate, however—though more pedantic—to call the feature a *serliana*, after its inventor Serlio.) Finally came a classical cornice of brackets or dentils (so called because they resemble teeth), and perhaps a cresting of carved urns as well.

(Such was the "Georgian" house, although the term is not universally accepted. Properly speaking, the term is chronological and dynastic, not architectural, and it describes the first four Hanoverian kings who reigned in England beginning in 1714, each of whom was named George. Since the heyday of Palladian classicism coincides neatly with the reign of the first three of these kings, however, the term has won general acceptance.)

After the middle of the century, the Georgian house became even more proudly monumental and formal. The key feature was a two-story pavilion, capped with a pediment, which projected from the main block of the house to form its architectural climax. The feature is not found in early Georgian houses, such as that of Isaac Royall [21]. In the grandest examples a prominent hipped roof crowned the composition, all four sides sloping toward the balustrade-crowned top. All these features are employed in Mount Pleasant, the lavish country house built by James McPherson in what is now Fairmount Park, Philadelphia [31].

McPherson was a Scottish sea captain and privateer—in effect, an authorized pirate—and his house made a determined bid for social respectability. Its theme of stately formality begins at a distance, where flanking dependencies frame the view and extend the central axis of the house into space. Nor does the sense of formal resolve and balance end here. Each of its interior walls is fully resolved as a balanced and symmetrical composition, complete with an entablature, and even the fireplace and the doorways are themselves conceived as miniature buildings [32]. Such a formal conception of the wall—looking as if it were a handsomely composed page in a pattern book—could not be farther removed from the plastered walls of Parson Capen's house.

Nothing about Mount Pleasant is provincial, and it might have stood in the English countryside without embarrassment. Perhaps its designer was an English architect, whose plans McPherson procured on one of his voyages. Several such instances of long-distance architectural practice are documented, and there must be countless others that are unknown. At any rate, on the eve of the Revolution American merchants were sophisticated enough to know the latest currents of English taste and prosperous enough to afford it.

31 and 32 Mount Pleasant, Fairmount Park, Philadelphia, 1762–65. Like their Welsh Quaker ancestors, Philadelphians preferred an architecture of solid masonry, building in brick in the city and stone in the country. Mount Pleasant is typical, a building of massive rubble that has been stuccoed and scored to simulate cut stone, while brick is used for the sturdy corner quoins and the massive belt course around its middle. So insistent is its frontality and formal symmetry, even in the interior, that sham doors were placed to either side of the parlor fireplace, purely to balance the composition (below).

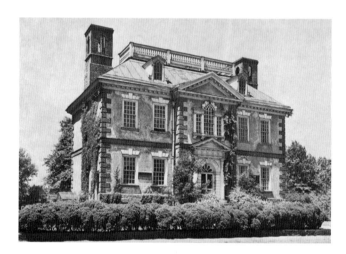

33 **Joseph Blackburn**, *Isaac Winslow and His Family*, 1755. This painting provides indirect evidence that its author was a drapery specialist in London. Its extravagant play of glistening fabric is partial compensation for his inability to make a true group portrait. Unlike John Smibert, who joined his figures in a pleasing unity, Blackburn composes by simple addition, connecting what are in effect three independent portraits. The note of pleasing artifice and of weightless gesture was new in Boston, and immediately popular.

American painting shows a similar abrupt leap in quality. Certainly the time was ripe for fresh stimulus. The Baroque tradition that Smibert and Hesselius had introduced had become diluted in the hands of their successors and had lost its vitality. Smibert's own career shows a pattern that frequently happened with Colonial artists: a slow but inexorable decline, once an artist had been taken from the competitive community of other artists. Without the benefit of ongoing contact to new impulses and stimulation, Smibert gradually settled into rote and repetition, and none his work of the 1740s could match the flair and facility of his *Bermuda Group* [20]. He certainly got no stimulation from his local competitors, other than Feke. His chief rival was Joseph Badger (1708–65), a lackluster draftsman who doggedly turned out one undistinguished portrait after another, mechanically reproducing the same two or three stiff poses.

A shot of inspiration now came from a new wave of émigré artists who flourished in the 1750s: John Wollaston, Joseph Blackburn, and William Williams. Collectively they brought a new artistic sensibility to America, the lighter and more graceful manner of the rococo. In place of the Baroque palette of Smibert, with its rich and intense reds and greens, the palette now lightened, preferring silver and pink and blue pastels [33]. To make a color a pastel, one simply adds white; much the same keying up occurred in the architectural palette of the era, and is to be found in the interior of houses such as Mount Pleasant.

Wollaston, Blackburn, and Williams are sometimes disparaged as "fabric painters," a term which refers to the studio assistants who painted the gowns and backgrounds for more talented painters. This is sheer speculation, for all that is known of any of their training is that Wollaston did study for a time in London with a drapery painter (Joseph van Aken). But the accusation is plausible, for all of them brought a splendid ability to render the luster and sparkle of satin, shimmering with reflected light. At times the costumes are more vivacious than the bodies within them. Wollaston, for instance, did not seem to be a particularly acute observer of faces, and he had a formulaic way of assigning the same features to his sitters, curious almond eyes with emphatically outlined lids [34]. But he also had the rococo feel for grace and amusement, and his figures seem to have relaxed from their rigid poses. Although he painted from formula, it was a winning one, and when the treatment of a delicate beauty was in accord with the sprightly play of fabrics, the results could be very successful. Their home-grown rivals could hardly compete against such a display of facility. It would take but a glance at such a vivacious painting to realize just how rigid and wooden the formal set pieces of Badger were, and of Feke as well.

Wollaston and Blackburn were artistic vagabonds, exhausting the patronage of a town and then moving on. Blackburn took the northern beat, painting in Newport, Boston, and Portsmouth before returning to London in 1763. Wollaston took the southern, moving from New York, Maryland, Virginia, and Philadelphia—leaving in 1758 for India (with a brief return visit in 1767 on his way back to England). Although the stays of Wollaston and Blackburn were short, they sharply reinvigorated the artistic culture of the colonies. They established the more sophisticated taste and demand for art

34 **John Wollaston**, *Mrs. John Dies*, c. 1750. Wollaston painted perhaps 300 portraits during his stint in America, indicating an enormous public demand for these icons of status and respectability. Many of the artists of the next generation, including West and Peale, took his work as their point of departure. Wollaston painted Mrs. John Dies along with her husband during the course of his two-year stay in New York.

under which the next generation of artists thrived, especially the duo of Benjamin West and John Singleton Copley, the first American-trained artists to find success in Europe.

The European success of West and Copley showed that an American background, for all its provincial deprivation, might also convey some advantages—if properly exploited. One of these was the American's innocence of all academic authority, and independence from the huge machinery of patronage, education, and tradition that in Europe restricted artistic invention into certain formal channels. This independence permitted a certain freedom of mind. Occasionally the untutored amateur makes a discovery in medicine, science, or engineering that the professional does not, usually by serendipity or simple unreflective observation. And this was the accomplishment of Benjamin West (1738–1820), that pioneer of the modern history painting.

West was born to a Quaker family near Swarthmore, Pennsylvania, and received painting lessons from several itinerant artists in Philadelphia, including William Williams. In 1760 his patrons donated funds to send him on a prolonged study trip to Italy. There he shrewdly played up his American identity, especially when it served him. Despite his smattering of formal lessons, he preferred to tell rapt listeners that he had been shown how to make red and yellow pigment by the nearby Indian tribes. During the years when Rousseau's doctrine of the Noble Savage captivated European salons, West was also quick on his feet. When he had an audience in the Vatican, it was arranged for him to see the Apollo Belvedere in the expectation that the sight of real art would overwhelm him. Anticipating the jest, West turned the tables on his hosts and nodded knowingly, saying that he recognized the stance: "It is a Mohawk warrior." It was a devastating rebuke, which simultaneously excused West's ignorance of European art history while implying that he was far closer to the living reality of antiquity than the desiccated connoisseurs of Europe.

By 1763 West was in England, where he practiced for the rest of his life, continuing resourcefully to exploit his Americanness. His most celebrated work, *Death of General Wolfe*, rests on the notion that the American painter need not feel humbled by antiquity. West's subject was the successful British attack on Quebec, which took place in 1759 at the height of the French and Indian Wars. He depicted the tragic climax of the battle, when the general learns at the very moment of his death that his attack has been victorious [35].

35 **Benjamin West**, *The Death of General Wolfe*, 1770. This is the first major painting to depict a contemporary event accurately, with carefully researched costumes and topography. Of course, West could not know the exact poses of the central figures so he borrowed them from familiar models. The dying Wolfe reclines as in a *Pietà*, comparing his death to that of Christ, while the stoic American Indian, impassively watching the scene, assumes a Greek pose. In this West was only following accepted artistic convention; it would not be until the rise of intense life drawing in the second half of the nineteenth century that artists would derive fresh poses from living models.

West faithfully rendered the scene in strictly contemporary fashion, refusing to treat it as an allegory or to dignify it with ancient costume. Such allegories often portrayed modern events in terms of classical antiquity, a comparison that was meant to enhance the status of the event. But for West, Wolfe's triumph was sufficiently epic in its own right, an event on the magnitude of any in the ancient world. The surrender of Quebec permanently wrested Canada from the French, and gave military control of the North American continent to the English. It had had no need to genuflect to antiquity.

West justified his unconventional treatment with an appeal to historical truth: "The classic dress is certainly picturesque, but by using it I shall lose in sentiment what I gain in external grace. I want to mark the time, the place, and the people, and to do this I must abide by the truth." Time, place, and people, each shown truthfully: here was the essence of modern history painting. After his portrait of Wolfe, West made a career of history paintings, producing one sumptuous set piece after another. In short order, the Quaker artist becomes an establishment figure in London, winning the patronage of King George III and becoming president of the Royal Academy. For all this, West was never a painter of the first rank. His formal training came too late and was too uneven, and he never achieved the fluid grace of Gainsborough or the solid realism of Raeburn. Lord Byron scorned him, referring to "the dotard West/ Europe's worst daub, poor England's best," managing in a few choice words to condemn both West and all of English art.

Unlike his portrait-painting rivals, West labored under the conviction that painting must serve a useful purpose, perhaps the legacy of his pragmatic Quaker upbringing. This resulted in increasingly larger and self-important religious epics of his late work. Behind his back, West's own pupils mocked his grandiose "ten-acre canvases." But their jibes were affectionate, for West was a big-hearted benefactor, and offered friendship and support to every American artist who showed up in London for the next fifty years [36]. Three generations of American painters—Peale and Pratt, Stuart and Trumbull, Sully and Morse, to name only the most important figures—benefited from his tutelage and advice. West effectively made London the epicenter of the American art world for half a century.

36 **Matthew Pratt**, *The American School*, 1765. American informality and Quaker simplicity made West an unusually accessible figure in Georgian London. He was already the center of a lively artists' colony by 1765, the year in which Matthew Pratt painted *The American School*. It gives a vivid glimpse of West's method, its geniality and Quaker informality, as he administered conversational criticism in small groups.

West was even generous to a far better painter, John Singleton Copley (1738–1815). A brilliantly gifted autodidact, he was born in Boston and raised by his stepfather Peter Pelham, the English-born engraver, who died when Copley was thirteen. Smibert died in the same year and shortly thereafter Feke vanished, leaving him no tutors in Boston and forcing him to rely on mezzotints for his education. Through them he acquired the linear precision and control of tonal contrast that marked his style to the end. But he also had some innate abilities, including a splendid capacity to capture a likeness and a sure and instinctive sense of color. The color sense was reinforced by Blackburn, who arrived when Copley was seventeen and charmed Boston with his sprightly rococo palette. This was his last formative experience. Within a few years, while still in his teens, he was the finest portrait painter in America.

As Copley prospered, he soon became indignant at the lowly status of the American artist. To a friend he confessed that "the people generally regard it no more than any other useful trade, as they sometimes term it, like that of a Carpenter tailor or shoemaker, not as one of the most noble Arts in the world. Which is not a little Mortifying to me." By 1766 the mortified artist was considering moving to England, although he was apprehensive about how he would fare in competition with European professionals. To test the waters he first sent one of his paintings to be exhibited in London. This was his *Boy with a Squirrel*, a tranquil study of his stepbrother Henry Pelham seated at a desk, his pet flying squirrel beside him [37]. The subject was carefully chosen to show off his versatility and it is filled with a great variety of textures, including fabrics and fur, the watch chain and the glass of water, and the polished table in which all of these are reflected.

The painting came to the attention of the great Joshua Reynolds, England's most important painter, who called it "a very wonderful performance," better than anything West had ever done. West, however, spotted its flaws: "a little Hardness in the Drawing, Coldness in the Shades, An over minuteness, all of which Example would correct." In short, West discerned an utter lack of painterly qualities, precisely what one would expect from an artist raised on mezzotints. But in some sense, the defect was also a virtue. Copley's extreme clarity of form—his starched taut volumes in airless spaces—is the very essence of his style, one of emotional restraint and the highest workmanlike standards. It is the expression of high quality in a mercantile culture that had little tradition of sensuous expression but had very high standards for quality of workmanship for silver, fabric, and furniture, where the finish of surface and texture was a matter of great concern indeed.

This ambivalent reception, echoed in a series of kindly letters sent by West, made Copley hesitate. He remained in America for eight more years, during which he painted his strongest work. Having long since dispensed with the readymade poses of European prints, he portrayed the bodies and characteristic body language of his sitters, rather than simply attaching their heads to stock figures, and he depicted them in their studies and workshops, rather than fictive settings. Among the best of these were forceful portraits of the Revolutionary leaders Samuel Adams and Paul Revere [38]. His own politics were staunchly loyalist, however, and in 1774, as the war was impending, he fled to England.

37 **John Singleton Copley**, *Boy with a Squirrel (Henry Pelham)*, 1765. Copley had a flair for memorable composition. In this work, the flying squirrel is a miniature emblem of the boy: two pensive creatures companionably share the same gesture, both lost in thought. It was in the making of these simple arresting compositions that Copley triumphed over his naive empiricism, making his paintings far more than a compilation of minutely painted objects.

38 **John Singleton Copley**, *Portrait of Paul Revere*, 1768. Here was a new kind of painting. Instead of aristocratic subjects in settings of leisure, Copley portrayed merchants and artisans who were not ashamed of their status or their manual labor, aristocrats of commerce. Revere holds one of his silver teapots in one hand as he prepares to incise it with decoration while the other holds his head, as if to suggest that he earns his livelihood by both his hands and head.

Copley was in his late thirties when he felt for the first time the full sensory experience of European art, rather than the meager and puny version available in prints. The effect on his work was overwhelming. *Watson and the Shark* [39], his first major painting after his arrival, shows him struggling mightily to learn the new lessons. The painting, like West's *Death of General Wolfe*, depicts a New World event: in his youth Brook Watson, the future Lord Mayor of London, fell into the water at Havana and promptly lost a leg to a shark. Copley re-created the scene at the moment of greatest drama, just before the rescue, as the shark returns to finish off the injured Watson.

Watson and the Shark was composed according the strictly empirical method of Copley's American work, involving detailed portrait studies of all the figures, including a superb one of the black man at the apex of the composition. Only where he had no tangible models, as with the maw of the ravening shark, did he falter. But the sense of grandeur—the elevation of a gruesome accident into an epic—was something new for Copley and is the result of his exposure to monumental European art. With this thundering debut, Copley went on to a lucrative English career and, like West, he never returned to America. But as his painting grew even more proficient and lost much of the "liney" quality that Reynolds and West had criticized, it belonged increasingly to the fashionable world of English art and less to that of America.

It is remarkable that Copley today looks far less dated than virtually all of his contemporaries. In comparison, rococo rivals like Blackburn seem too mannered and vapid, while history painters like West seem too bombastic. Perhaps that is because photography has trained us to appreciate Copley's dry sense of form, his sharp-focused factuality. But he also is in peculiar and intimate harmony with his society. His art was derived from the graphic language of the print—with all its linearity and schematic flatness—and was made for clients whose idea of form was developed through that same graphic language, and who saw form, texture, and outline much as he did. This graphic language, brought to a high pitch of development in the eighteenth century, did not vanish at that century's end. It has remained a crucial component of the American visual experience, and recurs repeatedly, as it did in the twentieth century with Precisionism and later with Pop Art. Copley was the first to show that linearity, respect for blunt facts, and tactile information, need not be provincial liabilities but might be the basis for great art.

39 **John Singleton Copley**, *Watson and the Shark*, 1778. Made after a year-long trip through Italy, this painting flaunts its knowledge of art history. The pose of the flailing Watson comes from the Apollo Belvedere, which Copley had admired at the Vatican, while the strictly pyramidal composition suggests Raphael, who liked to arrange a painting's significant elements at the salient points of a triangle. The painting was instantly popular and was published as a mezzotint.

Chapter 3   The Grand Manner

As the American Revolution drew near, art was pulled inexorably into the service of politics. Henry Pelham (the subject of Copley's *Boy with a Squirrel*) made an engraving of the Boston Massacre of 1770 that forever shaped the public image of the event, a disciplined file of British soldiers firing at point-blank range into a defenseless crowd. To make such visual propaganda, it was not necessary to be a good artist, or even an artist at all. Benjamin Franklin made a print in 1754 that depicted the American colonies as a dismembered snake, cut into separate writhing sections, with the emphatic caption "*JOIN, or DIE.*" As graphic art it was crude, but in political art crudity can be a virtue.

After the United States won their independence—declared in 1776 and recognized at last by a peace treaty with England in 1783—political imagery of a more serious and profound nature was required. Even a culture indifferent to art had need of government buildings, paintings, and statuary to adorn them, and a city in which to place them; there was also need for currency, seals, flags, and other symbols of national identity. Here timing was helpful. The United States came into being at about the same time as Neoclassicism, the radical new aesthetic philosophy of the second half of the eighteenth century. Neoclassicism looked beyond the forms of Renaissance and Baroque to their ultimate origins, the art of classical antiquity. And the United States themselves, in some sense, were a creation of Neoclassicism, an amalgam of Greek democracy and Roman republican virtues. As a result, the central historical and symbolic depictions of American nationhood are thoroughly Neoclassical, both in subject matter and in spirit.

The artistic ideal of Neoclassicism was ancient Greece, which had achieved the greatest clarity of form and line—or so it was believed. Neoclassical painters sought expressive outlines and clearly delineated figures; architects valued simple volumes and

40 **Charles Willson Peale**, *The Artist in His Museum*, 1822. This is the quintessential expression of the American belief that art is an empirical process, the accurate transcription of observed facts, and therefore of a kind with science. The portrait is far more painterly than his usual work, creating suspicion that the aging artist was assisted by his son Rembrandt. Only the flamboyantly upraised arm is an obvious afterthought, with no logical relationship to Peale's shoulder.

geometric solids, such as cubes, cylinders, and spheres. In either case, the writhing and contorted forms that the Baroque enjoyed—whether in buildings or bodies—were decisively rejected.

Formal purity went hand in hand with moral purity in the minds of Neoclassical artists, who strove to promote civic virtue with their monumental didactic paintings in the Grand Manner style. Their insistence on virtue gave urgency to the new taste. What would otherwise have been a mere oscillation of fashion—away from the froth and frivolity of the rococo toward simplicity and clarity—took on a bracing sense of moral purpose.

Finally, Neoclassicism brought fresh visual ideas. The repertoire of artistic forms was greatly expanded as enterprising architects excavated and measured ancient buildings and then promptly used the new motifs in their own work. In 1762 the British architects Nicholas Stuart and James Revett began publishing their *Antiquities of Athens*, which first made the public aware of the crucial differences to be found between Greek and Roman architecture. To contemporary eyes, which mainly knew classical architecture in its Renaissance version, genuine Greek architecture was shockingly primitive, particularly the Doric order, which placed its thickset columns directly on the ground without an intermediate base—barefoot as it were. Yet even as the book was in production, Stuart built such a Doric temple as a garden folly at Hagley, England. Other architects found their inspiration at the opposite end of antiquity, from late Roman examples: Robert Adam took the ruins of the Emperor Diocletian's palace at Split, the ancient seaport on the Dalmatian coast, which he published in 1764, as the prototype for his Adelphi Buildings in London (1768–72).

There was virtually no time lag before these innovations were known in the colonies. A certain William Williams sailed from Philadelphia to London around 1770 to "study Architecture in its various branches" and upon his return boasted of his familiarity with the celebrated Adam. According to his advertisement in the *Pennsylvania Packet* (January 4, 1773):

> [He] humbly hopes, from his practice and experience, to give the highest satisfaction to such as shall be pleased to employ him, in a new, bold, light and elegant taste, which has been lately introduced by the great architect of the Adelphi Buildings at Ducham Yard; and which is now universally practiced all over Britain. He also fits up shop-fronts in the nicest manner, from the plainest and most simple to the most elegant and tasty, according to original plans taken in London.

While Williams could serve up "tasty" ornaments in the mode of Adam, he could not bring to America that one essential component of architectural Neoclassicism, which was masonry construction. The forms of Neoclassical buildings were conceived in the geometric language of stone, of carefully dressed ashlar blocks and finely fitted vaults, and required a technical skill lacking in the colonies. This was especially telling when it came to the shaping of interior space. English Neoclassicists like Adam and John Soane gave their rooms various shapes and sizes—round, octagonal, apse-ended—to create spatial sequences of drama and excitement. Their model was the planning of Roman baths, which employed domes, barrel vaults, and groin vaults in order to roof their various rooms. The Romans had done this for practical reasons but for Neoclassical architects the motivation was often nothing more than a sincere love of the abstract beauty and variety of geometry.

In America, however, Neoclassicism was normally expressed in the dry and planar language of wood. Forms became more slender and attenuated, and graceful vertical elongation became the rule. To be sure, some of the new innovations lent themselves easily to wood, particularly the ornament of Robert Adam, whose highly calligraphic linear style derived from Etruscan tombs and the new discoveries at Pompeii. In wood-building New England, this helped to produce a distinctive variant of Neoclassicism for which there is no clear European counterpart: the Federal style.

The Federal style flourished roughly between 1780 and 1820, and its leading figure was Samuel McIntire (1757–1811) of Salem, Massachusetts. A furniture maker and joiner by training, when he later came to design buildings he treated them with a delicacy and precision that derived from woodworking, as if they were nothing more than unusually large items of furniture. Even when building in brick, he never thought to convey the heaviness and severity of a masonry wall, as European Neoclassicists loved to do. In buildings such as the Gardner-Pingree House [41], his brick walls have the lightness and buoyancy of wood. If anything, the wall is a neutral field for him to embellish with his passages of virtuoso carving, as in the handsome semicircular portico and the elliptical fanlight beneath it. Its sense of fragile delicacy differs poignantly from its Georgian predecessors, such as Mount Pleasant [31], even though the basic scheme of columns, entablature and fanlight is the same.

McIntire's career was confined to the vicinity of Salem but the forms and proportions of the Federal style were carried throughout

41 **Samuel McIntire**, Gardner-Pingree House, Salem, 1804–5. Interior.

America. In 1797, Asher Benjamin (1773–1845) published *The Country Builder's Assistant*, which rendered the classical orders in wood and simplified them for consumption by fellow carpenters. Similar pattern books followed in growing numbers, beginning with *The Young Carpenter's Assistant* (1805) by the Philadelphia builder–architect Owen Biddle. This too was widely distributed (one bookseller in Lexington, Kentucky, then on the frontier, ordered ten copies). In this way pared-down wooden versions of the orders were carried right to the edge of the settlement.

McIntire, Benjamin, and Biddle were builders who made their way gradually toward professional architecture; Charles Bulfinch (1763–1844) approached from the other direction, as a gentleman–amateur. A Harvard-trained civic leader in Boston, Bulfinch acquired a dilettante's love of architecture during the course of a grand tour of Europe. Later, as an amateur architect, he invested in his own speculative housing project (a mistake no architect should make) and was bankrupted. He presents the curious spectacle of a man who, destroyed financially by his hobby, did not renounce it but embraced it as his profession.

Bulfinch admired Neoclassicism for its stereometric quality—that is, for its plastic language of rectangular and spherical solids, for its expressive shapes and its eloquent shadows. A wall did not need columns before he could admire it; its melancholy grandeur was a sufficient credential. In this he differed from the pedantic

Palladians. With time and practice, his work grew confident and even original. Three successive houses in Boston, built between 1792 and 1806 for Harrison Gray Otis, record his growing sophistication. Each was a taut brick performance, rising to a flat roofline that emphasized its contained cubic mass. Each succeeding one was more elegant in rhythm and proportion, however, until the last achieved a superb papery lightness. The dimensions of the windows contributed much to this, such as the graceful triple-hung windows of the main story, three times as tall as they are wide [42].

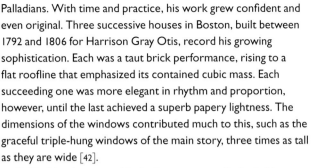

Bulfinch's talents—and limitations—are on display in his Massachusetts State House (1795–98), his most famous work and America's first great public building to sport a dome [43]. The entire scheme comes from Somerset House in London, just completed by Sir William Chambers: a porch with a screen of Corinthian columns prefaces a sturdy pedimented block which rises to a dome of distinctly ovoid form. So the prototype was composed but, as usual, the American version stiffened and simplified in translation. Bulfinch substituted brick for stone, giving the outer wings a starkness reminiscent of the Harrison Gray Otis House. And he eliminated Chambers's sculpted ornament in order to exploit the sheer planes of the wall, setting the central arches of the wings within larger blind arches—a favorite device of Robert Adam that lent the wall a laminated quality.

While the Massachusetts State House drew its inspiration second hand, from printed illustrations, its counterpart in Virginia resulted from direct experience of one of the great monuments of the ancient world. From 1785 to 1789 the American minister to France was that extraordinary gentleman–architect, Thomas Jefferson (1743–1826). He had already designed and built his own house, a clever but rather literal Palladian essay, but now he saw the real thing. At Nîmes he visited the celebrated Maison Carrée, a virtually intact Roman temple, and was enthralled. He described the encounter rather indelicately to Madame Tesse, the cousin of Lafayette: "Here I am, Madam, gazing whole hours at the Maison Quarree, like a lover at his mistress."

42 **Charles Bulfinch**, Third Harrison Gray Otis House, Boston, 1806. Even more dainty than the Gardner-Pingree House, it dispenses with the belt courses of McIntire's house and makes its dominant lines vertical, grouping its windows into elegant tiers that gracefully diminish in proportion with each story.

Jefferson evidently wanted to keep gazing at it: he copied it for the Virginia State Capitol at Richmond (1785–99), the first American building based directly on a monument of classical antiquity. But he also admired modern French architecture, and the revolutionary Neoclassicism of Claude-Nicolas Ledoux and Étienne-Louis Boullée (who built Madame Tesse's villa). He took intelligent note of the elegant refinements of French houses, such as the custom of building grand public rooms of double height, while the private wings tucked two more intimate stories into spaces of the same height.

Shaken out of his Palladian complacency, Jefferson at once redesigned Monticello, his house near Charlottesville, transforming the original bookish essay into a highly personal Anglo-French synthesis [44]. Here was no New England timber-building sensibility but a Neoclassical study in lucid geometry: an octagonal dome, a rectangular main block, a pair of triangular porticoes. But Jefferson's Neoclassicism was not slavish, and he sited his house with the seasoned eye of a surveyor and a planter.

43 **Charles Bulfinch**, Massachussetts State House, Boston, 1795–98. For all its refinement and elegance, this is still the work of a paper architect. Like most amateurs, Bulfinch found it easier to make lovely two-dimensional walls than to make satisfying, fully resolved spaces. His interior is parceled into rectangles of various sizes, with none of the oval, domical, or apse-ended rooms that gave contemporary English architecture its spatial ingenuity and delight.

44 Thomas Jefferson,
Monticello, Charlottesville,
1769–84; 1796–1809. Nowhere
is the perennial American tension
between the ideal and the practical
resolved so successfully as at
Monticello. While its exterior
is a Neoclassical essay in ideal
geometrical form, the interior
presents a functional array of
ingenious contrivances and
gadgets. Most remarkable was
Jefferson's built-in bed: placed in
a narrow alcove between two
rooms, it benefited from the
tendency of air to accelerate
as it moved through narrower
channels, an application of the so-
called Venturi principle, to produce
a form of passive air-conditioning.

Unlike French houses, which generally treat their grounds as a
formal extension of the architecture, his hugged its hilltop site;
he sank its supporting functions—a U-shaped array of arcaded
passages, kitchens, and outbuildings—out of sight below the crest
of the hill to preserve views to and from the house. In Georgian
houses such as Mount Pleasant [31], these dependencies were
part of the grand show, dominating the formal approach, but
for Jefferson geometric purity counted for much more than
procession and pomp.

Jefferson's architecture, like his Declaration of Independence,
was premised on reason, on the belief that certain truths were
self-evident. One was the truth of geometry, another was moral
truth and civic virtue, which architecture might serve to teach.
Both beliefs are embodied in his University of Virginia (1817–25),
for which he designed both the curriculum and the campus.
In many ways, the University was a monumental version of
Monticello, in which an interlocking array of functions was
resolved into an ideal form, presided over by a culminating dome.
The composition was a continuous U-shaped colonnade, open to
the south, that was punctuated by ten separate pavilions, which
housed classrooms below and apartments for the professors
above [45]. Each was in a different classical order—Corinthian,
Ionic, Doric, Composite, and Tuscan—to make a kind of outdoor

45 Thomas Jefferson, with **Benjamin Henry Latrobe**, University of Virginia, Charlottesville, lithograph, 1856. Thomas Jefferson's University of Virginia is not only a design of abstract clarity but it also plays with the laws of optics. Its pavilions are not spaced evenly but spread out as they move away from the library, distorting the effect of perspective. Looking north, the distant pavilions seem squeezed together, which exaggerates the perspective and makes the distant library seem bigger than it is. Looking from the library, on the other hand, the wider spacing counteracts the perspective, making the lawn look smaller and more intimate.

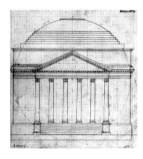

46 Thomas Jefferson, Southern Elevation of the Rotunda, Library of University of Virginia, Charlottesville, before 1821. Jefferson's original elevation drawing for the library uses his characteristic graph paper. Here too ideal geometry converges with the most prosaic concerns, enabling Jefferson to describe the Platonic forms of his buildings even as it lets him calculate the cubic mass of the walls and the precise number of bricks needed from his kilns—the chronic worry of the cash-poor planter.

schoolroom of architectural history. Between these pavilions and behind the colonnades were the rooms of the students, who could use the lower level of the passage to reach their classes while the faculty could use the upper.

The rotunda at the north end was a reduced version of the Pantheon, using that most rational of shapes, a sphere, to contain that most rational of functions, a library. Such a U-shaped arrangement, anchored by a grand centerpiece at one end, is a staple of European classicism, but here too the formal geometry is inflected with a reverence for the natural landscape not usually found in monumental classical compositions. While the rotunda [46] to the north shows Platonic form and reason, the open view to the south suggests the infinity of nature, its bounty and its goodness.

One aspect of French culture that Jefferson did not admire was its enthusiasm for urban life. His deep appreciation of landscape went with an equally strong distrust of the city:

> I view great cities as pestilential to the morals, the health and the liberties of man. True, they nourish some of the elegant arts, but the useful ones can thrive elsewhere, and less perfection in the others—with more health, virtue & freedom—would be my choice.

Here was an anti-urban sentiment of an intensity that would not be matched until Frank Lloyd Wright in the twentieth century. Using his political power, Jefferson sought to influence the design of Washington, D.C., along anti-urban lines. In 1791, he proposed a brilliant grid in which alternating diagonal squares were reserved as public parks—making the plan a vast alternating checkerboard of city and country. The only formal note was the monumental axis between the Capitol building and presidential mansion; clearly his native Williamsburg [15] was on his mind.

Jefferson's idea that nature might render the city more humane was prophetic; it is the first articulate expression of an anti-urbanism that would lead to the American park movement in the nineteenth century. But it was too advanced for its time, and the city was instead designed by one of George Washington's former officers, the French-born architect Pierre Charles L'Enfant (1754–1825). L'Enfant's 1792 plan was a rich and odd hybrid of the European Baroque and the pragmatic American grid [47]. He had available prints of the great Baroque schemes of Europe—the radiating diagonals from Versailles, Sixtus V's rebuilding of Rome, and Christopher Wren's visionary plan for reconstructing London after the fire of 1666—but he seemed to feel that the Baroque was the spatial expression of absolutism, and not of a largely Protestant mercantile republic. Instead of bringing his converging axes to a central place of power, he dispersed them across the enormous city, so that each state might have its own forum, a decentered and federalized vision of the Baroque. Between this large lattice of diagonal boulevards, the land was simply gridded for ease of property division, giving the city two different scales—a functional pragmatic scale for its local streets which was overlaid with an armature of diagonal axes that lent it civic grandeur and formality.

Architectural competitions were held for the Capitol building and the presidential palace, with mixed results, confirming that monumentality was beyond the ability of American architects [48].

47 **Andrew Ellicot**, after **Pierre Charles L'Enfant**, *Plan of the City of Washington in the Territory of Columbia*, 1792. The plan overlaid the American grid with a lattice of dynamic Baroque diagonals. Although it looks like a two-dimensional planning exercise, perfected in the abstract and on paper, it was based on meticulous surveys of the topography, so that all of its principal nodes are placed on the highest terrain in the city, giving them commanding prominences.

48 Phillip Hart, Rejected Competition Design for U.S. Capitol, Washington, D.C., 1792. The 1792 competition to design the United States Capitol drew a grab bag of carpenters whose entire experience was in the making of houses. Phillip Hart's design showed an oversized Palladian house with separate entrances for congressmen and senators. His one original idea was a bad one: to exchange the conventional row of classical statues on the balustrade for a tribe of unhappy Indian warriors.

The competition for the Capitol was won by the amateur architect Dr. William Thornton, whose mighty domed block suggested the grandeur and massive scale appropriate to a national capitol [49]. Since Thornton had no professional training, and could not safely convert his drawings into solid brick and plaster, the execution of his project was delegated to a French émigré architect who, perhaps inevitably, quarreled with him. The project languished and would have been a complete botch had it not been turned over to a superb architect, Benjamin Henry Latrobe (1766–1820).

Latrobe was a European professional, having trained in London with S. P. Cockerell, a Neoclassicist of the first order. Before coming to America in 1796, he had already designed some important houses; had he remained in England he would certainly

49 William Thornton, Design for the East Front, U.S. Capitol, Washington, D.C., c. 1793–95. Thornton was a physician whose preparation for designing the U.S. Capitol consisted solely of reading and self-study: "I lamented not having studied architecture, and resolved to attempt this grand undertaking and study at the same time. I studied some months and worked almost day and night." For all his structural ignorance, Thornton appreciated the symbolic requirements of a national capitol and he was the only competitor who designed a true civic building and not a house.

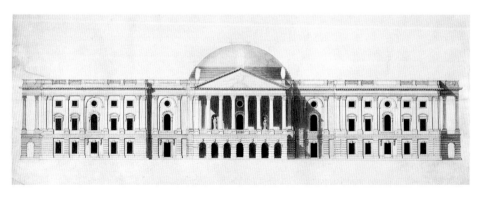

50 **Benjamin Henry Latrobe**, *Perspective of Front and Side of Bank of Pennsylvania, Philadelphia*, (detail), 1798–1801. This was Latrobe's first American building. Here he treated the banking room as a domed rotunda, clearly expressed on the exterior. This marble temple, with its air of restrained and rather austere elegance, set the stage for civic architecture in America. It also invented the enduring image of the American bank building, which sought to suppress commercial crassness in favor of civic grandeur.

have been a significant figure. But in America he was dominant. By virtue of his impeccable training, he was able to think fluidly in three dimensions, something no American architect had done before him; he was able to resolve the triad of interior form, exterior expression, and physical structure in an organically unified whole. Moreover, he could accurately convey the appearance of a building beforehand in graceful watercolor renderings, showing patrons what their buildings would look like when built, attractively set into their surroundings. These represented an enormous stride over the labored and charmless perspectives made by his predecessors.

Latrobe's American career was launched by his Bank of Pennsylvania in Philadelphia (1799–1801); here for the first time the plan is revealed faithfully and expressively on the exterior [50]. The domed rotunda of the banking space, vaulted in brick, forms the central space of the building as well as the principal feature of the exterior. Unlike a pattern book facade like Peter Harrison's Redwood Library [17 and 25], it is conceived in terms of space and structure. Moreover, its classicism was immaculate, a Greek Ionic portico that Latrobe drew from memory, rather than squinting at a woodcut. This creative essay was the beginning of the end of the Palladian supremacy, and architects now looked to classical Greece for their forms rather than the modified version of the Renaissance that had served them for a century.

No one was better qualified to appreciate Latrobe than President Jefferson (whom he assisted in the design of the University of Virginia). Through Jefferson's patronage, Latrobe became the architect of the Capitol, which he completely revised from 1803 to 1817, making a resolved whole out of Thornton's cumbersome and additive composition. Much of the exterior was already in place, with its overlay of ornamental pilasters; had Latrobe been there from the beginning it would have doubtless been a sheer-walled affair, austere and self-contained [51]. As it was, his most important contribution was to the interior, which he completely reshaped, creating an animated sequence of spaces of different shapes, vaulted in masonry and ingeniously lighted and ventilated. His House of Representatives (now Statuary Hall) was a semicircular auditorium, a kind of half-Pantheon that was inspired by the revolutionary Paris School of Surgery. But most popular was his vestibule outside the Senate, a skylighted rotunda which he ornamented with capitals modeled after the ears of corn. Had he known more about American taste for the literal he would not have been surprised that this little display of patriotic realism earned him "more applause from the members of Congress than all the works of magnitude."

It is remarkable that the architect of America's most monumental building of state belonged to a religious sect remarkably free of hierarchy or authority. Latrobe came from a family of Pietist Moravians (his mother was born in Pennsylvania), had attended a Moravian school in Germany, and spoke fluent German. This made the Low Church part of American culture accessible to him, which contributed much to the communal and congregational character of American democracy. His monumental public architecture, while using the trappings of Imperial Rome as well as democratic Athens, were in essence Protestant vessels, and beneath the regalia of antiquity was the strong sense of shared communal experience of a meeting house.

Latrobe revolutionized another crucial aspect of architecture. He is generally regarded as America's first professional architect, whose role was to plan buildings, not to build them. For this he expected a fee, which custom had set at five percent of the cost of construction. His clients, however, knew no such custom; they were used to paying bricklayers and carpenters for their material and labor—but not for their professional advice—and Latrobe was constantly forced to demand payment from his indignant clients. While his supremely able and eloquent classicism exerted

51 **Benjamin Henry Latrobe et al.**, U.S. Capitol, Washington, D.C., 1803–17. Benjamin Henry Latrobe revised Thornton's awkward Capitol interior, achieving a remarkable degree of spatial poetry. Much of his work was destroyed during the War of 1812 or despoiled by later additions, but the former House of Representatives (1815–17) survives as Statuary Hall, and the vestibule to the original Senate retains its famous corn-cob capitals.

an immediate influence on his contemporaries, his introduction of professional standards of practice was perhaps an even greater service. His office also turned out two of the leading figures of the next generation of architects, William Strickland and Robert Mills, whose pupils in turn established a long dynasty of ardent professionals, eager to champion their prerogatives.

At this same moment painting was undergoing similar changes; training was becoming more formal and regular, and there was a distinct rise in the social rank of the artist. Up to the end of the eighteenth century, the painter still had the status of a lowly artisan. As late as 1796, two miniature painters were mortified to have their invitation to a ball in Albany rescinded because, according to the rules of the association, the event was for gentlemen and "no mechanics could be admitted." (The anecdote is in William Dunlap's 1834 *History of the Rise and Progress of the Arts of Design in the United States*, the first American history of art.)

The painters of the next generation, however, were no mere mechanics. Having starved for a century on amateurs and England's castoffs, America now acquired three painters of genius, John Trumbull, John Vanderlyn, and Gilbert Stuart. Each had received a thorough professional training, was able to handle the human figure skillfully, to think in terms of color and glazes, and to make compositions of great pictorial vigor and drama. Like Peale, all three had passed through Benjamin West's halfway house for aspiring artists. But, radically different in temperament and character, they adopted very different career strategies.

52 **John Trumbull**, *The Death of General Montgomery in the Attack on Quebec*, 1786. Drawing his cues from the lush Baroque art of Rubens, John Trumbull (1756–1843) quickly surpassed Benjamin West. This painting is a brilliant paraphrase of West's *The Death of General Wolfe*, but while West's figures are additive and static, Trumbull's are enlisted in a superb compositional and coloristic harmony, conceived in color rather than line. For West, color was typically an afterthought, for which reasons his works lose little in black-and-white reproduction, but Trumbull's color was essential to the very conception of the painting.

53 **John Trumbull**, *The Declaration of Independence, July 4th, 1776*, 1786–1820. A large group portrait is often inert or additive, but Trumbull deployed the figures of this work in an emphatic arc, giving it all the spatial drama of his battle scenes. Because of its forest of white-stockinged legs, Trumbull's painting was mocked as a "shin picture." This is the superior early version; the much larger version in the Capitol is generally regarded as lackluster and careless.

Trumbull's strategy was to make himself the painter of national identity, a task for which he had splendid credentials. A prodigy who graduated from Harvard at the age of sixteen, he had seen many of the events of the American Revolution firsthand. He was present at the Battle of Bunker Hill and served later on Washington's staff, rising to the rank of Lieutenant Colonel. Trumbull was petulant and impulsive, however, and he resigned over the unbearable insult of a misdated promotion, sailing as an art student to England, where he was promptly arrested as a spy.

West helped free Trumbull and generously took him under his wing. He inculcated in him the principles of Grand Manner painting, above all the idea that paintings ought to have a high moral purpose and address the great episodes of history. Trumbull was a born painter, and the pupil quickly surpassed the master. Painting what he knew and drawing on his military experience, he produced the stirring *Death of General Montgomery in the Attack on Quebec*, his first mature work [52].

Trumbull had an overweening ambition and even before the painting was finished, he decided to produce a grand cycle depicting the principal events of the American Revolution. He knew there was scarcely any demand for monumental public art— or even buildings in which to house them—but he also knew there was a sizable market for prints, that great medium of the middle class. He decided to paint small canvases and have them engraved so that he could sell them by subscription to an enthusiastic public. Or so he imagined. Within two years he had completed six of his projected thirteen [53]. These were far better than West's dry work, and showed an intelligent response to Rubens, both for his color sense and his spirited sense of movement. Compare Trumbull's *Death of General Montgomery* with its inspiration, West's *Death of General Wolfe* [35]. The subjects and compositions are nearly identical, and yet West's is a static array of petrified statues, while Trumbull's is a thrashing tempest of movement.

Brandishing these works, Trumbull should have taken America by storm when he returned home in 1789. His prospects seemed radiant but his sense of timing was terrible; interest in the war had already faded and sales were disappointingly mediocre. After another stint in Europe and an unsuccessful attempt to make a go of it as a portrait painter in New York, he returned to London in 1808 where he took up the Grand Manner once more, treating biblical and historical subjects. He met with indifferent success and in 1816 returned to America.

54 **John Vanderlyn**, *The Death of Jane McCrea*, 1804. Rather than creating the historical event, this is a highly literal interpretation of a passage in Joel Barlow's epic poem *The Columbiad* (1787/1807), depicting the moment before Jane's death:

She starts, with eyes upturn'd and fleeting breath,
In their raised axes views her instant death,
Spreads her white hands to heaven in frantic prayer,
Then runs to grasp their knees and crouches there…

Even Jane's lover, hurrying *"with bounding leap"* in the upper right, derives directly from the poem.

By now the rotunda of the Capitol building was complete. There could be no more appropriate space for the display of monumental art on the great national themes of war and peace, and the founding of America—which Trumbull had already treated in his series on the Revolution. He easily won a commission from Congress to enlarge four of his small canvases to monumental scale, 12 by 18 feet (3 by 5 meters), for each of which he would receive eight thousand dollars. The commission ought to have been the summit of his career, and of Grand Manner painting. But Trumbull's talent seems to have burnt itself out. Compared to the vibrant originals, the enlarged versions were tepid and lackluster, and works envisioned for the small format of prints failed to work at monumental scale; the public was unimpressed.

A similar fate met Vanderlyn, a painter of equal ambition but even more talent. From 1796 to 1801 Vanderlyn studied in Paris, an unusual choice for an American of his generation. Here he came under the influence of Jacques-Louis David, the luminary of French

Neoclassicism. David's forte was moralizing history painting, idealized versions of incidents from classical antiquity. His compositions were finely drawn, with figures shown in active and expressive silhouette, with a clarity of line that was derived from Greek art and that rejected the turbulent foreshortening of the Baroque, which masked the proportions of the human body.

Vanderlyn swiftly absorbed this. In his *Death of Jane McCrea* he applied the technique of David to the themes of the American Revolution [54]. The painting shows a historical event, the 1777 killing of a Tory woman by her Huron Indian abductors, but Vanderlyn's treatment is thoroughly Neoclassical. The pose of each figure derives from a Greek sculpture in the Louvre, turned so as to maximize the linear drama of the silhouette. Vanderlyn's art historical knowledge was impressive, but the painting was still vaguely incongruous. The stately poses that were appropriate to events of classical antiquity did not seem quite so natural when recounting modern atrocities.

The simple fact was that Vanderlyn had educated himself beyond the grasp of American patrons. While Napoleon himself might award a medal to Vanderlyn's melancholy *Marius Amidst the Ruins of Carthage* (1807), his American audience never quite appreciated him. This was true of his masterpiece, *Ariadne Asleep on the Island of Naxos* [55]. Vanderlyn had traveled in Italy, where he came under the sway of sixteenth-century Venetian art, and his

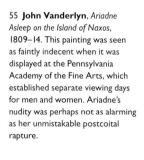

55 **John Vanderlyn**, *Ariadne Asleep on the Island of Naxos*, 1809–14. This painting was seen as faintly indecent when it was displayed at the Pennsylvania Academy of the Fine Arts, which established separate viewing days for men and women. Ariadne's nudity was perhaps not as alarming as her unmistakable postcoital rapture.

Ariadne was painted under the immediate influence of Titian. The story is from classical mythology: Ariadne has freed Theseus from the labyrinth and the Minotaur, and in return for her troubles has been seduced and abandoned by Theseus, who quietly sneaks away in the lower right. Such is the nominal subject but its actual subject was the human body, splendidly painted, its luxuriantly glowing flesh given the rich Venetian treatment.

Vanderlyn's triumph brought him no wealth, however, and, like Trumbull, he scrambled to find ways to make art pay in America. His first impulse had something of the circus in it, a specially built round structure in lower Manhattan in which he exhibited his paintings as well as a gigantic panorama of the palace of Versailles. But this too misfired and by the time Vanderlyn finally had a chance to paint a work appropriate to his talent and training, a mural for the Capitol rotunda, the spark had gone out. His *Landing of Columbus* (1839–46) was just as uninspired as Trumbull's adjacent murals. Both men had come back from Europe in a blaze of talent and promise, but away from the constant impetus of competition with like-minded artists and the encouragement of informed patrons, they were as cut flowers. By the time there were opportunities for their talents they had withered.

It is generally assumed that the chronic shortcoming of early American art resulted from the poor training of its artists. But the tragedy of Trumbull and Vanderlyn was one of patronage, not education. They had been given European skills, but not European patrons. Both their ambitions and their canvases were too large for American conditions, which still preferred portraits to voluptuous nudes or classical grandiloquence. Of their European-trained cohorts, it was only the charming rogue Stuart, dashing off his lively portraits, who was consistently successful.

Gilbert Stuart was indeed a rogue. A profligate, he routinely amassed debts that he could not pay, and he had to flee both London and Dublin ahead of the debtors' prison. In 1775 West took him in, exchanging drawing lessons in return for Stuart's assistance in finishing portraits and painting drapery. But Stuart was impatient and abandoned his drawing lessons as too demanding. In the end, however, the impatience would prove a strength. He turned to portraits, which he could knock off with haste, a valuable skill for a chronically debt-ridden artist. His artistic models were Gainsborough and Reynolds, although he soon outdid them in spontaneity and vivacity; in 1782 he captivated London with a daring painting of a skater [56].

56 **Gilbert Stuart**, *The Skater (Portrait of William Grant)*, 1782. Exercise was hardly a subject for polite art in the eighteenth century, but Gilbert Stuart dignified it by presenting it as fluid and effortless. The subject was William Grant, a friend of Stuart's; the painting was the hit of the 1782 Royal Academy exhibition and established Stuart's reputation.

Once back in the United States, Stuart concentrated solely on portraits. Virtually all were busts and he rarely did full-length figures again; critics jested that he did this to conceal his imperfect mastery of anatomy, joking that he was only reliable "down to the fifth button." Unable or unwilling to make careful preliminary drawings, he painted directly on the canvas, with a scintillating immediacy that was startling to patrons accustomed to the meticulous Copley.

Compared to Copley's exquisite draftsmanship and gleaming polished surfaces, Stuart could indeed look rough, but he compensated for this with an unerring mastery of color. He was the first American painter to grasp the three-dimensional nature

of color and of glazing. "Look at my hand," he once told Trumbull. "See how the colors are mottled and mingled ... good flesh coloring partook of all colors, not mixed, so as to be combined in one tint, but shining through each other, like the blood through the natural skin." *Like blood through the skin:* there can surely be no better definition of what the skillful layering of glazes can achieve.

Ever fickle, Stuart seldom stayed put for very long, meandering from New York (1793–94) to Philadelphia (1795–1803), Washington (1803–5), and finally Boston, where he remained until his death. His finest and most careful portraits came in the 1790s and he might have gone on making them, had he not discovered a lucrative cottage industry in George Washington imagery [57]. While dissolute

57 **Gilbert Stuart**, *George Washington*, 1796. Stuart dashed off his portraits with rapid-fire aplomb. The spontaneity is apparent in his "Athenaeum-type" portrait of George Washington, so called because of its purchase by the Boston Athenaeum. Recognizing the commercial potential of the image, he deliberately left it unfinished and worked up finished copies of it whenever he needed ready cash. (Estimates range from fifteen to seventy-five copies, which vary considerably in quality.)

with lenders and patrons, he was just as unfailingly generous to fellow painters as West was. At various times he aided Trumbull, Vanderlyn, Allston, Morse, and Sully, among others. If American art rapidly overcame its legacy of lineiness and flat coloring in the years after 1800, a lion's share of the credit must go to Stuart, who raised the abilities of artists and the expectations of patrons in every city in which he practiced.

Nonetheless, the Colonial tradition died hard. Even when offered the alternative of lush painterly portraits, many Americans preferred tight lines and flat surfaces, and would have declared Copley a superior painter to Stuart, if only for his self-evident precision. These patrons ensured a long afterlife for the Colonial mode. Ralph Earl (1751–1801), for example, trained with West but reverted to a tight Colonial style because his patrons in western Connecticut seemed to expect it. And naive painters like Ammi Phillips (1788–1865) carried the linear Colonial mode well into the second half of the nineteenth century.

The Colonial legacy is apparent in the career of Charles Willson Peale (1741–1827), whose gifts were not of the order of Stuart's or Vanderlyn's but who possessed a phenomenal capacity for work. As a painter, Peale was essentially an artisan. He had trained in Annapolis as a saddlemaker and was an inveterate tinkerer, building clocks, practicing taxidermy, and even inventing a "smokeless stove." Having easily mastered these trades, he regarded painting in much the same terms, a mechanical art whose rules could be learned by study and due diligence. He seems to have learned to paint by memorizing certain formulae and rules, and he never shook his habit of drawing a head by first making an egg shape [58].

Peale's friends raised funds to send him to study in London with West, who was helpful as always. On his return to America he established himself in Philadelphia as a fashionable portraitist, working in the tight liney mode of Copley. Serving with George Washington in the Revolution, he painted several full-length portraits of the general, which are among the first expressions of American political history in artistic terms. Dignified, fastidious, and fact-filled, they also betray Peale's chronic inability to arrange four limbs, a torso, and a head into a plausible body. When Stuart arrived in Philadelphia in 1795, Peale saw the futility of competition; he relinquished art for science, perhaps to the benefit of both.

With his encyclopedic interests, Peale was an ideal museum director. He opened a portrait gallery in 1784 and by the 1790s was devoting all his energy to it; after 1802, when he moved into the upper story of Philadelphia's Independence Hall, its focus

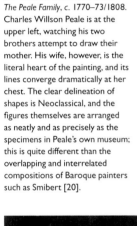

58 **Charles Willson Peale**, *The Peale Family*, c. 1770–73/1808. Charles Willson Peale is at the upper left, watching his two brothers attempt to draw their mother. His wife, however, is the literal heart of the painting, and its lines converge dramatically at her chest. The clear delineation of shapes is Neoclassical, and the figures themselves are arranged as neatly and as precisely as the specimens in Peale's own museum; this is quite different than the overlapping and interrelated compositions of Baroque painters such as Smibert [20].

shifted to natural history. This was America's first public museum, and its interior is recorded in a striking self-portrait of 1822 [40]. In it, Peale dramatically flings back a curtain to reveal the long gallery, lined below with the animals of North America and encircled by his portraits of the signers of the Declaration of Independence. He was careful not to pull the curtain too far back, and he kept his star attraction carefully veiled: a mastodon skeleton excavated by him and his sons in upstate New York. The histrionic gesture of the astonished woman in the middle ground, however, lets us know we are missing something very big indeed.

We might wonder at this indiscriminate mixing of revolutionary heroes and stuffed waterfowls, but for Peale there was no discrepancy: painting and taxidermy were two different mechanical arts, each of which preserved useful information in a realistic facsimile. Peale found a winning formula to unite art, science, and commerce—which was precisely the insight that a young French refugee would take from him. This was John James Audubon (1785–1851), whose celebrated *Birds of America* (1827–38) was America's most ambitious commercial exploitation of painting and naturalism, Peale's twin interests.

Peale groomed his eleven children to be artists and he burdened them with prominent names to which they were expected to live up; most achieved distinction in art or science, particularly Rembrandt (1778–1860), who trained in France and became a facile portrait painter, and Raphaelle (1775–1824), a still-life painter. Perhaps the most striking aspect of the Peale family was that everyone, whether male and female, was encouraged to draw. Four daughters of James Peale, Charles's brother, became painters. Of these, Anna Claypool Peale (1781–1878), a popular miniaturist, was the most talented.

Peale performed one other service to American art. He was a founder of the Pennsylvania Academy of the Fine Arts (1805), America's first art museum and school of fine arts. In this effort he was joined by William Rush (1756–1833), America's first native-born sculptor. Sculpture was the last of the great arts to flourish in the new republic, where there was no tradition of public statuary, apart from a few statues of the king that

59 **William Rush**, *The Schuylkill Chained*, 1825. One thinks here of Prometheus, who was punished by the gods for giving man the secret of fire, and was chained to a rock where an eagle would feast upon him. But for Rush it is water and not fire whose secrets have been revealed: his shackled captive graced Philadelphia's new public waterworks, showing how the fierce Schuylkill River was subjugated by a system of locks and dams, and made useful. The banks of the river now resound with industry and, rather than feasting, the bald eagle spreads its wings to vanish.

were toppled in the early days of the Revolution. Nor was it a field where the gentleman–amateur could hope to accomplish much. The first competent sculptors were French and Italian visitors who came for short visits to model George Washington, hoping to win a large public commission: Jean-Antoine Houdon (in 1785) and Giuseppe Ceracchi (in 1791/92).

Without formal education, Rush learned his craft as a carver of ship's figureheads, and his work only makes sense in these terms. His figures were vigorously animated, their swirling lines and billowing drapery carrying easily at a distance, a necessity for figureheads. And while he painted them white to simulate marble, their deep undercutting and gouging betrayed their wooden nature. In its rollicking lines and general sense of frothiness, Rush's work was rather more rococo than Neoclassical [59]. This may be because figurehead carving was a highly conservative art, and rococo conventions survived there (as they have in the decoration of today's wedding cakes). In the end, Rush made the most out of the hand that was dealt him, and he produced a respectable body of pious allegorical work for public buildings, but in artistic terms he was still on the level of Feke. It was not until Americans began working in Italy in the 1830s that sculpture was able to move beyond the realm of the craftsman and the amateur.

Given this great unevenness of quality, it seems as if there was nothing wrong with American art that could not be remedied with better formal training. Once artists were trained to European levels of accomplishment, then art might flourish. But a successful and robust artistic culture is a question of both supply and demand, that is, of both artists and patrons. And where patronage is not supportive, informed, and wealthy, the artist produces in vain, and lacks the spur of intelligent criticism.

American art had failed, not in the sense that it had not produced great and stirring works. Vanderlyn's *Ariadne* and Trumbull's *Death of General Montgomery* were works of a high order indeed. And yet their careers were ultimately failures. They had failed to produce a movement with sufficient ideas and cultural energy behind it to have an autonomous life of its own, which might sustain itself, and to be more than a passing fashion. In the end these bombastic epics were as much unsuited to American taste as they were to the scale of the American parlors for which they were destined.

Chapter 4   Landscape and Sentiment

A clean break separates the art and literature of the late eighteenth century from its immediate predecessors. Great changes in public taste and attitudes took place against the backdrop of the American and French Revolutions, which, if they did not cause these changes certainly reinforced them. The values of refinement and taste upheld by the earlier generation were now jettisoned in favor of passion and sentiment. In every form of art the effects of this change are visible. In poetry it produced Lord Byron, John Keats, Percy Bysshe Shelley, and Samuel Taylor Coleridge; in painting, John Constable and J. M. W. Turner in England, and Caspar David Friedrich in Germany; and in architecture, the far-reaching movement known as the Gothic Revival. Collectively these developments comprise the movement known as Romanticism.

An art of pure imagination, which thrilled at scenes of unbridled passion, madness, and terror, could not unfold in the United States as in Europe. It is true that Washington Irving and Edgar Allan Poe created an American school of Romantic literature; Benjamin Henry Latrobe imported the architecture of picturesque eclecticism; and the landscape paintings of John Trumbull and John Vanderlyn showed a romantic preference for irregular and picturesque scenery. And yet American Romanticism remained resolutely idealist. If it appealed to the imagination, it had an obligation to promote moral uplift and improvement, using the devices of Romanticism in service of the Christian agenda of personal redemption. The unhappy career of Washington Allston (1779–1843) shows the ambivalence of the American response to the Romantic movement.

Born in South Carolina, Allston graduated from Harvard and subsequently spent about fifteen years in Europe (1801–8, 1811–18). There he trained with the venerable Benjamin West, who was still grinding out heroic tableaux in the conventional

60 **Washington Allston**, *Moonlit Landscape*, 1819. Allston was less interested in heroic or exalted events than in exalted states of mind. This work is typical of his sentimental reveries, both in its introspective qualities and its nostalgia for the Italian landscape. Also characteristic of Allston is the luminous color sense and the richly glazed surfaces.

Grand Manner. Allston belonged to an age that saw West's work as bombastic rather than grand, however, and he yearned for art that addressed the imagination rather than art that promoted civic virtue. He soon befriended Coleridge, with whom he traveled through Italy and whose introspective and visionary poetry was the opposite of West's epic art. Allston, like Coleridge, sought to create a mood or suggest a state of mind; his most successful works were wistful reveries that took place in a gauzy ideal landscape [60].

But Allston never shed the conviction that art must be useful to justify itself. Once back in Boston, he struggled to combine his personal introspective voice with the formal demands of didactic Grand Manner painting. His masterpiece was to be the mighty *Belshazzar's Feast*, derived from the Old Testament book of Daniel, in which the vainglorious Babylonian king Belshazzar shrinks in fear as the finger of God writes on the wall. Allston chose the moment of high drama when the prophet Daniel revealed the meaning of the letters, a favorite motif of Romantic artists. But the colossal scale was not congenial to his talents, which were more suited to the introspective and personal. From 1817 to 1843 he labored in fits and starts over the painting, which was still unfinished at his death.

Allston's career could not differ more from that of his contemporary Thomas Sully (1783–1875), the Philadelphia portrait painter and the most successful of the Romantic era. While the perfectionist Allston was still agonizing over his *Belshazzar*, Sully managed to churn out 2,631 works, according to his own handwritten ledger. But his career is also a case study in the difficulty of learning to paint in the United States. After brief training with his French brother-in-law, a painter of miniatures, Sully switched to oil painting, bungling his early efforts by using olive oil (which never dries). In desperation, he paid for portraits by Henry Benbridge and John Trumbull, simply to watch how they painted. Others were more generous: Gilbert Stuart gave him three weeks of free lessons in 1807 and Benjamin West characteristically gave him the run of his studio during his 1809–10 trip to England. But he learned the most from Thomas Lawrence, the English painter whose works achieved a glowing richness of flesh, and a softness and delicacy of expression that formed Sully's ideal through the rest of his career.

Sully was one of several talented Romantic portrait painters, along with John Wesley Jarvis (1781–1840), Chester Harding

(1792–1866), and his son-in-law John Neagle (1796–1865). Sully stood out among them by virtue of his idiosyncratic method, and the extreme rapidity and thinness of his painting. In essence, he translated the conventions of miniature painting to oil painting. He generalized features to make them more elegant and decorative, suppressing bone structure and anatomy (a miniaturist does not need to know much anatomy) in favor of flowing lines and contours. So fluid is his sense of form that his figures often seem boneless, as in his portrait of Eliza Ridgely [61]. Even his approach to the handling of paint itself was that of a miniaturist, as his advice to his pupils suggests: "Paint freely, as if you were using

61 **Thomas Sully**, *Lady with a Harp: Eliza Ridgely*, 1818. This portrait showed Sully at his most elegant and fluid, although no plausible anatomy can account for the extraordinary length of fifteen-year-old Eliza's thigh, and her correspondingly short calf. But what does not work anatomically works aesthetically: the painting makes a charming visual pun between her exquisitely elongated form and the equally exquisite harp she is tuning, her delicate fingers absent-mindedly clasping the tuning key above.

62 **Hiram Powers,** *The Greek Slave,* c. 1843. Powers, whose earliest training was in modeling figures in wax, clay, and plaster, moved permanently to Florence in 1837. The plight of his slave is encapsulated in her chains, from which her Christian cross dangles. At a time of growing Abolitionist sentiment, many would read this as a commentary on American slavery as well.

watercolors, not too exact but in a sketchy manner." As a result, Sully was able to finish most portraits in six sittings—letting his wife and twelve children serve as stunt doubles for the clothing and hands between sittings.

The elegant elongation of Eliza Ridgely and her high-clinched waist suggest a new standard of beauty, that of Greek art. This was a radical change. During the late eighteenth century, enlightened patrons had admired the virtues of Republican Rome, their martial ardor and their public spirit. After the French Revolution and the defeat of Napoleon in 1815, however, enlightened taste everywhere turned to Greece. After the bombastic imperial imagery of Napoleon, Greek simplicity seemed a relief. And to a society recoiling in horror from the dawn of the Industrial Revolution, its Arcadian allure was irresistible. Greek meander friezes, palmettes, Greek furniture, even Greek clothing and hairstyles: all came into common use. The spirit behind this was the same languid aestheticism of John Keats's "Ode on a Grecian Urn": Beauty is truth, truth beauty, – that is all / Ye know on earth, and all ye need to know.

The Greek Revival was an international movement, which in its heyday—roughly, from 1815 to 1845—raised up errant Doric temples from Edinburgh to St. Petersburg to the Mississippi. In the United States it took on a political cast, inspired by the example of the modern Greek nation. The Ottoman Empire had ruled Greece since the fifteenth century but in 1821 Christian Greeks rose up against their Muslim rulers; the ensuing Greek War of Independence lasted until 1832. For Americans, who were aware of the ancient Greek origins of democratic government and who had likewise fought for independence, these wars aroused tremendous sympathy. Although Americans, unlike Lord Byron, typically did not fight and die alongside the Greeks, they marked the American landscape with their sympathy. This is the fringe of Greek place names on the American landscape, from Syracuse and Ithaca, Homer and Troy, all the way to Athens, Georgia. A line drawn between them shows the line of settlement during the first quarter of the nineteenth century; they form a physical map of the American frontier at the time of the Greek Revival.

The enthusiasm for the Greek cause produced a great deal of classicizing sculpture during the 1830s and 1840s, some of it good. It helps to explain the colossal success of Hiram Powers's *Greek Slave* [62] the first American work of art to receive the equivalent of a blockbuster tour. In the *Greek Slave,* ancient and modern

3 **Horatio Greenough**, *George Washington*, 1840. Like Powers, Greenough was an expatriate American sculptor, who went to Florence in 1825, and trained with the Danish Neoclassical sculptor Bertel Thorvaldsen. Both Powers and Greenough used allegorical devices to make their meaning legible. Greenough here shows Washington turning his sword round, indicating his surrender of military power.

Greece collided. The pose was that of the most celebrated statues of Greek antiquity, the *Knidian Aphrodite* (fourth century BC). But the story was contemporary: a Greek Christian woman has been captured by Turkish pirates and brought to the slave bazaar, where she has been stripped naked for inspection and auction. In an astutely crafted text, Powers explained that the slave's nudity was forced upon her, and therefore had no taint of shame or indecency. He was seconded by the Unitarian minister Orville Dewey, who wrote that the slave offered a lesson in Christian forbearance: "I would fain assemble all the licentiousness in the world around this statue, to be instructed, rebuked, disarmed, converted to purity by it!"

Greek Slave succeeded because its aesthetic idealism imparted a clear moral lesson. The other great Greek statue of the decade, Horatio Greenough's *George Washington*, did not, which helps to explain the scorn it aroused. The statue ought to have been a triumph: Congress commissioned it in 1832 from Greenough, an American sculptor living in Florence. He worked on it for nearly a decade, unveiling the result in 1841. Greenough's Washington was a Greek god, draped in a toga in the heroic pose of the fifth-century statue of Zeus at Olympia by Phidias [63]. The face, however, was a scrupulous composite of Gilbert Stuart's portraits of the president. The American public found this mixture of idealism and realism unhappy. One excessively literal critic suggested that Washington was "too prudent, and too careful of his health" to appear in this state of undress. After a brief term in the rotunda of the Capitol, the statue was discreetly removed.

Powers and Greenough each adapted a celebrated model from antiquity to serve a modern function; in architecture, much the same process took place.

Greek forms had long been a part of the repertoire of Neoclassicism, usually in combination with Roman domes and arches, but the line between Neoclassicism and the Greek Revival is crossed the moment that architects seek to re-create Greek buildings and not merely to use Greek forms. This can be marked with precision: on May 13, 1818, the building committee of the Second Bank of the United States invited architects to design "a chaste imitation of Grecian architecture in its simplest and least expensive form." No longer was a building to be a free and imaginative architectural essay, as in Neoclassicism, but literally an "imitation."

The instigator for the bank's program was evidently Nicholas Biddle (1786–1844). Although he would not be named director of the bank for a year, Biddle was already active behind the scenes. He had traveled extensively in Greece, one of the first American intellectuals to do so, where he was appalled by Lord Elgin's stripping of the Parthenon sculpture. Later he edited *The Port Folio*, an influential literary journal that he used to promote Greek architecture. The Greek Revival could have found no more eloquent or powerful patron [64].

The commission to design the bank was won by William Strickland, a pupil of Latrobe. Strickland "chastely imitated" the Parthenon, taking it line for line from the pages of Stuart & Revett's *Antiquities of Athens* [65]. Certain modifications were necessary. First, the bank was hoisted upon a great Roman podium, a kind of artificial Acropolis on a business street. The colonnades along its sides were eliminated, giving it two porticos but no continuous peristyle. Finally, the pediments were purged of sculpture, giving the facades a bone-dry austerity.

64 **Thomas Sully**, *Nicholas Biddle*, 1826. Sully painted Nicholas Biddle not as a banker but as a poet, a long-haired romantic gazing in dreamy reverie. He was about forty at the time of the portrait, suggesting that Sully was following the advice of his own treatise on painting: "it was well to increase the beauty of the complexion and give the appearance of youth, as this in a measure compensates for the want of life and motion."

65 **William Strickland**, Second Bank of the United States, Philadelphia, 1818–24. This was the first of a long line of American public buildings to have a true Greek portico. Its historical accuracy did not extend much beyond its two show facades, which served as fashionable frontispieces. But unlike Peter Harrison's Redwood Library of the previous century [17 and 25], these facades were no flat billboards; Strickland's building was a prodigy of rational construction, vaulted in brick and faced with marble. Its main banking room worked admirably, the central space reserved for the customers and marble counters for the tellers inserted between the columns.

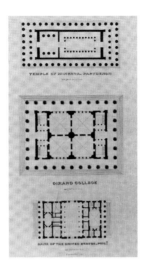

66 Thomas U. Walter, *Comparative Plans, Temple of Minerva; Parthenon; Girard College; Bank of U.S.,* undated. The central dilemma of the Greek Revival is encapsulated in this diagram: how to make a modern functional building out of the house of a god? The Parthenon, at top, contained a windowless cell with the statue of Athena at one end and a treasury at the other; it was not a public building. The Second Bank, at bottom, required a variety of well-lit and accessible rooms. To allow windows, it dispensed with columns along the sides. Girard College, at center, did not, which made the building far more accurate historically—and far more disastrous functionally.

67 John Neagle, *Portrait of William Strickland,* 1829. This portrait shows the effect of Neagle's training with Thomas Sully. The feathery touch, the delicate tilt of the head, the glazed ruddiness in his cheeks, even the starched and crisp shirt color, whose accented solidity offsets the softness of the face: all are part of the dashing Sully method.

Strickland's interior was a triumph of spatial imagination. Into the rectangular footprint he shoehorned an array of vaulted rooms, which culminated in the main banking room, a central barrel-vaulted space athwart the main axis. This vault was 28 feet (9 meters) in diameter, an extraordinary feat of brick construction, carried on two rows of slender Ionic columns. It was completely unexpected, a Roman space lodged in the depths of a Greek temple. In this respect it differs from its prototype, the Bank of Pennsylvania: Latrobe worked to make his interior volumes legible on the exterior, Strickland cleverly concealed them behind the all-important image of the temple [66].

The bank cemented Strickland's fame. An attractive portrait by John Neagle shows him before his great work, drawing board in hand [67]. Despite the casual stance, the composition was carefully disposed to show that the architect was a professional rather than a mechanic. The bank's portico is centered behind his head, reminding us that it is the product of both his hand and his mind. This was Latrobe's great cause and, indeed, Strickland succeeded Latrobe as America's principal architect of public buildings. Among his local works were the Philadelphia Mint, the Naval Home, and the Merchants Exchange; farther afield he designed the Tennessee State Capitol, the greatest of all the Greek state capitols.

Strickland's influence was immense, for the Second National Bank was emulated by its branch offices, which raised similar Doric temples from Boston to Erie to Savannah. For the first time, an American corporation achieved a visible national presence by means of architecture. The government and the national economy were now associated with Greek forms, indelibly (to this day, a pedimented portico adorns the American Social Security card). The decorous Palladian and Roman classicism of the early republic now gave way to Greek severity. During the next two decades, many of the principal buildings of the federal government were remade in a Greek image, including the Treasury Department and the Patent Office, both begun in 1836 by Robert Mills (1781–1855).

Mills, like Strickland, was a protégé of Latrobe although a less graceful designer and not a spatial thinker ("A wretched designer," Latrobe complained). Mills was no paper architect, though; his buildings were always conceived as completely resolved structural systems, each room vaulted in fireproof masonry. His Treasury Building is an assembly of groin-vaulted, cubic cells, arranged along a T-shaped array of corridors. To mask the immense flank on Fifteenth Street, Mills drew on the Ionic order of the Erechtheum on the Acropolis. And indeed, his 466-foot (142-meter) Ionic colonnade is sublime, stopping just before monumentality tips over into monotony [68].

Contemporary critics scolded these buildings for sacrificing archeological accuracy to function. Ever acerbic, Horatio Greenough made sport of eloquent facades that spoke eloquent

68 Robert Mills, Treasury Department, Washington, D.C., 1836–42. Although Mills's Treasury Building has been altered, its essential character has survived; the pedimented wings to either end were designed by Thomas U. Walter in 1855 and Mills's brownstone columns were later replaced with granite. The building helped establish the mighty civic scale that has stamped the national capital to the present. Mills followed his triumph with the Post Office (1839–42), a Roman Renaissance design, and the Washington Monument (1845–54).

Greek while "a huge brick chimney rising in the rear, talks English." Greenough may have missed the point: the aesthetic interest of every Greek Revival building usually lies in the intelligent negotiation between image and reality. The best work came when architects strayed from precedent. The New York Customs House (1833), by Town and Davis, daringly conflated the Pantheon and the Parthenon, squeezing a circular Roman dome into a Greek temple. Ammi B. Young repeated the feat with his Boston Customs House (1837–47) but pushed his dome above the roof to crown the building. Of course, the U.S. Capitol had already made a visible dome indispensable for a monumental public building. Town and Davis capitalized on the formula, building state capitols in North Carolina, Illinois, and Indiana, all of which placed conspicuous domes atop otherwise thoroughly Greek buildings. Commercial buildings played even more loosely with their prototypes. For the Providence Arcade in Rhode Island (1828), James C. Bucklin and Russell Warren used two Greek temple fronts as bookends to a modern skylighted shopping mall, lined by cast-iron galleries [69]. Most abstract of all was Town and Davis's design for the Astor Hotel in New York, a cage of pearly marble pilasters, through which the slender cast-iron railings of the balusters thread their way [70].

69 **James C. Bucklin** and **Russell Warren**, Providence Arcade, Rhode Island, 1828. Not every Greek Revival building was a retreat from modern industrial reality. The Providence Arcade arrayed three tiers of stores to either side of an enclosed street, fronted at either end by an Ionic portico in rugged granite. Although architects Bucklin and Warren played loose with their historical models, they achieved something that was more truly Greek in spirit than most of their contemporaries, making a modern version of the Greek colonnaded public building (or *stoa*).

A similar freedom and naivety is apparent in Greek Revival houses. Its most decisive influence was to change the orientation of the Colonial house, whose gable traditionally ran parallel to the street. Now the gable was turned to become the formal facade, its roof pitch lowered and wood pilasters placed at the corners; with a few such alterations a Georgian house became an abstraction of a Greek temple. This vernacular type is to be found across the United States. The temple front was usually a flat frontispiece, and did not go around the side of the building, except in the South where a covered colonnade suited the climate (and where social conditions ensured that the Greek Revival would flourish right up until the outbreak of the Civil War). There are a few northern exceptions, including the inspired Wilcox-Cutts House in Vermont (1843), which carries its colonnade around the sides of the house before it dies into the rear wings, a lovely vignette of an American parlor encased in a Greek cage [71].

This freewheeling invention shows an utter disregard for academic rules. It should be remembered that, unlike the gentleman–amateurs of the Palladian Revival, virtually all of the Greek Revival architects had originally trained as carpenters and bricklayers. If they too kept their noses buried in books, they

70 **Town and Davis**, Design for the Astor Hotel, New York, c. 1830. This is a triumph of architectural rendering—and subterfuge. Note how Davis keeps the windows out of sight, leaving nothing but an abstract wall of bone-white pilasters. This was the Greek Revival at its most modern absolute, which is surely the reason it was rejected for the usual classical pastiche.

71 Wilcox-Cutts House, Orwell, Vermont, 1843. Like its Georgian predecessors, the Greek Revival house retained the graphic quality of the carpenter's eighteenth-century pattern book, its details showing the crisp flatness of timber framing.

appreciated Greek architecture not only as beautiful form but also as intelligent construction. And their own buildings reflect a similar intelligence. While Greek temples were built of marble or limestone, American architects used materials that were either flimsier (wood) or stronger (granite). The work of carpenter-turned-architect Alexander Parris, the designer of Quincy Market, Boston (1823–26), is characteristic. Previously granite had been quarried only in small blocks but improved shipping and cutting had recently made possible the transportation of enormous blocks. Parris's enormous market hall (535 feet [163 meters] in length) is a rugged cage in which every pier and lintel was formed from a single monolithic slab of granite. The sheer physical heftiness of the building was palpable—as if Stonehenge had been built during the Industrial Revolution, and turned to commerce. At the same time, Parris used cast-iron columns in the interior to make the building fireproof.

So long as the Greek Revival made buildings that were functional and fashionable, the movement flourished. One building proved to be neither functional nor fashionable, however. And this was the legacy of Nicholas Biddle, who had presided over the rise of the Greek Revival, and would be personally implicated in its collapse. This occurred with the most spectacular of all modern Greek monuments, Girard College in Philadelphia.

Girard College was the bequest of Stephen Girard (1750–1831), the eccentric one-eyed merchant who made his fortune financing the War of 1812. His will remains one of America's single greatest acts of private philanthropy, which provided over two million dollars to found a school for "poor male white orphan children." Girard was obsessively meticulous; having dispatched many trading vessels to the Far East, he knew how to send instructions from beyond the grave. His will specified every aspect of his school, from the content of its curriculum to the thickness of its walls. The main building was to be a grid of four classrooms to a floor, each measuring 50 by 50 feet (15.2 by 15.2 meters), with a stair hall to either end. Everything was to be built "in the most permanent manner, avoiding needless ornament."

If Girard envisioned a utilitarian box, he made a mistake in appointing as his executor that great champion of all things Greek, Nicholas Biddle. Biddle promptly held an architectural competition which drew most of America's leading architects, the most important such contest since that for the Capitol building. The result was a stupendous Greek prodigy, a mighty Corinthian temple with a complete peristyle, built of white marble. Biddle's architect was Thomas U. Walter, who toiled on the building from 1833 to 1847 [72]. He also designed a house for Biddle, a Doric temple called Andalusia, perched on the banks of the Delaware River; scarcely an aspect of Biddle's life remained that did not take place beneath a Greek pediment.

72 **Thomas U. Walter**, Girard College, Philadelphia, 1833–48. This is the most sublime of Greek Revival monuments, Greek archeology devoted to philanthropy, costing nearly two million dollars—if only it had worked. Its architect was Thomas U. Walter (1804–87), a former bricklayer who helped build the great barrel vault of the Second Bank of the United States; later he was trained by William Strickland. Walter culminated the architectural dynasty that had begun with Benjamin Henry Latrobe, and which established American architecture as a profession. Walter's work at Girard College has been overshadowed by his work at the U.S. Capitol, including its great cast-iron dome.

73 **Francis William Edmonds**, *The City and the Country Beaux*, c. 1839. A master of homey genre scenes, Edmonds loved to exaggerate familiar types for comic effect. The rival suitors are exaggerated to the point of absurdity. The rural type is homespun but uncouth, wearing his hat indoors and sitting in a vulgar open-legged stance. His urban rival is unctuous and supercilious, with an exaggerated show of manners. Though Edmonds's painting is without malice, it shows the lines of social conflict that were exploited in the populist politics of the day.

For all its lavish expense, Biddle's monument did not work; the square classrooms with their lofty marble ceilings were an acoustic calamity. Walter was a gifted engineer but even he could not save the classrooms of the third story, masked by the massive entablature so that light could enter only from an oculus above or from windows at ankle level. Biddle may have argued that Greek architecture was the style of reason and utility; the evidence of his building argued otherwise.

The timing could not have been worse, for Biddle and his bank were under attack during the years of the college's construction. A central national bank had always been controversial and even, in the opinion of many, unconstitutional. And the strict probity with which it managed its affairs made it unpopular with those who favored a policy of easy credit. These forces found a champion in Andrew Jackson, America's seventh president and the first to practice deliberate class warfare. Jackson entered office in 1829, at a time of growing tension between the established classes of the eastern cities and the entrepreneurs and settlers of the frontier, and between agrarian and industrial wealth. This is the tension captured by the genre painters of the era [73]. Jackson also introduced the spoils system, whereby the victorious party replaced much of the upper tier of the Civil Service with people loyal to it, thus rewarding political supporters with patronage. Biddle's refusal to cooperate earned him Jackson's enmity.

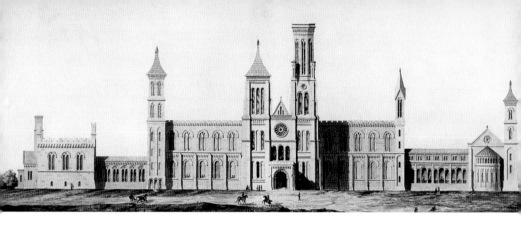

Jackson campaigned against the Second Bank continuously from 1829 to 1837. His withdrawal of government deposits ultimately led to the bank's failure and Biddle's public disgrace. In the course of his campaign, the bank's Greek architecture became a symbol of arrogant luxury. If the Greek Revival of the 1820s had evoked democracy and Arcadian ideals, by the 1840s it was associated with fraud, insolvency, and chastened pride. The death knell came in 1847, just as Girard College opened.

In that year the Smithsonian Institution opened on the Mall in Washington, D.C. Funded by a bequest by British scientist James Smithson, the institution and its building were the brainchild of Robert Dale Owen, a congressman and social reformer. Like Girard College, the Smithsonian was educational in purpose, and equally nostalgic in style: it was a rambling towered castle in red sandstone, its details borrowed from the great Romanesque cathedral at Speyer in Germany [74]. Unlike Biddle, however, Owen was no Romantic but a modern utilitarian, and his Romanesque was chosen by purely rational criteria. The freedom and irregularity of medieval planning made it possible to group laboratories, classrooms, and offices in a functional manner, and even the picturesque welter of spires, used to conceal the laboratories' water towers, were essentially rational. Unlike Girard College, here there was no tension between program and image.

Girard College and the Smithsonian were finished at roughly the same time, and Owen was happy to compare them. In 1849 he published *Hints on Public Architecture*, which tabulated the cost of America's principal public buildings. After the Capitol in Washington, Girard College was the most expensive building in America, costing $1,933,621. Owen took great glee in breaking down the figures for the thirty-four sumptuous Corinthian columns of the building's peristyle, or colonnade: "The cost of the

Girard College peristyle alone would have sufficed to erect two Smithsonian Institutions, and have left a hundred and sixty-seven thousand dollars to spare." The attack was devastating; judged purely on financial grounds, the Greek Revival was a catastrophe.

But styles seldom fail because of one factor but because of a convergence of forces. In the case of the Greek Revival, it was a combination of a general fatigue over Greek temple fronts, the taint of financial scandal that hung over the Second Bank and Girard College, and the abject functional failure of the college. So the stage was set for the Medieval Revival of the 1840s and such buildings as the Smithsonian. This required a considerable mental leap. Before American Protestants could reclaim the Romanesque and Gothic architecture of the Middle Ages (which still held worrisome Catholic associations), a fundamental shift in artistic values had to take place first. This shift, one of the great revolutions in American art, took place in the realm of land and landscape.

In 1811, the city of New York reached no farther north than Twenty-third Street and had barely expanded beyond the limits of the old Dutch settlement. But prescient citizens could already see that the four-mile length of the island of Manhattan would one day be entirely covered with buildings. Rather than letting this occur in piecemeal fashion, they proposed a comprehensive street plan for the island, all the way north to a hypothetical 155th Street. This was the notorious Commissioners' Plan, a plan as ambitious as it was stupefyingly unimaginative: an unvarying grid of 200 by 920-foot blocks was unrolled across Manhattan as if it were a giant bolt of fabric, taking no heed of topography or the need for public space [75]. Its underlying philosophy was utilitarian, in which land is regarded solely as a commodity—as real estate, and not as landscape or as nature.

Utilitarianism was the unofficial national philosophy in Andrew Jackson's hustling and speculating America, which was convulsed by a collective enthusiasm for "improvements," the all-embracing

75 John Randel, Jr., *Map of the City of New York and Island of Manhattan as Laid Out by the Commissioners*, 1811. The plan explicitly rejected "those supposed improvements by circles, ovals, and stars" that animated the plan of Washington, D.C. Instead, its authors asked New Yorkers to "bear in mind that a city is to be composed principally of the habitations of men, and that straight-sided and right-angled houses are the most cheap to build and the most convenient to live in." Their grid was a grimly efficient diagram for the division of real estate, without the theological significance that it had in New Haven and Philadelphia.

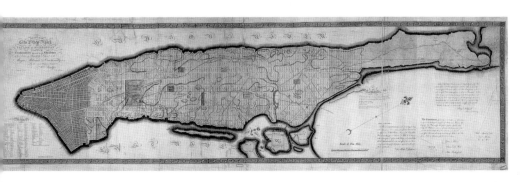

76 Thomas Cole, *Landscape with Tree Trunks*, 1828. Cole was inspired by the landscape painters of the seventeenth century, primarily Claude Lorrain and Salvator Rosa. From Claude came his pastoral mode, although he supplanted the classical ruins and Arcadian shepherds with settler's cabins and Indian braves. From Rosa came the drama: the turbulent atmospherics, the convulsive topography, the tormented trees. He is the source of this painting, its obligatory lightning-struck tree writhing in the foreground like a soul in perdition.

77 Thomas Cole, *View from Mount Holyoke, Northampton, Massachusetts, after a Thunderstorm (The Ox-bow)*, 1836. Cole depicts the celebrated scenic view from Mount Holyoke, showing where the slow-moving Connecticut River eroded its banks to meander into a curve. This natural feature shows the antiquity of the landscape but also its fragility. Two storms are crossing the land from right to left, the westward-moving rainstorm also a human storm, felling the primal forest and leaving behind a trail of tidy fields and small wood cabins.

term for those highways, canals, and railroads that were tying together the old seaboard colonies into an interlocking national economy. This culminated in 1825 with the opening of the Erie Canal, which cut across New York State to link Lake Erie to the city of Troy on the Hudson. Now the internal waterways of the United States became a great funnel, which collected the wealth of the interior and conducted it to its spout, the harbor of New York. From this moment, New York was the epicenter of the national economy and culture, and Philadelphia's long decline began.

A psychological milestone followed the economic one. Shortly after the opening of the canal came the fifty-year anniversary of the Declaration of Independence, on July 4, 1826, a day on which both Thomas Jefferson and John Adams famously died. The revolutionary generation was passing into history, along with its physical landscape, and nostalgia now flared up around preindustrial colonial America. Two artists resourcefully exploited this nostalgia in 1826: the writer James Fenimore Cooper published *The Last of the Mohicans*, and the painter Thomas Cole held the first public exhibition of his landscape painting. The focus of both men was the romantic topography of the Hudson River.

Thomas Cole was born in Lancashire, England in 1801, the son of a failed textile manufacturer. He emigrated to the United States at sixteen, studied briefly at the Academy of Fine Arts in Philadelphia, and moved to New York in 1825. Soon thereafter he took a fateful sketching tour along the Hudson, admiring its spectacular scenery while also noting the first lumbering boats steaming downriver with their booty from the interior. The works which resulted from this trip surprised and delighted three members of the National Academy of Design: John Trumbull, Asher B. Durand, and William Dunlap. With their approval and imprimatur, Cole became the artistic sensation of 1826.

Cole's subject matter was the rugged scenery of the Catskill Mountains, their gorges and waterfalls, and lonely granite ledges [76 and 77]. He did not invent landscape painting, but drew freely from Dutch and Italian sources, from Jacob Ruysdael, Claude Lorrain, and Salvator Rosa, whose work he knew, like most American painters, almost exclusively through prints. Inevitably, he thought in terms of tone and line, not color, and his technique reinforced this: he made pencil sketches on site, with cursory notations as to color, which he subsequently worked up into finished oil paintings in his New York studio. Cole may have been a realist, but he disdained slavish topographic fidelity. He insisted

that that he could "never paint successfully until I have generalized," which meant that in the studio features were conflated and details improved in order to arrive at the "essential truth" of a landscape. The realism of the sketches yielded to the idealism of the finished canvases.

Cole's work appealed to religious sentiment but in a general, nondenominational Protestant way. Each of his works could be read as an allegory of Christian redemption, expressed in the foliage at every state of life from blossom and maturity to death, decay, and rebirth. His chief insight was that the natural wilderness of the continent might be treated as a moral text, a visual sermon in line and pigment. This message found a receptive audience. The impulse to find a moral allegory in any given text is a deeply innate American habit of mind. After all, Protestant America, as in the Puritan meeting house of the seventeenth century, was still sitting down Sunday after Sunday to hear a short scriptural reading which was then subjected to prolonged formal analysis, and from which a moral lesson was drawn. Such exegesis was the nation's fundamental literary experience. It would be a dullard indeed who could not see the presence of God in a golden sunrise, or the wrath of God in a lightning-blasted tree—or look at a solitary cabin by a pristine lake and not see Adam's house in paradise. Here at last was an art that presented no dangerous "graven image," whose homily was not delivered in terms of saints and miracles but in terms of that great American preoccupation, the land.

Cole's art is essentially elegiac and it is suffused with a sense of intense personal distress at the vanishing of the American wilderness. He summarized his philosophy of landscape painting in his 1836 "Essay on American Scenery," published in the *American Monthly Magazine*. There he proclaimed that "the most distinctive, and perhaps the most impressive, characteristic of American scenery is its wildness," which distinguished it from the ancient settled landscape of Europe. Its wildness meant that it was poor in historical associations, but for Cole this was a blessing; it merely meant there was "no ruined tower to tell of outrage—no gorgeous temple to speak of ostentation." Instead, "American associations are not so much of the past as of the present and the future," and those who contemplated his serene landscapes were not intended to ponder what had once happened there but rather the civilization that was to come.

Cole's attitude to this was ambivalent. While he viewed the conquest of the landscape as predestined, he felt palpable physical distress at the process: "the ravages of the axe are daily increasing—the most noble scenes are made desolate … [t]he wayside is becoming shadeless" [77]. This bundle of ideas was contradictory—the imperative of progress and conquest collided with Cole's reverence for the divinity of nature—but out of their tense confrontation there arose the great landscape architecture and town planning of the nineteenth century that are one of the central achievements of American culture.

Cole was a facile draftsman but he was acutely aware of his artistic weaknesses; he never mastered, for example, the human figure (he learned to keep them small). Hoping therefore to augment his limited education, he sailed to Europe in 1829 for a three-year study trip. On the eve of his departure, William Cullen Bryant, the celebrated nature poet, dedicated a sonnet to Cole, which offers a succinct statement of the difference between the landscapes of America and of Europe, as understood by the Hudson River School:

> Thine eyes shall see the light of distant skies
> Yet, Cole, thy heart shall bear to Europe's strand
> A living image of thy native land
> Such as on thy glorious canvas lies:
> Lone lakes – savannahs where the bison roves –
> Rocks rich with summer garlands – solemn streams –
> Skies where the desert eagle wheels and screams –
> Spring bloom and autumn blaze of boundless groves.
> Fair scenes shall greet thee where thou goest – fair,
> But different – every where the trace of men,
> Paths, homes, graves, ruins, from the lowest glen
> To where life shrinks from the fierce Alpine air,
> Gaze on them , til the tears shall dim thy sight;
> But keep that earlier, wilder image bright.

Like many American artists, from Copley to Bingham, whose isolation and provincialism was a source of freshness, Cole was unsettled by his encounter with Europe. His technique did not change appreciably—for that he was too rigid—but his themes grew more elevated and ambitious. He projected several complex cycles in which landscape painting took on the pretense and swagger of the Grand Manner. After the grandiloquent *Course of Empire* (1834–36) came *The Voyage of Life* (1840–42), in which the journey of a single life is told in terms of four different landscapes [78]. Cole's sentimental didacticism was exactly pitched to popular taste, and both cycles were resounding public successes. (If the

78 **Thomas Cole**, *The Voyage of Life: Youth*, 1842. Cole's greatest public success was his *Youth*, the second painting of the four-part *Voyage of Life* series. It shows the figure of Youth taking over the rudder of his own destiny and setting course for dream castles in the air, not noticing that the river will soon carry him into violent cataracts. Distributed in the thousands by the Art Union, the image conveyed antebellum optimism at its most innocent and sentimental. Cole himself was no longer so optimistic. Perhaps thinking of slavery, and how it could not end without violence, Cole was already predicting for the United States "scenes of tyranny and wrong, blood and oppression such as not have been acted since the world was created."

Aesthetic Movement of the late nineteenth century would come to despise these cloying works, it never succeeded in creating anything nearly as popular.)

Cole died young in 1848 but he had already accomplished his goal, having made landscape painting the main channel of American art, which attracted the strongest talents and the most enlightened patronage. Under his leadership, the movement had grown from an artistic fad to a comprehensive intellectual movement, undergirded by the Transcendental philosophy of Ralph Waldo Emerson and embracing the fields of painting, architecture, literature, and landscape gardening. These various strands converge in Asher B. Durand's sentimental tribute to Cole, *Kindred Spirits* [79]. Durand depicted Cole and William Cullen Bryant, the Romantic poet, in symbolic conversation, contemplating the sublime landscape of the Catskills. The painting was prophetic, for at that very moment Bryant was aggressively lobbying for a municipal park in New York, issuing forth a torrent of editorials in the newspaper he owned and edited, the *New York Post*. *Kindred Spirits* captures this instant, as the Hudson River School moved from canvas to landscape to produce its grandest monument: Central Park.

79 Asher B. Durand, *Kindred Spirits*, 1849. Durand's posthumous tribute to Thomas Cole telescopes together the late painter's favorite sites, Kauterskill Falls and the Catskill Clove, in a single perfected view. Cole bids farewell to his friend William Cullen Bryant, and points with his brush to his ultimate destination. From now on his journey will be spiritual, and the soaring eagle—the focus of the principal lines of the painting—seems to suggest the release of his captive soul.

Well before Central Park, Americans had begun to take notice of the picturesque movement that began in eighteenth-century England. The doctrine held that land could be shaped and composed like a picture, to delight with those elements of picturesque design: irregularity, contrast, and surprise. Its devices were the meandering path, scattered clumps of artfully grouped trees and sudden unexpected vistas. This was the aesthetic vocabulary of the picturesque landscape, but in the United States it acquired an additional layer of meaning: the moral. Wild primal state was a moral good, simply by virtue of its wildness. The task of the gardener and the artist was to preserve this wildness or—

as Thomas Cole did by moving around trees and hills to find its essential truth—to simulate it.

The picturesque English fashion was brought to America at any early date. Already in the late eighteenth century, the grounds of private country estates were laid out along romantic and irregular lines. Evergreens were arranged in casual clumps to contrast with swaths of broad meadow, while frail pavilions and gazebos directed the view and served as eye-catchers. The first public parks to embrace the style came later, oddly enough in the form of cemeteries, where aesthetic and hygienic motives neatly aligned. The rural cemetery was not only healthier than the crammed urban churchyard, but it also looked salubrious. A trio of great rural cemeteries was built in the 1830s—Mt. Auburn, Cambridge, Massachusetts (1831), Laurel Hill Cemetery, Philadelphia (1836), and Greenwood Cemetery, Brooklyn (1838)—establishing the picturesque model that American cemeteries have continued to follow to this day.

These cemeteries were later followed by picturesquely landscaped suburbs, beginning with the exquisite settlement of Llewellyn Park, West Orange, New Jersey (1853). A planned suburb for inhabitants of "modest means," it scattered quaint Gothic cottages on serpentine streets, whose winding lines hugged the contours of the land. At the heart of Llewellyn Park was the Ramble, an undulating course of wild and undeveloped terrain, a new kind of public space that expressed the idea of the New England town common in the terms of pristine landscape. Llewellyn Park's main contribution to the American landscape was its insistence on visual continuity: no fences or landscaping was permitted to separate the lots from one another, so that the

80 Alexander Jackson Davis, Llewellyn Park, West Orange, New Jersey, 1853. Llewellyn Park ushered in a new kind of community, the commuter suburb. With the advent of the railroad it was now possible to live in the same wild surroundings that Cole celebrated—or at least a plausible fiction of them—even while working in the hustling mercantile city. Llewellyn Park instantly codified the elements that would define American suburban planning for the next century: winding streets, elm-shaded sidewalks and tree lawns, and a variety of picturesque architectural styles. So strong are its philosophical and formal ideas that they are still recognizable, a century later, even in their radically pared-down version in such suburbs as Levittown.

81 **A. J. Downing**, A Lake or River Villa in the Bracketed Style, from A. J. Downing, *The Architecture of Country Houses*, 1850. According to this book, a house must be truthful to its site as well as its materials. A craggy mountainous setting required a craggy roofline, as here, while a flatter site required broad spreading forms and generous verandas. Even the color should be local, and determined by overturning a nearby clump of earth and examining the clay. This was the most readily available natural pigment even as it served to unite the house visually with the local geology. Here, lofty flights of Transcendentalist considerations mixed with suggestions of utmost practicality, a characteristic mixture for Downing.

houses sit on a strip of unbroken green within an intact landscape. Here romanticism made its peace with utilitarianism; land could still remain as landscape, at least optically, even as it was converted to real estate [80].

A picturesque landscape called for a picturesque building, and Andrew Jackson Downing, America's foremost landscape gardener, provided both. Downing popularized picturesque landscape gardening in his journal, *The Horticulturalist*, and a series of influential architectural pattern books, including *Cottage Residences* (1842) and *The Architecture of Country Houses* (1850). The linchpin of Downing's thought was truth, that buildings had a moral scope and needed to be true in their use of materials and their expression of function. In cost-cutting America, these were revolutionary insights. Builders had long taken delight in rubbing sand on painted wood in order to simulate stone: Peter Harrison did it in his Newport Library, George Washington at Mount Vernon, and Thomas Jefferson at Monticello. Downing was not impressed by this noble pedigree and thought the practice deplorable, a "sham."

The doctrine of truth was not limited to materials, and it found its highest expression in the site itself. If Thomas Cole sought to extract the essential truth of a landscape, Downing felt that a house should be in harmony with that truth. His books provided choice examples for every type of topography and climate [81]. Here he aimed at a sublime metaphysical unity between a landscape and the objects within it, much as Cole had when he placed his symbolic figure of Youth in a setting of luxuriant high summer.

Downing was not himself an architect, and to illustrate his ideas he drew from the work of collaborators, such as Alexander Jackson Davis, who built most of the Llewellyn Park cottages. Now liberated from his partnership with the classicist Ithiel Town, Davis indulged his appetite for the picturesque, designing the era's most picturesque Gothic villas [82]. These buildings meandered and sprawled descriptively, "truthfully" showing the function of each discrete part. Here again, a moral rationale reinforced the aesthetic impulse—in this case, to make the house as variegated and charmingly irregular as possible.

Both Downing and Davis attached particular importance to the porch or veranda, which had already become a distinctive hallmark of American architecture but which now assumed a social, even a moral role. For Downing, the porch was the place of family gathering, "where the social sympathies take shelter securely under the shadowy eaves." With the open porch, the enclosed box of the house was rendered social and gregarious. Architecturally, it served the same function as the granite ledge in Cole's paintings, the viewing promontory which thrust the lone observer into the very landscape that he contemplated. So persuasive was Downing's gospel of the porch that it took two consequential inventions—the television and air-conditioning—to supplant its social and physical functions in the middle of the twentieth century.

82 **Alexander Jackson Davis**, Lyndhurst, Tarrytown, New York, 1838. Davis referred to himself as an "architectural composer," and he designed his houses as if they were paintings, their towers, gables, and bays arranged to make a lively and dynamic silhouette. The most celebrated is the sprawling and romantic Lyndhurst, built for the merchant William Paulding. Davis could do more than simply dream up clever facades; the interior offers an enchanting pageant of spaces, each different in shape, ornament, and character.

83 **Vaux & Olmsted**, Central Park, New York, 1863. Central Park is the picturesque antidote to the city's prim utilitarian grid of 1811. Olmsted advocated the radical idea that the urban park should serve as the one place where America's social classes might mingle and interact. Of all the competition entries, his offered the greatest expanse of open meadow, which he saw as essential to the park's social mission.

Downing's career, like that of Cole, was played out against the backdrop of the Hudson River. His death was ironic: having devoted his life to fighting the ravages of the Industrial Revolution and the steam engine, he was killed in 1852 when the boiler of the steamboat *Henry Clay* exploded. Although he had accomplished the work of several lifetimes, he was in fact only thirty-seven.

A few years earlier Downing had recruited an English architect, Calvert Vaux, to serve as his assistant; now Vaux inherited the practice. His cardinal achievement—and in a sense Downing's posthumous achievement—was Central Park. Here Vaux was aided by Frederick Law Olmsted, a journalist and fervent follower of Emerson who had recently become interested in the problem of landscape. Olmsted wrote a series of articles for the *New York Times* in the early 1850s, based on extensive travels through the American South. There he argued that the degradation of slavery went hand in hand with the atrophying of social institutions, and the weakening of community. He became convinced of the almost mystic connection between mental and physical freedom, a theme he would stress in his subsequent career as a landscape architect (a term he invented), which began at Central Park.

William Cullen Bryant's long years of lobbying paid off in 1858 when the city of New York held a design competition for Central Park. The conditions were baffling, requiring four major roads to be brought across the park without destroying the perception of untamed nature. This was the occasion for Vaux & Olmsted's greatest stroke of inspiration: they sank the road beds out of sight, carrying their footpaths across them on bridges, so that the park's visual and spatial continuity might be maintained [83]. Just as at Llewellyn Park, or in the paintings of Thomas Cole, the theme is the uninterrupted continuity of space. Olmsted said that it conveyed "the sensation of freedom itself," contrasting it with the degraded landscape caused by slavery. Thus Central Park overlaid the continental tradition of the picturesque with Transcendentalist themes to produce the landscape equivalent of philosophy.

The park made Olmsted a national celebrity and it became the chief prototype for America's public parks for the next half century and more. The best were built by Olmsted himself, including Prospect Park, Brooklyn, the Boston Fens, Golden Gate Park in San Francisco, and even Mount Royal Park, Montreal. And so the physical and psychic devastation caused by the Erie Canal gave rise to a school of landscape art that reached far beyond the Hudson River to become the American attitude toward landscape, with its themes of tragedy and idealism—and irony as well, for without the wealth produced by such enterprises as the Erie Canal there could have been no parks like Central Park.

The specter of the Industrial Revolution hovers constantly over the work of Cole, Downing, and Olmsted, who sought to heal the wounds and traumas of that revolution. It is this specter that gives their picturesque art its sense of unrequited yearning and of tragedy. Much the same might be said of the buildings of the antebellum era, which became ever more picturesque in appearance as their construction became ever more industrial.

In particular, two products of the Industrial Revolution—the steam saw and the mass-produced nail—utterly transformed the traditional wood house. Cheap mill-sawn boards eliminated the need for massive oak timbers, even as the receding forest was making those timbers scarce. Instead, a house could be assembled out of a light framework of thin boards, which did not become stable until propped against one another, as in a house of cards. This was the balloon frame, which could be swiftly nailed together without the laborious cutting and shaping of mortise and tenon joints in the traditional oak frame. This furthered the incipient planarity of American architecture, which startled Charles Dickens during his visit to the United States, and which forms a recurrent theme of his *American Notes*, where he puzzled over the "sharp outlines," "razor-like edges" and the "clean cardboard colonnades" of New England.

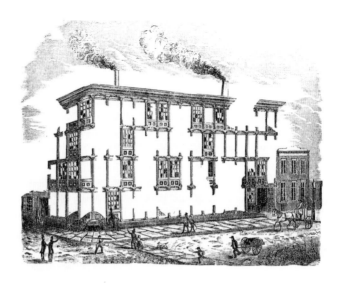

84 **James Bogardus**, Cast Iron Factory, 1849, from James Bogardus, *Cast Iron Buildings*. Bogardus's drawing of a cast-iron building, which peels away its walls to expose its iron components, is a tour de force of architectural rendering. But as advertising it is even more brilliant, making the impossible look possible, and suggesting that the building would be able to support itself even when reduced to a few slender columns. Even the doubtful viewer would carry away a sense of the irresistible strength of iron, which was Bogardus's principal selling point.

But the quintessential material of the Industrial Revolution was iron, not wood. Although iron had played a supporting role in architecture since time immemorial, the first all-iron buildings did not appear until the end of the 1840s. They were the creation of the New York inventor James Bogardus, a capricious prodigy who had invented the first efficient gas meter and the press for mass-producing postage stamps. In 1848 he turned his erratic mind to architecture, building himself a factory in New York that was perhaps the world's first cast-iron building [84]. He later claimed that the idea came to him during a visit to Italy, where he noticed how Renaissance palaces were composed of identical bay units, which were repeated as needed. His innovation was to adapt this modular system to iron, a material of limitless flexibility: it could be rolled into sheets to make floors, cast into molds to make structural columns, and variously hammered, cut, and stamped to make ornament and column capitals.

Rarely do the genius for inventing and the genius for marketing appear in the same person, and they did not do so in Bogardus, a catastrophe as a businessman. He was soon supplanted by Daniel Badger, a forceful entrepreneur who erected iron buildings in every major city in the country. The iron craze lasted until 1871, when the great Chicago Fire demonstrated in deadly fashion the limitations of the material: iron would not burn but it could indeed melt, and lose all its structural strength long before a timber beam failed. Not until the 1880s would architects regain the confidence to experiment boldly with metal construction.

Cast iron dramatically transformed the economics and technology of architecture but hardly touched its appearance at all. Bogardus and Badger used the material as a cheap surrogate for stone, and they poured it into shapes that made no sense in iron, such as round arches, to imitate the Renaissance forms then in vogue. The Industrial Revolution introduced new principles as well as new materials, however, and these did make for buildings of radically different form. Most revolutionary was the panopticon plan. Known in Europe since the late eighteenth century, it attached a series of radiating wings to a central hub, which permitted easy observation, a useful feature in a workhouse or an asylum. The English architect John Haviland encountered it before emigrating to Philadelphia, where he built the Eastern State Penitentiary (1821–36), the first monumental panopticon and the first building in America to be widely studied in Europe [85].

Any architecture that could be cogently explained, without sentiment, and on the grounds of objective principle, invariably found a positive reception in the United States; Haviland's panopticon was enthusiastically embraced. But an even more severely rational architecture was the octagonal house, the brainchild of Orson Squire Fowler. Fowler's insight, published in 1848, was breathtakingly simple: a circle encloses more area than does a square with an equal perimeter. A house in the shape of an octagon (not a true circle but a concession to the rectilinear nature of wood construction) would enclose considerably more space than a square one, given the same outlay in materials [86]. Of course, Fowler's elegant rationality revealed itself as spurious the

85 **Samuel Cowperthwaite**, *The State Penitentiary for the Eastern District of Pennsylvania*, lithograph, 1855. The formal geometry of John Haviland's Eastern State Penitentiary, Philadelphia has the cruel, attractive logic of a spider's web. Prisoners were placed in solitary confinement, where they would have the opportunity to repent their crimes (hence the term "penitentiary" instead of prison), rather than be degraded by contact with more experienced criminals. The prison was the highest expression of Quaker philanthropy, complete with indoor plumbing and central heating, although the isolation seems to have unhinged most prisoners, as an appalled Charles Dickens observed during his visit.

86 Orson Squire Fowler, Orson Squire Fowler House, Fishkill, New York, 1848. *A Home for All: or, the Gravel Wall and Octagon Mode of Building*, Orson Squire Fowler's odd treatise of 1848, caused a national mania for octagonal buildings. Fowler was not a professional architect but a practitioner of that nineteenth-century quack science, phrenology. But, like Bogardus, he was also that characteristic American type, the inventor or entrepreneur whose very lack of professional training gave him the mental freedom to consider alternative technologies. In a country where building was still largely unregulated and carried out in the flexible technology of wood, the amateur could dabble at form-making and space-shaping with no constraint other than those of his own imagination.

first time someone tried to push a rectangular bed into an oblique corner. Virtually every New England town has an octagonal house; virtually none has two.

The panopticon plan and the octagonal house—each as elegantly rational as a mathematical exercise, and as heartless—were manifestations of the doctrine of utilitarianism, which judged everything by the dispassionate criteria of utility and efficiency.

87 Samuel Sloan, Longwood, Natchez, Mississippi, begun 1860. With historicism, it was not necessary that the building be historically accurate, merely that it convey enough details to convey a general sense of its style. Such a doctrine invited theatrical exaggeration. The so-called Moorish style, for example, was invariably a wild burlesque of Islamic architecture, adapted to serve buildings then thought to have exotic functions: fraternal societies, synagogues, the house of an eccentric like P. T. Barnum. Dr. Haller Nutt's Longwood in Natchez, Mississippi, shown here, was designed by the Philadelphia architect Samuel Sloan, who applied its fantastic facade to that most rational of floor plans: Orson Squire Fowler's octagon.

Utilitarianism was not the only fiber in American thought, though. Offsetting it was a vibrant romanticism, rich in comforting and nostalgic visions of the preindustrial past. Both impulses might be expressed in the same building. Thus while Eastern State Penitentiary was a strictly utilitarian building in plan, in elevation it was thoroughly Romantic: a moody Gothic citadel, whose exaggerated battlements were meant to evoke all the terrors of a medieval dungeon.

Strangely, Haviland's next panopticon penitentiary, that in Trenton, New Jersey, was in the Egyptian style, which was also richly expressive of function. Here, it was implied, the unfortunate inmate would be incarcerated for eternity like a mummy. Such a careful alignment of style and building type is *historicism*, the doctrine that sanctions the use of the historical styles in order to convey mental associations. It is the source of the bewildering stylistic profusion that characterizes the architecture of the entire nineteenth century. In America, however, historicism took a rather different course than in Europe. There architectural style might be intimately connected with a country's sense of national identity, such as the Gothic in Germany or the Renaissance in Italy. This was not the case in the United States, where the styles were absolutely unencumbered by historical experience or patriotic association. For American patrons, the past was as open as the shelves of an emporium, and they ransacked its contents with the glee of the consumer [87].

Historicism was a permissive doctrine, and in a time of swift social and technical change, it helped to apply order to the visual clutter of the modern city. To the practical lobe of the American mind, this was immensely satisfying; to the moral lobe it was troubling. It preferred that style be based on principle, preferably moral principle, not caprice. And no style suggested moral principle more strongly than did the Gothic, which emerged as the strongest alternative to Greek architecture during the 1840s. Although the eighteenth century had once viewed the style in romantic terms, as a style of sentiment and irrationality, the materialistic nineteenth century was coming to view it in rational terms. Not only did the Gothic display its construction "honestly," flaunting its buttresses, arches, and ribbed vaults, but it had the merit of being associated with medieval piety and faith. Of course, these were only abstract arguments and it required the spark of a practical example for the Gothic fad to ignite: Trinity Church, New York (1839–46), by Richard Upjohn.

Manhattan's oldest Episcopal church, at the foot of Wall Street, Trinity Church was also America's most socially prominent church. This made respectable a design of radical novelty. There had been other Gothic churches, but Trinity was revolutionary in the historical accuracy of its forms [88]. They were mere classical boxes, decked out with pointed arches as an afterthought, but Trinity Church followed medieval practice punctiliously: the congregation assembled under a high central nave, flanked by

89 **Thomas Cole**, *The Architect's Dream*, 1840. The doctrine of historicism is neatly encapsulated in this tribute to the architect Ithiel Town. Cole cleverly reprises his divided composition in *The Ox-bow*, bathing the styles of classical antiquity in clear sunlight while plunging his medieval examples in Romantic obscurity. Most exotic, and most remote, was the Egyptian style, which had recently been dusted off to serve for cemetery gates and prison facades—both in some sense houses of the dead. (But here some critics drew the line, and objected that the Egyptian, the style of "embalmed cats and deified crocodiles," was ludicrous for modern America.)

lower side aisles, while the clergy performed their offices in the chancel, which was clearly delineated on the exterior as a distinct space. All was in a plausible fourteenth-century Gothic. Also medieval was the east-west orientation of the church (although the orthodox orientation was reversed so that the entrance tower to the east might dominate Wall Street). Even the material was revolutionary: brownstone, whose warm ruddy hue was the antithesis of the conventional marble or whitewash. Upjohn's revolutionary performance was soon emulated by Episcopal congregations throughout the United States.

Trinity Church made Richard Upjohn America's most important Gothic architect overnight; he would eventually design well over a hundred churches, nearly all of them for the Episcopal Church. As an English émigré, Upjohn gave his buildings a profoundly English character. Their form derived from contemporary English church architecture, especially that of A. W. N. Pugin, the great Gothic Revival architect and theorist. This Anglophilia is no surprise in a church for Episcopalians, the American counterpart to the Anglican church. But not all denominations followed English fashion. Episcopalians may have stood at the top of the American social ladder in prestige and wealth, but they were not a numerous elite. The vast bulk of Americans belonged to Low Church denominations that stressed the spoken word, not the ritual of High Church worship. These Low Church denominations included Puritans (which had split into Congregationalists and Unitarians), Scottish Presbyterians, German Lutherans, Methodists, Baptists, Quakers, and countless smaller denominations. Although their theology varied, these denominations were alike in their opposition to any architectural style that suggested Catholic ritual: long naves which stressed hierarchy and procession, pillars and aisles which interfered with clear lines of sight and sound. Hence the persistence of boxy, auditoriumlike churches throughout the nineteenth century.

We might find these sectarian distinctions trivial but the nineteenth century did not. Upjohn once refused to design a Unitarian church because he did not work for "heretics." For their part, Low Church denominations mistrusted the mystical connotations of medievalism, which they saw as undoing the work of the Reformation. Before they would embrace medieval architecture, it must first be stripped of all Catholic associations. One style that seemed to do this was the Romanesque, the round-arched predecessor to the Gothic. Without the intricate play of Gothic finials and tracery, the Romanesque was less mystical, less expensive, and more rational; its simpler forms evoked the purity of early Christianity while Gothic clutter evoked papist corruption—or so the argument ran. Such arguments are always literary artefacts, and have little to do with the intrinsic merits of a style. Still, much of Protestant America found the arguments convincing and in the late 1840s the Romanesque became a favorite style for churches, just at the moment when the Smithsonian Institution was making it a model for civic buildings.

Fortuitously, similar developments were underway in Germany, where architects had devised a modern Romanesque or *Rundbogenstil* (literally "round-arched style"); and just as fortuitously, events now brought a large number of these architects to the United States. During 1848 and 1849 Germany was wracked by a succession of revolutions, and universities, hotbeds of democratic and nationalist sentiment since the Napoleonic wars, were hard hit. Now great waves of political refugees—architects and engineers, scientists and artisans—came to America, bringing considerable technical skill, especially in precision work such as engraving.

90 **Frederick A. Peterson**, Cooper Union Building (Foundation Building), New York, 1853. The German *Rundbogenstil* used the round arch of the Romanesque for its abstract structural properties, and not because of its psychological associations. Since it did not need to mimic buildings of the past, the style was adept at serving such new building types as railroad stations. But Victorian audiences expected the style of a building to say something about its function, something the abstract *Rundbogenstil* could not do. After the Civil War it rapidly fell from fashion to become a mere utilitarian style for factories and warehouses. New York's Cooper Union was built during its brief heyday and shows its characteristic round arches and taut pilaster strips, giving its walls a crisp gridlike articulation.

Even before they perfected their English, these refugee architects came to dominate the profession. Of the several dozen professionals who emigrated, a few examples suffice. Gustav Runge went from Berlin to Philadelphia, building the Academy of Music (1855–57) in an up-to-date brick *Rundbogenstil*. Adolph Cluss was a political agitator and a confidant of Karl Marx, but in exile he worked in Washington, where he built numerous *Rundbogenstil* buildings for the federal government, including the Department of Agriculture Building (1868) and the Arts and Industries Building (1879). Another failed revolutionary was Frederick Peterson, who escaped from a Prussian prison to New York, where he designed the Cooper Union [90]. This building was not only progressive in its style and its iron construction but in its public education mission, yet another area in which modern Prussia was a pioneer.

The 1840s and 1850s were a period of great prestige for German science and technology. Germany had lagged behind England and France in the Industrial Revolution, but was now rapidly catching up. Unlike those countries, Germany was not a unified nation state and until 1871 was a collection of separate kingdoms and principalities. By modernizing late, Germany was able to modernize systematically, and was a leader in promoting universal public education, especially in Prussia. American schools of architecture and engineering such as Rensselaer Polytechnical Institute (RPI) and the Pennsylvania Polytechnical College modeled themselves on the German polytechnical system.

The prestige of Germany extended beyond architecture to painting. In 1849, John G. Boker, a Prussian diplomat, opened the Düsseldorf Gallery in New York to exhibit and sell works by German artists. At first, the gallery was met with bewilderment (New Yorkers were not certain if Mr. Düsseldorf was a painter or collector). In fact, Düsseldorf was the leading center of German art education, where the Neoclassical tradition of strong drawing flourished under Prussian patronage. Düsseldorf painters carried on the German idealistic tradition that originated with Johann Joachim Winckelmann, that eighteenth-century arbiter of classical idealism. Atmospherics were usually subordinated to the all-important criterion of visual clarity, which gives much Düsseldorf work a peculiarly airless quality. It also has a high quotient of theater, and a weakness for props and visual anecdote. This high illustrative component suits it well for engraving. At worst, though, the sentimentality and excessively literal storytelling reduces it to the level of genre painting.

America welcomed the artists shown at the Düsseldorf Gallery, such as Emanuel Leutze. His work was typical of the school, both in its microscopic detail and its foamy sentimentality. His swaggering historical epics captivated American audiences with detail and sentiment in a way that Trumbull's more formal set pieces did not. If an inferior painter, he was a better storyteller, and the public embraced his patriotic *Washington Crossing the Delaware* [91] and his *Westward the Course of Empire* (whose title derives from a poem by Smibert's patron, Bishop Berkeley). Leutze was soon joined by Albert Bierstadt (1830–1902)—a German émigré who came to the United States as a child but returned to study in Düsseldorf—and there arose a Düsseldorf–New York axis, with Leutze and Bierstadt both moving back and forth freely between the two cities.

As the prestige of Düsseldorf rose, American artists clamored to study there. Eastman Johnson put in two years, working with Leutze and enjoying the beer stashed behind *George Washington Crossing the Delaware*; likewise Worthington Whittredge and Richard Caton Woodville [92]. Even a successful painter well into his forties might study at Düsseldorf, as Bingham did, as a way of holding his own against younger, better-trained rivals.

The Hudson River School even came under the sway of Düsseldorf, and under the influence of Bierstadt it changed in mood and magnitude. Bierstadt's great achievement was to adapt the Hudson River School formula to the American West. In 1857, after spending several years painting Alpine scenery, he returned to the United States and joined an expedition to the Rocky Mountains, which he recorded in sketches and photographs. From this raw material he painted *Rocky Mountains, "Lander's Peak"*, whose tight German draftsmanship, unusual vertical format, and immense size (over 7 feet [2.1 meters] in height) made it the hit of the 1863 season [93]. Bierstadt was an astute businessman and he turned out many variants of the painting, augmented by several more expeditions to the West.

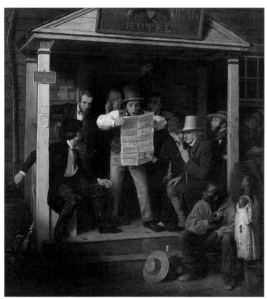

As stirring as such works are, they suffer badly from rote and formula. Bierstadt had the misfortune of having formulated his artistic language before he tackled the American landscape, so that what he saw was always interpreted in the light of Düsseldorf

91 Emanuel Leutze, *Washington Crossing the Delaware*, 1851. This is the greatest of all the theatrical tableaux produced by the Düsseldorf School. Typical of the school is the fussy clutter of props and details, the enormous scale (16 by 20 feet [4.8 by 6 meters]) and the overwrought sentimentality. Nonetheless, it is superbly effective as a composition, in which its wealth of pictorial incident is subordinated to the all-dominant figure of Washington.

92 Richard Caton Woodville, *War News From Mexico*, 1848. Painted in Düsseldorf, this was the most important painting inspired by the Mexican–American War, which had concluded in 1845. The highly finished surfaces are typical of the Düsseldorf manner as are the broadly theatrical gestures. Unlike Bingham's cartoonish black men, Woodville's black observer, who watches with bemused detachment, is treated with dignity and sympathy.

93 Albert Bierstadt, *Rocky Mountains, "Lander's Peak"*, 1863. Bierstadt successfully took the Hudson River School formula and adapted it to a landscape whose greatest contrast was *vertical*, from lush meadows and woodland below to mountains of almost arctic severity above. Its breathtaking rise is the vertical counterpart to Gifford's vast horizontal vistas. Such leviathans forced viewers to do precisely what they would need to do before the original: crane their heads to take in their panoramic sweep.

convention. Apart from its trees and wildlife, his Rocky Mountains do not differ as much as they should from the Alps. In this Bierstadt was unlike Cole who—though working within a much narrower compass—was able to delineate with great precision the differing character of the Catskills, Adirondacks, and White Mountains of New Hampshire. Here the naive artistic sensibility, working empirically and naively, had an advantage over Bierstadt, the well-drilled Düsseldorf professional, with his grab-bag of artistic conventions.

While Bierstadt exploited the American West, another group of landscape painters preferred coastal subjects, where the nature of the scenery invited compositions of great calm and clarity,

94 **Martin Johnson Heade**, *Approaching Thunder Storm*, 1859. The Luminists of the 1850s were not a true school but a group of independent painters with common interests, especially in the quality of light in a calm and ordered landscape. The most versatile was Martin Johnson Heade, whose work ranged from lovely studies of hummingbirds, painted on an expedition in Brazil, to ominous coastal scenes such as this.

95 **Fitz Hugh Lane**, *"Starlight" in Fog*, 1860. At the other end of the spectrum is Fitz Hugh Lane, a naive draftsman of a painter who loved to delineate the precise rigging of ships. But he tempered his old-fashioned linearity with an up-to-date interest in atmospherics and light. Both aspects inform this painting, in which ghostly ships emerge out of a pearly fog, backlighted by a gauzy sun.

organized in three horizontal bands of shore, sea, and sky. These were the Luminists, a useful term invented in the 1960s to describe the triumvirate of Fitz Hugh Lane (1804–65), John Kensett (1816–72) and Martin Johnson Heade (1819–1904). These painters were hardly a school, and scarcely knew one another, but had in common a concern for the presence of light in their paintings [94 and 95]. Here an abiding Colonial legacy was palpable, the same "lineiness" for which West had once upbraided Copley: a tradition of clearly delineated shapes, with strong outlines and boundaries, seen in a clear and even light.

The rise of the Luminists shows a change both in technique and in theology, or so it might be called. Artistically speaking, the depiction of light demands much more than facile draftsmanship.

A battery of sophisticated techniques is required: an understanding that reflected light contains color, the use of glazes to make shadows transparent, the ability to alter color values under the effect of atmospheric haze at increasing distance. All these made the works of the Luminists more truly painterly and less like illustration. This had theological ramifications as well. Stripped of its props and visual anecdotes, a Luminist painting was less suitable as a visual sermon. Its spiritual content no longer resided in the allegory it conveyed but in the general sense it gave of God's presence throughout nature, much as the Transcendental poets portrayed it.

By far the finest of the Luminists was the dashing Sanford Gifford, a pupil of the National Academy of Design. He made his public debut in 1847 although his artistic personality was not fully formed until the course of his 1855–57 journey to Europe, where he discovered the art of Turner. Gifford prowled the same Catskills trails as had Cole, but he enlarged their magnitude to the panoramic as in his 1862 masterpiece *Kauterskill Clove* [97]. Here the artist seems buoyed aloft, as in one of those observation balloons then being used in the Civil War. Gifford fought with distinction as a volunteer in the war, although he could not have known that it would bring an end to the sentimental idealism on which American landscape painting depended.

Gifford's career was launched by the Art Union [96], a profit-making institution that was the brainchild of John Herring. A New York entrepreneur, Herring was an inadvertent genius who,

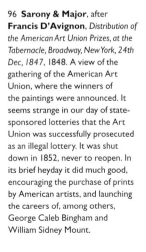

96 **Sarony & Major**, after **Francis D'Avignon**, *Distribution of the American Art Union Prizes, at the Tabernacle, Broadway, New York, 24th Dec, 1847*, 1848. A view of the gathering of the American Art Union, where the winners of the paintings were announced. It seems strange in our day of state-sponsored lotteries that the Art Union was successfully prosecuted as an illegal lottery. It was shut down in 1852, never to reopen. In its brief heyday it did much good, encouraging the purchase of prints by American artists, and launching the careers of, among others, George Caleb Bingham and William Sidney Mount.

97 **Sanford Robinson Gifford**, *Kauterskill Clove*, 1862. Gifford's hallmark was an extreme use of aerial perspective, the manipulation of atmospheric haze to suggest depth and distance. He liked to place the sun low in the sky so that it shimmered through a thick atmosphere of maximum humidity, a technique that culminated in his *Kauterskill Clove*.

working from strictly mercenary motives, did more to raise public interest in art than all the high-minded efforts of Peale, Vanderlyn, and Trumbull. In 1838 he opened an unsuccessful art gallery on Broadway, which promptly failed but which gave him a brilliant insight: if Americans were loath to spend twenty-five cents to see a painting, they were happy to spend five dollars on a lottery ticket for a chance to win it. To make the gambling less blatant, he gave each subscriber a fine engraving of a painting, and to make it sound less mercenary he called his business the Apollo Association.

In 1844 Herring reconstituted the association as the noble-sounding American Art Union and named William Cullen Bryant president. Herring's message was that the appreciation of the arts was an aspect of enlightened citizenship, an idea that resonated with the spirit of improvement that was a favorite theme of antebellum America. In this he succeeded spectacularly; at its peak the Art Union counted more than 16,000 subscribers and more than half a million annual visitors. Through its sponsorship, artists such as Gifford and George Caleb Bingham became household names.

Before the Art Union, household art was chiefly patriotic in nature, often limited to a framed print of George Washington above the family fireplace. Now genre scenes became a staple of middle-class family life. Sentimental and idealistic subjects were preferred, either accessible genre scenes, such as Bingham's rollicking *Jolly Flatboatmen*, or saccharine painted sermons, like Cole's *Youth*. The Art Union discovered that certain subjects were innately popular, scenes showing friction between social

98 **George Caleb Bingham**, *Fur Traders Descending the Missouri*, 1845. This was originally entitled *French Trapper and Half-Breed Son*, and was presumably renamed to be more genteel. The composition is unusually spare for Bingham, consisting only of the two figures with their cargo of pelts and their chained bear cub. So successful was the painting's reception that Bingham reworked it in the following years as *Return of the Trappers*.

99 **William Sidney Mount**, *The Power of Music*, 1847. Most genre painters are satisfied with the surface appearance of things, but in this painting William Sidney Mount accomplishes something more ambitious, a mental rather than a physical action: the experience of listening critically to music. A black laborer stops at a barn door to eavesdrop unseen to an impromptu fiddle serenade, listening with intelligence and evident pleasure. In classic genre means, Mount coaxes the story forward with easily legible props: the laborer's axe and his jug, and the carefully distinguished categories of clothing.

100 **Randolph Rogers**, *Nydia, The Blind Girl of Pompeii*, 1853. This was taken from Edward Bulwer-Lytton's *Last Days of Pompeii*, one of the nineteenth century's great potboiler novels. Here Rogers depicts the climax of the book, with Nydia seeking her friends in the storm of ash and cinder as Vesuvius erupts. Rogers, like Greenough and Powers, was an American sculptor living in Italy. Unlike their idealized Neoclassical compositions, however, his were vigorously animated, the energy of a locomotive in comparison to that of a sailing ship (a technological development that had already changed one's perception of the world and may account for the constant refrain of power in Victorian art).

classes or patriotic treatments of that great national subject, the conquest of the continent. The Art Union was also comically prudish, frowning, for example, on men with moustaches—which still seemed disreputable until Lincoln and the Civil War made facial hair fashionable.

The American Art Union helped reinforce the central role of prints in American artistic taste. Dutch and English prints had been widely available since the beginning of the eighteenth century, and offered a surrogate for the religious art that a Protestant society discouraged. Genre art was particularly suited to the language of prints, which, limited to line and tone, conveyed their messages through props and broadly drawn visual anecdotes. This was the formula of Bingham, the most important discovery of the Art Union and the most successful of all American genre painters. Like his Dutch prototypes, Bingham took his subjects from the mundane everyday: a polling place on election day, an overloaded raft floating downstream, a comic drunk losing his jug. But Bingham's sensibility was not so much Dutch as English, as embodied in the work of William Hogarth, whose boisterousness and jovial vulgarity he emulated.

Bingham was no great hand at life drawing or anatomy, although he kept a sketchbook in which he recorded strong and distinctive poses. His dynamic silhouettes and their exaggerated features verged on caricature and at worst look like flat cutouts, simply pasted on to the canvas. This weakness was also a strength, however, and it gave his compositions a strong graphic clarity. When he removed the clutter and incident, and concentrated on a few figures, he could produce a masterpiece like his *Fur Traders Descending the Missouri* [98]. Here he overcame his chronic vulgarity to produce the most splendid of American genre paintings; more than a mere vignette of the doomed lifestyle of the river fur trader, it is a poignant meditation on American life, in which solitary and autonomous individuals can author their own destiny, adrift in a boundless space.

Bingham's principal eastern competitor was William Sidney Mount who, in the more competitive artistic world of New York, became a much more competent painter. A lifelong inhabitant of Long Island, Mount specialized in humorous interactions between slightly bewildered participants, such as farmers and merchants, children, and black servants. Like Bingham, his popularity derived from his powers of exaggeration and caricature, but his works could also evoke deep human sympathy, as his *Power of Music* [99].

Both Bingham and Mount relied on easily recognizable stock types, including black men and women, who were a staple of their paintings. But they invariably appeared in light-hearted contexts, never in the context of slavery or Abolition, topics studiously avoided by the Art Union. Yet slavery was too dire a question to be kept out of American art. In 1852, the year in which the Art Union was dissolved, the novel *Uncle Tom's Cabin* by Harriet Beecher Stowe was published, a book which transformed Abolition, removing the taint of political fanaticism that had clung to it and making it a broadly respectable movement. As Abolition grew more powerful, so did the pro-slavery cause grow more entrenched and implacable. In 1854, the Kansas-Nebraska Act permitted the inhabitants of new states to decide for themselves whether or not slavery would be permitted, inviting campaigns of violence and intimidation from both sides. In 1856, the anti-slavery senator Charles Sumner was violently beaten by a pro-slavery congressman in the senate chamber, wielding a metal-topped cane. In 1859 came John Brown's abortive raid on Harpers Ferry, which was to have launched a slave insurrection.

Artists could not for long remain on the sidelines. Some continued to make escapist art, taking refuge in storytelling and genteel erotica [100]. Others embraced Abolition forthrightly, making art that was the visual equivalent of *Uncle Tom's Cabin*. The most important was produced by the enterprising sculptor John Rogers, whose feel for middle-class taste and values bordered on genius. From 1859 to 1893 he patented eighty different sculptural groups, which he reproduced in plaster and sold for between ten and twenty dollars. His first work, *Slave Auction*, appeared in December 1859, the very month in which John Brown was hanged [101]. As with the genre painters of the Art Union, the story is told is physiognomic terms: a defiant slave stands in proud contempt, while a lean jackal of an auctioneer settles his fate. Of course, moral politics is no guarantor of great art, and like much of Rogers's art, the work veers close to caricature. But he accomplished what Trumbull had failed to do: create a broadly popular and financially lucrative middle-class art.

Others artists shied away from Abolition, preferring to treat the plantation life of the South in sentimental terms. In this, music preceded painting. In 1851 the composer Stephen Foster sold the rights to his *Old Folks at Home* (*Swanee River*) because he did not think "Ethiopian music" (as it was then called) respectable. But one year later, in the wake of *Uncle Tom's Cabin*, the song had created a national craze, and he unsuccessfully tried to buy the rights back. Foster's

101 **John Rogers**, *Slave Auction*, 1859. Rogers was the first American sculptor successfully to exploit a mass market for sculpture. Most were pleasant and broadly sketched humorous tableaux, such as *Checkers up at the Farm* or *Fetching the Doctor*, the sculptural equivalent of Bingham and Mount's genre paintings. This overtly political sculpture is an exception to the general amiability of Rogers's work.

102 **Eastman Johnson**, *Negro Life in the South (Old Kentucky Home)*, 1859. Eastman Johnson (1824–1906) was a product of the Düsseldorf School, as this painting shows, with its maudlin mood and a composition framed like a theater stage. In terms of sheer technical competence, however, it far outpaces the naive work of Bingham and Mount, with their persistent Colonial stiffness and linear draftsmanship.

songs, such as *Massa's in de Cold Ground* and *My Old Kentucky Home* presented an idyllic reverie of Southern life, growing ever more sentimental as the war drew nearer. They were wildly popular, and when Eastman Johnson presented his painting *Negro Life in the South* in 1859, the public intuitively sensed that the view of plantation life was the same as that of Foster, and dubbed the painting *Old Kentucky Home* [102].

Such music and painting stressed the ties of affection between slave and master to an extent incomprehensible or offensive to modern sensibilities. And yet by stressing the common humanity of black and white, however indirectly or condescendingly, it may be that they strengthened the moral critique of slavery as much as any strident work of Abolitionist art. In any event, *Negro Life in the South* was to be the last of the great antebellum genre paintings. The Civil War began in the spring of 1861, and the reassuring social stability on which genre painting depends, with its insistence on stock figures and conventions, came to a mournful and abrupt end.

Chapter 5 Art for Art's Sake

Into the Civil War, truth and morality were still the touchstones of American art. Their most able champion, however, was an Englishman, John Ruskin (1819–1900). Ruskin was the dominant art critic of his day and his first three books, *Modern Painters* (1843–60), *The Seven Lamps of Architecture* (1849), and *The Stones of Venice* (1851–53), provided the most persuasive and eloquent, if not the most coherent, case for the moral basis of art. He spoke of art with quivering moral fervor, the legacy perhaps of his evangelical Protestant background. In any event, American readers proved themselves receptive as usual to aesthetic pronouncements made on moral grounds—even if the reasoning was spurious. For young artists and architects who found Düsseldorf theatricality and architectural eclecticism cloying, Ruskin offered an urgent sense of mission.

Ruskin cherished the art of the Middle Ages and the early Italian Renaissance, before growing religious skepticism robbed it of spiritual authority. Venice loomed large in his criticism, and not only for her richly colored buildings and paintings. The city was also the great international port of the Middle Ages, and offered suggestive parallels with modern England, another dynamic mercantile society with an intense religious life. His criticism had profound consequences. In painting, he inspired the Pre-Raphaelite movement, with its vibrant colors, scrupulous draftsmanship, and fidelity to nature; in architecture, the movement known as the High Victorian Gothic.

Ruskin's American admirers were concentrated in New York, where in 1863 they founded the Association for the Advancement of Truth in Art. Under this tongue twister gathered the landscape painter William Trost Richards, the architects P. B. Wight and Russell Sturgis, the critic Clarence Cook, and several lawyers and geologists (in Ruskin's vision of nature, geology was as crucial as botany). Their leader was Thomas Charles Farrer, a charismatic

103 **John La Farge**, *Magnolia Blossom, c.* 1870. Ostensibly a still life of a flower on a window pane, the true subject of this painting is color, the vibrating gorgeousness of green and white. This is the Aesthetic Movement in capsule form: no moral, no didacticism, no fussy storytelling, but simply a delightful exercise in lush color contrast.

104 **William Trost Richards**, *Corner of the Woods*, 1864. This shows why William Trost Richards was the most successful painter of the Association for the Advancement of Truth in Art. A pencil drawing, made with utmost deliberation, it fulfills Ruskin's admonition that "good and beautiful work is generally done slowly."

English painter who had studied under Ruskin. The members of the Association happily strapped themselves within Ruskin's artistic straitjacket, the architects practicing in the Venetian Gothic while the painters pledged themselves to Pre-Raphaelite precision, in which every object from the foreground to the distant background was rendered with the same exquisitely photographic crispness [104].

The Association published a pugnacious journal, *The New Path* (1863–65), which emulated Ruskin's blend of incisive criticism and malicious sarcasm. Artists who did not meet their lofty standards of truth were gratuitously insulted: Durand's landscape art belonged "to a past age, and a dead system" while Bierstadt was urged to undertake "ten years of study" before attempting to paint the Rocky Mountains again. Wight defended its belligerent tone in an editorial: "We exist for the purpose of stirring up strife; of breeding discontent; of pulling down unsound reputations; of making the public dissatisfied with the work of most artists, and better still, of making the artists dissatisfied with themselves." Although it lasted but two years, *The New Path* was a cradle of art criticism in America, producing two of the country's most important critics: Russell Sturgis went on to become the first art critic of *The Nation* while Clarence Cook wrote for *Scribner's Monthly*, the arbiter of fashionable society taste.

The Association for the Advancement of Truth in Art prided itself on its militancy but it was hardly unconventional to admire Ruskin. Even that establishment citadel, the National Academy of Design, was thoroughly Ruskinian—so much so that it built a new home that Ruskin himself might have designed [105]. The story is remarkable. In 1861 Durand, the Academy's longstanding president and the head of its building committee, conducted a competition to choose an architect. He ignored the designs of such seasoned professionals as Richard Morris Hunt in favor of a twenty-three year old unknown, P. B. Wight. Wight's proposal was a clever paraphrase of Ruskin's favorite building, the Doges' Palace in

Venice. For Ruskin, the palace balanced the three great architectural traditions—Gothic, classical, and Oriental—to become "the central building of the world," not a bad solution for a museum that was to house art from around the world.

The National Academy of Design was America's most thoroughly Ruskinian building, and a masterpiece of the High Victorian Gothic. Unlike the Gothic Revival of the 1840s, which conceived of architecture in terms of picturesque archeology, High Victorian design was dynamically synthetic. Looking beyond the thirteenth-century buildings of England, it borrowed from Italy, France, and Germany to produce an original amalgam. Instead of making its buildings look as old as possible, as the early Gothic Revival had done, the High Victorian Gothic preferred its forms to be sharp-edged, angular, and modern.

It also embraced color. The Academy was awash in color, produced entirely by the alternation of marble, brick, and sandstone in vivid contrasting bands. This too was Ruskin's doing. He insisted that architectural color should derive from the actual materials of construction, rather than paint or tinted stucco, which he despised as "sham." Ruskin's love of color went beyond his affection for Venice to a deep preoccupation with geology.

105 **P. B. Wight**, National Academy of Design, New York, 1862–63. Virtually every aspect of Wight's National Academy of Design derives from the theory of John Ruskin. The lively architectural color and the choice of the Doges' Palace as a model derive from *The Stones of Venice*. And the idea that the workmen should design their own ornament, closely copying natural specimens rather than imitating classical acanthus leaves, derives from *The Seven Lamps of Architecture*. Strangely, America's most electrifyingly polychromatic building was designed by an architect who was himself color-blind, although he claimed to have learned to compensate.

At a time when the most progressive science was geology, offering the greatest economic benefits but also the greatest challenge to traditional religious belief, a striped and layered stone wall inevitably took on metaphysical meaning. It suggested the implacable action of nature herself, and how geological time was calibrated in the patient accumulation of rock strata out of which the Earth was made.

Architects dramatized the play of stripes by increasing the color contrasts of their buildings, even to the point of stridency. There came into common use a rainbow of building stones, transported cheaply by the new national railroad network: yellow sandstone from Ohio, black marble from Tennessee, pink granite from Massachusetts, blue and purple sandstones from Pennsylvania, a state which also produced the electrifying green serpentine that the architect Thomas Webb Richards (brother of William Trost Richards) used at the University of Pennsylvania, further maximizing its intensity with contrasting red mortar joints.

These buildings were part of an international movement toward stronger color, in painting as well as architecture. The camera encouraged this, as painters exploited color, the one element that black and white photography lacked. With this came a growing tolerance for the intense and the garish. The first generation of nineteenth-century artists sought nostalgic refuge against the havoc of the Industrial Revolution, and compensated for the railroad by lining its tracks with Greek porticos. But their successors grew up familiar with the steam engine, locomotive, steamship, and telegraph, and they tolerated much greater intensity of expression. So the ante was raised.

If the Industrial Revolution may have increased the desire for stronger color, it also provided the means for satisfying that desire. The palette of colors available to Thomas Cole and the early Hudson River School painters was essentially the same as that used by Rembrandt: the traditional earth palette, made from pulverized mineral or vegetable matter. Diluted by impurities, these pigments were sharply limited in intensity, and an artist could only create intense, saturated color by implying it through the skillful manipulation of contrast and juxtaposition. But during the nineteenth century new chemical pigments began appearing at an accelerating tempo. First came emerald green in 1814, followed by artificial ultramarine (a substitute for lapis lazuli) in 1828, and cadmium yellow in 1846. There followed an explosion of colors: mauve, the first coal-tar color (1856), magenta (1859), cobalt violet

106 **Jasper Cropsey**, *Autumn—on the Hudson River*, 1860. Cropsey made the fullest possible use of the newly available chemical pigments. But while brilliantly iridescent, his color was additive, and not integral to the design. Foreground trees and the distant village show much the same sharpness and intensity of color. It has the glittering surface of mosaic, but also the mosaic's lack of depth.

(1859), cobalt yellow (1861), and artificial alizarin red (1868). These pigments had an intensity close to that made by a prism, pure refracted light, undiluted by baser matter. By the 1860s the artist had at hand something like the full range of the color spectrum, at close to maximum intensity.

Older painters, slow to draw the full consequences of the color revolution, tended to use the new pigments piecemeal. The color conception of Cole and Bierstadt, for example, was that of a draftsman: it was something to be added to a pencil drawing. (In fact, Bierstadt began his career in 1850 by giving lessons in "monochromatic painting.") Under the impetus of Ruskin, however, younger and more nimble painters seized the potential of the new pigments and two of them, Jasper Cropsey and Frederic Edwin Church, built their careers on color.

Cropsey was an architect who turned to painting in the 1840s, specializing in lurid autumnal scenes. During the course of a triumphant two-year jaunt in London, Cropsey painted his *Autumn—on the Hudson River*, a view of New Windsor, south of West Point. The painting stunned its viewers, earning Cropsey the sobriquet "the painter of autumn" [106]. It was even shown to Queen Victoria, who allegedly questioned its color-drenched foliage and the artist's probity (or his eyesight). Exultantly he sent for specimens. If true, the anecdote only shows how fundamentally naive was Cropsey's approach to color. It is not

107 **Frederic Edwin Church**, *Twilight in the Wilderness*, 1860. Church did not fragment his colors into intense local passages but subordinated them to an overall chromatic scheme, as seen here. As with a musical composition, there is a dominant key signature, against which contrasting harmonies resonate. The result was a ravishing color sensibility that falls somewhere between the didactic sentimentality of the Hudson River School and the sensuous languor of the Aesthetic Movement.

108 **Frederic Edwin Church**, *Cotopaxi*, 1862. For a generation preoccupied by the discoveries of Darwin and Agassiz, the natural world was no longer the benign wonderland painted by Cole. Church's *Cotopaxi* finds beauty in nature at its most menacing, as a spouting Ecuadorian volcano threatens to overwhelm a glowering sun. It also shows Church's genius for composition, in which his uncanny botanical realism is subordinated to the unified pictorial whole.

sufficient to hold a leaf against its counterpart on the painted canvas to demonstrate its color. That color will appear different at different distances, and its color will vary according to the light that is reflected on to it. This did not seem to trouble Cropsey.

Church was of a higher caliber. Trained as Cole's only pupil, he was that rare artist who is equally strong as a colorist and a draftsman. Although his drawing was impeccable, he never let meticulous detail or local color overwhelm the pictorial unity. And while he accepted Cole's conviction that a painting should have for its theme something lofty and sublime, he rejected the elaborate narrative programs of such portentous cycles as *The Voyage of Life* and *The Course of Empire*. Instead, he sought to make paintings that were resolved aesthetic wholes rather than mere illustrations [107].

Church also made his paintings depend in a decisive way on their color, and his chromatic curiosity led him to seek color everywhere, even the Arctic, where he painted a remarkable series of icebergs. These he rendered as translucent mountains, pulsating with reflected color, from the deep turquoise of the water to the faint violet of the Arctic sunset, a hint of divine presence even in the bleakness of the high latitudes. But Church also went to that part of the Earth where the colors of the prism naturally appear at high intensity, the Tropics. Modern transportation now put in easy reach the vivid birds, fish, insects, and flowers at the very moment when modern chemistry put in reach the means to depict their colors. Church traveled to South America in 1853 and 1857, producing the four sumptuous masterpieces on which his reputation rests: *The Andes of Ecuador* (1855), *The Heart of the Andes* (1859), *Cotopaxi* (1862) [108], and *Rainy Season in the Tropics* (1866). All were color essays of overwhelming skill and sophistication. One generation after the moralizing debut of the Hudson River School, with its tortuous chasms and prophetic tree stumps, it brought forth work as close to pure painting as anything yet produced in America.

Church's thought about color is embodied in Olana, the stunning and sumptuous house he built for himself overlooking the Hudson River [109]. This was a free Moorish design, an exotic towered affair blazing with color within and without. Church produced it in consultation with Calvert Vaux, and something of both men is present in the design. Church contributed the pictorial aspect of the house, designing its walls and surfaces, and conceiving it in terms of picturesque views. From Vaux comes something of Central Park, and the spacious and comprehensive treatment of the natural landscape.

Had they lived, Cole and Downing, the mentors of these artists, would have found both Olana and *Cotopaxi* alarming. Where was the appeal to morality in these hot-keyed pigments and stupendous sensory barrage? The punctilious and truthful

109 **Calvert Vaux** and **Frederic Edwin Church**, Olana, Hudson, New York, 1870–72/1888–89. During the course of an 1868 trip to Jerusalem, Church became enamored of Islamic architecture. He then collaborated with Calvert Vaux on Olana, his exotic villa high above the Hudson River. The house is a triumph of chromatic thought. Each room received an independent color scheme in keeping with its function and character, carefully distinguishing rooms of passage and reception from those of repose and reflection. In place of wooden baseboards and doorframes, Church simply painted broad bands of color that contrasted with the dominant hue of the room; further color accents completed the scheme, forming a triad of colors.

description of parts, essential to both Cole and Downing, was relinquished in favor of abstract chromatic effects. This heralded a titanic shift. The aesthetic criteria of truth and morality that had traditionally governed the American understanding of art were beginning to lose their authority. Such a shift was already underway in Europe but in America its course was traumatic, for it was punctuated by the four-year agony of the Civil War, in many ways the world's first modern war.

If America's painters had imagined that life would resume its natural course after the Civil War—that landscape and genre painting would flourish again, that the titans of art would reclaim their positions of leadership—they were to be sadly disappointed. Public taste had shifted in complicated and capricious ways between 1861 and 1865, and genteel sentimentality, that favorite stance of antebellum art, was now deeply unfashionable. In fact, the entire psychological foundation for American art patronage had now changed.

For one thing, the postwar landscape no longer carried quite the sense of pristine innocence it once had. Cole had contrasted the bloody topography of Europe with the innocence of America, where "you see no ruined tower to tell of outrage." But after the war, after the butchery of Gettysburg and Chancellorsville, this could no longer be said of the American landscape. Whether or not the public understood this consciously, it was no longer willing to spend as much for works by Church, Kensett, Cropsey, and Gifford, each of whom had the disagreeable experience of watching the demand for his paintings plummet. Church retreated to his Hudson River eyrie at Olana while Cropsey reverted to his youthful training as an architect: the "painter of autumn" performed the ignominious task of designing the stations for the Sixth Avenue Elevated Train.

The war thrust several new artists to prominence, including Matthew Brady, Thomas Nast, and Winslow Homer. Although they were respectively a photographer, cartoonist, and illustrator, they had one trait in common: a readiness to observe new facts, and drew logical consequences from them. And new facts could not long be hidden, especially the facts of modern war—not after the invention of photography. While cameras were still too cumbersome and film speed too slow to capture battle, they could still show all the other particulars of mass warfare, such as camp life, convalescing invalids, and scenes of violent destruction. And they could provide unsparing documentation of the carnage of battle, which photographer-entrepreneurs like Matthew Brady and Alexander Gardner ingeniously marketed to a mass audience. Timothy O'Sullivan's *Harvest of Death, Gettysburg* (1863) represented a new genre of popular photography, the post-battle tableau of the dead. O'Sullivan began the war working for Matthew Brady, whose practice of taking credit for the work of his staff photographers he came to resent. He left to work for Alexander Gardner, helping to complete his *Photographic Sketch Book of the War* (1866) [110].

Nast and Homer both become famous through *Harper's Weekly*, the illustrated newsweekly that flourished during the Civil War. Nast was a German émigré of decidedly liberal views who had marched with Garibaldi during the struggle for Italian unification. He was also a gifted cartoonist, whose robust drawing and intricate detail were firmly in the tradition of German caricature. By combining his uncanny visual inventiveness with his progressive politics, he created—virtually single-handedly—the modern profession of the editorial cartoonist [111]. During his long heyday in the 1860s and 1870s he coined some of the most familiar and enduring images of American culture: the Democratic donkey, the Republican elephant, and the definitive image of Santa Claus—each very much in use today.

The principal attraction of *Harper's Weekly* was its roster of sketch artists, whose battlefield sketches gave America its visual experience of the war. So much were they in demand that the painter Elihu Vedder later joked that "those were the times when we made drawings of battles before they had taken place." These artists scoured the front, making rough field sketches they would then work up into finished drawings in tents and hotel rooms, and ship to New York. At the massive office of Harper Brothers (one of the country's grandest cast-iron buildings), these drawings would be placed upon a treated panel of boxwood, and engraved into the wood. If speed was essential, the block could be sliced into squares and allocated to different engravers. Thus within a matter of days a Northern reader could look at relatively accurate scenes of battle from the South. Here, except for the speed of transmission, was modern photojournalism as we know it.

Wood engraving is a crude and unforgiving genre. Subtleties of line and tone are compromised or lost during the translation into wood, so that illustrations needed to be composed boldly enough to retain their graphic force, even when executed by hacks. This was Homer's genius. He knew how to let action unfold in large, broad gestures, carried by lively and forceful silhouettes [112].

110 **Alexander Gardner** and **Timothy O'Sullivan**, *A Harvest of Death, Gettysburg, Pennsylvania*, 1863. O'Sullivan took many of the most striking images for *Gardner's Photographic Sketch Book of the War* (1866), a landmark of photojournalism but a commercial failure: as Trumbull had unhappily discovered nearly a century earlier, a postwar society would often prefer to forget its recent traumas.

111 **Thomas Nast**, *A Group of Vultures Waiting for the Storm to "Blow Over". "Let Us Prey"*, 1871. With his cartoons in *Harper's Weekly*, Thomas Nast crusaded from 1871 to 1873 against Boss Tweed, the boss of New York's corrupt Tammany Hall political machine. Here Tweed and his cronies are portrayed as vultures that have devoured *law*, *justice*, *liberty*, *rent payers*, and *the city treasury*, which are represented by the gnawed bones strewn about their talons.

112 **Winslow Homer**, *The War for the Union, 1862—A Cavalry Charge*, 1862. Subtlety of line or tone are often lost in the carving of a woodblock, and Winslow Homer learned to make drawings strong enough to survive execution by even the most inept of woodcarvers. Published in *Harper's Weekly*, this is a typically spirited composition, its graphic energy deriving almost entirely from the silhouettes of a few boldly stenciled figures.

When he later shifted to oil painting, a few perfunctory lessons under his belt, these graphic qualities persisted. One early painting from the end of the war made him a celebrity: *Prisoners from the Front* shows a Union officer stand crisply to attention as he inspects three Confederate prisoners, whose body language runs the gamut from defiance to resignation [113]. This investigation of the differing physical reactions to captivity anticipates *The Burghers of Calais* by Auguste Rodin (who may have seen Homer's painting when it was exhibited in Paris in 1867).

It is remarkable that the painting manages to convey entirely different psychological attitudes, and does so more by body language that by facial expression. This would remain true throughout Homer's career; he was never a portraitist, and the meaning of his paintings never depended on a subtle likeness or a meaningful look. Instead he found great eloquence in the pose of the body itself, its postures and stances—which, after all, is the main instrument of the sketch artist.

Homer found himself artistically in 1881, during the course of a long stint in England. He lived for a year in Cullercoats, by Tynemouth, a hardy fishing village on the North Sea that provided him with a subject that neatly matched to his temperament: the

113 **Winslow Homer**, *Prisoners from the Front*, 1866. This struck a chord with the American public, who bought Homer's work as enthusiastically as it had Hudson River landscapes a generation earlier. Its finely observed realism suited postwar taste, evoking sympathy without stooping to sentimentality, a fitting tone after four years of mechanized mass slaughter.

brutal yet beautiful facts of life and death at the edge of the sea. During the war, he had learned the knack of locating a figure dramatically against the horizon line, a dangerous thing when snipers are near. He kept the idea of the fraught and vulnerable silhouette, and at Cullercoats he showed men and women fighting for their sustenance. He particularly enjoyed showing an object being acted upon by several forces at once, as in his *Inside the Bar* [114]. Here the woman steadies herself on the narrow bar, her skirt flapping crisply in the wind like the sail behind her, acted on simultaneously by wind and weight. This was no Düsseldorf vignette or genre scene, but a study of the physical facts of life at the violent shoreline, expressed in the language of weight and force, and drained of all superfluous detail.

Upon his return, Homer re-created the isolation of Cullercoats at Prout's Neck, Maine, where he built himself a simple shingled studio with a panoramic veranda, from which he could observe his rocky run of shoreline. Here he pursued ever more elemental dramas of conflict, gazing objectively, and rather pitilessly, at animals in the desperate work of hunting and surviving [145].

Homer's utter lack of sentiment put him in harmony with the cultural mood of post-Civil War America, which had no patience for judging art in moral terms. Before the war, Americans could still view art in essentially moral terms: to say that a painting or building was *true* was to award it the highest possible praise. After the war this was unthinkable. So serious were the moral issues of Abolition, secession, and emancipation, and so bloody their consequences, that moralizing art seemed a quaint affectation.

If art was not to be justified by the truths it told, or the lessons it taught, it might justify itself on its own terms: "art for art's sake." This was the insight of the Aesthetic Movement, the revolutionary movement that utterly transformed American culture between 1865 and 1900 and did so with the simplest of insights: art need not be true to be great, but it must be beautiful. Although this doctrine blossomed in the 1870s, its seeds had been planted much earlier, in 1855, when two American brothers returned to the United States following a decade of study in Paris. These were the painter William Morris Hunt (1824–79) and the architect Richard Morris Hunt (1828–95), two sons of a Vermont congressman. It is difficult to overestimate their influence, for the lessons they brought with them from France set the course of American art for the next half century.

Except for a brief interlude following the Revolution, France had not been of great importance to American art. Her Catholicism and her political radicalism were both suspect and only the occasional artist, such as Vanderlyn, strayed there. But in the wake of the revolution of 1848 a new and modern France

114 **Winslow Homer**, *Inside the Bar*, 1883. With its small format and spontaneity, the watercolor was a natural medium for Homer, and it built on his training as an illustrator. His earliest watercolors were still drawings, tightly rendered scenes where color was incidental. *Inside the Bar* shows him as a mature watercolorist, thinking in the liquid medium of color.

emerged. This was the Second Empire, ruled over by the emperor Napoleon III, a man whose ambition and insecurity were each limitless. Acutely aware that he had no more qualification than having Napoleon for his uncle, the new emperor worked anxiously to manufacture popular support. He embarked upon a great program of public amenities, which gave Paris a spectacular new opera house, a massively enlarged Louvre, and an array of grand boulevards that made her the showplace of Europe. When Boston, New York, and Philadelphia sought a model of fashionable urbanity, they found it in Paris.

Second Empire architecture deliberately evoked the glory days of the seventeenth century. The buildings of Napoleon III imitated those of the French Renaissance which, unlike their Italian counterparts, required high roofs and which provided them in the form of bulbous mansards. They were also vigorously plastic; the corners and centers of buildings were marked by proudly projecting pavilions while their rooflines were freighted with festive dormers. The walls themselves were articulated with segmental pediments and paired columns, which gave the facade the sense of overlapping planes, vigorously modeled in depth. Sculpture was used intensively and was closely integrated into the enframing architecture. Seldom was architecture so florid or fleshy. This treatment of architecture was rather antithetical to the American tradition of taut surfaces and flat walls, to the schematic approach to architecture of a wood-building culture without much experience in the expressive language of thick sculptural walls.

Nonetheless, the Second Empire instantly took hold in America after the Civil War, and did duty in countless courthouses, city halls (such as Boston, Providence, Baltimore, and Philadelphia), and state capitols (New York). It even became the quasi-official style of the federal government, which applied the same formula rigidly—and rather mindlessly—to buildings as different as the St. Louis Post Office and the State, War, and Navy Building in Washington, D.C. [115]. Both were by Alfred B. Mullet (1834–1890), the supervising architect of the United States Treasury, who built so many buildings during the presidency of Ulysses S. Grant (1869–77) that the style was nicknamed the General Grant Style. Placing so many buildings under the charge of one man inevitably made them rather schematic and standardized in detail, quite unlike France where an architect might lavish a decade or more on a single public building.

115 **Alfred B. Mullet**, State, War, and Navy Building, Washington, D.C., 1871–88. This colossal building is the forerunner of the Pentagon, both in function and in swagger. Now known as the Executive Office Building, it was built during the brief American heyday of the Second Empire and has all the hallmarks of its French prototype: a bulky mass broken up by projecting corner pavilions, topped with a mansard roof, bristling with dormers and paired columns. Nonetheless, unlike the graceful and elegant French version, this building is rather florid, and suffers in its details from a stiffness and hardness that its granite construction can only partially explain.

Mullet learned his French architecture at second hand, from photographs, but Richard Morris Hunt learned it at its source, the École des Beaux Arts (School of Fine Arts) in Paris, where he enrolled in 1847. Unlike the German polytechnical system, in which aesthetics were merely one component of a technical education, the École treated architecture as a fundamentally aesthetic enterprise, to which technical matters were subordinated. The heart of education was not the classroom but the *atelier*, which was run by the *patron*, a practicing architect, who groomed his students for the École's monthly design competitions. These consisted of a written program for a public building, such as a railroad station or a village church, for which the student had a fixed period of time to make a design. The essence of the design was the floor plan, which encapsulated the logic of the entire building in diagrammatic fashion, showing its public spaces, its clear paths of movement, and the masonry walls that enclosed them—all arranged with symmetry and evident visual clarity. The facades were designed last, and derived from the plan itself, which they were meant to express in rhetorical fashion.

From first to last, the mark of the École was an exquisite and thoroughgoing refinement of every aspect of a building.

Richard Morris Hunt trained in the *atelier* of Hector LeFuel, who was building Napoleon III's newly expanded Louvre. Hunt assisted him for a year, acting as job captain for the building's library pavilion, which required him to make the full-size drawings for each detail and decoration of the wing. This was the capstone of his education, and motifs of the building ricochet throughout his later work.

The Hunt brothers were no mere dabblers who ventured to Europe for a year or two of genteel lessons, after their taste and technique was already fixed and too late to redeem. Instead, after a full decade of study in Paris, they were for all practical purposes Frenchmen. Had they remained in Paris, each would have enjoyed a prestigious career. But in the winter of 1855, they returned to the United States, with the intention of founding a school of architecture and painting, modeled on the École des Beaux Arts. To this end, Richard built the Studio Building in New York, with magnificently large studios grouped around a spacious court [116]. At the base of the court, illuminated by skylights, was the main exhibition gallery (later claimed by William Merritt Chase for his own studio). Here Richard was to teach architecture and William painting, ending the long reign of German leadership in the arts.

From the beginning, the brothers worked to create in America the same sense of artistic community that they had enjoyed in Paris—a fraternity of like-minded artists joined in common purpose. Toward this end, they formed fraternal organizations. Richard helped found the American Institute of Architects (AIA) in 1857, the first professional organization of American architects. And in 1866, in order to raise the standard of artistic patronage, William founded the Allston Club in Boston; among his first acts was to buy a Courbet for Boston.

Unfortunately, the Hunt brothers' planned art academy never materialized. William backed out, leaving Richard to run a straightforward architectural *atelier*, which he did from 1857 to 1861, until he too abandoned the scheme of an American Beaux Arts. But though his *atelier* lasted but a few years, it produced five luminaries of American architecture: George Post, William Ware, Henry Van Brunt, Charles Gambrill (the partner of H. H. Richardson), and the idiosyncratic Frank Furness. Moreover, it changed the nature of architectural education, making it an

116 **Richard Morris Hunt**, Studio Building, 51 West Tenth Street, New York, 1857. Now demolished, this was America's first purpose-built art studio. Richard Morris Hunt designed it in the disciplined mode he had learned in Paris, an exercise in rational brick construction, generously lighted and ventilated. Some of America's most prestigious painters rented its studios, including Frederic Edwin Church, William Merritt Chase, John F. Weir, and John La Farge, while Hunt's architectural studio was on the top story.

academic process rather than the traditional system of apprenticeship and office training. Hunt's *atelier* was the direct ancestor of the Massachusetts Institute of Technology's architectural program, America's first modern school of architecture. Founded by Ware in 1867, it supplanted before long the German polytechnical model that had prevailed before the Civil War.

Hunt conducted his *atelier* on the École model: monthly projects were assigned and the results were critiqued, often savagely. But while his tutelage was rigorous, students were not drilled to imitate his designs. Because it was grounded in the floor plan, and in a penetrating analysis of movement and function, the École inculcated a method, not a style, and an architect who mastered that method could work in any architectural language. For the restless United States, where successive clients might demand Romanesque, Gothic, or Renaissance buildings, this flexibility would be decisive. This accounts for the striking individuality of Hunt's pupils. Post favored the Italian Renaissance, Furness devised a Greek–Gothic synthesis, and Ware and Van Brunt, working together, preferred the Ruskinian High Victorian Gothic. But beneath the wildest roofline and the gaudiest wall, each of their designs invariably revealed a symmetrical and disciplined floor plan, which gave integrity and logic to even the most frenzied design [117]. Only Hunt remained judiciously academic in his architecture, setting a standard of learning and refinement that did much to raise the general level of architectural quality—much as Latrobe had in his own day.

The effect of his brother, William Morris Hunt, on American painting was equally decisive and showed the same tendency: to raise standards, to impose academic values, and to promote an understanding of art that was aesthetic rather than moralizing or didactic. Likewise, he reoriented American painting from German influence toward the French. William Morris Hunt began his studies at Düsseldorf, on the recommendation of Leutze, but he quickly became disenchanted. His teachers there believed, he complained, "that the education of art genius, of a mechanic, and a student of science were one and the same thing—a grinding, methodical process for the accumulation of required skills." He abruptly moved to Paris, where from 1847 to 1852 he studied with Thomas Couture, who was a painter of historical scenes and portraits with a flair for lurid costume dramas as well as the teacher of Manet.

118 **William Morris Hunt**, *The Belated Kid*, 1854–57. When he painted this, the artist was at the peak of his Millet phase, with its rustic subject matter and feeling for the monumental solidity of the figure. The coarse subject matter and loose treatment of such works offended Boston critics, however, who accused him of "painting with a trowel." This charge wounded him, and subsequent portraits restored the smooth finish and sparkling color of Thomas Couture, his first teacher.

Hunt arrived in Paris when an American was still a novelty, not a dupe to be exploited. He gained entry into the highest levels of French artistic society, although he never absorbed its prejudices and deep distrust of innovation. Rather, he plunged directly into the French avant-garde. In 1852 he encountered Jean-François Millet, champion of the upcoming Barbizon School, whose work astonished him. Nothing could be farther removed from Couture's exuberant Roman orgies and billowing nudes. Millet's art confronted the prosy facts of rural life, of humble peasants and farmers, to whose tasks of sowing or harvesting he gave the exalted dignity of sacred rite. The antithesis of Couture, he suppressed all beguiling detail and incident, stressing the awkward bulkiness of his farmers and bestowing on them a heroic monumentality. Hunt was captivated. He purchased numerous works by Millet, including *The Sower*, for which he paid about sixty dollars; he arranged for friends in Boston to buy others. (This was the origin of the first-rate Barbizon collection of the Boston Museum of Fine Arts.) In 1853 Hunt moved to Barbizon to work with Millet—to Couture's intense displeasure—whose subject matter and technique he closely emulated for a time [118].

If training were everything, Hunt ought to have been the most successful artist of his generation. Instead, he became a fashionable portrait painter at the moment when portraiture was no longer the main channel of artistic progress. His ultimate importance was as a teacher, not a painter. His studio in Newport attracted an eclectic range of curious young figures: John La Farge, Frank Furness (taking a break from his architectural training), and the precocious brothers, William James and Henry James, both then considering a career in art.

Hunt's curriculum was something of a veritable one-man crusade against Düsseldorf, whose carefully drawn outlines he despised as only a former victim could. Students were made to disregard finicky detail and to think in terms of large masses of light and dark. In order to purge form of incidental and distracting detail, Hunt ordered them to draw from memory. When he caught students placing a set of measuring calipers on a photograph, he would explode in indignation: "Is your knowledge of art limited to what a pair of calipers can measure? Is Sumner's character confined to his nose? You need not do any measuring in my studio!"

119 **John La Farge**, *Portrait of Henry James, the Novelist*, 1862. La Farge befriended Henry James in 1860, when both were pupils of William Morris Hunt in Newport. Two years later La Farge painted the aspiring author. The soft indistinctness of outline and the shimmering and luminous surface color show a facility comparable to Hunt's although La Farge was too ambitious and restless a personality to confine himself to mere portraiture.

Such charming and maddening exhortations, poured forth in a glorious stream-of-consciousness reverie, comprised the essence of Hunt's teaching. One student, Helen M. Knowlton, surreptitiously transcribed his comments and published them as *Talks on Art* (1875/83), which enjoyed a minor sensation. By far his finest pupil was John La Farge (1835–1910), a talented but fiercely independent young man and a genius of color [103 and 119]. So strong was his love of spectral color that paint could not fulfill it, and La Farge almost naturally moved from oil paint to painting with light itself. In 1873 he designed the decorative stained glass for Ware and Van Brunt's Memorial Hall at Harvard. For this he invented opalescent glass, in which the color itself was integral to the glass, rather than painted on. The material was widely used by architects in the following decades. Lafarge's work was a high point of the Aesthetic Movement, the ultimate triumph of light and color over outline and contour, those staples of the Düsseldorf education.

Hunt himself was not as successful, or versatile, as his pupil. Despite success as a teacher, he struggled to find subject matter that befitted his talent. France had taught that the loftiest form of painting was monumental mural art for a public building, a form of art still uncommon in America. Not until 1878 did he receive such a commission: two large murals, 16 by 45 feet (5 by 14 meters), for the Assembly Chamber of the New York State Capitol in Albany.

Instead of a history painting, which might have inserted Henry Hudson or Pieter Stuyvesant in a theatrical tableau—as Leutze had done with George Washington—Hunt produced a complex and spacious allegory. On one mural was a figure of Columbus, representing science and progress; on the other Anahita, the Persian goddess of the moon, from a poem that had fascinated Hunt since the 1840s [120]. The work was an audacious study in dualities: Night and Day, Feminine and Masculine, Negative and Positive, Eastern and Western, each held in reciprocal and dynamic balance. This was a new kind of monumental painting in America, the academic mural, with a few large figures, drawn at large scale from life, in an allegory that challenged the imagination, rather than recreating a historical vignette. Hunt finished the work in a heroic sixty days, and the work finished him; within a year he drowned himself, shattered by feelings of personal and professional failure.

By the time of his death, however, Hunt had already transformed American art. The process was slow; well into the 1850s artists like Whittredge and Bingham preferred the sturdy, dependable German approach. But others began to follow Hunt's lead: after a few unhappy years in Düsseldorf, Eastman Johnson set out for Paris. Then in 1856 John La Farge came to Couture's studio. But by the 1870s, the stream had broadened into a torrent: throngs of aspiring painters enrolled in specialized *ateliers* like the Académie Julian, which made a lucrative business by crowding them into barnlike studios by the dozens, where they squinted at a distant model and waited for few hasty comments from the *patron* on his weekly visit.

Much the same happened in architecture. After Richard Morris Hunt, H. H. Richardson (1859), Charles F. McKim (1868) and Louis Sullivan (1874), and John Russell Pope (1896) each enrolled at the École, to name only some of the most distinguished. In fact, there were hundreds. For architects who could not afford to study in Paris, the Society of Beaux-Arts Architects was founded in New York in 1894 (renamed the Beaux-Arts Institute of Design in 1916).

Thus the two Hunt brothers changed the direction and orientation of American art, and largely through personal example. The vocabulary of *esquisse*, *atelier*, *concours*, *patron*, *Prix de Rome*, and so forth entered the common vocabulary, some of them, like *charette*—the term for the late night rush to finish a project—lasting to this day. Within a few years, the Hunts' idiosyncratic decision to study in Paris had become not only conventional, but virtually an obligation.

120 **William Morris Hunt**, *The Flight of Night*, 1877. William Morris Hunt painted this directly on the wall of the Albany State Assembly Chamber. Juxtaposed against a figure of Columbus, it depicts Anahita, the Persian goddess of the moon as she plunges "impelled by the dawn of civilization … into the dark and hidden caverns of superstition and barbaric thought." For Hunt, both figures were "suspended between faith and doubt," making the program a spacious treatment of the tragic nature of history. The tragedy was more than allegorical, alas: Hunt's pigments were unstable and flaked off under the building's leaky roof, and his design survives only in the form of preliminary sketches such as this.

Chapter 6   Academic Art

During the first century of its existence the United States brooded incessantly over the question of a national art: when would there be an art that was distinctively American?; what would its properties be?; how would it differ from the art of Europe? The subject preoccupied criticism, and artists were routinely praised on patriotic grounds and for their contribution to developing an American art. But as the successors to Cole and Powers became more sophisticated, and began to enjoy formal training in Europe, they shed the provinciality that was the primary constituent of their American identity. The Hunt brothers were prodigies but for all practical purposes they were French artists practicing in America. Americans now learned that they could have either great art or a national art, but not both.

This discovery was traumatic. Up to the Civil War, artists naturally assumed that every rise in wealth and sophistication would mean a corresponding rise in their own fortunes. And indeed, the bankers and merchants of the Jacksonian era were happy to buy American landscape and genre paintings. But their counterparts of the 1870s now started buying modern European art and Old Masters in preference to American landscapes. This was the privilege of wealth and success—they could now afford Old Masters—but it also reflected the ease of modern travel. The eight-day passage in a luxury steamer was now a pleasure rather than an ordeal, and after the Civil War the casual summer in Europe became a regular fixture of society life. All this gave the American patron a broader and more international outlook, greater familiarity with the artistic currents of Europe, and perhaps also a temptation to flaunt his cosmopolitan credentials. This lesson was driven home at the 1876 Centennial Exhibition in Philadelphia, America's first world's fair.

The exhibition, which commemorated the anniversary of the signing of the Declaration of Independence in Philadelphia in 1776,

121 **Furness & Hewitt**, Pennsylvania Academy of the Fine Arts, Philadelphia, 1871–76.

was an enormous boost to the prestige of the city. Philadelphia was still smarting after its loss of financial and population leadership to New York but it remained the nation's principal industrial city. During the Civil War it played a decisive role as the Union metropolis nearest the theater of battle in Virginia. In this way it recouped much of its pride and confidence, and wealth—a certain portion of which made its way into the new building of the Pennsylvania Academy of the Fine Arts (1871–76), which was planned so as to open on the eve of the great exhibition [121].

While the fair displayed America's dazzling technological prowess, with the first public exhibition of the telephone and the electric light, it was especially notable for the sheer volume of art that was exhibited. This was to be the largest exhibition of paintings and sculpture yet held in America, as well as the most eclectic. A total of 2,749 works of American art were shown, representing 787 artists. The judicious viewer would be able to take the measure of America's important artists, one after another, and to compare them in their totality to their European counterparts, who were represented in even greater number

(4,398 paintings, sculptures, and drawings). Here the public would be able to gauge the effects of the war, the recent collapse of the Hudson River School, and the new rage for European training—making possible a comprehensive appraisal of the state of contemporary American art.

The Exhibition was also a showcase of the art of Philadelphia and, in many ways, it seemed that the city's hour had now arrived. If public taste had turned emphatically realist, rejecting the antebellum doctrine that the role of art was to teach, uplift, or persuade, and preferring to be shown the world as it was, without sentiment or agenda, this was Philadelphia's strong suit. The city's realist tradition was of considerable antiquity, dating back to its Quaker origin. The Quaker religious service, or meeting, involves the congregation sitting in companionable silence until anyone feels moved to speak: since Quakers needed no formally trained ministers, they needed no universities to train them, and the city did not swiftly establish universities as did Boston, New Haven, and Providence. Instead, Philadelphia's higher education tended to be practical, oriented around useful trades or professions such as medicine. For abstract theoretical speculation, or for theory for its own sake, there was little place or sympathy. Although the Quaker population of Philadelphia shrank to a minority during the eighteenth century, their values still permeated the city: plainness, simplicity, and a dislike for rhetoric or pomp. By the time of the Civil War, the city was a center of printing, medical education, engineering, and industry—especially the building of locomotives—each of which was reinvigorated by the strenuous demands of the war.

Realism had a long pedigree in America, and not only in Philadelphia, but the realism of the postwar era had a different sensibility [113]. It shed the light-hearted tone of antebellum genre painting, and the comical characters and farcical situations that Bingham and Mount favored; its subjects were more likely to be industrial and urban than rural [122]. Postwar realists were typically trained academically, and they took much greater care with composition. Instead of additive and overcrowded cartoons, they produced well-studied and well-ordered arrangements of figures, sacrificing storytelling to composition.

A distinct melancholy tinged the new realism, particularly in the realm of the still life. The traditional still life depicted flowers and fruit, symbols of abundance and bounty; in a society where

123 **Lilly Martin Spencer**,
Raspberries on a Leaf, 1858. Lilly
Martin Spencer (1822–1902) was
not the first American artist to
raise her income by lowering her
sights. She was a commercial flop
with her Shakespearean and
allegorical subjects until a friend
advised to concentrate on her
own "peculiar" genre: "pictures
remarkable for Maternal, infantine
& feminine, expressions, in which
little else is seen but flesh, white
drapery, and fruits, constitute your
triumphs." There ensued an
uninterrupted stream of
confections such as this one—
pleasant, saccharine, and free of
all higher ambition.

124 **William Harnett**, *The Old
Violin*, 1886. William Harnett
(1848–92) trained in Philadelphia
and Munich, where he learned
his glistening, richly textured
technique. Its aesthetic force
comes from the contrast between
the strictly ordered background
and the elegant contours of the
violin, a voluptuous stand-in for
the human form.

wealth was still largely agricultural, this was only logical [123].
But after the war, the floral still life was dislodged by the *trompe
l'oeil* painting. These showed flat or nearly flat objects, often
painted on panel and painted illusionistically so as to trick—
literally, "trump"—the eye. Although some were clearly intended
as jokes (the owner might have the pleasure of seeing a visitor
try to pry a painted dollar bill from behind its painted string),
they had a darker meaning as well. Their subject matter hinted
at impermanence and decay: torn receipts, sun-bleached
photographs, and the ominous dangling watch [124]. These were
memento mori—reminders of mortality—which, according to the
ancient *vanitas* tradition, served to rebuke human folly and pride.
The Civil War had offered much of both, and it is easy to see how
these enigmatic compositions fascinated the public in the years
after the war.

The finest *trompe l'oeil* painters, William Harnett and John Peto, were both products of the Pennsylvania Academy of the Fine Arts, that crucible of realism. The Academy enjoyed the national spotlight at the Centennial, and visitors to Philadelphia gaped at its new building, a defiant essay in architectural realism [121 and 125]. The architect was Frank Furness (1839–1912), a designer of exceptional originality and perversity, and America's most modern architect of the post-Civil War era.

Furness, of course, was trained by Richard Morris Hunt in the rational Beaux-Arts method but he was also shaped by his family friendship with Ralph Waldo Emerson, whose Transcendentalism he applied to architecture. And Furness was the product of the Civil War; he served heroically as a cavalryman in the picturesque Rush's Lancers, the only regiment to ride into battle bearing lances—a military version of the Gothic Revival. After the war he seems to have been a larger than life character; "a horsy, flashy, tweedy sort of man," as the critic Lewis Mumford called him; there is a persistent legend that his mistress ran a brothel and that he once borrowed back the jewels he had given her so that he could pawn them in order to make his payroll.

125 **Furness & Hewitt**, Pennsylvania Academy of the Fine Arts, 1871–76. High Victorian art at its apex of chromatic and textural intensity. The columns are of red granite with black marble bands and blue marble bases, and they support Gothic arches of yellow sandstone. This is the palette of geology and above them is that of light itself, arranged in a star-flecked dome of red, blue, and yellow. These primary colors are centered at the hub of the Academy, providing an optical demonstration of the centrality of color in painting.

Something of the heightened violence of combat made its way into his buildings, especially the commercial work. Furness was alert to the financial forces underpinning modern life and he understood that capitalist clients were in lively and merciless competition with one another. He saw that buildings could advance that competition. Victorian architecture was already nervously eye-catching, relishing vibrant color and exaggerated form, but Furness pushed it to an extreme. He distorted conventional forms to express the agonizing structural tensions within a wall and he placed large elements on small buildings, where they might imperil the street and browbeat their neighbors [126]. The nation's great corporations—the Reading Railroad and the Pennsylvania Railroad, and that transatlantic steamship company, the Red Star Line—made good use of his arrogant pencil, and made Furness America's first successful corporate architect.

The Pennsylvania Academy of the Fine Arts, designed in partnership with George W. Hewitt, was also a rhetorical building but its theme was art rather than commerce. To show that the building was a storehouse of the art of different schools and nations, he made his facade a grand architectural encyclopedia: a trio of mansarded pavilions was arranged in a conventional Second Empire scheme but the walls, ablaze with color and sporting pointed arches, derived from the Venetian Gothic. Other motifs ranged even farther: stilted metopes (the square panels between triglyphs in a Doric frieze) conjured the Greek Doric, while the rectilinear portal quoted a North African mosque. It was as if Furness had taken the country's newest art institutions, the Gothic National Academy of Design and the Second Empire Corcoran Gallery, and violently collapsed them together.

Ruskin would have approved of the Venetian colors and the naturalistic foliage but he would have been appalled by Furness's flagrant use of architectural iron, brazenly displayed within and without in the form of riveted iron beams. This was the first use of exposed architectural iron on a monumental civic building in America, and perhaps in Europe as well. The French Gothic theorist Eugène-Emmanuel Viollet-le-Duc had already published visionary designs for iron and masonry buildings but they bore their first fruit in Philadelphia, a city congenial to industrial imagery. This was especially true of the Academy, which was administered by a board of the city's manufacturers and industrialists, including Furness's own brother-in-law, Fairman

Rogers, himself an engineer. (Very different was the case in New York, where the National Academy of Design was governed by the artists themselves.)

The realism of Furness's building is the physical manifestation of the Academy's distinctive curriculum. In fact, Furness was advised by Thomas Eakins (1844–1916), its most rigorous and influential teacher, and America's greatest champion of scientific realism. A pupil of the Academy in the early 1860s, Eakins had also taken classes in anatomy at Jefferson Medical School. There he derived his belief that the human body, understood as an expressive mechanical system, is the basis of all art. From 1866 to 1869 he studied in Paris under the dashing Jean-Léon Gérome, France's popular painter of Orientalist themes. Eakins absorbed Gérome's fastidious method, which was informed by research, photography, and a full array of costumes and props. A later six-month visit to Spain was equally influential. There he reveled in the dark palette and the Spanish predilection for painting in broad, bold masses:

126 **Frank Furness**, Provident Life and Trust Company Bank, Philadelphia, 1879. Furness drew from both the picturesque Gothic of the English Ecclesiologists and the rationality of French classicism, but his Provident Life and Trust Building looked neither ecclesiastical nor rational. Its brawny granite blocks and out-thrust bay belong to the world of military architecture—appropriate for a building waging financial warfare on its competitors. The Provident provided life insurance for Quakers, and boasted that their sobriety and longevity was a good investment; this muscular building is a kind of architectural parody of good health.

127 **Thomas Eakins**, *Miss Amelia van Buren*, c. 1891. A lesser painter would have concealed the strong planes of Amelia van Buren's forehead, but Thomas Eakins virtually caresses them, raking light across them to give them crisp definition. This is Eakins's skill: he begins by treating the body as a mechanical system, as so many volumes in space hung on pulleys and pivots, and ends by achieving a sense of vivid personality.

128 **Thomas Eakins**, *William Rush Carving His Allegorical Figure of the Schuylkill River*, 1876–77. Many of Eakins's best works are either investigations of the human body or depictions of great skill and prowess; this painting is both. Despite the title, the center of attention is not the artist (nor the patiently knitting chaperone) but the nude model, whose back is eloquently articulated with sharp highlights on the thigh and breast. The heap of clothes and undergarments call attention to the fact of her nudity, and struck contemporary viewers as indelicate. But they lift the painting up above genre art to give it a higher theme: the dependence of art on the dispassionate study of the human form.

"O what a satisfaction it gave me to see the good Spanish work so good so strong so reasonable so free from every affectation. It stands out like nature itself."

Back in Philadelphia, Eakins first made his mark with a series of rowing pictures, which showed athletes engaged in intense physical activity and mental concentration. Here was his lifetime's theme: the human body, either in action or repose, placed solidly in space and described forensically, even clinically, by raking light. His artistic insight was to treat the body as a complex mechanical apparatus of interlocking bones and muscle groups, capable of subtle flexure and inclination that could convey character. He did not work to charm his sitters into spontaneity and self-revelation, but let their posture and tilt of the head reveal personality, the unconscious deployment of muscles making visible the inner life. In his portrait of Amelia van Buren, a simple pensive slouch speaks as eloquently as any of Sargent's sprightly vivacious belles [127].

To realize this method fully required that the subject be nude, and here Eakins found resistance. Although a generation had passed since the success of Hiram Powers's *Greek Slave*, the American public was still alarmed by nudity, artistic or otherwise. Yet Eakins was convinced that great art must begin with the human form. With his *William Rush Carving His Allegorical Figure of the Schuylkill River* (1875–77), he made the case the only way he could, pictorially. The painting depicts an actual event: in 1814, the sculptor William Rush had carved a statue for Benjamin Henry Latrobe's Philadelphia Waterworks, and a young Quaker woman

129 **Thomas Eakins**, *The Gross Clinic*, 1875. This is Eakins's masterpiece, uniting the tight draftsmanship he had learned from Gérome with the sweeping dignity and drama of Spanish Baroque art. It is filled with magnificent passages: the brilliant and unexpected foreshortening of the patient, which dramatically compresses the urgent activity of the assisting surgeons; the radically narrow depth of field—an effect conceivable only after photography—leaves Gross alone in sharp focus, while everything in front of or behind him is somewhat soft-edged. Gross displays a magisterial calm, presiding over the ordered agitation like the captain at the helm of some great ship.

was enlisted as his model. Eakins recorded the physical facts as Gérome had taught him, reproducing the period costumes and making his own wax models of Rush's sculptures; he altered the crucial fact, however, and showed the model posing nude, which she certainly did not do. Eakins surely knew this, but he proclaimed the artistic and not the historical truth [128].

Eakins was a painter of considerable emotional reserve and detachment, but his works often give a distinct sense of great personal passion, kept veiled and held in check, which make them more than mere painted facts and surfaces. It is evident that he identified with Rush, a fellow member of the Pennsylvania Academy whose artistic struggles mirrored his own. He also clearly identified with Dr. Samuel D. Gross, the subject of *The Gross Clinic* (1875) [129]. Gross was a celebrated surgeon and an instructor at Jefferson Medical College, where Eakins had learned his anatomy. Ostensibly, the painting depicted Gross operating in

Jefferson's surgical amphitheater, demonstrating how to remove the dead bone splints caused by osteomylitis, a technique he had pioneered. As with *William Rush*, however, the true subject was the confrontation of the human mind and the human body. Again, Eakins makes the rhetorical point by means of pictorial composition: the figures are grouped as a loose pyramid whose apex is Gross's prominent brow, which emerges from darkness to be struck from above with a shaft of sunlight (from the operating theater's necessary skylight). This light on his splendid brow is juxtaposed against the poised hand with the bloody scalpel, indicating that Gross is a teacher who learns by doing, the blood on his hand ratifying the knowledge in his head. There could be no stronger defense of Eakins's own empirical method.

Eakins implemented this method at the Pennsylvania Academy when he became its director of instruction in 1879. No more would students spend years drawing from plaster casts of antique statues before they ever saw a living model; now they would draw from life almost from the beginning. But he pursued his method too eagerly and in 1886 he was dismissed for removing a male model's loincloth in a class that included female students. Nonetheless, even without Eakins the Academy remained staunchly realist, and through such successors as Thomas Anschutz, Robert Vonnoh, and Robert Henri, his inheritance was carried into the twentieth century.

Philadelphia's ultimate achievement in realism came in that most objective of artistic media, photography: Muybridge's monumental *Animal Locomotion* (Philadelphia, 1887). Eadweard Muybridge (1830–1904) was a San Francisco commercial photographer who in 1872 began photographing race horses for Leland Stanford, the president of the Central Pacific Railroad and former governor of California. Stanford wanted to know if a trotting horse ever had all four feet in the air; his were strictly prosaic interests—horse breeding and racing—but they inspired a revolution in high-speed photography. Muybridge developed extremely sensitive and rapid photographic plates as well as a shutter that could operate at a five-hundredth of a second. Using a battery of trip wires, he could take images in rapid-fire succession. To project these serial images he later devised the Zoöpraxiscope (1879), the first motion-picture projector.

Muybridge's efforts brought him into contact with Eakins and the Academy's president, Fairman Rogers (who was himself both a gifted horseman and an amateur photographer). Through their support, Muybridge was brought to Philadelphia in 1884 to undertake a systematic study of the body in motion. He set up an outdoor studio at the University of Pennsylvania, where he photographed a battery of human and animal subjects according to a strict experimental method: against a precisely ruled background, models performed a simple action, such as throwing a ball or pouring a bucket of water, while three cameras simultaneously recorded the event from different angles. Muybridge used a wide variety of models, including himself and Eakins; the hopping model for plate 185, shown here, was "the première danseuse of a Philadelphia theater" [130]. But he also photographed handicapped or deformed subjects, crucial to the usefulness of the book as a work of medical reference. The vast undertaking took three years and the full version of *Animal Locomotion* consisted of 781 multiple-image plates, with a total of nearly 20,000 separate photographs.

With the work of Furness, Eakins, and Muybridge, among others, Philadelphia's realist school was at its peak during the 1870s and 1880s. But by then the national mood was beginning to turn away from realism. Already at the Centennial there were signs that the blunt and brutal realism of Philadelphia was out of step with the national mood. Eakins's *Gross Clinic*, for example, was the most original and audacious American work of its day but to the judges of the Centennial Art Gallery it seemed merely vulgar.

130 **Eadweard Muybridge**, *Female Figure Hopping*, 1887. Although Eadweard Muybridge's *Animal Locomotion* was scientific in conception, it was hoped that artists would also use it as a reference. Nevertheless, its aesthetic influence went far beyond its role as an aid for drawing figures in motion. Modernist artists recognized that its fragmentary nature and sense of arrested motion had a peculiar aesthetic power. It is possible to draw a line between Muybridge's work and Marcel Duchamp's *Nude Descending a Staircase* [179].

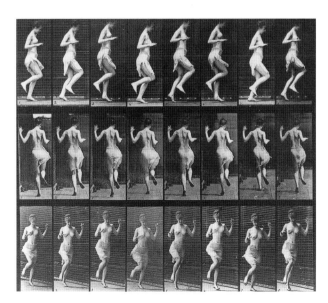

It must have come as a stunning rebuke to Eakins to see it relegated to a surgical display.

Nor was the Centennial a coup for Furness, whose work seemed incomprehensible to non-Philadelphians and whose Academy brought him no commissions outside the city. The architectural phenomenon of the Centennial was not Furness but H. H. Richardson of Boston, whose work (displayed in the form of photographs) drew an enthusiastic response. After a generation of Victorian eccentricity and wayward individualism, Richardson's calm and ordered designs were a revelation, as fresh and irresistible as the changing of a season. The Centennial offered other attractions for architects seeking alternatives to High Victorian excess. There was the Japanese pavilion, with its elegantly continuous roofline and delicate carpentry; and there were the English buildings, half-timbered and redolent of late medieval vernacular architecture—a great impetus for the American Queen Anne Revival of the next generation. Out of these separate ingredients emerged the tasteful architectural aestheticism of the next generation.

The fact is that the centre of gravity of American art was now moving toward Europe. Art criticism dropped its patriotic criteria of judgment and began to apply the cosmopolitan standards of continental criticism. The first sign of the changing of the guard came in 1871, when Henry James began writing art criticism for *The Nation*. There he took delight in kicking the dead horse of the Hudson River School, drubbing figures such as Frederic Edwin Church. James's artistic values had been nourished by his studies with Hunt and they were like those of his novels, in which mood and tone counted for more than narrative and moral. In 1876, James moved permanently to England, becoming one of the leaders of the large cultured expatriate class that would center in London and Paris, and whose intellectual and cultural viewpoint was thoroughly international. Besides James, Edith Wharton, and Henry Adams, it included three painters of the highest rank: James Abbott McNeill Whistler (1834–1903), John Singer Sargent (1856–1925), and Mary Cassatt (1844–1926). Just as Benjamin West helped to shape American art from afar in the late eighteenth century, so these three expatriates—though working and exhibiting in Europe—were a constant though vicarious presence in the artistic life of late nineteenth-century America.

They had much in common. All had lived in Europe as children (Sargent was born there), all were multilingual, and all had the

131 **James Abbott McNeill Whistler**, *Symphony in White, No. 1: The White Girl*, 1862. Whistler called this painting "one gorgeous mass of brilliant white." While its ambiguity and the lack of affect of its subject perplexed critics, and although the French Academy refused to exhibit it, it was the first suggestion of a new language of painting in which carefully modulated tones of a single hue would predominate, rather than the strong color contrasts on which most academic painting relied.

benefit of French academic training. But they were not merely French painters; as expatriates, they could move freely between the art worlds of France and England, something that neither French nor English artists could easily do. They contributed considerably to the internationalization of art in the late nineteenth century.

Whistler, the eldest, established the template for the others. At a young age he lived in Russia, where his father built the St. Petersburg–Moscow railroad. After an unsuccessful term at West Point and an equally unhappy one as a coastal surveyor—where he learned to make etchings—he went to Paris in 1856 to study painting with Charles Gleyre, the teacher of several young artists who would go on to become famous, including Renoir, Monet, and Sisley. His sensational debut came six years later with *The White Girl*, a distinctly unidealized painting of a wan young woman in white, standing on a white rug in a white room [131]. But Whistler's conception of his subject matter, or rather his indifference to it, was revolutionary. The mood of the painting, and its overall chromatic unity, counted for him far more than the woman—who was simply a formal element in the composition, much as the bear rug on which she stood. To underscore that the subject of the painting was not the woman but the abstract chromatic harmony, Whistler renamed the piece *Symphony in White, No. 1*, as if it were a piece of music.

The White Girl and its successors are the ultimate source of the movement known as Tonalism, which reached its peak in the 1880s. Tonalists suppressed pictorial incident and storytelling in their canvases in order to create a sense of overall mood, usually one of languorous reverie. They also suppressed sharp color contrast, reducing their palette to a single predominant color which they applied in varying—but only slightly varying—values. In the most typical work, a pale gauzy color, often pale green or yellow, hangs like a veil over the canvas. The most ethereal of the Tonalists was Thomas Wilmer Dewing, who spent four years in Paris in the late 1870s, and whose work can be seen as an elaboration of Whistler's. Dewing's languid women inhabit a strange world through which they wander as if sleep-walking, taking little notice of their surroundings, or of each another [132].

The most daring and radical aesthetic art, however, was made by Whistler himself. During the 1860s he became increasingly interested in the art of Japan, and its asymmetrical compositions, which juxtaposed a passage of exquisite drawing against large areas of empty space. In his printmaking, he developed an exacting sense for delicate gradations of tone and value, particularly in etching, where he insisted on having absolute control over line value, so much so that he occasionally applied the acid to the plate with a feather. In his campaign against narrative art, Whistler was drawn to subject matter that was inherently abstract, without a field of tangible objects, such as fog or moonlight scenes, or—as in the case of *Nocturne in Black and Gold (The Falling Rocket)* (c. 1875)—a fireworks display. The painting happened to come to the attention of Ruskin, whose violent reaction made it the single most notorious work of the Aesthetic Movement [133].

Enraged by the painting, Ruskin accused Whistler of "cockney impudence" and of "flinging a pot of paint in the public's face." His words occasioned a libel suit in 1878 which drew international attention, for it had wider cultural ramifications. Here the two great progressive movements of nineteenth-century art—the moral conception of art and the aesthetic—came to blows, represented by their principal proponents. Whistler scored the mortal blow. When he was asked if he demanded 200 guineas for the work of but two days (the amount of time it took him to complete the canvas), he replied: "No, I ask it for the knowledge which I have gained in the work of a lifetime." There could be no better statement of the aesthetic doctrine: that the artist was no mere artisan or transcriber of facts but followed a higher calling, a veritable priesthood, in which his aesthetic perceptions were carefully cultivated and heightened by a lifetime of preparation. Whistler's quip, a flippant remark at the time, would come to be the controlling idea of the artist in the next century.

Unlike Whistler, John Singer Sargent was no provocateur; by training and disposition he was a thoroughgoing academic. From 1874 to 1879 he studied in Paris with Carolus-Duran (Charles-Émile-Auguste Durand), a consummate teacher, under whose demanding tutelage he mastered academic painting. Later, like Eakins, he took a study trip to Spain that acted as an antidote to excessive refinement and preciousness. There he discovered Velázquez, whose work suggested how a painting might be structured in terms of broad masses of lights and darks, and how the poetic shadows surrounding a figure could be more than mere dead space, but might form an active and essential aspect of the composition [134].

Sargent's gift was portraiture, which formed the mainstay of his very lucrative career. He had an ineffable eye for pose, and a flair for making a single vivacious gesture—a dashing tilt of the head or a saucy lift of the chin—the point of departure for an entire composition [135]. His *Madame Pierre Gautreau (Madame X)* of 1884 shows why his patrons clamored for full-length portraits by Sargent. The entire figure is an essay in haughtiness: the falling dress, the disdainful arch of the shoulder, the coil of the body, all restate and reinforce the challenge of her bold aquiline profile. While Eakins's portraits presented his sitters in private, Sargent's invariably present them in public, their attitudes and persona on conspicuous display. For this reason, his full-length pieces are often called, and with justice, swagger portraits.

Madame X swaggered a bit too haughtily, alas, and French critics were scandalized. Sargent moved to England where he soon produced a pageant of dazzling aristocratic portraits, increasingly influenced by English portraiture of the late eighteenth century,

132 **Thomas Wilmer Dewing**,
Summer, c. 1890. By reducing
action and incident to the
minimum, Dewing elevated
the importance of the space
surrounding his figures, much like
a composer who finds beauty in
the silences and rests between the
musical notes. In *Summer* there is
but a single gesture—the leisurely
cast of the fishing woman—a stray
note of action in what is otherwise
a glowing, colorful mass of emerald
and turquoise.

133 **James Abbott McNeill
Whistler**, *Nocturne in Black and
Gold (The Falling Rocket), c.* 1875.
For "pure" painting, without the
distractions of recognizable subject
matter and the inevitable mental
associations to which they give
rise, there are few better subjects
than fireworks. This painting
presented light and color without
contours or boundaries, dispensing
with the need for the preliminary
drawing (although an oil sketch
might be made). Here was perhaps
the first of a long series of efforts
to find subject matter without hard
edges, that would lead ultimately
to the Synchromists of the next
century and Stieglitz's photography
of clouds.

134 **John Singer Sargent**, *The Daughters of Edward D. Boit*, 1882. This work brilliantly shows how a painting can depict no action whatsoever and yet still convey the keenest dramatic intensity. Sargent places the four sisters at the periphery and leaves a void near the center of the square canvas, so that their figures balance and offset one another, like the fragile balance of a mobile. The blue vases participate in the balancing act, mimicking the sisters' shapes, as does the dagger of scarlet to the right.

135 John Singer Sargent,
Madame Pierre Gautreau (Madame X),
1884. This painting was the scandal
of the Salon of 1884, as much for
the distinctly lavender hue of the
woman's powdered skin as for
her indelicate cleavage. Sargent was
devastated and, at the suggestion
of his friend Henry James, left Paris
for London, where he remained for
most of the rest of his career.

such as that of Thomas Gainsborough and Thomas Lawrence. Like many of his contemporaries, his palette lightened, and in the 1890s he fully embraced the animated light-dappled surfaces of Impressionism as well as its preference for lively and highly visible brushwork. His success and the attention surrounding his visits to the United States in 1887 and 1890 made him the ideal of the successful professional artist.

Like any alert young artist in France, Sargent imbibed the Impressionists' heady revelations about light and color; he spent his summers practicing *plein-air* painting, sometimes with Claude Monet, making effervescent color studies. Still, he never became a true Impressionist. His academic roots were too deep and he took too much delight in exploiting the full tonal range. But Mary Cassatt was not only a full-fledged Impressionist, she was among its founding figures, as much a figure of the French art world as of the American.

Cassatt is properly regarded as America's first woman artist of consequence. Although she was preceded by Henrietta Johnston, Mary Jane Peale, Lilly Martin Spencer, and others, they were lesser talents, and she was the first to be a major artist in her own right. From the beginning, she enjoyed a life of privilege. She belonged to an elite Philadelphia family who spent much time in Europe; her brother Alexander was an engineer and president of the Pennsylvania Railroad. Cassatt first studied at Pennsylvania Academy of the Fine Arts and then, in 1866, went to France where she remained (apart from a few brief trips) for the rest of her life. In 1877 she befriended Degas and exhibited with the Impressionists, the only American to do so. She embraced the high-keyed colors and mottled brushwork of the Impressionists as well as their fascination for scenes of modern life, such as driving a carriage or peering through opera glasses from a loge. But her characteristic theme was maternity, expressed in intimate cameos of mothers cradling their infants and toddlers; any cloying sentimentality underlying them was usually outweighed by their sincerity and overall lack of affectation, and the modern means by which she rendered them.

Her subject matter aside, Cassatt was highly innovative as a printmaker. In 1890 she was profoundly affected by an exhibition of Japanese prints at the École des Beaux Arts, and her response was a suite of ten prints in which the figures became gracefully patterned silhouettes, interacting with the other shapes of the background to form an abstract ensemble of form [136]. But the influence of Degas is also apparent, especially in the way that the face is turned from view so that one may concentrate on the play of flattened shapes without the distractions of character that a face can offer.

In 1879, Cassatt's work was exhibited at the Society of American Artists, the first Impressionist art to be shown in America. Virtually overnight, the cause of Impressionism was taken up by a band of young American painters, including John Twachtman, Robert Reid, Childe Hassam, and Abbott Thayer, all Paris-trained. While each emulated the bright colors, dappled light, and sparkling surface effects of their French counterparts, they specialized in different aspects of the Impressionist repertory. Reid painted vibrant nudes like Renoir. Twachtman painted rural scenes with a fragile, ineffable sense of light, recalling Monet. And Hassam became the most accomplished painter of the modern American city, depicting Boston as the tidied-up Paris it yearned to be [137].

136 **Mary Cassatt**, *The Bath*, 1890–91. A color print made with both drypoint and aquatint, this employs Japanese perspective: parallel lines do not converge toward a vanishing point but remain parallel, so that the bathing woman is not placed into three-dimensional space. Instead, she hovers on the surface of the image as a graceful and elegant silhouette.

137 **Childe Hassam**, *Rainy Day, Columbus Avenue, Boston*, 1885. A characteristic Impressionist subject: the bourgeois life of the modern metropolis, seen under the changing conditions of light and weather. The tonal range, however, is typical of American Impressionists. In place of the high-keyed pastels of French Impressionism, Americans were more likely to use darker colors, descending into the bass register, so to speak, of the palette.

Although they explicitly patterned themselves on the French Impressionists, these American painters—as a whole—evinced a different sensibility. For one thing, they lacked the forthright theoretical preoccupations of the French version. There is nothing in all of American Impressionism to compare with Monet's investigation of haystacks, painted at different times of day and in different seasons to study the effect of changing light. Nor was there anything like the partisan cohesiveness of the French Impressionists, railing against a sclerotic Academy and the mighty apparatus of state patronage. American Impressionists had no institutional oppression against which to recoil. In short, the American version was not a complete system of thought but simply a fashionable novelty—an attractive new color sensibility and a pleasing range of subject matter; in the words of one critic, the Americans were not so much Impressionists as *Impressionizers*.

Impressionism was only one fiber of the Aesthetic Movement fabric, which expressed itself as well in sculpture and architecture. There French aesthetic values penetrated more slowly, especially in sculpture where the tenets of Italian Neoclassicism still held sway. The public sculptors of the post-Civil War era—John Q. A. Ward, Henry Kirke Brown, and Daniel Chester French—still worked in the didactic and sentimental vein that Horatio Greenough or Hiram Powers had mined a half century before.

They conceived their statues as much as acts of civic piety as works of art. To the insights of the Aesthetic Movement they were completely impervious. From time to time their work achieved a majestic dignity, such as French's colossal Lincoln in the Lincoln Memorial, but many flailed in the unhappy twilight between realism and idealism. To this general pattern there was one great exception: Augustus Saint-Gaudens, the greatest of the Aesthetic Movement sculptors.

Saint-Gaudens descended from French stock and was culturally French, which eased his studies at the École des Beaux Arts from 1868 to 1870. On his return to America he befriended both John La Farge and Stanford White, a remarkable combination of the principal painter, architect, and sculptor of the Aesthetic Movement. All three worked on Richardson's Trinity Church and joined forces for subsequent projects. Saint-Gaudens and White collaborated on the Admiral David Farragut Memorial in Central Park (1876–81), which brought the sculptor instant celebrity.

Saint-Gaudens was the first major American sculptor who had no Puritan inhibitions about showing the human body as a supple, flexible, sensuous thing, which even in repose exuded the potential for graceful, even ecstatic motion. In this he was the opposite of his predecessors, most of them from New England, who inherited a certain reticence about showing the human body in its full sensuous reality, and whose statues—even when nude—seem to be standing stiffly to attention [62]. But Saint-Gaudens lent his figures a lithe and fluid grace, a quality common in the figural art of France but rare in American art before the 1880s.

Saint-Gaudens's masterpiece and that of the Aesthetic Movement was the Adams Memorial, in Rock Creek Cemetery, Washington, D.C. Saint-Gaudens was never better. The cause of the commission was the suicide in 1885 of Clover Adams, wife of the historian Henry Adams. Under the circumstances, the conventional props of Victorian funereal art, such as inscriptions, urns, inverted torches, and wreaths, were inappropriate. Instead, he modeled an enigmatic shrouded woman, and set her against a mute granite slab, designed by White [138]. As with the best art of the Aesthetic Movement, the work draws on non-Western art and not only for its motifs. During the design process Henry Adams traveled to Japan, and John La Farge seems to have urged him to give his monument an Eastern treatment. Thus while the cryptic woman herself derives from classical antiquity, her aesthetic sensibility—her reserve and ineffable detachment, and her remoteness from the world of Christian morality—is more Eastern in character.

This was the highest formal ideal for Aesthetic Movement artists, a synthesis of Japanese restraint and Greek simplicity, especially in the treatment of the human form. Although this was a rarefied and sophisticated intellectual doctrine, it came into the broadest public distribution through the populism of President Theodore Roosevelt, who in 1905 proposed the comprehensive redesign of American coinage. An admirer of Greek Hellenistic sculpture, Roosevelt proposed to Saint-Gaudens that American coins imitate its high relief and elegant lines. The sculptor devised a woman striding boldly forward, as on a mountaintop, as an emblem of progress for Roosevelt's Progressive Era. The figure appeared on the twenty-dollar gold piece, the so-called Double Eagle, generally regarded as America's most exquisite coin. After Saint-Gaudens died in 1907, his pupils completed the process,

138 **Augustus Saint-Gaudens**, Adams Memorial, Rock Creek Cemetery, Washington, D.C., 1886–91. This dispenses not only with all Christian symbolism but with all conventional funereal art. In his notebook, Saint-Gaudens scribbled: "Adams/Buddah/Mental Repose/Calm reflection in contrast with the violence or force in nature." Here the meaning is conveyed abstractly. At the center of the statue is a mysterious darkness, the shrouded impassive face of the woman drawing the curiosity of the viewer, and suggesting the enigma of death and suicide.

creating the Mercury Dime, the Buffalo Nickel, used from 1913 to 1938, and the Lincoln penny, still in use today. These coins, and the Beaux-Arts buildings of the new century, placed the stamp of French academicism upon the visual character of the federal government.

So completely and so thoroughly did French academicism transform American art at the end of the century that its triumph may seem inevitable. It did not seem so at the time. For a time during the 1870s Germany appeared at least as important, perhaps more so, having humiliated France in the Franco-Prussian War of 1870 and become a unified nation state in the process. German art rebounded in prestige, and in influence. Having once produced Europe's tightest and driest school of painting, that of Düsseldorf, Germany now produced its most luscious and painterly. This was the Munich School, where the very antithesis of the Düsseldorf manner flourished: deep, rich colors; a wet and hearty brushstroke; a love of thick, exotic atmosphere. The new method was introduced to a startled

139 **Frank Duveneck**, *He Lives By His Wits*, 1878. A typical specimen of Munich school painting: the face sculpted by a series of palpable individual brushstrokes, treated as a series of discrete planes; the dark and rich palette; and, above all, the stress on strong, forceful character rather than on beauty.

America in 1875 by Frank Duveneck, who, together with his friend William Merritt Chase, were the most important Americans to study in Munich [139 and 140]; others followed, including William Harnett, who arrived in 1880.

The Munich School was the beginning of a quiet revolution in the way that paintings were made. Traditional academic painting, as taught by Hunt or Eakins, was a sequential process. Images were built up gradually, layer upon layer, with thin translucent glazes, "like blood through the skin," as Stuart had described it to Trumbull. Thus the red of ruddy cheeks, for example, was not applied on top, like rouge over skin, but beneath the flesh tints and allowed to flicker through, just as it does in reality. Special care went into the shadows, which were made transparent as reflected light carried color into them. This gave a lustrous, layered richness, and a sense of depth to the painted surface.

Munich painters had begun to explore an alternative approach called direct painting. Instead of painting layer by layer, and working surfaces up to a fine glossy finish, they colored in opaque strokes; the slashing brushwork was allowed to remain visible.

William Merritt Chase was a master at this and he cultivated a bravura brushstroke, jabbing at the canvas like a swashbuckler. This fondness for rapid-fire execution led him to pastel-sticks of pure pigment—and he formed a society of pastel painters (a feat scarcely known today, given the growing reluctance of museums to display these frail works). The next generation of painters, led by Robert Henri, would retain the vigorous brush technique even as they despised Chase's vanity and aestheticism [140]. Direct painting offered a trade: the artist lost the complexity of layered color but in exchange received the directional energy of the visible brushstroke, and the expressive power of its agitated surfaces.

The leadership of the National Academy of Design, dominated by aging Hudson River School veterans, found the Munich School offensively slapdash but they correctly recognized its revolutionary implications. Munich paintings were given short shrift at their annual exhibitions, to the intense displeasure of younger artists. These in turn formed their own rival association in 1877, the Society of American Artists. The SAA was not limited to the Munich men but included any artist of aesthetic or

140 **William Merritt Chase**, *In the Studio*, 1882. Chase outfitted his studio with Chinese vases, animal-skin rugs and ornamental wall hangings—trappings that proclaimed to his sitters that he was a fashionable aesthete.

progressive tendencies, including Saint-Gaudens and the decorative artist Louis Comfort Tiffany. It also was the first to exhibit Cassatt's Impressionism. But its progressivism lasted but a generation. Once Aestheticism lost its revolutionary aura and became the conventional wisdom, and once the old guard of the National Academy faded away, there was no reason for having two distinct organizations. In 1906 the SAA and the National Academy of Design quietly merged, and circled the wagons against the newer artistic revolutions of the twentieth century.

In architecture, the Aesthetic Movement took a rather different course. Architecture remained a conventional art, its formal repertoire limited to the historical styles of the past. Its character was still literary, in which different styles carried with them a body of mental associations. Even within the styles of the past there was scope for purely aesthetic considerations, such as the abstract life of volumes and masses, and of line and color, and a sense for the living vitality of form. These considerations became paramount in the work of Richardson, who was the most original architect of the era.

Born in New Orleans, Henry Hobson Richardson (1838–86) was a Harvard graduate who studied at the École des Beaux Arts until the Civil War cut off his remittances from home. He worked for a time in an architectural office before returning to America in 1865. There he found a divided architectural culture. On one hand was the classical tradition, that of antiquity and the Renaissance, as refined and codified by France at the École des Beaux Arts. On the other hand was the medieval tradition, which flaunted the picturesque values of irregularity, contrast, and strong feeling; this school was best represented in the Gothic Revival of modern England. Most American architects fell into one camp or the other: Hunt and Mullett into the classical, Wight and Vaux into the medieval. Richardson transcended these parochial barriers and capitalized on the best of both schools, subjecting the English picturesque to French rationality—"disciplining the picturesque," in the words of one scholar. He did this by cultivating an architectural style that fell midway between classical antiquity and the High Middle Ages, the Romanesque of the twelfth century.

Richardson's first mature essay was Trinity Church (1872–77) in Boston. Dominating the city's Copley Square, the church presented a cruciform plan with three stubby arms under a squat tower, modeled after that of Salamanca's Old Cathedral in Spain. Richardson's strength was not his ability to quote history, however, but to deploy his masses freely and vigorously. The building's various parts—its nave, transept arms, and taut semicircular apse—converge to form an abstracted pyramid, to which all its copious details and decoration are strictly subordinated. In many respects the church followed High Victorian convention, such as its striped walls and contrasting colors, but the sense of latent force was absolutely new, and startling [141].

To execute his grand project, Richardson formed a brilliant team of artists and decorators, including Charles F. McKim, Stanford White, Saint-Gaudens, and John La Farge (who designed and executed the vast program of murals in 1876–77). Together they helped make the church America's most conspicuous model of aesthetic doctrine—an integrated ensemble of the arts, conceived entirely in terms of color, mass, and line, and without the slightest whiff of moralizing.

After Trinity, Richardson's work grew bolder and simpler. On the interior, room divisions were eliminated and spaces thrown

141 **H. H. Richardson**, Trinity Church, Boston, 1872–77. Although nominally Romanesque, Trinity Church in Boston shows a wealth of subtle refinements that are the architect's hallmark, especially the straightforward logic of the plan. This is a Greek cross with short stubby arms that centers on the pulpit, its centralizing character strongly reminiscent of a Puritan meeting house. This was deliberate, meant to showcase the speaking voice of its celebrated Episcopal minister, Phillips Brooks.

142 **McKim, Mead & White**, Low House, Bristol, Rhode Island, 1886–87. A fine example of the Shingle Style, together with Bruce Price's Travis C. Van Buren Residence at Tuxedo Park, New York. While the motifs are Colonial, the quality of abstraction derives from a close study of Japanese and Greek architecture, and the principles underlying them. Price, for example, knew that the Greek word *entasis* meant expressive tension, as when an arm bulges as it draws back a bowstring. Rather than using it as the Greeks did, to taper a classical column in order to convey suppleness and life, he shaped the entire house according to *entasis*, giving it a kind of living elasticity.

together; on the exterior, the masses were more tightly consolidated. Both space and surface were made to flow as continuously as possible, unlike the syncopated lines of Victorian composition. Even the roofline was simplified, and in place of the bulbous Second Empire mansard, with its top-heavy pomp and circumstance, the roof became a single fluid line, as delicate and personal as a stroke of calligraphy.

To achieve this seamless continuity, Richardson seized on one of the humblest and oldest of American building materials, the wood shingle. Able to sweep fluidly around corners and dormers, the overlapping skin of shingles blurred joints and transitions, as if a gauzy blanket had descended over the entire building. This was the Shingle Style, a term coined by Vincent Scully to describe the architectural language embodied by Richardson's Stoughton House in Cambridge, Massachusetts. Inspired by Richardson's example, architects such as McKim and Bruce Price seized on its abstract possibilities, and shook out the last lingering historical references [142 and 143]. In this their artistic goals were not far removed from those of John Singer Sargent, whose *Daughters of Edward Darley Boit* similarly deployed familiar forms in order to achieve a formal abstract unity. In each instance, formal balance and clarity governed the composition, rather than the demands of storytelling and anecdote.

Richardson's own shingled houses are suffused with Colonial nostalgia, conveyed by their Palladian windows and low-beamed ceilings, but in one the nostalgia reaches much farther back in time. In 1880 he built a gate lodge for Frederick L. Ames, the treasurer of the mighty Union Pacific, which completed the transcontinental railroad. Ames had an abiding interest in the natural landscape and in scientific horticulture (the gate lodge served in part as a winter garden). All these elements percolate in the building, which is at once poetic, scientific, and tragic.

In its most elemental terms the F. L. Ames Gate Lodge is simply a wall and an opening, defining the boundary of the Ames estate as

143 **Bruce Price**, Travis C. Van Buren Residence, Tuxedo Park, New York, 1886.

144 **H. H. Richardson**, F. L. Ames Gate Lodge, North Easton, Massachusetts, 1880–81. The Ames Gate Lodge is built of boulders so emphatically rounded that their outer edges project a foot or two beyond the face of the wall. The building is a collaboration between Richardson and Saint-Gaudens, Tiffany, and Olmsted, who contributed the imaginative landscaping. Across the site he randomly strewed submerged fieldstones, which quicken in tempo as they near the building and then seem to burst from the ground, as if the house itself were the dramatic by-product of some distant subterranean upheaval.

it formed an entrance to it [144]. Its three components of a plant house, arched passageway, and dwelling are arranged in linear fashion, culminating in the squat two-story wing that crouches at one end to form the fulcrum of the composition. All is logical and rational except for the materials of construction: enormous granite boulders, taken from the glacial moraine left behind by the last ice age and set directly into the wall, without dressing or tooling. The effect is that of a natural rock outcropping, erratic and accidental. This whimsical geological performance was not frivolous, however, for it touched on a truth of utmost profundity: that all New England once lay frozen under a massive blanket of ice, lifeless for millennia.

Such was the recent revelation of modern science, in particular of Louis Agassiz, whom Richardson knew at Harvard. His F. L. Ames Gate Lodge is a poignant essay on the history and destiny of the American landscape, as fervent and devout in its way as anything in the work of the Hudson River School. Still, this was not the view of nature held by Cole and Durand. It was not the traditional Christian interpretation, in which a personal God presided over a benign and unchanging nature, which offered an ever present allegory of spiritual redemption. This was nature as impersonal machine, ruled by inexorable mechanical forces: the inevitable disintegration of a mountain through erosion, the implacable march of glaciers. It is a vision of the universe composed of nothing but matter and the forces that act upon it. This is nature much as it appears in the mature works of Winslow Homer, whose late tragic seascapes ponder the unrelenting assault of the waves on the exposed jetties of Prout's Neck [145].

This change in the American view of nature had a distinct religious strain. Ames and Richardson were both Unitarians (as were Furness and Frank Lloyd Wright), the New England denomination that comprised the Puritan intelligentsia. Unitarianism encouraged skepticism toward tradition, and in its most radical form questioned even religion itself, but it was also quick to accept the discoveries of modern science, including those of Agassiz and Darwin. In this way the American preoccupation with landscape and nature could assimilate the lessons of nineteenth-century science. Instead of seeing God and science as rivals, Unitarianism could see them as identical; God was immanent in the very forces of the universe. So Cole's Christian understanding of nature evolved almost without transition into a generalized pantheism. And the megalithic Ames Gate Lodge is the most forceful relic of that change.

Richardson's work was equally important for the American city. His innate gift for representing vehement force suited the pulse and tempo of postwar urban life. His Marshall Field Wholesale Store in Chicago is his mightiest urban building, and the simplest—nothing more than a deep and muscular arcade, advancing the length of a city block, each story stating clearly and without flourish how it carries the weight of the one above it [146]. The sheer brute force of the design was widely imitated, and helped bring in the Richardson Romanesque that was the most dominant influence on American architecture during the 1880s and early 1890s, with its ubiquitous round arches, rusticated masonry, and clifflike massing.

Richardson's accomplishment was immense but it was primarily aesthetic—to apply formal clarity to the large modern building—and not in the slightest technological. Structural innovations, the potential of the steel frame, for example, held little interest for him. But in Chicago it was usually the other way around. There technology was exploited swiftly and ruthlessly. After the great fire of 1871, the city rebuilt itself at breathtaking velocity, and without the inhibitions of taste and convention that generally governed architecture in New York or Boston. In particular, Chicago seized the two technologies that made the skyscraper possible, the steel frame and passenger elevator. In 1884, William Le Baron Jenney built the Home Insurance Building, a ten-story building with a novel iron frame. Its walls were no longer load-bearing, and only needed to support themselves. A few years later, in his Leiter Building, the walls were freed even from this duty. Instead they were hung on the internal steel frame, a "curtain wall," and Chicagoans had the unnerving experience of watching the bricklayers begin their work in the upper stories of the building while the lower ones were still a naked skeleton.

Although innovative in their engineering, these buildings were almost comically awkward. A formula that was successful for a building of four or five stories produced grotesque results when applied to buildings twice as tall. Indeed, most early Chicago skyscrapers were Romanesque layer cakes, with a cornice inserted every few floors for visual relief, and having nothing to do with the inner workings of the building. Not until 1889 did Chicago produce a fully satisfying aesthetic solution, Daniel Burnham and John Wellborn Root's superb Monadnock Building.

146 **H. H. Richardson**, Marshall Field Wholesale Store, Chicago, 1885–87. America's boldest response to the problem of the large urban building. Once again, Richardson's stylistic sources are Romanesque (and Florentine Renaissance) but enlarged to meet the gargantuan scale of the Chicago city block. Typical of his late work is the exaggerated heft and texture of the masonry, every stone larger than it need be, and made to retain the rock-faced finish of the quarry instead of being dressed to a smooth finish.

147 Burnham & Root,
Monadnock Building, Chicago,
1889–91. "When the fates place
at your disposal a good, generous
sweep of masonry, accept it frankly
and thank God." The Monadnock
Building is a demonstration of John
Wellborn Root's own point, its
walls utterly blank except for its
clusters of bay windows. It is often
forgotten that its planning was
equally brilliant. Sixty-eight percent
of the floor space was rentable, an
unheard of amount when stairs
and corridors claimed much of
the interior of an office building.

A rental office building is primarily a device for
making money, and only secondarily a work of art—
and here Root did not let his clients down. Instead of
seeing these motives as contradictory, he showed
that a building might be beautiful without being lavish
or costly. Here he capitalized on one of the basic
insights of the Aesthetic Movement, the notion that
abstract shape itself might be beautiful [147]. He
refused to garnish the building with panels of carved
foliage, as architectural etiquette required, but
instead relied on silhouette and contours alone,
giving it the beauty of a nude body. The result was a
sixteen-story work of sculpture: the building bulging
massively at the base, then drawing in sharply to
ascend without intervening cornices or moldings,
only to flare outward once more at the crown,
opening like a flower. The subtle linear expression
again recalls the Greek doctrine of *entasis*—the
supple elasticity that distinguishes a healthy living
thing—as in the Shingle Style houses of Bruce Price.

Root designed the building for steel but at the last
minute his nervous clients, unable to forget the Chicago Fire,
ordered him to use brick and stone. As a result, the Monadnock's
walls measure an astonishing 6 feet 4 inches (1.9 meters) thick at
sidewalk level. Aesthetically resolved but structurally backward,
it was the diametric opposite of Jenney's building. It would take a
third architect to integrate their achievements. This was Louis
Sullivan (1856–1924), who can be regarded as the creator of the
skyscraper, at least in terms of its aesthetically and intellectually
resolved form.

When Sullivan began his partnership with Dankmar Adler
in Chicago in the early 1880s, the physical task of building tall
buildings had already been accomplished; what remained was
the graphic aspect of the task, to devise a fitting imagery for the
skyscraper, and to make it stick. Here his patchy education was
perhaps an asset. The classicism taught at the École was essentially
a horizontal language, and its best students foundered when
confronted with skyscraper projects. Sullivan found a satisfying
vertical language, quite unlike the gawky and verbose Romanesque
skyscrapers of his day. His pioneering work was his Wainwright
Building in St. Louis (1891), a sleek tower of red brick with lush
terracotta panels. It had the coherence of a single forceful

148 **Louis Sullivan**, Wainwright Building, St. Louis, Missouri, 1890. The Wainwright Building fulfilled Sullivan's demand that a skyscraper "must be every inch a proud and soaring thing, rising in sheer exaltation that from bottom to top it is a unit without a single dissenting line." To do this, he recessed the horizontal panels, or spandrels, accentuating the lift of the vertical piers. Root had already shown that intermediate cornices might be profitably removed but it was characteristic of Sullivan to invest his design decisions with metaphysical meaning, and to ridicule the classical cornice as an expression of naysaying dissent.

thought, and he bragged that it was "a sudden and volcanic design (made literally in three minutes)."

Like the Monadnock Building, the Wainwright was composed like a classical column, a simple tripartite arrangement of base, shaft, and crown [148]. This columnar theme had nothing to do with Greek Revival columns. Sullivan's stint at the École gave him a lifelong contempt for all academic classicism and its claim of historical authority. He argued not so much for Platonic form as for Darwinian: a building, like an animal, had a unique and distinctive physiognomy that suited the function it performed. This was the startling claim of his 1896 essay, "The Tall Office Building Artistically Considered," where he coined the phrase *form ever follows function*. Just as the beak of a bird or the proboscis of a mosquito reflected its function, so the components of the skyscraper reflected theirs: the base served as entrance and required large, inviting windows for its storefronts; the upper stories served as office space, and since each was identical on the interior, so must it be identical on the exterior; the uppermost level contained the elevator housing and other mechanical systems, and required yet another expression. The round windows of the Wainwright's cornice allude to this, and playfully evoke the turning of the elevator winch.

Sullivan is justly regarded as a prophet of modern functionalism. As the mentor of Frank Lloyd Wright, he was celebrated and his works closely studied in Europe. But his functionalism must not be mistaken for the rational process of engineering. He did not believe that a building should be an arid and emotionless affair; instead it should be "designed in a high pitch of sustained emotional tension" and should express the active mental force of its creator. This required something that was absolutely forbidden by functionalist doctrine of the twentieth century: architectural ornament.

Sullivan's insistence on ornament was somewhat self-serving: his earliest practice was as a decorative draftsman, for which his restlessly fertile imagination and facile pencil suited him. His first job was with Furness, whose buoyant idiosyncratic ornament he learned to imitate. Later he devised his own lush decorative language of terracotta ornament, quivering bouquets of foliage, alert with incipient life. Even his most rationally gridded building, the Schlesinger and Mayer Store in Chicago (now Carson Pirie Scott), was awash with opulent ornament [149 and 150].

At first glance this is a paradox: the architect who expressed most clearly the mathematical language of the grid also produced the most passionate rhapsody of ornament. But to a Transcendentalist, steeped in the writings of Emerson and Walt Whitman, there was no paradox: both the machine and nature expressed the same universal laws, and the curving lines of growth of one of Sullivan's flowers were no less rational than the urgent rectilinearity of a steel cage.

Here two perennial lines of American tradition converged— selfish individualism and romantic nature worship—to act as a counterweight to the general tendency of the age to move toward a rational functionalist architecture. The stubborn individualism was the legacy of dissenting Protestantism, which made a higher duty out of personal autonomy and expression. The appeal to nature as a source of authority and goodness was of equal antiquity, although now a nature widened to embrace modern

149 **Louis Sullivan**, Schlesinger and Mayer Store, Chicago, 1899–1904. Now the Carson Pirie Scott store, this is a landmark of early modern architecture. While modernists praised the rational expression of the building's steel frame, they were embarrassed by its writhing ornament: by the 1930s they were cropping photographs so as to show only the taut piers in the middle.

150 **Louis Sullivan**, Schlesinger and Mayer Store, Chicago, 1899–1904. Detail of entrance.

151 **George Inness**, *Home of the Heron*, 1893. No landscape painter journeyed farther artistically than George Inness, who began in the 1840s as a painter in the Cole mode and who ended as a painter of Aesthetic Movement mood pieces. *Home of the Heron* is the culmination, after he discovered how objects became blurred and indistinct by dusk or moonlight. Instead of the Hudson River School's loving inventory of natural facts, Inness presents no facts at all, focusing only on the generalized glow of twilight.

science. These two elements, expressed with special clarity in the work of Sullivan and Wright, do much to explain the crucial differences between American modern architecture and the collectivist and rational version of Europe.

Sullivan's preoccupation with nature began in his childhood, spent on a New England farm. Most Americans still led a rural life, although this was beginning to change with the massive immigration from eastern and southern Europe in the 1880s and 1890s, which poured into American cities. And just as Sullivan interpreted modernity in terms of nature, modern American painters of the late nineteenth century likewise found in nature their principal subject. This was not true of Whistler, Sargent, and Cassatt, who were almost entirely European in their aesthetic framework, but it was quite true of Homer, George Inness, and others who applied the ideas of the Aesthetic Movement to the American landscape.

The Hudson River School was already in an advanced stage of disintegration. Once precisely rendered landscape had lost its moralizing meaning, nothing was left but a dry inventory of trees and objects. Painters now looked to nature for the moods it inspired rather than the truths it taught—for its subjective rather than objective properties. The tight drawing of the Hudson River School was abandoned as well, and no longer did landscape paintings suggest colored drawings. Instead, the values of Tonalism, with its firm belief in the chromatic unity of a painting, came to prevail.

The new values are especially strong in the work of George Inness (1825–94), whose painting forms the landscape counterpart to Dewing [132]. Although trained as a Hudson River School painter, he had the benefit of several prolonged stays in Europe; he traveled to Italy in 1851/52, to France in 1853 for more two years, and then a lengthy stay in Rome (1870–75). Through his travels he became interested in the Barbizon School and its conviction that one must paint outdoors. This was attractive to Inness who, like Frederic Edwin Church, had a strong interest in the effects of light and atmospherics. So strong was his interest, however, that light came to dominate everything, overwhelming even the objects that it touched. He set his groves of trees directly before the setting suns or beneath the moonlight, so that there were no precise edges and all forms blurred in twilight obscurity [151]. During the 1890s he produced his most mature work, with the soft focus that Aesthetic Movement photography was at that time suggesting [176].

Inness's late art can be called Symbolist, the introspective and self-contained work of an artist working in isolation. In the intensity of its cryptic personal expression, it has something of the nature of private devotion, perhaps related to the artist's deep Swedenborgian faith. His fellow Symbolist Albert Pinkham Ryder (1847–1917) was even more introspective and hermitlike. Ryder's mysterious world was totally subjective, the product of his own shy and erratic invention. After an unsatisfying term as a landscape painter, he renounced fidelity to nature and began to paint large generalized scenes, particularly stormy oceans and forests by night [152]. For all his many artistic faults—his chronic indecisiveness, his

152 **Albert Pinkham Ryder**, *Jonah, c.* 1885–95. Albert Pinkham Ryder's eccentric method of painting and indecisiveness led him to paint and repaint his canvases, forming a thickly layered surface in which earlier phantom images sometimes flickered through. He worked on his *Jonah* off and on from about 1885 to 1895, and those foolish enough to sit for him waited years for their portraits.

crippling procrastination, his feeble draftsmanship, and his cloying romanticism—he was the only one of his generation to pursue an art entirely of personal imagination. Although his contemporaries came to view him as a laughable misfit, who might dither for a decade over a canvas, he was of great importance to the modernists of the early twentieth century, who saw in him a visionary and a prophet, the first American artist to emancipate the painting from its duty to describe facts and things.

Ryder's art, like much of nineteenth-century art, was essentially escapist—which was an understandable response to the stresses and convulsions of the Industrial Revolution. The first industrial generation, confronted with the steam engine, the paddlewheeler, and the railroad, took refuge in nostalgia for the rural landscape of the past. But things were not so simple for the generation that reached maturity after the Civil War. There were now fortunes of an entirely new order of magnitude. The tycoons of antebellum America had made their fortunes by making things or by selling them, but the new ones could do so by means of national monopolies or cartels, dominating the commerce of a continent. Cornelius Vanderbilt created a national railroad empire in the 1860s; John D. Rockefeller did the same with oil in the 1880s and J. Pierpont Morgan with investment banking in the 1890s. During the Depression these indomitable industrial magnates were given the name Robber Barons.

The new order of wealth posed a dilemma: how to live? America offered no models for wealth on this scale, neither architectural nor social. The European past, however, offered many: one might live like a Medici prince of the fifteenth century, or a French aristocrat of the seventeenth, or an English lord of the eighteenth. None was necessarily more plausible or spurious than the others, and eventually each was tried. The finest experiments were at Newport, which by the 1880s had become the showcase of the new wealth, and many were designed by America's most learned architect, Richard Morris Hunt.

Hunt designed four great houses for Vanderbilt's children and grandchildren. Two were for William K. Vanderbilt: a Loire Valley château on Fifth Avenue, New York (1878–82) and, at Newport, a variation on the Petit Trianon at Versailles, dubbed the Marble House (1888–92). For William's son, Cornelius Vanderbilt II, Hunt built the Breakers (1893), also at Newport, a fiction of a palace from sixteenth-century Genoa. But the mightiest of all was Biltmore, George W. Vanderbilt's grand mansion at Asheville,

North Carolina (1888–95). Here Hunt reprised the Loire theme, choosing as his model the early French Renaissance château of Blois [153] and inflating it to gargantuan size. The scale was simply staggering, a 250-room house on an estate of 8,000 acres, landscaped by Frederick Law Olmsted (whose Central Park was but a tenth its size). This was the zenith of Gilded Age display, and perhaps the only estate to have grounds vast enough to justify the pretense and scale of the house.

Hunt had an effortless facility, drilled in him at the École des Beaux Arts, for adapting historical prototypes to modern needs, and all his houses were remarkably well planned and coherent. Still, at some fundamental level, historical pastiches like Biltmore were a failure. For all their formal force and authority, they lacked the necessary conditions for the true ancestral estate, which were hereditary land ownership and a settled way of life. Few remained in family possession for more than a generation or two. Given American history and class structure, which had no tradition of

153 **Richard Morris Hunt**, Biltmore, Asheville, North Carolina, 1889–95. Biltmore was an intelligent and elegant paraphrase of a French château of the early sixteenth century. The animated roofline was pleasantly picturesque, especially when viewed from a distance, while the ground plan was a Beaux-Arts essay in tightly interlocking axes, organized about the central winter garden.

palatial life, the only enduring template for living was that of the middle class. Still, as a creative performance, as an architectural hypothesis on how a permanent and settled American aristocracy might live—before the income tax and the trust-busting activism of Theodore Roosevelt—there was nothing quite like Biltmore.

Another factor lay behind these swaggering houses: social insecurity. One is never more arrogant than when one is insecure, and the flamboyance of the nouveaux-riches reflects the constant awareness that their fortunes were but a generation old. Lacking family pedigrees, they surrounded themselves with pedigreed art and architecture. This accounts in large measure for the new cult of taste, something which did not especially trouble the antebellum merchants and traders, who were quite secure about their position in the world.

France was now the undisputed arbiter of fashionable taste, in architecture as well as painting, and American buildings became more self-consciously French once more. Architects such as McKim, Mead & White turned increasingly to the academic classicism of modern France. A dramatic herald of the new taste was their Boston Public Library (1887–95), a textbook example of Beaux-Arts doctrine [154]. Just as McKim's teachers had shown him, the building was a clear and logical expression of its program, rendered in terms of Renaissance architecture. The massive ground story housed the bookstacks while the second story, marked by the graceful stride of its arcade, declaimed the well-lighted reading room within. Its immediate model was the Bibliothèque Ste-Geneviève in Paris, Europe's most modern library when McKim studied there.

The Boston Public Library showed a concern for the aesthetic refinement of the details of a building that was absolutely unheard of in America. Every feature was a matter of thought and study: details were extracted from the photographs, travel sketches, and leather-bound portfolios that lined McKim's office, and then studied and restudied in drawings. This is not to say that the results were dry and bookish; McKim and White were animated by the Aesthetic Movement conviction that beauty was an abstract property, and merely one of formal correctness (as the bookish Palladians of the eighteenth century believed). McKim even built a full-size wooden mock-up of the cornice of his library, and had it winched into place so that he could look at it in strong sunlight, and judge whether its shadows and highlights had the proper degree of heft and spirit.

154 **McKim, Mead & White**, Boston Public Library, 1887–95. This is the fulfillment of the aesthetic revolution initiated by Richardson's Trinity Church [141], which stands directly across from it on Copley Square. Richardson's building began the process of applying order to Victorian architecture; the library completes the process, making architecture an affair of academic rules and proportions, rather than an instrument of personal expression.

The Boston Public Library introduced another innovation. Previously, civic buildings were usually decorated as an afterthought, as when statues and paintings were retroactively incorporated into the Capitol in Washington. But France had a longstanding tradition of harmoniously orchestrating the arts; murals and architectural sculpture were envisioned from the first as integral components of a composition. McKim put this into practice in his library, for which he devised a full program of allegorical art in collaboration with Augustus Saint-Gaudens and John Singer Sargent, who painted its great mural cycle, The *Triumph of Religion* (1890–1919). Other huge public buildings followed this practice, most notably the Library of Congress in Washington, D.C.

With the Boston Public Library, academic classicism gained a bridgehead in America; the World's Columbian Exposition of 1893 completed the conquest. This second great American world's fair, which definitively ended the Victorian era, might be thought of as the most glorious accomplishment of the Aesthetic Movement, for it showed that the city might itself be a work of art, shaped as much as any painting by the abstract properties of unity and repose.

155 Court of Honor, The World's Columbian Exposition, Chicago, 1893. The song "America, the Beautiful" memorably describes the White City of the Columbian Exposition: "*Thine alabaster cities gleam, undimmed by human tears.*" This "alabaster" was actually a technological breakthrough: unable to build the fair in traditional masonry construction in the allotted time, its architects exploited a new material called *staff*, a plasterlike compound of hemp that could be squirted on to a frame through a spray gun. The glistening surfaces were nothing more than a gorgeous sham.

The planning of the fairgrounds, a vast tract along the shore of Lake Michigan, was revolutionary. In Philadelphia, at the 1876 fair, the problem had been handled in picturesque Victorian fashion: different buildings in different styles were nestled into the landscape, in the visual jubilee that we know from the circus or the highway strip. To the planners of the Chicago fair, however, such disorder was deemed unacceptable. The task was entrusted to the city's principal firm, Burnham & Root, who promptly formed a committee of artists and architects including Hunt, Olmsted, and McKim, Mead & White. John Wellborn Root, as fiercely original a designer as Sullivan, might have offered a nonclassical alternative for the fair but he died in early 1891, having contracted pneumonia after the committee's very first meeting. This left the planning entirely in the hands of Beaux-Arts men, making the entire fair an exercise in French classicism.

In strict Beaux-Arts fashion, the grounds were organized along a controlling armature of formal axes. At the center was the main axis of the grand lagoon, dominated by the domed administration building, assigned for reasons of seniority to Hunt [155]. At the other end of the lagoon, toward Lake Michigan, was Daniel

Chester French's towering effigy of *Columbia*, a gilded statue on a metal frame based on the ivory-clad statue of Athena from the Parthenon. Around this axis was an ensemble of exhibition buildings by McKim, George B. Post, and other classicists, who followed the cue of Hunt's pavilion and produced a unified ensemble of classical buildings, linked by their common cornice height, classical character, and uniform white coloring. Such far-reaching architectural unity had never been seen before and an enthralled America instantly dubbed it the White City. The only dissenting note in the unity was Sullivan's colorful Transportation Building, which sulked at the periphery [156].

The Columbian Exhibition was a national triumph, and the millions of visitors who came to admire the replicas of the *Niña*, *Pinta*, and *Santa María* sailing back and forth across the lagoon and the debut of the Ferriss wheel took home with them certain architectural lessons. The ordered symmetry and coordinated classicism of the fair set into motion a new school of urban planning, in which the aesthetic considerations were as important as the utilitarian. This was the City Beautiful Movement, the influence of which was felt throughout the country.

156 **Louis Sullivan**, "Golden Door", Transportation Building, The World's Columbian Exposition, Chicago, 1893. A red, gold, and green dissenter amidst the regimented conformity of the White City. A brilliantly colored but functional shed, it played on the fundamental modernity of rail travel. America would never get closer to Art Nouveau than the sinuous foliage of its portal, which evidently inspired the modernists of France (which awarded Sullivan a medal for the building).

The greatest of all was the redesign of the national Mall in Washington, D.C., undertaken in 1902 by the McMillan Commission. The Mall in Washington still preserved the vestiges of a picturesque landscaping scheme by A. J. Downing, incompletely realized and now looking dowdy. But the McMillan Commission was stacked with the creators of the Chicago fair, McKim, Burnham, and Saint-Gaudens (Hunt and Olmsted had since died, although F. L. Olmsted, Jr. took his father's place). Their solution was an enlarged version of the White City: a monumental array of grand vistas and axes, each terminating in a classical monument or memorial. The axis from the Capitol through the Washington Monument to Henry Bacon's Lincoln Memorial is the progeny of the White City, built in permanent marble and serving as a national forum. For decades to come this plan guided the development of the Mall, and long after the deaths of McKim and his team, their aesthetic heirs were still adding the classic memorials they proposed [159].

During the heyday of twentieth-century modernism, this chapter of American architecture was mocked in retrospect as a ludicrous costume party, a laughable contrast to the rational planning of functionalism. But a Beaux-Arts architect was drilled in intelligent planning, and the best of them were able to handle complex architectural problems with sovereign clarity; they knew how to break a program into its component parts, to express these parts in a logical diagram, and to organize them along a firm axis. Only after the plan was settled was the exterior composed, the final act in the design process and the most rhetorical, in which the spatial logic of the interior was expressed in physical form.

So free and flexible was this planning that it could address the most complex and modern of building types, the large urban railroad station. In 1906 the president of the Pennsylvania Railroad, A. J. Cassatt (the brother of Mary), conceived the idea of tunneling underneath the East River. Previously train passengers had to shift to ferryboats to make the crossing. Cassatt was a trained engineer, whose buildings were typically daring, and he had until now relied on Furness for most of his buildings—such as Broad Street Station in Philadelphia, where a ten-story skyscraper surmounted the station. But Cassatt now rejected Furness's lumbering Victorian style. Instead, he chose McKim, Mead & White who showed that the Beaux-Arts method could be applied to the most complex of modern building requirements.

The building was entirely the work of McKim for, just before

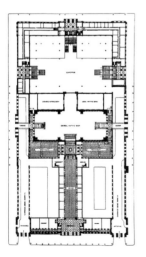

157 **McKim, Mead & White**, Plan of Pennsylvania Station, New York, 1906–10. Stretching from Thirty-first through Thirty-third Street, and Seventh through Ninth Avenue, the station's waiting room (*opposite*) took the form of an ancient Roman bath, a mighty hall with passage into rooms with pools of varying temperature. For a train station, which also must accommodate multiple paths of movement, this was the most sensible of models and McKim exploited its potential brilliantly. While in Rome, he paid Italian peasants to stroll about the Baths of Caracalla so that he could study their circulation, research of the sort that few architects are granted.

158 McKim, Mead & White,
Pennsylvania Station, New York,
1906–10. Main waiting room.

work began, White was murdered by the husband of his lover, Evelyn Nesbitt—one of the most coveted artist's models of the day. He died on the roof garden of his own Madison Square Garden, a fitting death for a voluptuary of the Aesthetic Movement, as much as Downing's death in a steamboat explosion befitted the Industrial Revolution.

McKim drew up an elegant Beaux-Arts plan, carefully segregating pedestrian from vehicular traffic, which he placed along the periphery. The principal axis was the east–west spine, a store-lined viaduct that marched passengers efficiently to the climax of the grand waiting room, which formed the cross axis and loomed well above the building [157 and 158]. Although the waiting room was Roman in theme, McKim was not indifferent to modern construction. He designed his building around a steel skeleton, and passengers descending to the subterranean train platforms passed beneath a canopy of steel and glass domes. In every respect, the building was a feat of spatial and structural acumen. Its mindless demolition in 1964 was the single greatest factor in creating the American historic preservation movement.

As the classicism of the Columbian Exposition swept the field, the Richardsonian movement instantly went limp. The nation's courthouses, schools, and state capitols were now invariably carried out in an august and often chilly Roman classicism, with a full complement of sculpture and mural decoration. This high pitch of civic dignity was out of place in residential architecture, but even here a kind of sublimated classicism was felt as a far-reaching Colonial Revival took place—by far the chief inspiration for American houses in the first half of the twentieth century. (The saltbox form was also revived at this time, a way of proclaiming Englishness and an ancient family lineage, very desirable qualities at a time of intensive immigration.)

Despite the epic reach of its influence, Sullivan could only regard the White City as an event of unspeakable tragedy. The fad for classicism that it unleashed was for him not a sign of cosmopolitan sophistication but of craven insecurity. With it America had surrendered its indigenous line of development, that of Root and Sullivan, in favor of a classicism that was already dead when it was first revived in the fifteenth century. Sullivan's final verdict on the fair was the following comment: "The selling campaign of the bogus antique was remarkably well managed through skillful publicity and propaganda, by those who were first to see its commercial possibilities."

159 **John Russell Pope**, Jefferson Memorial, Washington, D.C., 1939–43. The idea of the Jefferson Memorial dates back to the McMillan Commission plan of 1902, although John Russell Pope's building was not built until 1939–43. Throughout this period, the classical architecture of the French École des Beaux Arts served as the quasi-official architecture of the federal government of the United States, a role it would not relinquish until the end of World War II.

By this, he meant Burnham who, deprived of Root's counsel, now began to make buildings like the Flatiron Building in New York, skyscrapers wrapped in decorous classical skins. Alienated from his own society, Sullivan increasingly became a marginal figure. After the Schlesinger Mayer commission came no further work except for a handful of small rural banks, scattered through the Midwest. They show Sullivan at his best, terracotta-adorned jewelboxes, but they are a melancholy coda for the inventor of the modern skyscraper.

Writing his autobiography on his deathbed, *Autobiography of an Idea*, he continued to brood over the Columbian Exhibition. In the book he predicted that "the damage wrought by the World's Fair will last for half a century from its date…". In fact, the Jefferson Memorial, the last great monument of Beaux-Arts classicism and the fulfillment of the Washington Mall, was completed in 1943 [159]. Sullivan's prophecy was accurate almost to the day.

Chapter 7 Early Modernism

By 1900, American art was thoroughly and comprehensively academic. This did not only mean that artists were trained at a formal academy, either the École des Beaux Arts or one of its American imitators. It also meant that buildings and paintings were now judged by the standards and criteria of the academy. Rampant individualism and self-expression, those touchstones of Victorian art, were decidedly out. Instead, art was to be judged by its correctness, refinement, propriety, and even its bookishness. These criteria were enforced by a monthly deluge of sophisticated criticism in popular magazines, to which art buyers, architectural patrons, and museum curators all paid careful attention. For the first time in American history, there was an art establishment. And in short order, also for the first time, there was an avant-garde.

This avant-garde was the modern movement, which touched art, music, literature, and dance, each of which aspired to the same radical emancipation from traditional structures of form and authority. Many of the key components of early modernism—cultural and scientific as well as artistic—emerged in the span of a few years. In short order there appeared Sigmund Freud's *The Interpretation of Dreams* (1900), Albert Einstein's special theory of relativity (1905), the lurid and garish colors of Fauvist painting (1905), the earliest Cubist works of Pablo Picasso and Georges Braque (1908–9), Wassily Kandinsky's first fully abstract art (1911), and Igor Stravinsky's modernist ballet *The Rite of Spring* (1913). These were independent developments, to be sure, but taken collectively they had an overwhelming force, suggesting that the very nature of modern experience had radically changed, and that a radically new art was called for.

Modernist painting and architecture advanced along different paths. In painting, European leadership remained the rule, making early American modernism a rather derivative phenomenon. In the practical art of architecture, however, American experiments

160 **Stanton MacDonald-Wright**, *Conception Synchromy*, 1914. The goal of the Synchromists was to divest "art of all anecdote and illustration and to purify it so that the emotions of the spectator can become entirely aesthetic, as in listening to music." By this definition, *Conception Synchromy* is a happy success. Its subject is the conception of life, both biological and spiritual, which Macdonald-Wright presents by means of color rather than form. (Notice how he runs each of its concentric curves through a shifting spectrum of colors, making it impossible to read them as tangible, self-contained forms.)

with the skyscraper and steel construction had long since outpaced Europe; here the process was more one of cross-fertilization as influences flowed in both directions. The decisive figure, and certainly the most single most influential artist in American history, was Frank Lloyd Wright.

Frank Lloyd Wright (1867–1959) spent an unusually itinerant childhood, unusual even in a country where rootlessness was innate. His father was at times a lawyer, preacher, and musician, and repeatedly uprooted his family—from Wisconsin to Iowa, Rhode Island, Massachusetts, and back again to Wisconsin. This peripatetic existence shaped Wright in major ways. He keenly felt the lure of mobility, and was the first architect to take the invention of the automobile to its logical conclusion: the dissolution of the city itself. But his vagabond childhood also made him understand the lure of the home, and he gave it its most poignant expression in all of American art, centered on the elemental qualities of the hearth and the roof, warmth, and shelter—an image of permanence and solidity, precisely what he never knew.

From 1888 to 1893, Wright worked in Chicago with Louis Sullivan, whose functionalist doctrine he absorbed, and which he applied to houses, his responsibility in the firm (they did not interest Sullivan). In later years he named Sullivan as the only architect who influenced him. Instead, he attributed his success primarily to his formative childhood encounter with Froebel blocks. Invented by Friedrich Froebel, the Swiss pedagogue who created the Kindergarten movement, these used simple geometric components such as cubes and spheres to teach children manual dexterity even as they showed that the same principles of crystalline development learned through the blocks also appear in minerals, flowers, and mathematics. In other words, knowledge was acquired simultaneously through tactile and intellectual means. This was high romanticism, of course—the doctrine of the spiritual oneness of the universe—and by invoking it, Wright was indirectly praising himself. By insisting that he was beholden to no other architect, he

161 **Frank Lloyd Wright**, Larkin Building, Buffalo, New York, 1904. The Larkin Building was Wright's first masterpiece. It is also one of the first buildings to achieve a strong monumental character entirely by expressing the facts of its program and construction, without regard for historical prototypes. The mightiest element, the bulky pylons to either side of the building, actually encase the building's fire stairs; another architect might have hid these utilitarian elements but Wright made them the principal subject of the facade.

suggested a much loftier source of inspiration: the underlying order of the universe itself, that is, from God. Such an idea was quite congenial to his own Unitarian background , and his immersion in the pantheistic Transcendentalism of Emerson.

After Sullivan fired him (for secretly designing houses on the side), Wright rapidly blossomed as a designer. By 1904, when he designed the Larkin Building in Buffalo, New York, he was in full command of his powers [161]. The Larkin Company was a mail-order house, and required a well-lit and hygienic office building in which mail could be opened and orders filled. It also needed to be screened hygienically from its industrial context and nearby railroad sidings. Wright turned his building inward, placing a skylighted sleeve of space at the center, wrapped by five tiers of galleries. From these vantages, the employers could observe their workers below [162]. For all its progressive technology, the Larkin Building presented that abiding theme of Wright's career, the image of a family, united and sheltered.

162 **Frank Lloyd Wright**, Larkin Building, Buffalo, New York, 1904. Interior. The Larkin Building was extraordinarily modern in its services: modular steel furniture, built-in vacuum cleaning ducts in the wall, and even an early system of passive air-conditioning— allowing the building to be hermetically sealed from its brutal industrial site between factories and railroad sidings.

The same pattern holds in Wright's houses, reliquaries of family life in which modern materials and processes were used to create elemental sensations. The earliest ones cribbed from the Shingle Style of Bruce Price, although Wright soon grew more abstract, eliminating specific historical references such as the gable and the cornice. The Shingle Style also showed him the value of spatial continuity. His rooms flowed fluidly, one opening upon the other and even interpenetrating, showing the effect of his thoughtful investigation of Japanese architecture, with its sliding screens and flexible partitions. Here modern construction came to his aid. By using concrete slab construction, supported only by a few steel uprights (like a waiter carrying a tray on his fingertips, he explained), he eliminated the structural need for interior partitions, placing them only where needed to shape and sculpt space, or in order to achieve privacy. Only at the core was there a solid masonry mass, the place of family togetherness at the ever-blazing fire. Here Wright revived the seventeenth-century living hall, in feeling if not in form. (In this he did precisely the opposite of his colleagues, whose counterfeit Colonial revived the forms of the style, its Palladian windows, and elliptical fanlights, but showed no interest in the positive qualities of its intimate spaces.)

Spatial continuity was also the theme of Wright's exteriors, which virtually abolished the traditional distinction between inside and out. Slivers of wall (spur walls) slid beyond the volume of the house to define adjacent terraces. At the same time, the walls of the upper story were set well behind the projecting slab of the roof, creating spaces that were within the shelter of the roof but beyond the volume of the house. The result is an abstract composition of forceful stiff planes and shadowed voids, pinned to the earth by a massive masonry chimney that prevents its parts from cartwheeling into incoherence. Such a house was no longer a sculptural solid, set upon the land like a statue on its base, but was integrated so thoroughly with the land that it was simultaneously a work of architecture and of landscape [163]. The work of extending the house into the land, which had been begun by Downing and Davis a half century earlier with their spreading porches, was now consummated.

The predominant lines of these houses were horizontal, restating the topography of the Midwest, in recognition of which fact Wright dubbed them "Prairie Houses" in 1901. Prairie Houses were not merely a new *style* of house, like the Queen Anne or Colonial Revival, but an entirely new *type*, because, as Wright recognized, there was an entirely new type of American life, characterized by automobiles, telephones, electric appliances, and changing social mores. This was the end of the Victorian house, with its rabbit warren of specialist rooms, its libraries, parlors, sitting rooms, and reception halls. The intimate cocktail party soon replaced the formal machinery of Victorian entertainment, and social rituals would become even simpler and breezier after the imposition of a national income tax in 1913; the large retinues of domestic servants would shrink to a housekeeper, cook, and maid, or vanish entirely. Wright's clients— young and progressive entrepreneurs, like Fred Robie (a manufacturer of bicycle parts)— were especially alert to these changes.

Wright's unconditional rejection of historical prototypes was revolutionary but his principles were not. Most of the themes of the Prairie House would have been familiar to Downing, who argued that houses should harmonize with their landscape and that materials should be used truthfully. Even earlier, Horatio Greenough had spoken of the relationship between beauty and function, and how architecture needed to find forms that were as well suited to their function as the streamlined form of a clipper ship. Even Sullivan's doctrine of form following function was but an outgrowth of Greenough's insight.

163 **Frank Lloyd Wright**, Robie House, Chicago, 1908–10. The most splendid of Wright's Prairie Style houses; like his Froebel blocks, it is a delightful abstract play of intersecting planes. Fred Robie was typical of Wright's clients: a free-thinking and progressive young inventor and a manufacturer of parts for bicycles, then a national craze.

Indebted to this tradition (a debt he characteristically did not acknowledge), Wright coined the idea of an "organic" architecture, his term for the indissoluble unity of site, space, and structure. This did not necessarily mean that a building should look as if it was a part of nature (although it might); rather it meant that a building, in analogy with a living thing, should grow naturally from the inside out. This describes Wright's own design process, which began with its core and the spaces that clustered around it, so that the facades were the end result of the design process, rather than the start, as was often the case. Wright's organic method of design became a fundamental doctrine of modern architecture, and not only in America. In 1911 Wright traveled to Germany to arrange for the publication of his designs with the Berlin publisher Ernst Wasmuth. The so-called Wasmuth portfolio had a galvanizing effect on European architects, setting in

164 **Henry Mercer**, Mercer Museum, Doylestown, Pennsylvania, 1914. Henry Mercer (1856–1930) was an archeologist and anthropologist who set out to document the vanishing heritage of traditional crafts—many of them still surviving in the Amish countryside in Pennsylvania—which he arranged in his labyrinthine concrete museum, each of whose individual cells was devoted to a different trade. Fifty years later, this disorienting and richly layered architecture, a dream world of suspended objects, would have a startling effect on the postmodern architect Charles Moore.

165 **Greene and Greene,**
David B. Gamble House, Pasadena,
California, 1908–9. The exact
contemporary of the Robie House,
whose horizontality, flowing plan,
and freedom from historical
precedent it shares.

motion a series of developments that would ricochet back in the 1930s when many of these same European modernists found asylum in America.

There are parallels to Wright's architecture in other areas of the country, where vigorous regional schools also flourished, and where the use of modern materials was tempered by an awareness of local history, materials, and climate. In the hilly wooded landscape around Philadelphia, Wilson Eyre, William L. Price, and others drew on the local tradition of massive German and Welsh fieldstone farmhouses. Unlike Wright's horizon-hugging slabs, this architecture had a hefty solidity which stood up to the corrugated terrain of the region. It did not shrink from new materials, and from an early date concrete was exploited, but not to make flat slabs, as Wright had done. Instead architects exulted in the liquid language of the material, its ability to be poured into arches and vaults. At Doylestown, north of Philadelphia, the amateur architect Henry Mercer built a complex of a house, a tile factory, and a museum, each a free-form array of concrete domes, vaults, and parapets [164].

The landscape of southern California fostered a very different regionalism. The drier and warmer climate lowered roof pitches and opened up the interior to the outside; here the historical vernacular was Spanish Colonial, although there was also a vibrant curiosity about the architecture of the Pacific world, especially that of Japan. These forces converged in the exquisite bungalows of Greene and Greene. Charles Sumner Greene and Henry Mather Greene were eastern transplants who had worked in the successful firm of H. H. Richardson. They also attended an arts-and-crafts school in St. Louis, where they learned to work in wood, metal, and leather. Their designs were never mere paper exercises, and were conceived in terms of the specific properties of the materials to be used. In their best work every detail and joint is lovingly celebrated, showing the exquisite sensitivity to materials normally found only in fine furniture or musical instruments. Their masterpiece is the David B. Gamble House, with its exuberant play of visible carpentry that suggests their intelligent study of Japanese wood architecture [165].

Greene and Greene freed California architecture from its dependence on eastern fashions. They showed that the way to develop a modern indigenous architecture was not to mimic the forms of Spanish missions but to work intuitively from climate, conditions, and materials. Their work was of far more than mere local interest, however; in the permissive architectural culture of California, which was free of many of the historical and social constraints that hobbled eastern architects, they could respond with unusual speed to the changing social conditions of the new century. Like Wright, they recognized the need for smaller and simpler houses. Their response was the bungalow, a California innovation that became a national fad in the 1910s. In the course of a 1915 interview, Charles Sumner Greene explained the bungalow as the expression of a new California sensibility, in which the invention of the automobile played a central role: "Between the automobile mania and the bungalow bias, there seems to be a psychic affinity. They have developed side by side and they seem to be the expression of the same need and desire, to be free from the commonplace of convention. It is the growth of the germ of California's incentive, the mere joy of living, newly discovered."

This is one of the first expressions of that central theme of twentieth-century architecture, the problem and the potential of the automobile. By liberating the building from the need to be in the enclosed spatial order of the city, or even of the landscaped suburban development, the automobile encouraged the architect to treat the building as a freestanding object in space, with no duty to relate to adjoining buildings, or to the pedestrian. This is the essential freedom of roadside architecture. It is a defining characteristic of California architecture but it is more than a mere regional school. In a certain sense, it is the primal American architectural experience: the colonist in a new setting, uninhibited by existing social arrangements or architectural context. It is not surprising that Californian architecture would become ever more important over the course of the twentieth century, at the end of which the best-known American architect in the world was a Californian, Frank Gehry.

Early modernist developments in painting paralleled those in architecture. In both cases the most progressive artists were those who were most alert to the quickened pace of American life. This was the special insight of the Ashcan School, the innovative school of realism in the early twentieth century. Of course the Ashcan School was no formal school at all; the term was originally an insult, mocking the painters who seemed to find their subject matter in alleys and trash cans. But, as often happens, the insult became a badge of honor, and the name stuck.

The Ashcan School was the creation of Robert Henri (1865–1929), an artist with a eventful childhood. He was born Robert Cozad and grew up riding and hunting on the frontier in Nebraska, where his father was caught up in the perennial wars between homesteaders and cattleman, killing a man who had come to murder him. The family fled and Robert took his mother's name, Henri (pronounced *hen-rye*), keeping the secret throughout his life. He entered the Pennsylvania Academy in 1886, the year Eakins was fired, although his method lived on at the Pennsylvania Academy of the Fine Arts, upheld by his successors, Thomas Anschutz and Thomas Hovenden. Later Henri attended the Académie Julian in Paris, where he cultivated brushwork of swashbuckling energy. His rough and tumble youth did not seem to hold him back. On the contrary; it was an asset in an era that promoted a cult of vigorous masculinity in the wake of the Spanish–American War, and in which Theodore Roosevelt's charge up San Juan Hill made him a national hero. After an age of effete and suave dandies like Whistler and Chase, Henri stood out as a kind of plain-speaking cowboy artist.

In the mid-1890s, Henri assembled a circle of loyal pupils in Philadelphia, including John Sloan, George Luks, Everett Shinn, and William Glackens. These men belonged to one of the briefest of artistic generations on record: the newspaper sketch artists of the 1890s. Photoengraving had recently made it possible to print sketches directly in the newspaper, without first cutting them as wood engravings, as in Homer's day. Daily newspapers now became a graphic as well as verbal medium; their sketch artists were essentially journalists who filed their stories visually. Speeding from courtroom to railroad accident to apartment fire, they made terse, efficient sketches on site, which they finished in their offices, racing against the evening deadline. But their heyday was fleeting. Once the photographic half-tone became widely available after 1900, the photograph replaced the line drawing and newspapers emptied their studios.

Sloan and his friends found in Henri a natural mentor. Charismatic and articulate, he showed them how to make oil paintings without sacrificing the quivering spontaneity of the first sketch. His technique is the same direct painting that had been

166 **Robert Henri**, *Eva Green*, 1907. "Do it all in one sitting if you can. In one minute if you can." So Robert Henri urged in *The Art Spirit* (1923), his treatise on painting, which remains a readable manual today. This did not mean he was slapdash; he had a strong sympathy for his sitters and a gift for coaxing vivacity from children, as here in his portrait of Eva Green.

pioneered by Édouard Manet in France in the 1860s: no fussy glazing and built-up surfaces, a forceful, vigorously painted surface, and the cultivation of the palpable brushstroke as a means of expression. Henri's pupils learned, for example, that an eyebrow is not a multitude of individually painted lines but a single feature, raised by a single muscle—an action that might be depicted with a single emphatic stroke of the brush. And faces were faceted into distinct planes, each showing a particular value of light. The results were scruffier and looser than formal academic painting, but conveyed a sense of the nervous, restless energy of the sitter [166]. This was not the biological realism of Eakins but rather a sociological realism, portraying the truth of the highstrung modern city rather than the truth of the human body.

In 1900 Henri was summoned to teach at the New York School of Art, where he formed an odd couple with the debonair William Merritt Chase. His pupils followed him from Philadelphia, drawn to the modern metropolis with its lively immigrant quarters, its seedy demimonde, and fashionable nightlife. Each cultivated a distinct specialty: Glackens found his subjects in restaurants [173]

167 Everett Shinn, *The Orchestra Pit, Old Proctor's Fifth Avenue Theater*, c. 1906–7. It is unfair to say that the Ashcan School reveled in the sordid and the unseemly, but rather that they embraced life in its full range. This painting by Everett Shinn was characteristic of their approach, which was based on an eye for the vital instant, a skill honed during years of journalism.

168 George Luks, *The Wrestlers*, 1905. Having developed his skills by drawing the comic strip *The Yellow Kid*, George Luks was adept at maximizing the visual force of a scene. He liked bold or unusual angles: in *The Wrestlers* he places the body of the losing wrestler at a right angle to the picture plane, so that he is heroically foreshortened, all of the action telescoped behind his straining head.

169 John Sloan, *Sunday, Women Drying their Hair*, 1912. This painting shows the prying voyeurism that was Sloan's hallmark, the legacy of his days as an artist-journalist. Of the artists' group The Eight, he was closest to Henri, both socially and artistically, and his canvases shared Henri's distinctively scratchy surface—as if the slightest hint of prettiness in brushwork was a thing to be avoided at all costs.

and racetracks while Shinn lurked backstage at the ballet or in orchestra pits [167]. Luks was a rowdy, and his fascination with squalor and lowlife settings recalls the Dutch genre painters whom he admired [168]. Finally, Sloan was the most committed to painting the unremitting pulse of modern urban life, which he sought out on ferry boats and in storefronts, on tenement rooftops, and underneath elevated trains [169].

170 **Lewis W. Hine**, *Untitled (Girl in a Cotton Mill)*, n.d. This was made during an extensive documentary campaign investigating the horrors of child labor. A technical tour de force, it places the young girl in a shallow plane of sharp focus, isolating her within the deep thrust of the perspective. It conveys the dispiriting and repetitive drudgery of modern industry just as effectively as Weir had evoked its excitement [122].

The artists of the Ashcan School were not social reformers; they lacked the righteous indignation of Jacob Riis or Lewis W. Hine, then making his photojournalistic crusade against child labor [170]. They had the jaded eye of the journalist, free of sentiment and mawkishness. They were the pictorial counterparts of American literature of the time, especially Theodore Dreiser, whose scandalous *Sister Carrie* (1900) was then laying bare the stark lives of the modern city-dweller.

Also like Dreiser, the painters of the Ashcan School offended contemporary sensibilities. Without fail they were slighted in the annual exhibitions of the National Academy of Design, despite the best efforts of Henri, who was a prominent member. By 1908 he had had enough, and boycotted the show to organize one of his own. This he did not restrict to members of the Ashcan School; he did not want to exchange one parochial orthodoxy for another. Besides his own pupils, he invited Maurice Prendergast [171] and Ernest Lawson, two Post-Impressionists, and Arthur B. Davies, a Symbolist with a penchant for unicorns and sleepwalking nudes [172]. The exhibition was known only by the number of participating painters, The Eight.

The debut of The Eight caused a sensation out of all proportion to its commercial success, which was trifling. It effectively exposed the National Academy of Design as hidebound and laughably out of touch with the modern world: "no more national than the National Biscuit Company," Henri scoffed. There followed a rapid realignment of artistic allegiances. Some of America's most talented young artists now affiliated themselves with the Ashcan movement, including Edward Hopper (1882–1967) and George Bellows (1882–1925), a former semiprofessional baseball player [174].

171 **Maurice Prendergast**, *The Promenade*, 1913. Maurice Prendergast (1859–1924) is the most important of American Post-Impressionists. After three years in Paris and another in Venice, he returned to America as an accomplished and lyrical watercolorist, with a love for intense glowing colors. He brought this color sense to his later oil paintings, like *The Promenade*, where the effect is that of a mosaic: flat decorative patterns and a glistening jewel-like surface.

172 **Arthur B. Davies**, *Dream*, 1908. Davies continued the introspective American tradition that ran from Washington Allston and Elihu Vedder to Ralph Albert Blakelock and Albert Pinkham Ryder. A painter of sleepwalkers, he evidently sleepwalked through his own life, for he was a successful bigamist (as both his families were surprised to discover on attending his funeral).

The best perhaps and certainly the most enduring was Hopper, whose practice lasted into the second half of the century. His art is strongly reminiscent of Sloan, another artist whose years as a commercial illustrator taught him the art of the memorable composition. Hopper was even more gifted in finding eloquent architectural settings. His best work placed one or two figures, frequently women, in a stark and lonely room: a pensive usherette in the gloom of a movie theater or a wan secretary, toiling in solitude by night. Ironically, although Hopper escaped from the commercial grind, his work retained its commercial sensibility—its legibility, its bold graphic quality, and its economical formal structure—which has made it very easy to turn his paintings back into commercial products, such as the endless stream of calendars, postcards, posters, and coffee-table books derived from his work [175].

Hopper remained cheerfully indifferent to the innovations of the European avant-garde; if he was a modernist at all, it was the modernism of Freud rather than that of Picasso. Other Americans followed European events more avidly, and in the first decade of the new century, a growing number of American observers began to look not to the European academy but to the European avant-garde. Of course the most alert to these developments were those close to the center of events, like those sophisticated expatriates such as Gertrude and Leo Stein in Paris. But after 1905 the European avant-garde gained a toehold in New York, where the photographers Alfred Stieglitz and Edward Steichen opened a modest art gallery, which was soon known simply by its Fifth Avenue address, 291.

Stieglitz (1864–1946) was American-born but later moved to Germany, where he studied at the Technische Hochschule in Berlin. There he became an accomplished photographer, achieving an exceptional degree of technical expertise. Once back in America he joined with Steichen in 1902 to form the movement known as Photo-Secession. Of course the name was an affectation, since the European Secessionists on whom they modeled

173 **William Glackens**, *Chez Mouquin*, 1905. This painting depicts James B. Moore, a restaurant owner and something of a professional Casanova, with one of his "daughters" at a well-known New York nightspot. Both the subject and its handling derive from Manet's *A Bar at the Folies Bergère* of 1882, showing how American artists were still assimilating the lessons of French Impressionists in the new century.

174 **George Bellows**, *Stag at Sharkey's*, 1909. Bellows learned much from Luks, as his boxing paintings show. Here two clinching boxers and a referee are brought violently together to form a dynamic pyramid, a quivering mass of colliding heads and gloves, almost a kind of flattened *Laocoön*. Never was boxing rendered in such classical terms, and seldom did the classical pyramid contain so much kinetic energy.

175 **Edward Hopper**, *Morning in a City*, 1944. Hopper, like Vermeer, specialized in portraying pensive women, alone in a room and illuminated through a window. But Hopper mixed the insights of Vermeer with those of Freud. In *Morning in a City*, the customary props and storytelling devices of American genre painting have been stripped away, leaving few clues with which to reconstruct the narrative. We are left with only its enigmatic, solitary subject, whose rueful expression invites us to speculate about her state of mind.

themselves had an official academy from which to secede, but it nonetheless proclaimed their identification with the avant-garde of Europe. Stieglitz fretted throughout his life whether or not the camera was modern. If modern in its technology, it was conservative in its aesthetics, for it implied an objective realism. He rejected this, insisting that photographs should be evaluated according to their abstract formal structure, which made him an early champion of Pictorialism.

176 **Edward Steichen**, *The Flatiron*, 1904. Steichen's atmospheric photograph suggests what Whistler might have done had he used a camera instead of an etcher's copper plate. Steichen saw the distinctive bladelike form of the Flatiron, produced by its triangular site at the intersection of Broadway and Twenty-third Street, as a dynamic symbol of the modern metropolis, a building that looked as if it might like to move.

Pictorialism applied the doctrine of the Aesthetic Movement to photography. It favored soft and veiled tonalities, where everything seems obscured by a fine mist or a delicate veil, or a gauze—which was often literally the case, as photographers muffled the lens with gauze or threw it slightly out of focus to make dreamy and indistinct forms; in short, anything to overcome the natural tendency of the camera to produce definite forms and hard lines. Steichen championed Pictorialism into the 1920s [176] while Stieglitz [177] eventually came to find its decorative properties made it fundamentally unserious. Preferring a more abstract and rigorous modernism, he founded the journal *Camera Work* in 1913.

But it was at 291 where he enjoyed his greatest influence. Shortly after its founding in 1905, Steichen sailed to Europe, where he acted as Stieglitz's ambassador to the avant-garde, making the personal ties and connections that brought to the gallery its pioneering exhibitions of European modernism. These included the first American exhibitions of Henri Matisse (1908), Paul Cézanne (1911), Picasso (1911) and Constantin Brancusi (1914), among others. For regular visitors, 291 presented the volcanic birth of modernism in annual installments, almost as it happened.

But 291 was also supportive of American artists, and Stieglitz exhibited their work, provided them contacts in Europe, even loaned them money. His beneficiaries form a modernist honor roll, including John Marin, Max Weber, Charles Demuth, and Marsden Hartley—whose stint in Europe Stieglitz funded almost single-handedly. Even more intimate was his patronage of Georgia O'Keeffe, whom he married after first displaying her work. By the time he and Steichen quarreled in 1910, more on grounds of personality than aesthetic philosophy, he had done more than anyone else to give early American modernism its cosmopolitan and international character.

As important as Stieglitz was as an artist and impresario, his 291 reached only a select vanguard; the general public took little notice. This was not the case with the Armory Show of 1913, which stunned the American public, and which variously perplexed, infuriated, and amused its visitors. Its sensational effect is all the more remarkable as it was largely inadvertent.

The Armory Show was not intended to serve as the springboard for European modernists but rather to showcase the work of progressive Americans. In 1911 the Association of American Painters and Sculptors was established, intended to serve as a more democratic alternative to the hidebound National Academy. Arthur B. Davies was named president and he set about organizing an independent exhibition, much like that of The Eight. The European component was an afterthought. In 1912 Davies and the artist Walt Kuhn visited the celebrated "Sonderbund" exhibition in Cologne, Germany, and were astonished by the quality and variety of the work. They arranged to borrow a substantial portion of that show for their own, certainly not dreaming that this last-minute addendum would overshadow the American work on display.

Davies rented a large armory building at Twenty-sixth Street and Lexington Avenue from the New York National

177 **Alfred Stieglitz**, *The Steerage*, 1907. Alfred Stieglitz's most important photograph, this showed a quintessential Ashcan School subject—European immigrants arriving in New York harbor—but for him its true subject was the dynamic play of gangplank, funnel, and railing: "I saw shapes related to each other. I saw a picture of shapes and underlying that the feeling I had about life."

178 Armory Show, New York, installation photograph, 1913. Only a portion of the art displayed at the 1913 Armory Show was highly abstract but it was these works—such as Brancusi's *Madame Pogany* at center left— that scandalized the public and received the most attention. This photograph shows room H of the show's foreign section.

Guard's 69th Regiment. In its massive barn of space was displayed virtually every strand of modernist art except Futurism (the Italians refused to cooperate). Picasso was represented by some of his Cubist drawings; Matisse's *Blue Nude* represented Fauvism, while Brancusi's *Madame Pogany* represented the most progressive current of sculptural abstraction. But older works were displayed as well, beginning with Goya and Ingres, and then passing through Impressionism and Post-Impressionism. Davies and Kuhn did not merely present an assortment of contemporary art but laid out the historical pedigree of modernism. Such was the exhibition that opened to a startled and scandalized public on February 17, 1913 [178].

Only about a third of the 1,600 works of art on display was European, but it was these that perplexed and shocked the public. The American reaction was violently and overwhelmingly negative, among critics as well as the general public. The farthest that popular opinion would go in accepting modern European art was Odilon Redon, the commercial hit of the show, since his mysterious fantasias of color could be understood on Aesthetic Movement terms. Cubism could not be, however, and it quickly became a term of amusement and ridicule. Oddly enough, the most notorious item at the exhibition was not one of Picasso's Cubist drawings but Marcel Duchamp's *Nude Descending a Staircase* (1912). While Picasso's intimate drawings could be written off as decorative, Duchamp's factual title promised a reality that it did not deliver, which seems to have enraged the public. *Nude Descending a Staircase* became the public face of the Armory Show, to be repeatedly burlesqued in cartoons and lambasted in editorials—a "staircase descending a nude," one newspaper sneered—as the exhibition wended its way from New York to Chicago and at last to Boston [179].

But even as the public gaped and jibed, artists came and learned. In its broad effect on American practice, the Armory Show recalled how the Columbian Exhibition thrust Beaux-Arts classicism into the public consciousness twenty years earlier. There a traditional art had been showcased while now it was modernist art, but in both instances the same motives were in play in the public response. There was the inevitable fascination for a fashionable novelty but there was also a distinct feeling of provincial inadequacy, of being away from the center of things, a feeling that is as overpowering as fashion insecurity. In this respect, both the American avant-gardist of 1913 and the American academician of 1893 were similarly provincial, each willingly accepting the leadership of European masters.

One immediate result of the show was the fall of the Ashcan School. Compared with Duchamp and Brancusi, the gritty realism of Henri looked positively quaint, having been robbed of its power to provoke. But to the young artist in search of inspiration, the Armory Show was somewhat baffling. It did not offer one modernism but many: Cubism, Fauvism, Orphism, and various smaller ones. In the years after 1913, this tantalizing bouquet of possibilities caused many an American artist to lunge wildly from one to another.

A typically tentative response was that of Morton Schamberg (1881–1918), a pupil of William Merritt Chase. At the Armory Show, Schamberg exhibited a Matisse-influenced portrait, with strong black outlines and a green stripe running across the face. And yet after the exhibition he failed to find his artistic center: he experimented in turn with Cubism, Synchromism, Picabia-like mechanical abstractions, and finally a Dadaist phase in which an ordinary sink trap in a miter box was labeled *God* (1918). The range was remarkable but somehow it did not advance beyond a precocious display of proficiency.

Another artist of talent who vacillated was Max Weber (1881–1961). Weber's modernist credentials were impeccable: he studied in France from 1905 to 1908, was trained by Matisse, and twice exhibited at the progressive Salon d'Automne; there he met Picasso and joined the cadre of early Cubists. But when some of his works were rejected by the Armory Show, Weber was affronted. His works of the following two years seem a defiant attempt not only to confirm his modernity but to demonstrate that he could do everything that the Armory Show offered. His *Rush Hour, New York* translated Duchamp's *Nude Descending a Staircase* into the

179 **Marcel Duchamp**, *Nude Descending a Staircase, No. 2*, 1912. This work, by the French artist Marcel Duchamp (1887–1968) is an alloy of modernist styles: its armature of faceted planes is Cubist while the suggestion of blurred motion is Futurist.

180 **Max Weber**, *Rush Hour, New York*, 1915. This conveys the convulsive pulsating energy of the modern city through Futurist lines of force and repeated rhythmic patterns. Weber was also a devoted follower of Cézanne, as his delicately mottled yellow and green palette shows (he does not use strident red, for example, to suggest the nervousness of traffic).

181 **Max Weber**, *Chinese Restaurant*, 1915. Weber described the genesis of this painting: "On entering a Chinese restaurant from the darkness of night outside, a maze and blaze of light seemed to split into fragments the interior and its contents. … Oblique planes and contours took vertical and horizontal positions … the life and movement so enchanting! To express this, kaleidoscopic means had to be chosen." Here Cubist fragmentation is used not as a formal analytical tool but a way of conveying a psychological state.

staccato pulse of the modern city [180]; *Chinese Restaurant* was a Cubist collage [181]; *Spiral Rhythm* was a nonobjective work of sculpture, a bronze torso of writhing ribbons of force, a Cubist variation on Brancusi. All three works were produced in 1915, a dazzling display of proficiency, but Weber lacked follow-through. He eventually returned to figure drawing in the 1920s.

Weber was not the exception but the rule. Most artists who responded to the Armory Show treated it as a storehouse of stylistic novelties rather than as a complete system of thought. As with Impressionism, which came to America as a visual fad with little of its original sociological content, the various movements inspired by the Armory Show spread shallow roots.

In this general pattern, Marsden Hartley stood somewhat outside. Although trained by William Merritt Chase, he had strongly mystical tendencies that was encouraged by his encounters with the elderly Albert Pinkham Ryder, then living like a hermit in his New York tenement. Stieglitz later took Hartley

182 **Marsden Hartley**, *Portrait of a German Officer*, 1914. Hartley was in Berlin at the start of World War I when his friend Karl von Freyburg, a young German officer, was killed. *Portrait of a German Officer* captures this with the intensity of a lover's grief, with its cryptic symbols (the 4 refers to Freyburg's regiment and the 24 to his age), lurid Fauvist colors, and the fractured frontality of Cubism.

under his wing and sent him to Europe, where he remained from 1912 to 1915. There he came into contact with the principal modernist painters, particularly Picasso and Kandinsky, whose essay *On the Spiritual in Art* (1912) he admired and studied avidly. But he saw his own symbol-laden art as something entirely new: "It is not like Picasso—not like Kandinsky not like any 'cubism'—it is what I call for want of a better name subliminal or cosmic cubism." On another occasion he boasted of having created "the first expression of mysticism in modern art."

Hartley soon developed a distinctive personal language of painting, in which the formal sense is Cubist and the vaguely religious overtone closer to the mysticism of Ryder. Most suggest sublimated shrines: a central symbolic object is presented frontally, so that it crowds the frame while smaller, related symbols assemble around it—like the spurs, insignias, and epaulettes of his *Portrait of a German Officer* [182]. Although highly personal and painfully cryptic, perhaps because Hartley was acknowledging a homosexuality that he could not otherwise address, these paintings were enormously influential for other American modernists. They showed that one might draw deeply from the formal experiments of European avant-garde painters without relinquishing some of the perennial themes of American art: recognizable objects, the natural landscape, and a certain vague religious longing.

This was the pattern for most early American modernists. The key figures were all forty or older at the time of the Armory Show: John Marin (1870–1953), Arthur Dove (1880–1946), Marsden Hartley (1877–1943), Joseph Stella (1877–1946), and Charles Demuth (1883–1935). Each had had a serious grounding in academic art before encountering the avant-garde of Europe: Marin and Demuth studied at the Pennsylvania Academy; Hartley at the National Academy of Design, and Stella at the New York School of Art. In each instance, their academic grounding acted as an anchor, and kept them from completely abandoning tangible subject matter to create a fully nonobjective art. Although they might simplify and abstract from an object, or stylize it through rhythmic patterns or extend and repeat its contours in space, not one of them ever eliminated it entirely, or sought to.

These first-generation modernists were still preoccupied by nature and the modern city, those perennial themes of American art. Although the stylistic expression often showed the mark of avant-garde practice, the underlying themes would not have been unfamiliar to Cole or Homer: that the city was a place of throbbing intensity, tumultuous change, and a vague underlying sense of menace; and that the natural wilderness was a place of mystic goodness. Of course, the pulse and cacophony of the city lent itself to modernist abstraction, and Cubist fragmentation.

At the same time, American artists felt free to combine at will the insights of movements that in Europe were deeply hostile to one another, such as Cubism and Futurism. The Futurists, for example, despised the Cubists for their static compositions and for not portraying the "beauty of speed," the Futurist ideal. Demuth and Stella happily fused the two movements to make what might be called a Cubo-Futurist synthesis, fragmenting their compositions into discrete faceted planes which they then overlaid with Futurist "lines of force." But they applied these devices to subject matter that was quite tangible. For Stella, it was the Brooklyn Bridge, or factories and gas tanks, whose vast industrial hulks gave him a readymade Futurism [183]. For Demuth,

183 **Joseph Stella**, *The Voice of the City of New York Interpreted: The Bridge*, 1920–22. "Many nights I stood on the bridge … deeply moved, as if on the threshold of a new religion or in the presence of a new DIVINITY." So proclaimed Joseph Stella, for whom the Brooklyn Bridge was the physical embodiment of American modernity, which he revered with the fervor of a poor Italian immigrant. In *The Bridge*, part of a five-panel polyptych, he invested it with religious character, showing it frontally as a kind of neo-Gothic altarpiece, its steel suspension cables erupting outward like Futurist lines of force.

it was still lifes of pears, vaudeville performances, or architecture that reminded him of the crisp Pennsylvania Dutch architecture of his native Lancaster [184]. They might be called tangible modernists, profiting from the stylistic devices of modernism but retaining a respect for solid form and the essential objecthood of things.

This was certainly the case with Marin. On the one hand, his work showed the intimacy with the European avant-garde that is to be expected after his 1906–11 stint in Europe. It was strongly marked by the French Fauves and by Robert Delaunay: just as Delaunay ruptured the Eiffel Tower into melting shards of form, so Marin exploded the Woolworth Building. On the other hand, he turned in the 1920s to those perennial American subjects, seas and mountains, which he treated reverentially as sources of elemental and unfathomable power. His favorite haunt was the Maine coast, the one area left in the East where something like Cole's ideal of primal wildness survived. As with Cole, these meditations on nature were strongly personal even when playing whimsically the Cubist doctrine of pictorial flatness. Marin frequently drew a second frame within the picture frame, recalling the Renaissance idea of painting being a window on to a world, even as his

184 **Charles Demuth**, *Trees and Barns: Bermuda*, 1917. After studying at the Pennsylvania Academy of the Fine Arts, Demuth traveled to Europe in 1907–8 and again in 1912–14, where he befriended Gertrude and Leo Stein and was introduced to avant-garde circles. *Trees and Barns, Bermuda* shows a typical mix of Futurist and Cubist devices, but it also demonstrates his characteristic elegance of color and line: the delicate contours of the trees and the mottled texture, caused by carefully graded blotting of the watercolor.

185 **John Marin**, *Maine Islands*, 1922. The genre of watercolor is normally intimate and lyrical but John Marin showed that it could be a modernist medium. *Maine Islands* is typical, Cubist in its attention to flatness and its geometric scaffolding of form, but rich with passages of jewel-like color. It is painted rather dryly, another Marin hallmark, the brush dragged across the tooth of the paper to underscore its coarseness, and to add vigor to his line.

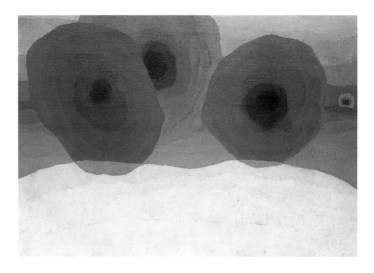

186 **Arthur Dove**, *Foghorns*, 1929. Dove was a Symbolist, who was strongly affected by Odilon Redon and Robert Delauney during the course of a 1907–9 trip to Paris. He could just as easily be called a Symbolist-realist, however, for his subjects were invariably grounded in tangible phenomena, although often nonvisual ones, such as the sound of wind rushing along a hill. In *Foghorns*, a blaring honk from out of the darkness is answered by a much fainter echo in the distance. Here Dove's composition is fully abstract even as it is absolutely literal to the nature of a foghorn.

obviously painted frame exposed the whole thing as a contrivance. For the same reason, he learned to leave large areas of the image unpainted so that the viewer, whose imagination yearns to penetrate into the depth of the picture, inevitably collides with the implacable flatness of the surface [185].

The difference between American and European attitudes toward abstraction is encapsulated by Arthur Dove (1880–1946) and the Russian artist Wassily Kandinsky. Some time around 1910, Kandinsky made the first fully nonobjective art, the first to be entirely abstract. At the same time, Dove also began to make improvised abstractions, similarly free and spontaneous in execution. But while Kandinsky's improvisations had no specific subject matter, Dove's continued to cling to natural phenomena, such as sounds and sensation, if not to natural objects. Thus no solid object is depicted in his *Foghorns*, although the whole painting can be read quite literally as a diagram of an echo [186].

The first Americans to liberate themselves fully from subject matter were Stanton Macdonald-Wright (1890–1973) and Morgan Russell (1886–1953), who were in their twenties at the time of the Armory Show in 1913. Studying in Paris at the time, they created an experimental mode of painting they called "Synchromism," meaning simply "with color" [160]. That summer they presented it at an exhibition in Munich and later in Paris; in 1914 a third exhibition followed in New York.

Synchromism was a truly nonobjective art, the first American art that did not imitate or abstract from objects in the natural world, as Dove did. A self-consciously theoretical movement, it applied analogies drawn from music and sculpture to painting. From music came the concept of pure abstraction: just as the note F sharp is simply a frequency of vibration, which lacks inherent meaning until it is juxtaposed with another note, so the color yellow becomes expressive only when contrasted against blues and reds. From sculpture came another kind of abstract expressiveness, the dynamic play of solid and void. Out of these two notions Macdonald-Wright and Russell devised the idea of a painting of pure colors, in which the projection and recession of warm or cool colors recalled the plasticity of a statue. Russell had studied sculpture with Matisse, and his earliest Synchromist works were a deliberate attempt to translate the dynamic force of Michelangelo's sculpture into chromatic terms.

In some sense, Synchromism was an inversion of Cubism. While Cubism stressed its architectural lattice of lines and proclaimed the flatness of the canvas, Synchromism dispensed with line entirely, working to make its forms plastic solely through highly saturated spectral colors. Synchromism was enormously influential and the artists were exhibited repeatedly in New York, culminating with the Forum Exhibition of Modern Painters of 1916. For a time Thomas Hart Benton and Morton Schamberg both became Synchromists. The expressive range of Synchromism was fundamentally limited, however, and the response of critics can be summed up as, "if you've seen them all, you've seen one." The war helped to disrupt the movement and by 1916 it was essentially finished.

Another strand of modernism also fell on rather rocky soil in America, the absurdist art of Dada. Marcel Duchamp moved to New York in 1915, where he cut a mischievous figure, making light of the pretense of the art world in general. Most notoriously, he submitted a urinal as a readymade art to the New York "Independent Show," giving it the confrontational title of *Fountain* (1917). He gathered a circle of admirers and acolytes, who joined him in his nihilist gestures and visual puns. Most important was Man Ray, the photographer and painter, whose *Le Violin d'Ingres* (1924) was a typically amusing example [187].

Man Ray's version of Dada was light-hearted and unserious— quite unlike the apocalyptic, deadly serious version of Europe. There World War I (1914–18) had toppled three empires, throwing into question the inherent meaning of Western culture. The shock waves have lasted into our own time. The Dada of

Europe might make a jolly spectacle with its absurdist humor but at its core was a grim seriousness, and more than a hint of nihilistic despair.

All this was different in the United States, scarcely touched physically by the war. If anything, in terms of culture, the war was a widening experience for most Americans. For the first time, millions of soldiers from the middle and lower classes were exposed to the culture of Europe, including its more tolerant sexuality. "*How 'Ya Gonna Keep 'Em Down On The Farm (After They See Paree?)*" one of the popular songs of the era wondered. The America of the postwar era was not ravaged and in a state of existential hopelessness, but reinvigorated and revitalized to an almost gleeful extent.

Because of this gulf in experience, the worlds of American and European modernism—which had been converging during the 1910s—sharply and decisively diverged after the war. The war made European modernists even more radical; it suggested the failure of civilization itself. Instead of building on the organic modernist tradition from Manet through Cézanne and Picasso, there was now a sense that all of history should be swept away. The architect Le Corbusier (Charles-Édouard Jeanneret) made the audacious and daft proposal to demolish medieval Paris and replace it with serried ranks of rational towers. To a continent mutilated by four years of cruel trench warfare, the impulse to start all over again was understandable. It is this revulsion at recent history that lies behind the insistent quest for purity in 1920s modernism, its yearning for a hygienic and clean Utopia, and forms of an immaculate and antiseptic whiteness.

In 1920s America, however, civilization and its technology were not threatening but benevolent. If the products of modern civilization were barbed wire, aerial bombardment, mustard gas, and submarine warfare, the American was more conscious of technology in its benign consumer applications: the family automobile, the cinema, and the radio. Perhaps more than any other innovation, the radio changed the nature of the American experience of modernity. Once regular broadcasting began in 1920, people across the country could share in the same collective feeling

187 **Man Ray**, *Le Violin d'Ingres*, 1924. This photograph was typical of the mischievous punning humor of Dada. The Neoclassical painter Ingres was an amateur violinist of considerable skill, and to say that someone could "play the violin like Ingres" was to pay a great compliment. Here Man Ray photographically creates Ingres's violin out of the back of one of his gracefully elongated nudes, displaying a blasé awareness of the Western art tradition, a favorite posture of Dada.

188 **Charles Sheeler**, *Classic Landscape*, 1931. With Precisionism, as in other times of artistic transition, America turned again to realism and precise draftsmanship. Sheeler's *Classic Landscape* implied that the chimneys, storage tanks, and railroad sidings of modern industry were like the aqueducts and temples of the Roman countryside: the achievement of a great civilization expressed in concentrated geometric form. His friend Demuth made the same point when he whimsically called his painting of cylindrical grain elevators *My Egypt*.

at the same time. As Frederick Allen Lewis memorably described in his 1931 book *Only Yesterday*, the new sense of simultaneous experience was electrifying. During the 1927 Gene Tunney–Jack Dempsey heavyweight boxing match, five radio listeners are said to have died of heart attacks in an agony of suspense over the referee's celebrated "long count."

Cubism may have radically transformed the act of seeing, but the automobile achieved this far more comprehensively and pleasurably. The visual experience of speed served to fracture form and space, but it fractured social dimensions as well. Now Americans could quickly escape their neighbors and enjoy instantaneous social freedom in nearby towns where they were strangers. The automobile affected art in more tangible ways as well, as it changed the color sensibility of the era. In 1923, a Packard automobile showroom in Los Angeles turned on the first neon sign, which soon became commonplace. Three years later, Ford introduced a new palette for its cars; previous models had been painted in drab browns and blacks but now bright colors came in and were given a high gloss by the new pyroxlin finish (much as freshly varnished pictures look brighter). In either case, speed became psychologically associated with vibrant, highly saturated colors, and artists who wished to assert their modernity sought colors with the chromatic intensity of neon.

The public mania for automobiles climaxed at the end of 1927 when Ford unveiled the new Model A, with its revolutionary hydraulic brake system, to riotous crowds. Ford carefully planned its advertising campaign, engaging Charles Sheeler to photograph the complex at River Rouge where it was manufactured. His role was purely that of a commercial artist but the immensity of the site and factory overwhelmed him. Sprawling over 1,100 acres, it had a sense of colossal scale like that of Egyptian pyramids or the cathedrals of medieval Europe. And like those monuments, the factories seemed to embody physically the great social forces of the age. Even the throngs that mobbed the Model A showrooms were motivated by something comparable to religious faith. It is easy to see why Sheeler concluded that these factories were "our substitute for religious expression."

He soon began to make paintings based on his photographs, imitating not only their compositions but their photographic character: their crispness, and their sense of both objectivity and of abstract geometric forms in almost airless space [188]. In this way he looked both forward and back. The insistent linearity certainly recalled earlier American art; on the other hand, the palpable delight in sharp planes and facets shows the impact on Sheeler and his generation of Cubism, and, to a certain extent, works such as *Classic Landscape* may be regarded as Cubist found objects. The new mode of expression adopted the values of the machine—clarity, precision, razor edges, and clean form—became known as Precisionism, the leading school of American realism in the art of the 1920s and 1930s.

Sheeler was not alone in reverting from abstraction to realism. Thomas Hart Benton, Georgia O'Keeffe, and Charles Demuth—each abstract in the 1910s—all turned dramatically back to recognizable subject matter. Of these, Demuth was closest to Sheeler in his hard-edged forms and industrial subject matter, and his *My Egypt* (1927) might have been painted by Sheeler himself. But there was something new. Demuth had always been attracted to the sensory phantasmagoria of the circus, with its swirl of light and motion, and now he found something similar in the shrill neon and advertising clutter of the modern city. In particular, he enjoyed the attention-getting crassness of posters and billboards. This is the theme of his painting *The Figure 5 in Gold* (1928), a visual realization of a short poem by his friend William Carlos Williams [189].

189 **Charles Demuth**, *The Figure 5 in Gold*, 1928. This is one of Demuth's "poster portraits," in which he symbolized one of his friends in the graphic terms of an advertising poster. It is his most famous work; ironically, its hard-edged Precisionism suppressed his greatest gift as an artist, his frail and elegant hand, best seen in his intimate watercolors and still lifes.

Williams wrote the poem immediately after being startled by a speeding fire truck on a New York street, and its theme is the sudden sensory barrage of noise and light, diminishing in the distance even before it can be fully perceived: "Among the rain / and lights / I saw the figure 5 / in gold / on a red / firetruck / moving / tense / unheeded / to gong clangs / siren howls / and wheels rumbling / through the dark city." Demuth's overlapping fives capture the receding form of the truck as well as its diminishing clangs, even as the shrill reds and yellows make a visual analogue with its howling siren.

The central theme of *The Figure 5 in Gold* is the raucous tumult and clamor of contemporary New York, which for Demuth was not in the least oppressive; rather it was the embodiment of modern life itself, rapturous and ecstatic. A similar sensibility pervades *Manhatta* (1920), a short experimental film made by Sheeler and Paul Strand, a photographer and protégé of Stieglitz. The film depicts a day in the life of New York City, accompanied by passages from Walt Whitman's *Leaves of Grass*. Beginning with throngs of morning commuters arriving on the Staten Island ferry, the day unfolds with a kind of insistent mechanical exactitude, as if boats, trains, and skyscrapers were merely the component parts of some colossal machine, and pedestrians just the raw materials that it processed.

Manhatta demonstrates how freely inspiration flowed between painting, film, and photography during the 1920s. On the one hand, Precisionist painting aspired to the clarity and objectivity of photography; on the other hand, these same paintings prompted photographers to sharpen their focus and to render objects so tightly that their edges look like cutting instruments. The atmospheric soft-focus photography of the Aesthetic Movement now fell abruptly from fashion. Even Steichen removed the gauze from his camera, and joined the J. Walter Thompson advertising agency where he became a champion of hard-focus photography.

The most influential of the Precisionist photographers was the Californian Edward Weston, who had begun to experiment with sharp focus as early as 1922. He sought out the narrowest lens aperture then available, f/64, the setting that gives the greatest possible depth of field. In other words, every single object in the picture frame would be in hard focus, from the pebbles at the photographer's feet to the most distant mountains [190]. He also photographed on clear days without atmospheric haze, to counteract the effect of depth produced by the humidity

190 **Edward Weston**, *Tomato Field, Monterey Coast*, 1937. This shows the razor-sharp quality of photographic Precisionism even as it plays on the modernist obsession with flatness. Unlike Hine, who narrowed his depth of field to isolate his subject from its background [170], Weston kept everything equally sharp, suppressing the sense of depth. Instead his rows of tomatoes flatten to make a wavy abstract pattern, like a decorative design printed on a fabric.

that Luminist painters had cherished [97]. When Weston photographed sand dunes, fields of crops, or even a toilet bowl, he did it to explore its abstract properties, such as surface patterning or volumetric form, and not to call forth psychological associations with the subject depicted.

Weston's example inspired other photographers to explore the pictorial possibilities of sharp focus and razor edges. Many of them, including Ansel Adams, Imogen Cunningham, and Willard Van Dyke, worked in California, which played the same role for photographers as the Hudson River had for painters a century earlier. In 1932 they loosely formed themselves as the f/64 group. They wrote a brief manifesto, pledging themselves to practice "pure photography," which they defined as that "possessing no qualities of technique, composition or idea, derivative of any other art form," unlike photography that imitated painting (that is, Pictorialism) or graphic arts.

Those artists who remained faithful to the tenets of Cubism had been made self-conscious about national identity by the war, which had diminished the prestige of Europe. The sense of cultural inferiority that educated Americans had felt toward Europe since the day of Henry James and Henry Adams, and the dread of being provincial, had vanished, if only for the time being. This is apparent even in an abstract artist like Stuart Davis (1894–1964), who

191 **Stuart Davis**, *Egg Beater Number One*, 1927. Stuart Davis described in his memoirs the artistic breakthrough that produced this painting: "The culmination of these efforts occurred in 1927–28, when I nailed an electric fan, a rubber glove, and an eggbeater to a table and used it as my exclusive subject matter for a year. The pictures were known as the Eggbeater series … even though they retained no recognizable reference to the optical appearance of their subject matter." Here he found his own formula for overcoming any residual interest in the objects he painted: to paint them for so long that they lost all their fascination as physical forms with distinct mental associations, becoming mere shapes.

192 **Elie Nadelman**, *Dancer*, 1920–24. A peculiarity of Elie Nadelman's sculpture was his habit of joining the head, limbs, and body of a figure together to make one continuous shape, with no articulation of the separate parts. *Dancer* is carved from a piece of cherry wood, a dense and richly grained wood that lends itself to the fine, smooth contours that Nadelman desired.

193 **Gaston Lachaise**, *Walking Woman*, 1922. Lachaise obsessively reworked the theme of the alluring female form, the rounded contours exaggerated into continuous flowing curves as here, in a process he called "simplification and amplification." Its stylized form was derivative of the European abstractions of Brancusi and Modigliani, although the high erotic quotient was his own contribution.

encountered the Armory Show at a formative age and became a faithful Cubist. But he too was now swept up in the experience of American modernity; in 1922 he ostentatiously declared that all of his future work would be "rigorously logical American not French." While he drew from American Precisionism, his Cubist instincts remained strong, however, compelling him to flatten his subjects into planes. Although he sought out American subject matter, he was especially drawn to graphic imagery, which was already flat and planar—such as advertising signs and cigarette packs. By the end of the 1920s, he arrived at a personal synthesis of Cubism and Precisionism with his celebrated *Eggbeater* series [191].

Precisionism was a graphic language and by its nature was not easily applied to sculpture. The sculpture of the 1920s continued to develop on the abstract themes of the Armory Show, and the example of Brancusi and Archipenko in particular. But even here there was a turn toward strong outlines and simplified contours that was Precisionist in spirit. The Polish-born sculptor Elie Nadelman (1882–1942) met Picasso in 1908 and became one the first sculptors to employ Cubist devices in his sculpture. After moving to America in 1915 to exhibit with Stieglitz, he too turned to traditional sources of inspiration, and began collecting American folk art. Renouncing the self-conscious analytical tools of Cubism, he began to look for unconscious approaches to abstraction. These he found in the simple forms of archaic Greek

sculpture but also in the naive wood carving of American folk art. Merging the two, he created his own sleek and enigmatic modernism, which had much in common with the faceless figures of Surrealism [192].

Nadelman's contemporary Gaston Lachaise (1882–1935) developed in much the same direction, toward rounded and simplified forms, although in his case this involved a monomaniacal interest in the female form. Born in Paris, where he studied sculpture, he traveled to New York in 1906 in pursuit of a married American woman he met, wooing her for a decade before she divorced and married him. He later described her as "the primary inspiration which awakened my vision and the leading influence that has directed my forces. Throughout my career as an artist, I refer to this person by the word 'Woman'." His lifelong preoccupation with the same subject matter, whose forms grew progressively more generalized, produced something quite unusual in American art: a sculpture that was frankly erotic but also had a dignified monumentality [193].

Lachaise's voluptuously rounded nudes seemed to go against the spirit of Precisionism's absolute edges and planes, but they also share some of the same underlying impulses: a desire to define and contain shapes as tightly as possible, without ambiguity or the haziness that Tonalists equated with sensual feeling. An interest in crisply defined shapes is also at work in the era's architecture, which produced the most conspicuous of all artefacts of 1920s modernity: the setback skyscraper.

Since Sullivan's boldly functional Wainwright Building [148], American skyscraper design had become more adventurous technologically but more cautious stylistically. Since the Columbian Exhibition, the carcass of their engineering was likely to be encased within a Beaux-Arts skin, usually in creamy white terracotta. Classicism did not naturally lend itself to extreme verticality, and most of the Beaux-Arts skyscrapers were boxy affairs that terminated in a deep cornice. An exception was the Woolworth Building (1910–13), an imaginative essay in the Gothic by the architect Cass Gilbert. The Woolworth Company, one of the world's wealthiest corporations, wanted a corporate headquarters that would also provide a conspicuous symbol at the prow of Manhattan. According to legend, when Gilbert asked Frank Woolworth how high the skyscraper should be, Woolworth retorted "How high can you make it?" When Gilbert replied that this was the client's decision, Woolworth asked that it be 50 feet (15.2 meters) higher that the Metropolitan Life Tower, then the world's tallest building. Obediently, Gilbert delivered a building 792 feet (241.4 meters) high, the tallest in the world [194].

When the Woolworth Building was built, skyscrapers were still permitted to rise without limit, to blacken the streets below and to cast their neighbors to the north into permanent shadow. In 1916, however, New York passed a remarkable zoning ordinance that sought to protect property rights by restricting the height and bulk of skyscrapers. At each prescribed increase in height, a

194 **Cass Gilbert**, Woolworth Building, New York, 1910–13. Cass Gilbert was a protégé of Stanford White and most of his work showed a handsome academic classicism, as in his U.S. Supreme Court Building and Minnesota State Capitol. But his Woolworth Building is a brilliantly resolved Gothic essay, which smoothly integrated its twenty-nine-story main mass with its fifty-eight-story tower so that the two forms did not appear to be stacked on top of one another; instead, the tower emerged logically and forcefully from out of the base, evoking a strength and urgency missing in the conventional Beaux-Arts classical skyscrapers of the era.

195 **Hugh Ferriss**, *Studies for the Maximum Mass Permitted by the 1916 New York Zoning Law*, c. 1925. The extraordinary draftsman Hugh Ferriss showed how it was possible to make living art out of arid legislation. Beginning with the maximum dimensions allowed under the terms of the 1916 zoning law, he chiseled away at the envelope of space to generate the form of a skyscraper whose crisp telescoped shape was suggestive of contained power. Fortuitously, these setback skyscrapers recalled the step pyramids of the ancient Maya, which were then receiving their first systematic study. Pursuing this logic to its incongruous conclusion, some architects draped their skyscrapers in angular neo-Mayan ornament, whch was a charming decorative fad of the 1920s.

building was required to step back a certain number of feet (depending on the width of the street below); only on one quarter of its footprint could it rise without constraint. The result was the characteristic chiseled silhouette of the modern skyscraper [195]. Here was an absolutely new architectural form, every bit as distinctive as the Colonial saltbox and, as with the saltbox, the skycraper's form was not the product of conscious artistic invention but of adaptation to necessity. Its forceful and animated contour was nothing more than hard-earned armistice line between the appetites of real estate and the constraints of legislation.

There was no question that the setback skyscraper was modern, but it was of a different order of modernism than that developed at the Bauhaus in Germany, the progressive school of design founded by Walter Gropius in 1919. At the Bauhaus, modernism was conducted as a theoretical and experimental enterprise, which applied rational analysis to such problems as the modern demand for mass-produced housing. But the modernism of America's skyscrapers was empirical, produced by the mammoth forces of real-estate speculation and the need for corporations to distinguish themselves from one another. It was an organic and uncoordinated modernism—a modernism that was without manifesto or program.

There are two variants of modernism, the theoretical and the empirical, and they had an opportunity to scrimmage in 1922. In that year, the *Chicago Tribune* newspaper sponsored an international competition for designs for "the most beautiful and the most distinguished office building in the world." A total of 263 submissions arrived, some by the leading modernists of Europe, including Gropius, Eliel Saarinen, Bruno Taut, and Adolph Loos. The American competitors, long inured to the needs of commercial representation, typically submitted overwrought historical pastiches, hoping they would prove eye-catching. The European entries were more consciously modern but lacked the aggressive imagery an American corporate client required. But the *Tribune* preferred swagger to modernism, and the European

luminaries were snubbed [196 and 197]. In the end, John Mead Howells and Raymond Hood won with their quirky neo-Gothic project, a distant offshoot of the Woolworth Building.

Saarinen's design, though unbuilt, was fruitful. The way its carefully modulated setbacks concentrated and focused its energies was a revelation to American architects. Louis Sullivan, with only months to live, put aside his customary petulance to praise it as "some titanic seed, planted deep in the earth." Even Raymond Hood quietly learned from Saarinen. His American Radiator Building in New York, built two years later, was a deliberate and subtle development of the *Tribune* project. He first beveled its corners so that it appeared as a muscular shaft in space, rather than a planar facade. Then he chose black brick, highlighted in gold, so that both the walls and the voids of the windows would read as a continuous black surface, and the building would not seem a spindly cage of piers, interrupted and weakened by its window openings. Finally, he shaped and sculpted the building's crown, giving it a supple plasticity that provided a deeply satisfying resolution to the architectural tensions below. It even looked like an abstracted radiator, a bonus for a building that served as a corporate symbol. This was not lost on Georgia O'Keeffe, who painted it as a great living furnace, glowering ominously in the night [198].

The American Radiator Building is neither Gothic nor Beaux-Arts, although it has elements of both. For want of a better term, it has been classified as Art Deco, a name derived from the influential "Exposition Internationale des Arts Décoratifs et Industriels Modernes." This was a Paris exhibition of 1925 devoted to sumptuous luxury wares such as jewelry and furniture; in the United States the term has been assigned to the commercial modernism of 1920s and 1930 architecture, which is distinguished by its geometric ornament and its abstracted use of industrial or mechanical motifs—such as streamlining, the use of parallel flutes and reeds, and turbine or enginelike forms. As a commercial language, it found its widest use in office towers, restaurants, and movie theaters, but almost never in civic commissions, where the demands of formality still mandated the three-piece suit of classicism.

196 (top) **Eliel Saarinen**, and 197 (bottom) **Walter Gropius** and **Adolf Meyer**, Competition Entry for the *Chicago Tribune*, Chicago, 1922. The design of the *Chicago Tribune*'s new headquarters was chosen in one of the most celebrated contests of the century. The most progressive entries came from the circle around the Bauhaus, including the joint entry of Walter Gropius and Adolf Meyer. A brilliant study of rectilinear abstraction, its flat roof, modular grid, and free play of cantilevered balconies were reminiscent of Mondrian's disciplined geometric paintings. Oddly, only one European exploited the possibilities of the American setback: the Finnish architect Eliel Saarinen (1873–1950), whose splendidly tapered design won second prize. Buoyed by his near victory, he came to the United States where he helped found the Cranbrook Academy of Art in Michigan, introducing principles of modern design that were similar to those of the Bauhaus.

198 **Georgia O'Keeffe**, *Radiator Building—Night, New York, 1927*, 1927. Whether painting flowers, cattle skulls, or skyscrapers, Georgia O'Keeffe invariably employed the same technique: she enlarged her subject until it filled the picture plane, making it frontal and monumental, charging it with a mystic force. Her *Radiator Building—Night, New York, 1927* treats the building reverently, as a kind of sublimated altar of modernity, which is much how Wood likely regarded it.

Unlike other architectural styles, such as the Gothic Revival or Bauhaus modernism, Art Deco produced virtually no literature or theory. But then, neither did the short skirts or bobbed haircuts of the 1920s. Each belonged to the world of fashion, where change and oscillation are always the law, and well-timed novelty is always justification enough. Art Deco was a fashionable novelty, therefore, but like the short skirts of the Flappers, it was associated in the public mind with a new and liberated spirit of the age, and a rather delicious sense of rule-breaking. In fact, since the country was then engaged in stubbornly defying the alcohol ban of Prohibition (1919–33), it may be said that the entire decade was an exercise in collective and joyous rule-breaking. Of course, this was all sustained by unparalleled economic prosperity, and when it came to an end in 1929, the sense of mad glee that runs like an electric charge through the art of the Roaring Twenties vanished instantly with it.

Chapter 8   The Rise of Formalism

On October 29, 1929, the day known as "Black Tuesday" in American history, the stock market plummeted violently in value. Investors who had been buying to the limits of their credit suddenly found their margins eliminated, and were force to dump their holdings; as they did so, stock values plunged further. Within days came the foreclosures as each defaulting business, bound to others by a chain of debts and loans, dragged its neighbor into the abyss. The process would take years to reach its full extent but well before then the confidence and optimism of the Roaring Twenties had evaporated—and with it the prestige of capitalism. Earlier panics and bank runs had discredited politicians or specific bankers but the Great Depression sullied the image of American business as a whole. Unlike previous depressions, this was a crisis not just of subsistence but of identity—and therefore of art.

With the exception of banking, the Depression ravaged no institution so thoroughly as architecture. At once there came a violent, stupefying contraction in building activity. One example from T. E. Tallmadge's *Story of Architecture in America* (1936) shows its magnitude. In 1927 the city of Chicago approved 12,025 building permits, for a total value of nearly $353,000,000. In 1932 the figure was only 467 permits, valued at $4,000,000—barely one percent of the pre-Depression activity. The figures for New York are similar. The Empire State Building, begun in 1929 and finished in 1931, was the end of the line. By then most architects were unemployed. The whole world of twenties eclecticism, of faience-tiled movie palaces, neo-Mediterranean villas, and streamlined *moderne* stores, had vanished, along with the capitalist patronage that had sustained them.

As private and commercial patronage stagnated, the state became by default the principal patron of architecture. Instead of skyscrapers, the most important commissions were for public buildings, such as post offices, schools, and hospitals. These were

199 **Mark Rothko**, *No. 9 (Dark over Light Earth/ Violet and Yellow in Rose)*, 1954. Rothko wanted paintings like this to arouse the highest spiritual exaltation: "The people who weep before my pictures are having the same religious experience I had when I painted them. And if you ... are moved only by their color relationships, then you miss the point."

200 **Paul Cret**, Federal Reserve Bank, Washington, D.C., 1935. The stripped classicism of the 1930s is visible in this building, where the marble cladding is quite obviously a veneer applied to a steel frame. Born in France, Cret taught at the University of Pennsylvania, which he made the leading center of Beaux-Arts classicism in America. His numerous banks, museums, and public libraries represented the pinnacle of civic elegance during the 1920s and 1930s. Ironically, his work was later disparaged for its resemblance to Nazi architecture.

201 Public Works Administration, Williamsburg Houses, Brooklyn, New York, 1938. A pioneering social housing development that followed the "tower in the park" image beloved of European modernists: twenty-three acres were obliterated to create four large super-blocks, oriented toward the sun rather than the city grid. The flat concrete roofs and austere buff brick walls were typical of the International Style.

built in that late and spare version Beaux-Arts style sometimes called stripped classicism [200]. But the most revolutionary building type was the enlightened social housing project. Although perhaps the central preoccupation of European modernism during the 1920s, it had received little notice in laissez-faire America, where housing had been left to private development. This now changed, and the first government-sponsored housing projects were undertaken by the Public Works Administration. Even skyscraper architects like Richmond Shreve and William Lescaze, authors respectively of the Empire State Building and the P.S.F.S. Building, were happy to collaborate on a project like the Williamsburg Houses [201].

In many ways, the American architectural landscape now recalled that of Europe in the years after World War I, modernism's formative decade. European modernism had then seemed remote from American concerns but the Depression gave it instant relevance and urgency, and its stature soared. Timing was fortuitous. In 1933 the Bauhaus, Germany's modernist school of design, was closed by the Nazis, and within a few years its key figures made their way to the United States. Walter Gropius became head of Harvard University's Graduate School of Design,

202 Howe & Lescaze, P.S.F.S. (Philadelphia Saving Fund Society) Building, Philadelphia, 1929–32. With its cantilevered upper stories and the dynamic interplay of horizontal windows and vertical piers, the P.S.F.S. Building was America's first skyscraper in the International Style. But it was also a commercial building, a bank run by Philadelphia Quakers, and it bluntly acknowledged this fact in a way that satisfied both the demands of modernism and of Quaker plain-speaking. Instead of the typical sculpted crown, Howe and Lescaze capped it with a large electric sign, the first building to terminate in a graphic logo.

which he remade on Bauhaus lines, and Ludwig Mies van der Rohe supervised architecture at the influential Illinois Institute of Technology (IIT). Other architecture programs followed suit, and by the 1940s all of America's major schools of architecture had systematically purged their faculty of their Beaux-Arts teachers.

Even before the arrival of the Bauhaus men, Americans had begun to turn for leadership to the new European modernism. In 1932 it was the subject of a major exhibition at the Museum of Modern Art, curated by Henry Russell Hitchcock and Philip Johnson. Hitchcock and Johnson identified its principles: "a concern with volume as opposed to mass and solidity, regularity as opposed to axial symmetry, and the proscription of 'arbitrary applied decoration.'" Drawing on a wide variety of recent German, Dutch, and French buildings, they showed how these principles were embodied in the progressive architecture of postwar Europe. Here Hitchcock and Johnson made their

provincial vantage point into an asset. Like the hero of Thomas Cole's *Architect's Dream* [89], who was free to use any style without regard to its national origin, they too could view the modern architecture of Germany, Holland, and France with detached impartiality, able to draw on the whole of it at will. In recognition of the movement's collective and international character, they titled their catalog *The International Style*, a term that quickly passed into common use.

Only a few American buildings made the catalog. The P.S.F.S. Building in Philadelphia did, satisfying the authors' strict criteria; but the delightful Chrysler Building was snubbed, as were all other Art Deco towers [202 and 203]. For such baubles, Hitchcock and Johnson had only contempt. Instead of exalting American sophistication and might, and shaping the modern skyline, these buildings were vulgar acts by vulgar clients—nothing more. In his preface to the catalog, Alfred H. Barr, who had founded the museum in 1929, did not even try to mask his scorn: "We are asked to take seriously the architectural taste of real

estate speculators, renting agents, and mortgage brokers."
Of course it was easy to scoff at capitalism in 1932 when it lay
prostrate. Only after their owners were penniless did the jaunty
forms of Art Deco skyscrapers start to look ludicrous [204]. The
Empire State Building was discredited not by the fanciful zeppelin
mooring mast on its summit but by the apple vendors huddling
around its base.

The trough of the Great Depression came in 1932, when
unemployment neared thirty percent—*One-Third of A Nation*,
as the title of a contemporary Broadway play put it. But if the
Depression had discredited Big Business, it tended to discredit
modern art as well. Modernism, like the Aesthetic Movement
from which it emerged, had always been hostile to narrative and
didactic content; it tolerated no agenda for art beyond form itself.
As the misery of the Depression deepened, this aloof stance
seemed a kind of abdication of moral responsibility. To make a

203 **William van Alen**, Chrysler
Building, New York, 1928–30.
In America's competitive
architectural culture, buildings
regularly try to top one another
but the Chrysler Building is the
only one to have done it literally.
William van Alen designed it to
be the tallest building in the world,
a title for which the Bank of
Manhattan was simultaneously
vying. His initial design showed a
height of 925 feet (281 meters), but
once its competitor was finished at
a slightly greater height, van Alen
boldly extended the retractable
spire that had been concealed in
the dome, rising to a final height
of 1,048 feet (319.4 meters).

204 Queensbridge Houses
Project, Queens, New York,
1939–40. A study of photographic
manipulation to promote this
47-acre development with over
11,000 residents. Its merits are
displayed visually: the rational
geometry of modern architecture
is contrasted with the ludicrous
visual disorder of skyscrapers, and
instead of exciting forms against
the skyline, there is a jumble of
flailing gestures. The implication
is that skyscrapers attract air
pollution whereas progressive
housing blocks repel it.

205 **John Steuart Curry**, *Tornado over Kansas*, 1929. John Steuart Curry depicted the humble chapters of life of the prairie, such as hogs trampling a snake or a full-immersion public baptism, in order to show its vitality as well as its perils. *Tornado over Kansas* shows the desperate race for the storm cellar, and was evidently the inspiration for the famous tornado scene in the 1939 film, *The Wizard of Oz*.

purely abstract painting in the mid-1930s, an era of bread lines and soup kitchens, evoked Marie-Antoinette's call to "let them eat cake" in the French Revolution. It suggested a sublime disregard for the spirit of the age—and to express the spirit of the age, after all, had been the challenge of modernism since its inception.

While a few stalwarts clung to abstraction, most artists were swept up in the emphatic turn toward realism. There they fell into one of two factions, the Social Realists and the Regionalists (known also as the American Scene painters). It is not exactly correct that one was leftist and the other reactionary. True, the Social Realists were to a large extent Communist in their sympathies, but the Regionalists were hardly pro-business; instead, suspicious of banks and of the city in general, they imagined an America before the rise of the cities and corporations during the Gilded Age. It is better to say that the two schools represent the urban and rural versions of the same sentiment: both strongly anti-capitalist, both of them imagining cooperative alternatives to the failed economic system. And both took part in the same progressive causes, making art for the labor movement and for the anti-lynching crusade.

The Regionalists were a decentralized rural movement, their principal figures dispersed across the Midwest: Thomas Hart Benton in Missouri, Grant Wood in Iowa, and John Steuart Curry in Kansas [205]. Although their subject matter was largely rural, they objected vehemently to the charge that they were

233

propagandists of farm life. Wood, their chief spokesman, argued that they only painted those subjects that aroused their strongest and deepest emotions. Since one's strongest impressions are formed in childhood, it was inevitable that they painted scenes of their own environment [206].

Though painting in the provinces, the Regionalists were hardly provincials. Benton, for example, had impeccably modernist credentials. From 1908 to 1911, he had studied with modernist teachers in Paris where he befriended Stanton Macdonald-Wright and tried his hand at Synchromism. But he confessed that "I just couldn't paint George Washington as a rainbow," and he soon strayed. The lessons of abstraction, however, stayed with him. Instead of merely placing solid objects in space, in academic fashion, he retained the Synchromist habit of charging the entire surface of the canvas with pictorial energy. Every object upon the picture plane, from earth to clouds, seems possessed by a collective rubberiness, as if pulsating with latent force [207]. Even in his preliminary studies, he described these forms as abstract diagrams of force and movement. Here Benton was using abstract means to pursue realist ends—a lesson that was not lost on his chief assistant at the time, Jackson Pollock.

The Regionalists were essentially apolitical and regarded politics with bemused, cynical detachment. The Social Realists, on the other hand, were thoroughly political. They soaked up their radicalism from their surroundings, the ravaged cities of Depression America, with their concentrated unemployment and large immigrant populations. Some were themselves immigrants from Eastern Europe, such as Isaac, Moses, and Raphael Soyer. Others, like Ben Shahn (who in 1932 depicted the execution of the anarchists Sacco and Vanzetti as a kind of secular martyrdom), were the children of immigrants.

For most leftist artists, however, there was little explicitly leftist art to serve as inspiration. Mexico was the great exception. There a spirited school of mural painting flourished in the wake of Mexico's recent revolution. At its center was the dashing trio of Diego Rivera, José Orozco, and David Alfaro Siquieros, with their vividly colored and rather furiously painted monumental peasant figures. All three received commissions in the United States. Most significant was Rivera's 63-foot (19.2-meter) mural for the RCA Building in Rockefeller Center (1933), for which he was assigned the impossible title "Man at the Crossroads Looking with Hope and High Vision to the Choosing of a New and Better Future."

There Rivera overplayed his hand: confident of Rockefeller family support, he gave a prominent place to a reverential portrait of Lenin. Even worse were the microbes that hovered over the heads of card-playing debutantes, but which proved to be enormous syphilis and gonorrhea bacilli—not the allegory of medical progress originally envisioned but an allegory of the sickness of capitalist society. The appalled Rockefellers paid Rivera off and had the work destroyed.

As the decade wore on, politics and art intermingled ever more intimately. In 1935 Stalin launched the Popular Front, the Soviet-led campaign to unify all liberal and leftist factions in an international struggle against Nazism and Fascism. Rather than warring against each other, progressive movements should make common cause, and writers and artists should lend their services as well. In the United States, the American Artists' Congress Against War and Fascism was formed, with over 400 members. Because of its centralization and strong party discipline, Communist influence became dominant behind the scenes, with serious consequences for the art. Previously, Cubism and abstraction were regarded as the most progressive tendencies in art; now they were deemed a decadent and bourgeois indulgence. For a progressive artist, the only acceptable style was that which promoted world revolution: Social Realism. (In the Soviet Union, where the style was compulsory since 1934, it was known as Socialist Realism.)

In Social Realism the class struggle was presented in graphic terms and its subjects were conventions of Marxist doctrine: the heroism of the working class, the exploitation of the capitalist, the violence of its strike-breakers and police, the debauchery and degeneration of the idle rich. It did little to pioneer artistic technique, for its generating impulse was political rather than aesthetic; technically, much of it recalled the Ashcan School. At its best, it poignantly evoked the dispiritedness of Depression-era America [208]. But it frequently turned shrill and schematic, and simplified the political moral to the level of a cartoon or a political poster—which in fact it was.

Although most Social Realists affected radical or revolutionary politics, they found their most dependable patron in the United States government. Here too, as with architecture, the government came to dominate patronage. President Roosevelt's New Deal first addressed unemployment among artists in December 1933 when it organized the Public Works of Art

206 **Grant Wood**, *American Gothic*, 1930. Grant Wood's celebrated painting is neither an affectionate tribute nor a cruel lampoon; its strength is its ambiguity. The stiffness of expression and hard-edged drawing (it was painted on board) is reminiscent of early Colonial painting, which enjoyed a patriotic revival during the Depression. But beneath the seemingly careless pose is a rigorous formal structure: the vertical boards of the farmhouse are reprised in the farmer's shirt, while a duplicate of the pitchfork is concealed in the farmer's overalls. The painting was immensely popular, to the distress of its models: Wood's sister and his dentist.

207 **Thomas Hart Benton**, *The Ballad of the Jealous Lover of Lone Green Valley*, 1934. Much like El Greco, Thomas Hart Benton learned to elongate the bodies of his figures, and to make their limbs ripple and undulate eloquently. This painting is a characteristic extravaganza of linear energy: virtually every single line of the composition is stretched and made to revolve around two hubs, the sun to the left and the wheel of color made by the fiddler's bow.

208 **Isaac Soyer**, *Employment Agency*, 1937. Although the Social Realists admired the technique of the Ashcan School, they did not emulate its journalistic detachment and they invested their work with explicit political meaning. *Employment Agency* evokes the hopelessness of the Great Depression, then in its eighth year. Like much of Social Realist art, it is a protest poster that requires no caption.

Project, hiring nearly 4,000 artists to produce works of art for the federal government. Two years later the program was reorganized as the Federal Art Project of the WPA (Works Progress Administration). Although other branches of the government commissioned art—particularly the Treasury Department, which supervised all federal building projects—the term WPA came to be applied generically to all painting and sculpture in the public buildings of the 1930s, regardless of its origin.

The WPA employed many of the future luminaries of postwar art, among them Jackson Pollock, Willem De Kooning, and Mark Rothko. Most of their WPA work was in the Social Realist camp, and as a whole was not especially noteworthy. Pollock's involvement was typical; he received a monthly stipend from 1935 to 1943, during which time he painted perhaps fifty canvases for the government (none of which seems to have survived).

In general, the public art of the Depression was emphatically realist, especially its photography. Here the legacy of Precisionism was still strong, with its preference for hard edges and clearly described volumes, but the subject matter was the physical and psychological ordeal of the Depression. Although the photographers' agenda was largely the same as that of the social realists—to document misery as a step toward alleviating it—they could venture where their urban counterparts could not. Dorothea Lange photographed the migrant farmers dislodged by the Dust Bowl, the photographic counterpart to John Steinbeck's *The Grapes of Wrath* (1939). And Ben Shahn, working for the Farm Security Administration, documented the lives of hardscrabble Appalachian dirt farmers.

A few photographers preferred to veil their political commentary in traditional subject matter, as Ansel Adams did. A member of the f/64 group, Adams became the best known of all American photographers, probably because he pegged his career on the same theme that Thomas Cole did, the American wilderness in its most pristine form. For him the Rocky Mountains served as the Adirondacks had a century early, as the physical manifestation of American power, immensity, and goodness. His *Winter Sunrise, Sierra Nevada from Lone Pine, California* (1944) is instantly accessible because all its conventions are those platitudes of the Hudson River School: the exaggerated division into foreground, middleground, and background; the sense of sublime mystery in the dark band at the center; and even the stray note of the corral, which hints at man's intrusion into paradise [209].

209 **Ansel Adams**, *Winter Sunrise, Sierra Nevada from Lone Pine, California*, 1944. Adams's conception of the landscape owed much to the Hudson River School, and he found ways to accomplish photographically what earlier painters had done through draftsmanship. For this photograph he narrowed his aperture and lengthened his exposure time to give his forms their razor-sliced edges, producing the photographic equivalent of Thomas Cole's tight pencil drawing.

Adams remained aloof from politics; like the best artists of his day, he bridled at having to subordinate aesthetic decisions to the dictates of politics. In the end, however, the heyday of Popular Front art was brief. After the Moscow show trials of 1937/38 (the Great Purge of Joseph Stalin's political opponents, whose public trials ended in predetermined guilty verdicts), many were appalled at how the American Artists' Congress parroted Soviet propaganda. The last straw came in 1939 when members were forced to salute Stalin's temporary alliance with Hitler (the Soviet–German nonaggression pact) and the Soviet invasion of Finland. This was too much for all but the most political of painters, and the Popular Front shrank into irrelevance.

There now set in a deep and visceral disgust with political imagery in politics, whether of the left or right. The Utopian admiration for the Soviet Union had vanished, and no political goal seemed worthwhile enough to attach an artistic movement to. This is the great separation of art and agenda—which prevailed from the 1940s into the 1960s, and which set the stage for America's artist leadership after World War II. In place of politics, modernism now turned in a new direction for inspiration: to the human psyche, and to the insights of modern psychology. During the 1930s, the new practices of psychiatry and psychoanalysis achieved widespread acceptance, and Sigmund Freud and Carl Jung became household names.

210 **John B. Flannagan,** *Jonah and the Whale*, 1937. Flannagan was drawn to primal themes, such as birth, captivity, and escape, which were restated in his own physical struggle to liberate the figure from its stone mantel. His *Jonah and the Whale* invites comparison with Ryder's treatment of the same theme [152].

Freud was the first to analyze the subconscious, his collective term for those incessant workings of the mind carried on beneath the level of conscious awareness. These activities were invisible except when they escaped the filters and inhibitions of the conscious mind, to reveal themselves in the form of dreams or slips of the tongue. This insight had swift consequences for European art and literature. In 1924 André Breton conceived Surrealism, in which subconscious impulses would be liberated from "all control exercized by the reason and outside all aesthetic or moral preoccupations." Its principal device was automatism, in which the subject wrote or sketched furiously in a stream-of-consciousness process. This gives to Surrealist art, even when drawn with painstaking realism, the sharp and vivid quality of dreams.

Surrealism gained a foothold in America after the Nazi conquest of France in 1940, which prompted artists such as Yves Tanguy, Roberto Matta, and Joan Miró to seek refuge in New York. There their success was modest. In a country where art was expected to do something, Surrealism offered neither insight nor moral uplift, nor did it even make attractive decoration. Apart from a few followers, such as Peter Blume and Edwin Dickinson, who painted dream landscapes of fragmented forms and melting parts, America produced few true Surrealists. Still, Surrealism preoccupied artists, for it suggested the possibility of an art of complete personal authenticity, which laid bare truths unknown even to the artist himself.

While the theories of Freud stressed the individual subconscious, Jung stressed the collective. His doctrine of racial memory held that millennia of repeated human experience created patterns, or archetypes, that expressed themselves as myths. Though primitive art was farthest from us in time, it was therefore in intimate contact with the most fundamental of life forces; it was not so much primitive as primal. Of course African and Polynesian sculpture had inspired artists since the time of Paul Gauguin and Picasso, but Jung suggested that the very earliest forms of art, recorded as rock carvings, runes, and hieroglyphs, were still somehow contemporary, speaking to us through the common language of racial memory. At a time when Western civilization appeared to have failed in a fundamental way, first with the Depression and then with World War II, there was great willingness to reconsider the primitive and the archaic.

During the 1930s the prestige of primitive art soared. The Museum of Modern Art in New York devoted exhibition after

exhibition to the subject, presenting "African Negro Art" (1935), "Prehistoric Rock Pictures in Europe and Africa" (1937), "Twenty Centuries of Mexican Art" (1940) and "Indian Art of the United States" (1941). Artists rapidly incorporated the lessons of these exhibitions into their work. Sculptor John B. Flannagan (1895–1942), for example, gave his work a deliberate, purposeful archaism [210], choosing the simplest of tools and the most unyielding of materials, such as granite, which he carved directly. The results were crude but had the sense of mysterious power of the strongest Paleolithic sculpture, such the Venus of Willendorf, or of indigenous totems.

After the start of World War II, the lure of the primitive and the archaic grew even stronger. The violence and agony that now engulfed the modern world seemed to defy all artistic response, at least in the terms of traditional realism or Cubist abstraction. Only primitive art seemed to offer something vital. Or so argued Adolph Gottlieb, Mark Rothko, and Barnett Newman, three New Yorkers who earlier dabbled in Social Realism and found it wanting. They began a newspaper and radio campaign in 1943, arguing for the need to reconnect modern art with the world of myth. Gottlieb, their chief spokesman, noted the strong affinities between the modern world and its primitive forebears: "All primitive expression reveals the constant awareness of powerful forces, the immediate presence of terror and fear, a recognition of the brutality of the natural world as well as the eternal insecurities of life. That these feelings are being experienced by many people throughout the world today is an unfortunate fact and to us an art that glosses over or evades these feelings is superficial and meaningless." Gottlieb's own paintings during the early 1940s were in this spirit, cryptic hieroglyphs suffused with a sense of tragedy and suggesting a secret alphabet of forms and symbols [211].

211 **Adolph Gottlieb**, *Pictogenic Fragments*, 1946. "We are for flat forms because they destroy illusion and reveal truth"—so Adolph Gottlieb and Mark Rothko declared in a celebrated 1943 letter to the *New York Times*, a remarkable statement of artistic principles as well as self-justification. They argued that the stenciled figures and hieroglyphs of rock carvings, like modern Cubist painting, respected the integrity of the flat picture plane, which made them kin. *Pictogenic Fragments* uses Gottlieb's characteristic array of stylized faces, eyes, and spirals, inspired by the American Indian imagery that had fascinated him since MoMA's 1941 exhibition.

In contemporary sculpture there was the same turn to mythic and arcane symbols. Isamu Noguchi had trained in the 1920s with Brancusi, one of the luminaries of the Armory Show, who taught him the compact and elegant forms produced by streamlining. But in the 1940s Noguchi also came to realize that the ancients also knew how to work abstractly, and with no less force. His marble *Kouros* took its name from that category of archaic Greek sculpture in which the rigid human figure awakens for the first time into potential motion [212]. In its handsomely rounded contours it is indeed like a kouros, but it also has the sense of a pictogram, seeming to bear an urgent meaning that cannot quite be deciphered.

The turn to primitive art exposed a deep and gnawing dissatisfaction with the alternatives available to the modern artist, either Surrealist or Cubist. The one was too personal, the other too impersonal, for taking the measure of a cataclysm that affected whole peoples and nations. On the other hand, neither artistic mode could be discarded. Surrealism offered the promise of an art of personal authenticity, modern in its psychology if not in its forms. Cubism still represented the most vital and fecund language of modern form, and showed itself capable of infinite further development. The situation remained fluid in 1942, as influential trendsetters like Peggy Guggenheim, the art dealer who ran the Art of this Century Gallery, kept their options open. On one famous occasion, presumably to confound those who looked to her for a sign of coming trends, she wore two different earrings: a Cubist one by Calder and a Surrealist one by Tanguy, as if to say that her own head was torn between the two alternatives.

In Europe, Cubists and Surrealists fell into separate camps: Surrealists inhabited an utterly separate mental world than Cubism, and had nothing but contempt for what they regarded as the polite and fussy business of adjusting line and form into decorous compositions. In New York's ever more cosmopolitan artistic culture, however, the lines were not so dogmatic. American artists had long ago learned to pry styles away from their accompanying ideological baggage, and to combine them at will, even such mutually hostile as Cubism and Surrealism. One of the first to do so was that pioneer of kinetic sculpture, Alexander Calder (1898–1976).

Calder trained with John Sloan and George Luks, and his flair for fluid caricature—"I seemed to have a knack for doing it with a single line"—won him a stint as illustrator for the *Police Gazette*.

From 1926 until 1933, he lived mostly in Paris, where he established cordial relations with the leading abstract artists. His formative experience was a 1930 visit to the studio of Piet Mondrian, an immaculate white cell hung with movable rectangles in the primary colors. Calder "suggested to Mondrian that it would be fun to make these rectangles oscillate." Mondrian thought that that was a bad idea ("No, it is not necessary, my painting is already very fast") but Calder took the idea to its logical limit.

The following year he made his first kinetic sculptures, frail affairs of wires and struts that moved at the turn of a hand crank, or an electric motor. This mechanical movement was too repetitive, however, and a year later he began to suspend his sculptures so that their aluminum panes might swing freely in the wind; when he asked Marcel Duchamp what he should call the new work, he was told *mobiles*. With their nervous quivers and pivots, Calder's mobiles were distinctly comical, and after he started to give their pieces an abstracted kidney shape, they became more so. This particular shape derived from the Surrealist creatures that swam through the canvases of Miró, yet another artist with whom Calder was on friendly terms. Miró and Mondrian were hardly on civil terms but Calder's tolerant mind could embrace both, and he used the biomorphic whimsy of the one to relax the faceted geometry of the other [213].

Another who navigated between Surrealism and Cubism was the painter Arshile Gorky, a figure of tragedy. Gorky was born in Turkish Armenia, where he barely survived the massacres of 1918, fleeing on a long trek during which his mother perished. Making his way to the United States, he acquired the immigrant's elastic sense of identity. Virtually everything about him was invented, including his name (he was born Vosdanig Manoog Adoian) and purported study with Picasso. The same fluency is evident in his stylistic shifts, as he lunged from the Cubism of Picasso to the Surrealism of Miró. He liked to flaunt his virtuosity, and at a time when most WPA murals were done in a Social Realist manner, his was an unusual essay in Cubism. This was a cycle for the Newark, New Jersey airport on the theme of aviation, for which he found a kind of readymade Cubist collage in the abstract shapes of wings, rudders, and airelons.

But Cubism, with its tight geometric lattice of forms, was too emotionally cold an artistic medium for Gorky. In the early 1940s he devised his own personal language in which biomorphic shapes, sporting tufted crests, and lacy tendrils, swim through a kind of

213 **Alexander Calder**, *Yucca*, 1941. After developing the hanging mobile, Alexander Calder developed the earthbound *stabile*, exchanging monumentality for movability, although they retained the quivering sense of line of his early pen sketches, as in *Yucca*. During the final decades of his life, the stabiles grew to colossal dimensions and were widely used as outdoor civic sculpture.

primordial ooze [214]. These whimsical creatures were fished from out of his own subconscious, in Surrealist fashion, but they also showed a strong formal organization: large and boldly colored shapes rested on the picture plane, and the flatness was only occasionally disturbed by a discrete cast shadow or a hint of modeling. One can view it either as a sinuous variant of Cubism or as a formally ordered Surrealism, but in either case, Gorky had found a way of making intense private feeling into strong and arresting form.

Gorky's dilemma—how to reconcile Cubist abstraction with the psychological insights of Surrealism—was the central question of American art in the early 1940s. Painters like Jackson Pollock and Willem De Kooning were struggling along the same lines. By the time they achieved a fully resolved synthesis, some time around 1948, New York had displaced Paris as the world's most vital artistic center. That this could happen at all—that the provincial and aesthetically indifferent United States should become the center of world art—was in part the accident of the war, and the great shift of artists and artistic energy to New York. But it was also due to the exceptional strength of American criticism in these years, which took the inchoate eclecticism of American modernism and gave it a piercing intellectual rigor. Chief of these was the art critic for *The Nation*, who soon became the chief arbiter of modernist orthodoxy: Clement Greenberg.

Greenberg emerged as an art critic with his pioneering essay in *Partisan Review*, "Avant-Garde and Kitsch" (1939), which introduced into English the German word *kitsch*, meaning vulgar or sentimental art, usually mass-produced. In it he argued that any art that sought to convey any extraneous meaning, any narrative or message, was not art but literature, or kitsch. This was why fine art in both the Nazi and Soviet regimes, despite their opposing ideologies, had degenerated into surprisingly similar political kitsch. Art could only remain art by remaining aloof from politics, and concentrating on the all-important matter, form: "Content is to be dissolved so completely into form that the work of art or literature cannot be reduced in whole or in part to anything not itself." Such was the doctrine of formalism, which for the next three decades, through the 1960s, was the principal idea governing modern art.

Greenberg's formalism insisted that each genre of art was autonomous and had certain specific and characteristic properties: in sculpture, plasticity and volume; in painting, the flatness of the

214 **Arshile Gorky**, *The Liver is the Cock's Comb*, 1944. This is Gorky's lush and sensuous depiction of joyous personal fulfillment, perhaps erotic. His own life, which began and ended in tragedy, denied him that fulfillment. In 1948, having been abandoned by his wife, losing his studio in a fire, and breaking his neck in an automobile crash, he killed himself—just at the moment when his Cubist–Surrealist amalgam was becoming the dominant force in American painting.

picture plane. The artist should aspire to assert those properties; the painter, for example, must shun all spatial illusion, anything that might make the canvas into a window. Here Greenberg was popularizing ideas absorbed from Hans Hofmann, the European modernist whose painting classes he attended and who was his principal teacher about the language and nature of paint.

Although Greenberg rejected all political content in art, his formalism was nonetheless strongly tinctured by his youthful flirtation with Trotskyism and Marxism. From Marxism came his dogmatism, his vocabulary of objectivity, and his appeal to historical inevitability—the idea that history proceeds according to certain imperative laws, which one is bound to follow. To resist historical inevitability made one a reactionary, whether of the political or aesthetic persuasion. Such a neat division into progressives and reactionaries was a commonplace in leftist politics, but Greenberg made it a principle criteria for judging art and artists.

Greenberg declared that historical inevitability was on the side of abstraction, not Surrealism, which he mocked as a "confusion of literature with painting." (Famous for his hot temper and fisticuffs, he once protested that he "only beat up Surrealists.") But he also felt that Surrealism had been a necessary historical phase, which had helped show how the full force of the artist's creativity must be released. Only abstraction, however, was free of any narrative content that might be corrupted by entanglement with politics. Such were Greenberg's theoretical demands, which seemed to be fulfilled in the sudden, startling appearance of Jackson Pollock.

Pollock was a pupil of Thomas Hart Benton, with whom he spent five years, and whose influence he never fully shook off. In artistic terms, he was a late bloomer. He had passed through the phases of 1930s art, taking inspiration variously from regionalism, Cubism, the Mexican muralists, and the myth-making art of Gottlieb and Rothko. He later disavowed this work, including his studies for the WPA, and he seems to have destroyed most of it. In his restless quest to stake out his artistic identity, Pollock recalled Gorky, another self-invented figure with a troubled, itinerant youth. He too, like Gorky, made much of his childhood experiences; during a stint in the Southwest he claimed to have watched American Indians painting with colored sand. Here Pollock replayed the scenario of Benjamin West, who also boasted of having been taught to mix paint by Indians—a claim that put him in contact with the primal sources of art, rather than its pale and over-refined academic products.

Around 1938, while undergoing psychoanalysis and suffering from incipient alcoholism, Pollock began to experiment with Surrealism and with Jungian archetypes. Automatism let him pour out his personal anguish in a way that none of his other artistic modes had allowed, and his drawings and paintings soon overflowed with wolves, snarling animal heads, moons, knives— mythical symbols of the sort that Gottlieb had proposed [215]. Pollock was by temperament more a draftsman than a painter, and he put his force into his lines, first imitating the swinging curves of Benton's rubber-limbed figures and then becoming ever more agitated and explosive—and abstract. By 1943, when Peggy Guggenheim commissioned a major mural from him, his paintings no longer contained any recognizable subjects at all. Already Greenberg was calling his work "the strongest abstract paintings I have yet seen by an American."

Pollock's breakthrough came in 1947, when he first began to pour and drip paint directly on to the unsized canvas. He placed it on the floor of his Long Island studio, attacking from all sides so that there was no longer any top or bottom, and stomping across it so that cigarette butts and bits of broken glass worked their way into the surface. Paint was applied in a way that celebrated its fluid

215 **Jackson Pollock**, *Untitled (Naked Man with Knife)*, c. 1938–41. This shows Pollock as he was moving from Benton's Social Realism in the direction of a high-strung, intensely personal expressionism, haunted by tormented, struggling figures and cryptic symbols. These recognizable objects gradually faded from the work but the turmoil remained constant.

and viscous nature, either flung from the tip of a brush, leaving an arc of droplets and splatters, or poured it directly from the can, so that it puddled in long thick rivulets.

Pollock did not invent the technique of pouring paint. Hans Hofmann had been doing this perhaps as early as 1940, but only as a way of exploring the Surrealist's "happy accident," not as the ordering principle for an entire painting. Pollock's drip, however, was both technique and subject matter [216]; it liberated the creative act from the filter and censorship of the conscious mind, and gave it the absolute psychological freedom that the Surrealists had desired. Before Pollock, the making of a painting could be divided cleanly into first conception and then the process of execution—that is, into thought and action. But now conception and execution were joined so closely that they were almost simultaneous, as in an improvised dance.

The new painting was given several names, depending on which aspect was at issue. In geographic terms, it was the New York School. Greenberg, always conscious of artistic pedigree, said it was "abstract expressionism," which acknowledged its twin roots in Cubist abstraction and early twentieth-century Expressionism. Others, noticing that the canvas no longer distinguished between figure and ground, called it an "all-over painting." The painters themselves squirmed at these titles and De Kooning warned, "it is disastrous to name ourselves."

The most durable name, however, came from the critic Harold Rosenberg's "The American Action Painters" (1952), which not only coined the term Action Painting but provided its most memorable definition:

At a certain moment the canvas began to appear to one American painter after another as an arena in which to act—rather than as a space in which to reproduce, redesign, analyze, or "express" an object, actual or imagined. What was to go on the canvas was not a picture but an event.

Obviously Rosenberg was describing Pollock at work—as documented by the 500-odd photographs taken by Hans Namuth in the summer of 1950. These showed Pollock stalking and

216 **Jackson Pollock**, *Autumn Rhythm: No. 30, 1950*, 1950. This 17-foot- (5.1-meter-) long work, the culmination of his drip method, was his largest and most ambitious canvas. The painting began as a lacy scaffolding of black lines, which he built up in successive layers of muted browns and whites. The scale of the arcs and loops is established by Pollock in long fluid sweeps that carried his arm through its entire range of motion, so that the painting preserved a vivid sense of a fully engaged body, not just the carefully controlled actions of wrist and fingers.

brooding over the canvas as an existentialist poet, and then hurtling himself into action. They made clear the intimately personal quality of his canvases, which recorded his inner turbulence as faithfully as a seismograph vibrating with the force of a distant tremor. Rosenberg was as much interested in Pollock's exalted state of being as the art that issued from it, possibly more so. It was pointed out at the time that his analysis, although a rollicking account of the new art as a whole, provided no criteria for distinguishing between a good action painting from a bad. All this had far-reaching and unintended ramifications. By subordinating the picture to the event (a few years later he would have used the word Happening), he unwittingly summarized the central premise of performance art.

Pollock brought about the most thorough revision of the public image of the artist since Whistler. Instead of playing the wit and dandy, Pollock struck a pose of surly delinquency, sporting cowboy boots, a T-shirt, and the ubiquitous cigarette (airbrushed out of the commemorative stamp recently issued to honor him). The surliness was much like that of young Marlon Brando and James Dean, those intense movie stars who were Pollock's contemporaries. Brando and Dean practiced Method Acting, which sought to tap directly into pent-up reserves of emotion from earlier traumas, and to harness them for scenes where the same feeling was required. Rather than feigning an emotion, the actor would attempt to induce it. As with Pollock, the caliber of the performance was directly linked to the sincerity of the felt emotion and it was not always evident to the viewer if one was judging the art or the emotion. Today, half a century after the fact, this appeal to emotional authenticity seems quaint, but at an age still dazzled by the discovery of the subconscious, it was deliciously revolutionary.

Pollock's rivals were affected by his sudden celebrity and they responded to it in different ways. The most successful were those who developed strongly marked personal styles—mannerisms—within the parameters of Abstract Expressionism: the choppy and mauled figures of De Kooning, the monumental black-on-white scribbles of Kline, the iridescent color planes of Rothko. This deliberate cultivation of idiosyncratic, instantly recognizable styles is not unlike that which advertisers call branding, the differentiation of products to aid consumer recognition.

The trademark of Willem De Kooning (1904–97) was the human figure, especially (but not exclusively) women. De Kooning was born in Holland and in 1926 he emigrated illegally to New York, where he shared a studio for a time with Gorky. Here he came under the influence of Surrealism, although like most of his contemporaries he cribbed from Picasso as well. By 1948 he achieved his mature style and there followed a series of increasingly agitated portraits of women, which brought him rapid fame [217]. In them, as with Pollock, mutually exclusive visual languages were reconciled: Surrealist passages of descriptive drawing, like the cartoon faces of his women, alternate with flat Cubist planes of unmodeled color, such as those of the shoulders and the breasts. De Kooning brought off this extraordinary fusion by strength of his unifying surface treatment, an outrageously thick and soupy mass of paint, sometimes runny and sometimes clotted. For this extraordinary finish he was unwilling

217 **Willem De Kooning**, *Woman I*, 1950–52. Willem De Kooning insisted that "flesh was the reason why oil painting was developed," although the flesh in his *Woman* series is rather monstrous. *Woman II* is a leering temptress, a modern Gorgon's head under a mane of yellow hair and wearing what appears to be a cocktail dress and a hat—an image of sexual attraction and revulsion made all the more unsettling by the discordant fillips of color that play across the surface of the canvas.

218 **Franz Kline**, *New York, N.Y.,* 1953. Kline, like Pollock, was a draftsman at heart and he conceived his paintings in terms of a rugged frame of lines, which convey the idea of force, pressure, and resistance. *New York* offers an abstract salute to modern city life in its imagery of ladders, girders, and angular buttresses.

or unable to provide any theoretical justification, merely that "I like a nice, juicy, greasy surface."

The New York School was thoroughly urban in sensibility, and free of pastoral or picturesque qualities. Its anxieties and forces were those of the city: of traffic and industry, of electricity and rasping noise, of the constant friction of contact with strangers. The urban pulse and mood is the subject matter of Franz Kline (1910–62), whose scratchy, forceful lines look like a small detail of a Pollock painting magnified to colossal size. And so in a sense they were; in 1949, Willem De Kooning lent Kline a projector in order to show enlarged images of his pen and ink drawings on the wall. The magnification isolated stray passages of drawing, detaching them from their descriptive function, even as it coarsened the line quality. What had been a dainty arabesque revealed itself when enlarged to have the quality of a mighty buttress. This chance discovery gave Kline his pictorial language: a spare and incisive structure of black lines on a white ground (which he also painted) that would recall an inked Chinese character were it not so tense and belligerent [218].

If Kline's was an art of line, that of Mark Rothko (1903–70) was one of color. He had the same mongrel pedigree of his artistic generation: Cubism and Social Realism in the 1930s, Surrealism in the 1940s. In between came his brief immersion in mythic art with Gottlieb. The end product of the cross-fertilization was a clarified and monumental abstraction, in which a few shimmering planes of color float in space, divided by strips of another color [199]. The edges are left feathery and indistinct, so that the planes do not lie in the same plane but overlap in space, ambiguously advancing and receding. It is noteworthy that his paintings are unsatisfactory in reproduction, which Rothko would have taken as a compliment.

The more a painting can be appreciated from a black and white photograph, the more it tends toward illustration, a story told in lines and symbols; Rothko's effectiveness, however, was entirely a matter of scale and precise color value. The visual experience of his paintings was not transferable to other media, which fulfilled the formalist demand that each genre of art should embrace the conditions of its own making.

For all their differences—De Kooning's dissected figures, Kline's pugilistic jabs of line, Rothko's pools of color—the painters of the New York School had much in common. Like Pollock, they cultivated a large and monumental art, impossible to be taken in, needing to be experienced at a proximity that made it loom physically. There was also an interest in an "all-over" treatment of the entire picture plane, and a love of jagged visceral forms. Above all, there was a sense that spontaneity and intuition counted for more than calculation. In this, their minds were still half-Surrealist. Even in sculpture, an architectonic medium where spontaneous creation was difficult, artists like David Smith (1906–65) aspired to the psychological liberation of Surrealism. In appropriately Surrealistic fashion, his *Hudson River Landscape* began with an accidental ink spill [219].

219 **David Smith**, *Hudson River Landscape*, 1951. This work grew out of David Smith's weekly railroad trips between Albany and Poughkeepsie, during which he constantly sketched the river: "While drawing, I shook a bottle of India ink and it flew over my hand. It looked like my river landscape. I placed my hand on paper. From the images that remained, I traveled with the landscape, drawing other landscapes and their objects, with additions, deductions, directives, which flashed unrecognized into the drawing, elements of which are in the sculpture."

Smith shows how far New York School artists had progressed in their effort to make serious and lasting art out of the haphazard urges and impulses of the subconscious, Surrealism's raw material. But he also shows the limits of Surrealism, at which one after another of his generation arrived sooner or later. Surrealism may have been psychologically authentic, but aesthetic quality and authenticity were not quite the same thing. Unless refined by a process of conscious control, subconscious impulses might remain at the level of the self-indulgent or trivial. One way to avoid this was to work serially, treating the same theme again and again in an extended campaign of work, in which the initial impulse was disciplined and ordered, and raised to monumental stature. Perhaps the greatest serial enterprise was Motherwell's *Elegy to the Spanish Republic*, more than 140 canvases on the same theme, produced over the span of two decades.

Robert Motherwell (1915–91) was the most literate and intellectual of the New York School painters, having studied philosophy as a graduate student at Harvard and, later, art history under Meyer Schapiro at Columbia University. He came under the influence of Matta and the Surrealists, and learned the technique of automatism, the source of the abstract fluid shapes that recur in various arrangements throughout his protracted *Elegy to the Spanish Republic* [220]. But the overall tone of the series is strength and simplicity, in which a few bold black limbs dominate the white canvas, expressing the yearning for monumentality that colored the entire New York School.

Nowhere in America was there anything like the concentration and density of the New York art world, giving it an authority and dominance that made other schools, however original or imaginative their work was, into provincial footnotes. To be sure, a distinctive West Coast school was now emerging and flaunting a distinctively western sensibility, more mystic in character and without the urban aggression of the West Tenth Street milieu; its most interesting figures were Mark Tobey and Morris Graves, who practiced in and around Seattle. But this remained an art of talented individuals, practicing mostly in isolation, and without

220 **Robert Motherwell**, *Elegy to the Spanish Republic, LXX*, c. 1961. The swaggering masculine character of Abstract Expressionism was often understood as an explosive expression of male potency but only Robert Motherwell supplied the phallus itself, albeit a defeated and flaccid one. This painting is a forlorn tribute to the leftist republic that was destroyed in the Spanish Civil War.

221 Andrew Wyeth,
Christina's World, 1948. Frequently misunderstood as an image of teenage longing, *Christina's World* actually depicts fifty-five-year-old Christina Olson, paralyzed from the waist down by a degenerative disease. A brilliant composition, its most powerful element is present only by implication: the riveting axis between Christina's upturned head and the distant farmhouse.

the coordinated force of a coherent school. To the main story it was a sidelight.

The triumph of the New York School may have seemed irrevocable but even in 1948, at the very moment when Pollock, De Kooning, and Kline were arriving at their definitive personal styles, there were signs that pictorial realism was still alive. In that year, to the astonishment of many of its supporters, the Museum of Modern Art purchased Andrew Wyeth's bittersweet painting, *Christina's World* [221], a work as far removed from the formalist preoccupations of Abstract Expressionism as can be imagined. Of course, one could argue that the methodical stippling of the work's tempera surface was a kind of "all-over" surface or that its melancholy spatial disorientation expressed psychological modernism, but these would be rationalizations; the truth is, Wyeth's *Christina's World* was realist art. In its assured academic draftsmanship it seemed to repeal even the insights of the Aesthetic Movement, let alone those of Cubism.

The heyday of Abstract Expressionism would last no more than a decade. In retrospect, it is hard to imagine a movement less in keeping with the historic trajectory of American art: it offered no moral instruction or social commentary; it was far removed from the world of solid objects and tangible forms that had constituted the subject matter of most American art; its technique was sensuous and complex, lacking a clear delineation of outlines and edges; above all, it was difficult and challenging, rather than accessible and lucid. In short order, these temporarily ignored values would reassert themselves, massively and irresistibly, in that strange modernist-realist hybrid known as Pop.

Chapter 9   The Fall of Formalism

The high point of formalism came around the year 1950, when its prestige and authority was at its maximum. A decade earlier, it had seemed impossible that the formal insights of Cubism could ever be reconciled with the psychological liberation of Surrealism. But now Gorky, Pollock, and De Kooning had succeeded in amalgamating the two in their painting, and Smith and Calder in their sculpture. The result of their grand synthesis was Abstract Expressionism, a rigorously formal art that had no narrative or moral content, nor any content at all beyond its formal properties. At the same time, a vibrant and fiercely intellectual culture of criticism had come into being to champion formalist art, led by Clement Greenberg, Harold Rosenberg, and Meyer Schapiro, among others. To observers at the time, the triumph of Abstract Expressionism seemed to have epic historical significance, on a par with the Italian Renaissance, a claim that would have been presumptuous except for the general sense that these were epic times in every respect. World War II ended in 1945 with the dropping of the atomic bomb, and in 1949 the immensely more destructive hydrogen bomb was tested. In that year the Cold War between the United States and the Soviet Union began in earnest, and for the next generation the possibility of mutual nuclear annihilation was a constant possibility. In such apocalyptic times it seemed logical that the era's artistic breakthroughs should be equally apocalyptic.

Likewise in architecture; there the success of the International Style seemed similarly freighted with historical meaning. If World War II was the result of the mad nationalism of 1930s Europe, then peace in the postwar world would be achieved by deliberate and dedicated internationalism. It was therefore of great symbolic importance that the United Nations Secretariat (1947–50) in New York be built as an International Style box, designed by an international team that included the American architect Wallace

222 **Frank Lloyd Wright**, Solomon R. Guggenheim Museum, New York, 1956–59. The Guggenheim was the elderly Wright's final monumental rebuke to Mies van der Rohe. Here he countered the remorseless Miesian rectilinearity with a building that had no right angles at all. The consensus at the time—that it was lovely as sculpture and a failure as a building—was summed up in the title of the New York Times's 1959 review of it, "Wright vs. Painting."

K. Harrison, Le Corbusier, Oscar Niemeyer, and others. For a moment, the choice of a flat roof and a steel frame had idealistic, even utopian ramifications.

In many ways, the International Style fulfilled the demand of formalism that each medium must develop in a way that expressed its intrinsic quality. The essential property of a painting was its flatness while that of a building was its manipulation of space, and each suppressed features that masked or contradicted these properties. Just as paintings systematically purged themselves of narrative, perspectival illusionism, and moral instruction, so buildings were to be purged of ornament and historical references. In some ways, however, architecture took a different course than painting. Architecture is a social act, requiring the investment of land and capital, and it needs a client as well as an architect; it is seldom an instrument of purely personal expression. This was especially true of modernism, which, because of its roots in the war-ravaged Europe of the 1920s, professed a sense of collective moral responsibility. Modernism, in its grandest form, aspired to far more than just to make better buildings; it simultaneously pursued three interrelated goals: the reform of architecture, of the city, and of society itself. In this high-minded work of reform there was no place for the existentialist fury of the Abstract Expressionist.

Much of the ideology of European modernism—especially its strongly theoretical and intellectual program, and its association with revolutionary politics—was alien to the American experience. Of course, Americans had long since learned to unburden European movements of their theoretical content, as they once had with the *Rundbogenstil* and with Impressionism. But other elements of modernism were quite congenial to the American spirit. One of these was the eager embrace of new technology and new materials. Another was the durable idea that art and architecture ought to contribute to moral improvement. Here two entirely different sets of ideas, resting on entirely different foundations, converged: the Puritan legacy of supporting art with a didactic mission and the utopian social program of European modernism. Out of this came the intellectual energy for urban renewal, the movement that would transform the character of most American cities between 1945 and 1975, and fill them with social housing projects of European pedigree.

Nonetheless, while the federal government pushed through its great national project of slum clearance and urban renewal,

American society remained fundamentally capitalist and commercial. In fact, in the full swell of postwar prosperity business now reclaimed much of the bluster and confidence lost in the Depression. And far from shunning modernism because of its socialist origins, capitalism made adroit use of it, directing it away from the task of reform toward that of corporate advertising.

In many ways, modernism was an ideal fit for the postwar corporation, which desired an image of efficiency, professionalism, and vaunting technological prowess—qualities that flat roofs, slender steel beams, and pristine glass curtain walls seemed wonderfully suited to convey. They offered an imagery quite different from that of the chiseled setback towers of the 1920s. Those embodied corporate power in terms of heroic sculpture, projecting a strutting, swaggering arrogance [203]. After the calamity of the Depression and the fall of the Robber Barons, however, swagger and arrogance struck precisely the wrong note. Instead of evoking the idiosyncratic taste of an F. W. Woolworth or a Walter Chrysler, the corporate buildings of the 1950s were sleekly impersonal, and projected the collective sobriety of the modern professional boardroom.

Such was the character of Lever House (1950–52) in New York, the first of the great modernist corporate headquarters [223]. The designer was Gordon Bunshaft of Skidmore, Owings & Merrill (SOM), and he neatly turned the New York zoning law on its head. While Hugh Ferriss had capitalized on the sculptural possibilities of the setback, Bunshaft concentrated on the provision that exempted twenty-five percent of the site from any height restriction whatsoever. This produced a twenty-two-story rectangular slab rising from a two-story pedestal, making the design itself a kind of upright lever. Bunshaft's theme was light, not structure: he set his steel columns well behind the wall membrane so that the facade consisted wholly of window elements: blue-green heat-resistant glass, opaque wire glass spandrels, and slim stainless steel mullions—compressed into a thin plane that looks as if it has been sliced with a blade. The windows were inoperable, fastidiously sealing out the gritty air of the city, and required a comprehensive air-conditioning system, much as Wright's Larkin Building (161 and 162).

As novel as Lever House was, within two years it was surpassed by a building placed diagonally across from it on Park Avenue; this was the Seagram Building (1958), the crowning work of Ludwig Mies van der Rohe, and of the International Style in general [224]. Prior to this, Mies van der Rohe had built the Farnsworth House in Plano, Illinois, and a pair of pioneering apartment houses on Lake Shore Drive, Chicago. He also designed the new campus of IIT (Illinois Institute of Technology), for which he conceived 28 buildings between 1941 and 1956. But the Seagram Building stood apart. It took center stage on New York's Park Avenue, and it had behind it enlightened patronage and great personal wealth. It showed what the International Style was capable of, provided there were nearly unlimited resources and an architect as methodical and perfectionist as Mies van der Rohe.

223 **Gordon Bunshaft (Skidmore, Owings & Merrill)**, Lever House, New York, 1950–52. Bauhaus purism enlisted in the merchandizing of soap: the steel skeleton of the Lever House was configured so that the platforms of window-washers could ride along tracks set in its stainless steel mullions—conveying a hygienic cleanliness appropriate to the imagery of a company that made soap and detergent.

The Seagram Building precisely reverses in architecture what Pollock achieved in painting. Pollock had managed to extirpate every bit of content and subject matter from his art so that nothing was left but the purely personal; at the Seagram Building, personal expression is brought to the irreducible minimum. Even the basic composition was the result of a relentless series of calculations: its footprint was mandated at twenty-five percent of the site, which determined an optimum ratio between the elevators and the office space they served; the building then rose to the maximum height that eight banks of elevators could serve, which was thirty-seven stories. (This was not quite enough space,

224 **Ludwig Mies van der Rohe** and **Philip Johnson**, Seagram Building, New York, 1958. "God is in the details," Mies van der Rohe famously proclaimed. One of these details is the way the ground story of the Seagram Building is set back behind its metal frame, since it requires nothing but an elevator lobby. Here the building lifts its curtain wall to show its legs, standing on tiptoe, showing that independence of volume and structure, a cardinal doctrine of the International Style.

as it turned out, and an eight-story wing was incorporated behind the tower, and nicknamed "the bustle.") Within these givens, Mies van der Rohe subjected every aspect of the building to a prolonged process of study, refinement, and clarification, conducted with almost monastic devotion. For him, every successive simplification of the program and form was an improvement—"less is more," as Mies van der Rohe's motto would have it.

The Seagram Building, unlike Lever House, does not conceal its structure behind its skin; on the contrary, it pushes its structure—actually, a facsimile of it—in front of the wall. Here Mies van der Rohe struggled against New York's fire code, which insisted that the steel skeleton be encased within incombustible insulation, where it could not be seen. Instead he affixed a second set of mullions to the face of his building, which served nominally to stiffen the windows but actually fulfilled a more important rhetorical function: to make the hidden engineering comprehensible to the viewer and to establish the rhythmic order that is the essence of every framed building. These mullions were not of mere stainless steel but of oiled bronze, an extravagant material, and their glistening surface counteracted any sense of utilitarian poverty in the building's expression.

For abstract artists who were uneasy with the impulsive caprice of action painting, Mies van der Rohe's quest for purity was appealing. Barnett Newman (1905–70), in particular, responded to the Miesian call to purity. Beginning in 1948 he started to make "zip paintings," in which a single wavy line divided the canvas into precisely calibrated rectangles, proportioned as scrupulously as any Miesian grid [225]. Newman's geometric restraint and self-control made him one of the few Abstract Expressionists whose popularity remained intact in the 1960s, when taste shifted away from personal effusions and toward the discipline of hard-edged painting.

Purity was also the subject of the most celebrated of all Miesian tributes, the Glass House of Philip Johnson. Mies van der Rohe was not registered as an architect in New York, and he required a local collaborator for the Seagram Building. This was Johnson, the historian who in 1932 had coined the term International Style. Since then he had become a late-blooming architect and, because of his social connections and considerable personal wealth, one of the most influential exponents of that style. As a designer, he lacked the monkish dedication and perfectionism of Mies van der

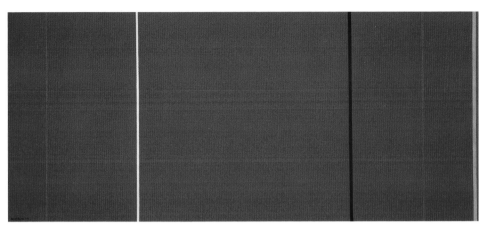

225 **Barnett Newman**, *Vir Heroicus Sublimus*, 1950–51. This is one of Barnett Newman's "zip paintings," organized around a single vertical line, and quivering like a portal about to open on a place of secret knowledge and revelation. Its Latin title means "Man, heroic and sublime," and it recalls that Newman had once joined with Gottlieb and Rothko in their crusade for a mythic, timeless art, dealing with the great themes of birth, life, and death.

Rohe. His work was elegant and suave, but could not be said to aspire to Platonic perfection. On the other hand, he had a rare genius for publicity, and an effortless way of making the International Style palatable to corporate executives. He came to enjoy the patronage of the Rockefeller family, the most important supporters of the Museum of Modern Art, for which he designed a series of additions. In these buildings, modernism lost the last scintilla of its revolutionary origins and became a kind of architectural language of the establishment.

Johnson was in the rare position of being able to act as both patron and architect, and in this capacity made the purest demonstration of the International Style, his Glass House in New Canaan, Connecticut [226]. Mies van der Rohe had pursued the goal of "universal space," the idea that space might flow freely and partition-free beneath a space-frame truss, so that no room would be confined to a function by the straitjacket of its walls. Johnson's house realized the Miesian ideal with a one-story, one-room box of glass, achieving the ultimate in dematerialization and transparency; only the brick core of the bathroom relieved its flagrant exhibitionism. Such a building was the zenith of International Style purity and rigor—but it was also rather funny. After all, the large acreage owned by Johnson guaranteed a measure of privacy that few other clients could match. Here the International Style reached a point of self-consciousness, of almost deliberate self-parody that within a few years would begin to dissolve it.

One should not overstate the importance of the Bauhaus and of European modernism, even during its high water mark of the 1950s. Historians typically devote more attention to architects working from theoretical programs, because it is always easier to write texts if one has texts. Bauhaus modernism was indeed ensconced in the academies, and enjoyed the prestige of institutional and establishment patronage, but much of America remained cheerfully impervious to it, and its social program and intellectual foundation.

Commercial architects might enjoy long profitable careers without ever dipping into modernist ideology. Morris Lapidus (1902–2001) strewed gaudy wiggling hotels across south Florida that were the very antithesis of the Miesian credo of "less is more." Lapidus mischievously entitled his autobiography *Too Much is Never Enough*. His Las Vegas counterpart was Martin Stern, Jr. (1917–2001), who built a practice on the design of casinos, for which his sole credential seems to have been his stint as a Hollywood sketch artist; his visual sources were amusement parks, cinema, and Art Deco, with hardly a whisper of Bauhaus influence. These architects practiced much as America's commercial architects did before the arrival of modernism: using new materials because they were cheaper and making innovative form in order to shout down their neighbors—and not because of any moral imperative. In this they are the true heirs of Frank Furness and Raymond Hood, who happily accepted the commercial nature of American life, and played by its rough rules.

226 Philip Johnson, Glass House, New Canaan, Connecticut, 1949. If "less is more," there could hardly be much less than Philip Johnson's Glass House. It shows the International Style at the cusp, just at the moment when the impulse to transparency and formal purity threatened to tip over into parody. When in residence, Johnson himself preferred to stay in his nearby guest house.

But the strongest resistance to European modernism was offered by Frank Lloyd Wright, the most self-consciously American of architects, who took the triumph of the Bauhaus as a personal affront. In 1932, he founded the Taliesin Fellowship and withdrew somewhat from private practice to concentrate on teaching and writing. When Mies van der Rohe and Gropius came to America three years later, he was 68 years old, but their arrival galvanized him, spurring him to two decades of furious activity—in effect, a second career. Just as Sullivan had once resented America's wholesale capitulation to French classicism at the Chicago Exposition, so Wright protested the similar capitulation to German modernism. His work of the 1930s can be looked at as a magisterial critique of that modernism, in which he turned over one after another of its tenets, and then rejected each out of hand.

If European modernism exploited the possibilities of concrete slabs and steel frames to standardize workers' housing and make them identical, Wright used these same materials to individualize the house. If Europeans sought to revive the city through enlightened social housing projects and through density, he sought to abolish the city by means of single-family houses and dispersal. In 1932 he published *The Disappearing City*, arguing that the automobile had made the traditional city obsolete. In fifteen minutes, he suggested, one could now drive fifteen miles, permitting stores and businesses that once needed to be densely concentrated to sprawl across the landscape. Wright was able to draw the most radical and far-reaching consequences from the automobile, that creation of modernity, because he understood the most traditional and ancient of American cultural patterns. Drawing on a long legacy of anti-urban thought, reaching back to Thoreau and Jefferson, and beyond, he envisioned an entirely new form of decentralized settlement. He called it Broadacre City, although it was hardly a city at all but a kind of continuous suburb, populated at a density of one acre per person.

To build Broadacre City low-cost houses were required and in 1936 Wright made the first of them, the Herbert Jacobs House at Madison, Wisconsin; eventually he would build more than one hundred. The Jacobs House displayed the crouching one-story horizontality of his Prairie Style houses, as well as the bold overhangs; it also compacted the dining and living rooms into a unified social space, centered on the ubiquitous hearth. He called it a Usonian house, invoking his term Usonia, a conflation of the United States of North America and of Utopia.

In his campaign to decentralize, Wright was inadvertently aided by a European modernist. In 1938, the Austrian architect Victor Gruen (1903–80) fled the Nazis and established himself in New York as a commercial architect. In Edina, Minneapolis, he devised the first indoor shopping mall (1952–56), a building type that did more to change the American city than all the urban renewal initiatives of the past half century. Previously, shopping centers had fronted on parking lots but Gruen turned them around to face interior streets, and gave them a roof. These malls have done more than anything to transform America into Broadacre City, where the majority of people now live neither in cities nor farms, but in concentric rings of suburbs, from which they commute to still other suburbs. As might be expected, Wright was not grateful when he saw Gruen's mall: "What is this," he exclaimed, "a railroad station or a bus station?"

While developing his ideas for Broadacre City, Wright designed the finest house of his career, Fallingwater (1935–39). The client was Edgar Kauffman, the owner of a Pittsburgh department store, and the site was Bear Run, Pennsylvania, a secluded mountain setting crossed by a lively waterfall. With his turn-of-the-century Prairie Houses, Wright began his campaign to "destroy the box," and at Fallingwater he completed the process. The Robie House had pried apart the walls and rooms of the traditional house, opening itself to nature like the petals of a flower, but it still dominated its site [163]. At Fallingwater it was the other way around. The house is an improvisation upon the site, oriented diagonally to its 30-foot (9.1-meter) waterfall and culminating in its two cantilevered balconies, set at right angles to one another [227]. Just as Wright's boulder-anchored cantilevers hold the building in physical equilibrium, it is held in visual equilibrium by this tight triangle of forces at its core: the two balconies straining upward and the downward flowing water, forming the hypotenuse of the triangle. This three-dimensional coil of precisely balanced forces gives the house its sense of serene resolution, and anchors what would otherwise read as a centrifugal frenzy of parts.

Wright, certain that he had irrevocably exploded the box, both as form and as idea, was aghast to see it return in its Bauhaus incarnation during the coda to his long career. He railed against the Seagram Building, and all "boxes put up on such skinny legs." This gave his commission for the Guggenheim Museum (planned in 1943 but not begun until 1956) the heightened drama of a

227 **Frank Lloyd Wright**, Fallingwater, Bear Run, Pennsylvania, 1935–39. At the Glass House, nature was tamed and framed as in a picture, but nature and architecture are married so intimately at Fallingwater that one can no longer distinguish between them. Here Frank Lloyd Wright brilliantly summarized a century of American thought about nature and architecture. While he regularly updated his stylistic sources—cribbing here from European modernists (and his pupil, Richard Neutra) for his fluid plan and cascading tiers of balconies—his vision of nature essentially remained that of Downing, Olmsted, and Richardson, with their poetic-mystic reverence for the American landscape.

showdown, in which the champions of International Style modernism and organic architecture squared off in the arena of Manhattan. Wright's concept of organic architecture was always analogical, suggesting that a building might learn the lessons of nature, but at the Guggenheim it literally looked like an organism, a giant snail or nautilus. By using a single continuous form—a tightly coiled spiral—he integrated form and structure so completely that there was no longer any meaningful distinction between them, the same elemental shape providing the floor plan, the physical structure, and the formal composition [222].

Of course, the Guggenheim's ostentatious display of form following function was fraudulent. Wright had made a building that was perversely nonfunctional, in which it was impossible to stand at the proper distance from a work of art. One could only view works from close range or across the rotunda, but never from the middle distance that large Abstract Expressionist work required.

228 **Eero Saarinen**, TWA Airline Terminal at JFK International Airport, New York, 1956. The lessons of Eero Saarinen's training in Paris as a sculptor carried over into his architectural practice, where he designed buildings through models, rather than on paper. The result, in New York's TWA Airline Terminal, was a remarkable fluid plasticity. Such expressionist architecture has less to do with the cool rationality of Mies van der Rohe [224] than the impulsive gestures of the Abstract Expressionists [217].

Even at the time it was recognized as an appalling attack against modern art, but the protests of modern artists seem only to have delighted him. It was a wry curtain call to Wright's career but in the long run his meditations about the city and the suburb were more prophetic, and more influential, although in a far less benign way than he had imagined.

If Wright had shocked New Yorkers by dropping a mighty congealed mass of concrete on to Fifth Avenue, he was only reflecting the general tendency to stress weight and mass in the late 1950s. By this time, Le Corbusier's late work, much of it executed in deliberately coarse concrete (*beton brut*), offered a sculptural and richly tactile alternative to the International Style. Even Walter Gropius was affected by the shift to buildings of strong physical expression, and his own Pan Am Building (1956–62) sported an assertive beveled contour.

This marked the return of architectural expressionism, a strand of early twentieth-century modernism that had been especially vibrant in Germany. Although Expressionism came to be viewed as self-indulgent and arbitrary during the socially preoccupied 1920s and 1930s, it was never fully extinguished, and the triumph of Abstract Expressionist painting restored its stature. By far the most expressionist of American architects was that master of poured concrete, Eero Saarinen (1910–61), the son of Eliel Saarinen. His buildings rose in sweeping gestural arcs, as if Franz Kline had dipped his brush in concrete. At once bold and lyrical, this was a splendidly visceral language but it was not one for office towers, and his most distinctive work was in lively building types that were inherently expressive, like his TWA Airline Terminal in New York [228], his Yale University Hockey Rink, or his Gateway Arch in St. Louis, Missouri.

When Saarinen died, apparently from overwork, his highly idiosyncratic style died with him. More influential was Brutalism, a burly concrete style derived from the New Brutalism of postwar Great Britain. Its leading figure was Paul Rudolph, architect of Yale's forbiddingly corrugated Art and Architecture Building (1959–63). The vocabulary of Brutalism was self-consciously humanist, insisting that buildings might have a tragic dimension, and that they might address a part of the human spirit that required more than reliable plumbing and so many square feet of sleeping space. Here concrete took on metaphysical meaning. If the pristine and weightless forms of the steel frame suggested rationality, the weighty and tactile properties of concrete conveyed timeless and poetic qualities. This was the insight of America's most important late modernist, Louis I. Kahn (1901–74).

A Russian émigré, Kahn came as a child to Philadelphia, where he studied under Paul Cret. He was among the last to learn the full Beaux-Arts classical system, sincerely and without irony. He worked for Cret in 1930, helping to detail some of his modern classical buildings [200]. But with the Depression, he lost both his job and his faith in classicism, and turned to European modernism. For a time, he worked in partnership with George Howe, whose P.S.F.S. Building was America's first International Style skyscraper [202]. Kahn had a lifelong interest in the formal order of architecture, and he became fascinated for a time with the modular geometry of Buckminster Fuller, who believed that a new and free architectural language might be made from abstract geometric principles, much as wasp nests are based on interlocking tetrahedrons [229].

229 **R. Buckminster Fuller**, U.S. Pavilion, Montreal Expo, Montreal, 1967. This Pavilion was the capstone to a life of experimentation with structural systems, beginning in the 1920s with his Dymaxion system. As with Orson Squire Fowler's octagonal house, Fuller believed that abstract geometric principles might bring about a new architecture. His Expo pavilion was a geodesic dome, a spherical space frame that comported well symbolically with 1960s ideas of universal global peace.

From the 1930s into the mid-1950s, Kahn tried vainly to suppress his Beaux-Arts roots, and stubbornly pursued a modernist ideal that he could not bring to a happy resolution. It was not until he ceased struggling against his classical training that he found his personal voice. This began, tentatively and uncertainly, in 1951. During the course of a fellowship at the American Academy in Rome, he returned to the classical antiquity that had been the core of his education. He sought out those ancient buildings without classical orders, the mournful hulks of Roman baths and *insulae*, stripped of their marble cladding and ornament, buildings that achieved a kind of mute monumentality through scale and space alone; further excursions took him to Greece and Egypt. In short order his own work grew more solid and substantial—and more archaic—as he restored to architecture those two basic elements that modernism had virtually abolished, the discrete room and the solid wall.

In 1957 he designed the Richards Medical Research Laboratory at the University of Pennsylvania, in Philadelphia, a modest building that managed to challenge virtually every sacred doctrine of Miesian modernism. In place of the "universal space" of modernism, Kahn's space was insistently, remorselessly particular. He divided the building into laboratory blocks and the ventilation and plumbing towers that sustained them, sharply distinguishing between "served" and "servant" spaces, creating a hierarchy where International Style modernism had insisted on a lack of hierarchy. And while he might have worked to pare down the program to make a simplified and visually composition, he instead took evident pleasure in the jumble of brick towers, and called attention to their straggling roofline in a gesture that can only be described as picturesque [230].

Kahn was nearing retirement age when he hit his stride in the mid-1960s. Concentrating on civic and public buildings (his domestic projects were less successful), he revisited the lessons

230 **Louis Kahn**, Richards Medical Research Laboratory, University of Pennsylvania, Philadelphia, 1957–64. During two prolonged stays in Italy (1928–29 and 1951), Louis Kahn repeatedly drew the picturesque hill town of San Gimignano, with its welter of plucky brick towers, admiring their faceted cubic geometry. His Richards Medical Research Laboratory is among the first modernist buildings to quote from a historical source in this way, and to do so frankly and unashamedly.

231 **Louis Kahn**, Exeter Library, Philips Exeter Academy, Exeter, New Hampshire, 1965–71. In the 1960s, Louis Kahn found his characteristic subject matter: monumental spaces of human gathering, which he gave the dignity of archeological ruins. The central compartment of his library for Philips Exeter Academy is wrapped by the tiers of the book stacks to make movement through the building a metaphor for enlightenment: readers using the library take their books to the carrels along the outer perimeter, moving to the light.

that Cret had taught him, applying them now as abstract principles, shorn of their columns and cornices, and the rest of their Beaux-Arts formal vocabulary. One of these abstract devices was the formal axis, which modernists had banished as the laughable relic of Beaux-Arts formality. At the Salk Institute in La Jolla, California, he organized an entire research village about a single axis extending to the sea, aspiring, like that at Stonehenge, to infinity, and striking a note of eternal and timeless values that was missing in most functionalist modernism. In other buildings, such as his dormitory at Bryn Mawr College (1960–65) or his library at Philips Exeter Academy, New Hampshire (1965–71), he treated the wall as a thick masonry solid, punctured by deep reveals to allow the eye to gauge its depth.

Kahn liked to claim that "architecture is the thoughtful making of space," but he did not so much make space as discrete rooms. At the core of his buildings he liked to insert a ceremonial chamber, bathed in natural light and surrounded by a mantle of subordinate rooms [231]. These invoked the permanence and weight of the great buildings of the past, but also a certain grave solemnity, like that conveyed by ruins in which long-forgotten sacred rites used to be performed.

To the end, Kahn was a modernist but one of peacemaking stripe. Unlike the International Style in its militant phase, he did not seek to begin architecture again at some fictitious year zero, dismissing everything that had been built, drawn, or imagined before that moment. By the time he found his voice he was old enough to have seen that all styles, sooner or later, will date. And an absolute up-to-date contemporary style dates fastest of all. His goal was the opposite, not an architecture of radical contemporaneity but one of radical timelessness. Here he had much in common with his contemporaries Rothko, Gottlieb, and Newman, whose cultural background he shared, and who also sought a timeless and mystic art—without the altars and thrones that had traditionally given monumental Western art its meaning.

While architecture was struggling in the 1950s on the fault lines of functionalism and expressionism, or nationalism and internationalism, a sudden rapid change took place in painting. Up through Gorky, Pollock, and De Kooning, the hallmark of Abstract Expressionism was sincerity, the idea that the work of an artist was an expression of absolute personal authenticity. It could hardly be otherwise in an age riveted by Sigmund Freud and Carl Jung, and the understanding of man as a psychological creature. According to this understanding, Pollock's stream-of-consciousness canvases could even be superior to the work of a Renaissance master, since they streamed directly from his id, without first being filtered by the superego. Here the goals of painting and psychoanalysis became virtually indistinguishable.

It was precisely this indissoluble merger of artist and work that the next artistic generation came to find ridiculous. Here, in twenty generations of American artists since the seventeenth century, was the most rapid and complete change in temperament ever experienced. Although the two succeeding generations were not far apart in years, they were absolutely far apart in life experience. The principal Abstract Expressionists were born within a few years of 1910, such as De Kooning (1904), Kline (1910), and Pollock (1912). They were in their teens during the Depression and in their twenties during World War II. They achieved artistic maturity during an age of hyper-masculinity, the postwar culture in which returning combat veterans set the tone.

The next artistic generation was born around 1930: Robert Rauschenberg (1925), Andy Warhol (1930), Jasper Johns (1930), Claes Oldenburg (1929). The war was over while they were still in their teens, and they spent their youth under the continuously widening horizons of postwar prosperity: the automobile, television, sexual liberation. Their attitude was entirely different fromthat of the Abstract Expressionists. Instead of seriousness and self-importance they offered irony, flippancy, and charm. If a drip painting was a Rorschach projection of personality, the next generation turned the process on its head, making compositions of ostentatious impersonality.

In this galvanic change of attitude, a key figure was Robert Rauschenberg—the first significant artist to look at the moral seriousness and self-importance of the Abstract Expressionists and to laugh at it. For members his generation, looking to stake their own artistic claims in a world dominated by Greenberg's protégés, came as a relief and an emancipation.

Rauschenberg was a veteran who used the G.I. Bill to study art; he spent a half year at the musty Académie Julian in Paris, perhaps the last American artist of note to do so. His intellectual awakening took place later, at Black Mountain College in North Carolina, where every aspect of modern art, dance, theatre, and music was subjected to the most radical critique. Although the school eventually failed in 1953, it was at a pitch of intellectual fervor during its final years. Its remarkable faculty included the choreographer Merce Cunningham (born 1919), the composer John Cage (1912–92), and several refugees from the Bauhaus, among them the painter and theorist Josef Albers (who took color so seriously that he once sent a letter to Coca-Cola, explaining that its corporate logo did not use the proper hue of red to induce thirst). In 1951, Rauschenberg joined the college's faculty and partook of its radical rethinking of modernism, producing a revolutionary series of all-white paintings.

Although Rauschenberg, like everyone of his generation, was under the influence of Pollock, he drew from him quite different, and much more radical conclusions. For Rauschenberg, the image of Pollock strutting and charging across the space of his Long Island studio—as recorded in the Hans Namuth stills and film of him at work—was far more arresting than any canvas that resulted. Building from this, he and his colleagues began to put together works in which the performance itself comprised the aesthetic point. In 1952 Cage improvised an untitled event in which

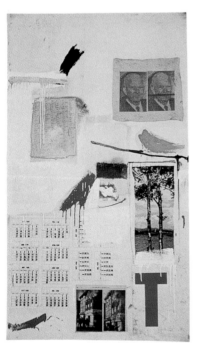

he delivered a lecture while Cunningham danced spontaneously beneath Rauschenberg's white paintings while a poet simultaneously declaimed poetry from atop a ladder, the entire event taking place without division between performers and audience. Such spontaneous performances had occurred at the Bauhaus and in Dada circles, but this was the first in the United States. The event is generally regarded as the first Happening, although this term would not be coined until 1959.

Shortly thereafter Cage produced his celebrated 4'33", a silent piece that required the pianist to sit motionless at the keys for four minutes and thirty-three seconds. The work was the musical equivalent of one of Rauschenberg's all-white paintings, creating a silence in which the accidents of stray sounds and throat-clearing came to take on musical value. Out of these events two distinct artistic lineages unfolded: the Happening and Minimalism. The Happening was art that resulted in no permanent object—in other words, "art that cannot be sold"; Minimalism was that radically reductive art that was distilled to an absolute minimum of complexity. Rauschenberg, in large measure, was at the head of both movements.

The joyous anarchy of the Happening was well suited to puncturing pretense, a quality that Abstract Expressionism had in abundance. In 1953, Rauschenberg spent several days erasing a drawing by De Kooning, returning it to its all-white state. Here he turned Abstract Expressionist doctrine against itself: if the impulsive pour of a paint can be a valid artistic gesture, then why not the action of an eraser? Four years later he took aim at another tenet of Abstract Expressionism: its conviction that the gestural stroke was an expression of personal authenticity, tracing the inner workings of the mind as like the quivering needle of a polygraph. Rauschenberg made a passable drip painting, complete with embedded shards of newspaper, which he called *Factum I*; he then made a meticulous copy of it, drip for drip and splatter for splatter, calling it *Factum II* [232]. Sincerity, evidently, could be faked.

232 **Robert Rauschenberg**, *Factum I* and *Factum II*, 1957. The paint spatters on this look as unpremeditated and spontaneous as any work of Pollock, yet Rauschenberg matched them, drip for drip and drool for drool, on his *Factum II* (below) so that the works were nearly indistinguishable. Rauschenberg's point was that every artistic act, in the end, was one of studied artifice.

Rauschenberg's *Factums*, like his erased De Kooning, are perhaps best considered as Happenings. With them, he kicked over the whole spurious edifice of authenticity and sincerity on which Abstract Expressionism was grounded. Rauschenberg had only derision for Greenberg's formalism, and in his work he seemed to go out of his way to provoke the critic. If Greenberg insisted on the autonomy of each genre of art, Rauschenberg promiscuously mingled them in his *combines* [233]. Such garish assemblages were known from Dada, and Rauschenberg's art was then described as neo-Dada, but the context was different. While Dada was made to shock the sensibilities of a bourgeois and academic art, Rauschenberg's was meant to shock the modernist establishment, and its dainty formalism.

The innovations of Rauschenberg would not enter the mainstream for a decade; in the 1950s, formalism was still the prevailing ideology for respectable art. But formalism did not remain stagnant. By 1952, Pollock has passed his zenith; taste was starting to turn from aggression and force, just as it had done after the Civil War. In that year came the first hint of a new sensibility, with Helen Frankenthaler's petite *Mountains and Sea* (1952), a reticent and understated landscape composed of wisps of delicate color. While it was technically a drip painting in the Pollock mode—made on the floor and worked on from all sides—the actual handling of the painting was quite novel, suggesting a mist of color rather than a puddle [234].

233 **Robert Rauschenberg**, *Monogram*, 1955–59. This work glories in its decrepit materials: a tattered stuffed goat is thrust through an old tire, resting on a painted platform cluttered with debris. In sensually abstemious America, it is perhaps the first art object that looks as if it might smell. Such combines are classified as Assemblage, although the older term Junk Art better conveys its scorn for art gallery hygiene.

Mountains and Sea was immediately influential. A year after its completion Morris Louis (1912–62) saw it and was thunderstruck, and he invented an entirely new manner of painting, in which he removed from Frankenthaler's gentle pours the last remnant of personal gesture. His method was to stain the canvas, applying acrylic paint in thin films, so that it bled into the unsized canvas to produce a fragile "veil" [235]. His shapes generally grew from the

234 **Helen Frankenthaler**, *Mountains and Sea*, 1952. To make this, Helen Frankenthaler emulated Pollock's drip technique, carefully trickling turpentine-thinned paint on to an unsized canvas. But her light touch removed from the pour all sense of aggression and force, and with it the sense of psychological anguish that permeates the Abstract Expressionism of the 1940s.

235 **Morris Louis**, *Tet*, 1958. The work of Louis is as close to pure painting as Whistler's *Nocturne in Black and Gold (The Falling Rocket)* [133]. Its fine mist of overlapping tints can only be fully experienced in person and at close proximity.

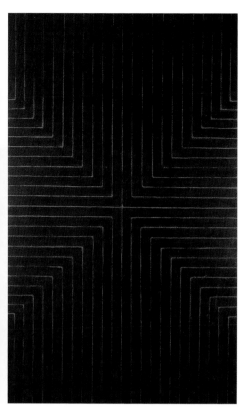

bottom of the canvas and swelled outward in the shape of a funnel, as if spreading by their own volition. He also inflated Frankenthaler's intimate stain paintings to immense size; his *Tet* (1958) measures 12 feet 9 inches (3.9 meters) in width.

Such work was abstract but it could no longer in any meaningful sense be called expressionist; indeed, its principal feature was the way that it checked and restrained personal expression, making it less psychologically revealing. Some critics, noting the purely chromatic basis of the new school, called it color-field abstraction. But Clement Greenberg dubbed it Post-painterly Abstraction, because it had renounced all the values of traditional painterly art: tactility, touch, surface lushness. Color was to be detached as much as possible from the physical materials that carried it, and the slicker, more anonymous the colored surface, the better. Among the key figures of the movement were Jules Olitski, Ellsworth Kelly, and Kenneth Noland. Kelly and Noland were much less ethereal painters, working with knife-edged lines rather than blurred edges, but they shared with Louis the same reaction against Pollock's generation and the same scorn for the gestural line.

The sense of personality in Frankenthaler and Louis is subtle and elusive, but their successors recoiled ever farther from Abstract Expressionism to achieve a kind of absolute and impervious impersonality. In 1958 Frank Stella, who had just graduated from Princeton University, made the first of his "black paintings." He methodically laid down parallel lines in enamel paint, restating the flat rectilinearity of the canvas in a composition that presented a repetitive mechanical figure, devoid of individual expression. Among the earliest was *Die Fahne Hoch* ("Raise high the flag"), a canvas of complete blackness but for the pale slivers of unpainted canvas between the black bars [236]. The sardonic title is from the first line of the Horst Wessel Song, the Nazi Party anthem, and serves to distance Stella from his own work—further mocking the idea that a painting was a projection of the self.

236 **Frank Stella**, *Die Fahne Hoch*, 1959. This is Frank Stella's inversion of Abstract Expressionism: instead of a personal signature, it offers an impersonal hard-edged pattern; instead of strong and distinct forms, a juxtaposition of black against slightly darker black. Here were many of the elements of Abstract Expressionism except for the emotion, whose elimination from painting began the process that led ultimately to Minimalism.

Stella may have gotten the impulse to make *Die Fahne Hoch* from his visit to the New York gallery of Leo Castelli, where he was among the first to see the work of his friend Jasper Johns. In 1958 Johns had finished the first of his *Flags*, showing the American flag (then still bearing forty-eight stars). Although the flag was the subject, it was not treated in illusionistic terms, as a form in space. Rather, as a flattened graphic symbol it was already close in form and format to a painted canvas. As Johns noted, the minute a flag was painted on a canvas, it actually became a flag, rather than a picture of a flag. According to a celebrated anecdote, a critic told Jasper Johns, "I see. It's a painting, not a flag." "No," Johns supposedly retorted, "it's a flag, not a painting."

Johns followed up his flag painting with a welter of other flat graphic imagery: targets, numbers, alphabets, maps of the United States [237]. Each was enlarged to fill the entire canvas, so that there was no distinction between figure and ground, which there still was, for example, in a work by Franz Kline. In this way, Johns took evident delight in lampooning Greenberg's insistence that painting should confront the essential flatness of the canvas. By choosing subject matter that was intrinsically flat, Johns lived up to the letter of formalism but not its austere spirit; the fundamental unseriousness of his work transgressed formalist decorum and seriousness. And yet Johns also drew from all-over painting, in the way he produced a highly agitated surface by his technique of combining wax encaustic with shredded newspaper and fabric. (Even here he seemed to having fun at the expense of formalism, inverting the usual process by which abstract painters used flat shapes to create the illusion of depth; he used thick and turbulent paint to create an illusion of flatness.) These ingredients—the appropriation of familiar imagery, the graphic boldness and accessibility of the art, and the pervading tone of irony—constituted the recipe for Pop Art, which received its name in 1956.

Pop Art defined itself in opposition to Abstract Expressionism and its intellectual tumult, its *Sturm und Drang*. In place of the soupy complexity of the Abstract Expressionist canvas, it offered instant

237 **Jasper Johns**, *Target With Four Faces*, 1955. This is at first glance a straightforward translation of an item of flat graphic imagery into a flat painting. In fact, its seething encaustic surface, through which shreds of newspaper can be read, is nearly as sculptural as the four plaster casts of eyeless faces that are solemnly arrayed above. In the juxtaposition of unlike parts, it recalls the *combines* of Robert Rauschenberg, with whom Johns once worked as a window dresser at Tiffany's in New York.

238 **James Rosenquist**, *President Elect*, 1960–61. This shows Rosenquist's practice of taking source material from advertisements and glossy magazines and arranging them in collages of overlapping fragments. Inevitably, strange resonances are created between the fragments. Rosenquist's predecessors are the enigmatic still lifes of Peto and Harnett [124], but now suffused with modern anxieties and inflated to the scale of a billboard.

legibility, like that of the advertising logos and the highway billboard. In fact, one of the best of the Pop painters was himself a seasoned sign painter, James Rosenquist, who had painted billboards on Times Square. Used to painting at the largest scale (his *F-111* of 1964–65 measures 86 feet [26.2 meters] in length), Rosenquist rivaled the largest Baroque wall cycles. Like those sprawling Baroque allegories, his works used symbols of political power in dynamically orchestrated compositions; his *President Elect* (1960–61) juxtaposes John F. Kennedy against images of postwar prosperity and consumerism [238].

Pop Art was not hostile to capitalism. Far from it; it embraced American life in all its tacky consumerist glory, finding an inexhaustible treasury of imagery in the highway strip, the glossy magazine, and the packaging of consumer goods. It also drew its artists from the world of commercial art and advertising; of these, the most important was Andy Warhol (1928–87). Warhol stood in a long tradition of commercial illustrators, from Homer to Sloan to Rockwell. But unlike them, Warhol did not aspire to rise above the commercial; rather to he brought to the world of high art the qualities of modern advertising: its slickness, anonymity, and mechanistic repetition. And despite his fetching and consummate draftsmanship, at an early date he stopped making original designs and drawings altogether.

Rather than making a single stray line that might imply personal self-expression, Warhol limited himself to pre-existing images, such as photographs of Marilyn Monroe or Elvis Presley, which he manipulated through the silk-screening process. Further

239 **Andy Warhol**, *100 Cans*, 1962. This is one of many paintings in which the same commercial logo was rendered in various colors, assembled into panels of four or more, and otherwise subjected to mass production. The flat, shrill colors show the neon Dayglo palette that Pop artists used in order to distinguish themselves from the Abstract Expressionists, with their layered and interpenetrating colors.

suppressing the personal, he chose subject matter that had been drained of all sentimental association through excessive familiarity, such as soap boxes and soup cans [239]. To borrow or appropriate imagery in this way—today known as "sampling"—has become standard practice in art and music, but it was not in Warhol's day. According to the code of personal authenticity to which the Abstract Expressionists subscribed, this was sheer heresy. In this he was closer to the mezzotint pirate Robert Feke than to Pollock.

In fact, Warhol's entire public persona was an inversion of Pollock. Instead of letting his emotion pour out in sullen interviews and drunken fisticuffs, he permitted himself no public display of emotion, and appeared as an utterly impassive and aloof figure. Rather than identifying himself with his work, he held himself aloof from it: bland, taciturn, bemused; and refusing to offer any comment on his work beyond the simplest platitude. Even his physical presentation, dominated by the unruly platinum wig that became his trademark, was as much an ironic gesture as Pollock's cigarette, jeans, and cowboy boots were meant sincerely. But like Pollock in the 1940s, and like Whistler in the 1870s, Warhol created the persona of a new kind of artist, in which the strongest note was one of ironic detachment.

This new persona was far removed from the high-testosterone masculinity of the Abstract Expressionists. Even at the time it was recognized that the new artistic sensibility of the 1960s was distinctly homosexual (the term "gay" did not come into general use until about 1969) or, in the vocabulary of the era, campy. The critic Susan Sontag described this sensibility, and named it, in her 1964 essay "Notes on Camp": "the essence of Camp is its love of the unnatural: of artifice and exaggeration." For her, "homosexuals, by and large, constitute the vanguard—and the most articulate audience—of Camp." And indeed, many of the key figures of post-Abstract Expressionist art were indeed homosexual, including Warhol and Johns, and collaborators such as Cage and Cunningham.

Other Pop artists found other categories of pre-existing imagery to exploit; the speciality of Roy Lichtenstein was the comic book and the cartoon. Appropriating single panels from comics, he would make minor alterations to the composition and then paint them at large scale, using the Ben-day dots of commercial illustration. Typically he would isolate a moment of high melodrama, such as an unexpected marriage proposal or a German U-boat commander ordering the firing of a torpedo [240]. The exaggerated storytelling recalls the genre painting of the nineteenth century, with one crucial difference: the paintings of William Sidney Mount and George Caleb Bingham suggested a complete self-contained story, while Lichtenstein's are the fragmentary and incomplete images of the television age, the experience of changing the channel and being plunged into the middle of a disorienting story.

240 **Roy Lichtenstein**, *Torpedo... Los!*, 1963. Roy Lichtenstein's Pop paintings, such as this one, were inspired by the shorthand storytelling of action comic books, although he took pains to alter his source images and to concentrate the action. He began by appropriating popular imagery, but soon began to create his own, working as a commercial artist and making covers for *Time* magazine. After Pop Art closed the circle, there would no longer be a distinct and separate genre of popular art for highbrow artists to mine.

If Lichtenstein made comic books into art, Claes Oldenburg reversed the process, making monuments into comic books. Oldenburg's domain was the comic enlargement of the familiar. Around 1962 he made the first of his "soft sculptures," in which a solid object such as a cheeseburger, toilet, or typewriter would be sculpted out of inflated plastic, and at a grotesque scale. While the giant objects loomed self-importantly in the gallery, their sagging and drooping deflated—literally deflated—their pretense. The sensibility was that of the mock heroic, that of Don Quixote rather than Jean-Paul Sartre. In Claes Oldenburg's world, everything is subject to ironic subversion, which is why his grand works of public art are to be viewed as anti-monuments rather than monuments [241].

241 **Claes Oldenburg**, *Proposed Colossal Monument for Park Avenue, N.Y.C.—Good Humor Bar*, 1965. Oldenburg's sculptures begin life as quirky notebook sketches and something of their graphic cartoonish quality passes into the finished work: the monument as doodle. His unbuilt *Design for a Monument* is a study of absurd grandeur, a colossal melting Popsicle wedged between the skyscrapers of Manhattan.

242 **Norman Rockwell**, *The Problem We All Live With*, 1964. This painting depicts the forced integration of a New Orleans school in 1960. The black child, six-year-old Ruby Bridges, is accompanied by federal marshals past the taunting crowd, which is conveyed indirectly by the graffiti and the thrown garbage. Rockwell cleverly places us at Ruby's eye level, cropping the heads of the adults so that we are able to experience the event from her vulnerable perspective.

Oldenburg was much like Warhol in that he preferred to tease American capitalism rather than condemn it, as the crusading artists of the Depression had done [208]. For his best-known work, *The Store* (1960–61), he rented an empty storefront and filled its shelves with his brightly painted oversized sculptures, as if they were so many goods for sale. More absurd than vicious, it had the effect of an affectionate parody of a neighborhood store. Like many innovative works of the early 1960s, it cheerfully blurred artistic categories: it was both a sculptural installation as well as a rather goofy performance piece, in which Oldenburg played the deadpan role of a sales clerk. And while it lampooned capitalism, it showed no special reverence for art either, treating it as merely another kind of commodity, with no more intrinsic value than the price tag that was affixed to it.

The success of Pop Art brought about the re-evaluation of other types of art. Even pictorial realism, that laughingstock of modernists, could now be enjoyed—if only ironically. One could enjoy, for example, if only for his kitsch value, Norman Rockwell, the popular artist known for his *Saturday Evening Post* covers, who had been shunned by respectable opinion for his sentimentality and patriotism [242]. But in many cases ironic appreciation turned into the real thing, and by the 1970s Rockwell was critically appreciated for his consummate realism and even his crusade for racial integration. His durable success, even during a half century of modernism, revealed just how much American popular taste was still fundamentally that of the nineteenth century, preferring crisp inventories of fact, delivered with humor, and a gentle dollop of moral instruction.

Pop Art represents the return to patterns of patronage that had a long pedigree in American history, reaching back its Colonial origins: to appropriated images, to bold graphics, and even to clearly drawn forms with hard outlines. The blithe indifference to theory was also an old American habit. After three decades of rarefied aesthetic theory, ultimately European in origin, Pop required no theoretical program to understand it. In many ways this recoiling away from European theory recalled the similar movement of American art in the 1920s, which also returned to Precisionist linearity and commercial subject matter.

The Pop mood also made itself felt in architecture. In 1962 the architect Robert Venturi built a house comprising little more than a gable and a chimney—inflated to comic proportions as in an

Oldenburg sculpture [243]. It might have been a child's drawing of "a house for mommy," which in fact it was, designed for the architect's mother, Vanna Venturi. The house was revolutionary, and so it was understood at the time. By exaggerating the roof and chimney, Venturi called attention to the primal duties of a house—shelter and warmth—so that as it served those functions it also proclaimed them symbolically; in other words, it both *acted* and *spoke*. Here Venturi called attention to the language of signs and symbols that underlies all architecture—all architecture, that is, before the International Style, which in its most formalist phase insisted that architectural forms could represent nothing other than themselves [226].

Venturi was a protégé of Kahn, who inculcated in him a humanist understanding of architecture. But their critique of modernism took entirely different paths; Kahn confronted the modernist box with the archeological ruin, Venturi with the highway billboard. His house—and subsequent buildings like his Guild House (1962–65)—had the graphic character of a sign, with the simplification of form necessary for recognizing an object at a great distance, or when moving at a great speed. Even his materials were billboardlike: the arch over the entrance is simply a flimsy wooden appliqué, and is placed upon the concrete lintel as if it were a refrigerator magnet.

243 **Robert Venturi**, Vanna Venturi House, Chestnut Hill, Philadelphia, 1962. Throughout history, architects have always quoted from their predecessors, but Robert Venturi typically lets the quotation mark show. In his Vanna Venturi House the exaggerated play of roof and chimney quotes Charles McKim's Low House [142], while the mannerist distortions and shifts of scale invoke Frank Furness, whom Venturi celebrated in his book, *Complexity and Contradiction in Architecture*, helping spur the Furness revival of the 1960s.

Venturi expounded his theory in two important books. His *Complexity and Contradiction in Architecture* (1966) explored the multiple meanings and ambiguities that make great buildings rewarding and challenging, and lamented how the clarity and universality of the International Style had impoverished architecture's expressive power. In the sloganeering and protest-pin-wearing fashion of the 1960s, he summarized his argument with his own anti-Miesian slogan, "less is a bore." In his next book, *Learning from Las Vegas* (1972), he examined what was widely regarded as the most vulgar architecture in America, but one which he found obeyed a strict code of signs and meaning. By concentrating on signs and meaning—semiotics was an intellectual fad during the 1970s—Venturi blithely abolished the hierarchical distinction between high and low art, and made it possible to judge a Greek temple and a roadside hamburger stand according to the same criteria.

Venturi's quiet assault on the International Style had much in common with the Pop Art assault on Abstract Expressionism. Each was a lighthearted attack on a self-important establishment; each was broadly tolerant and eclectic in its sources—as free to borrow from McDonald's as from Michelangelo; and each liked to exaggerate forms to the point of caricature. But in certain aspects, Venturi's design revolution did not challenge modernism. He kept the structural and spatial innovations of modernism, changing its skin, not its bones. He recognized that buildings would continue to be built as metal-framed boxes with flat roofs; he only proposed that the box be faced with a billboard, making it—in his words—a "decorated shed."

Venturi's language was new but the insight was not. Since the eighteenth century, American architects had regularly built decorated sheds, draping a thin screen of architecture over a simple framed box of timber or iron [21, 25, 84]. His contribution was merely to point this out at a time when most architects believed implicitly that the facade must express the frame, and that if any ornament at all were to be applied to it, it must be—as at the Seagram Building—a facsimile of the frame. Venturi opened the door to motifs drawn from across the history of architecture, although flattened and simplified into slender panels. This was not a specific historical revival, like the Greek and Gothic revivals of the nineteenth century, when certain styles were rehabilitated because of their intrinsic social or religious meaning, but a comprehensive opening up to all of history, a promiscuous historicism in the spirit of Cole's *Architect's Dream* [89].

244 Michael Graves, Portland Services Building, Portland, Oregon, 1980–82. More than any other postmodernist, Michael Graves had a flair for the playful manipulation of scale. His Portland Services Building is a teasing exercise in architectural gigantism, a keystone and arch inflated to the size of a whole building.

Venturi's ideas captivated the young architects of the 1960s and set in motion the postmodernism that would explode a decade later. Michael Graves and Charles Moore were by far the most influential [244]. Their buildings shed their glass curtain walls for a festive skin of stripes, cutouts, and polished stone panels. During the 1930s, modernists had scorned the colorful Beaux-Arts renderings out of existence but now eye-catching renderings returned to the scene, and architects like Graves and Moore became almost as well known for their colourful drawings as for their buildings.

The signal that the architectural establishment accepted postmodernism came in 1979, when Philip Johnson, whose Glass House was a veritable sacred relic of International Style modernism, designed the ATT Building in New York. This was a tall carton of a building, capped by a gigantic broken pediment that gave the whole affair the character of an eighteenth-century Chippendale high chest. The striking silhouette recalled the flashy crowns and spires of the 1920s, Johnson's penance, perhaps, for the abuse he heaped on Art Deco skyscrapers during his youth.

In sculpture—as in painting and architecture—the authority of formalism eroded quickly in the 1960s. At the start of the decade it still enjoyed immense authority. Greenberg championed David Smith for his tough, masculine art as enthusiastically as he once had Pollock. By now Smith had outgrown his early interest in Surrealism and automatism, to Greenberg's pleasure, in favor of a ruthlessly abstract and earnest language of simple geometric forms, executed in burnished or wire-brushed stainless steel. He defended his preference for steel on the grounds that it "possesses little art history. What associations it possesses are those of this century: power, structure, movement, progress, suspension, destruction, brutality." These terms might all be applied to Smith's magisterial *Cubi* series, on which he began working in 1960 [245]. Haughty and strenuous, they are the culmination of formalist principles in sculpture— and Smith was still working on them in 1965 when he was killed in an automobile accident.

But even as Smith was producing his *Cubi*, formalism was coming under fire and from the high ground of the establishment itself. In 1961 the Museum of Modern Art held an exhibition on "The Art of Assemblage," highlighting nearly 140 sculptors whose only common trait was their habit of working with found materials or through a process of collage—that is to say, their disinterest in formalism. Besides Rauschenberg, the roster included such dissimilar figures as Louise Nevelson (1899–1988), with her walls of painted wood, or Edward Kienholz (1927–94), with his creepy dioramas of mental patients and groping couples in automobiles. Here perfectly normal objects were made strange, even frightening, by unexpected juxtapositions and combinations. Kienholz practiced in Los Angeles and his work displayed a distinct West Coast sensibility, both in the ideological fault lines that divided his counterparts on the East Coast and its delight in visual spectacle and fantasy of a cinematic sort.

245 **David Smith**, *Cubi XVIII*, 1964. This is one of the last of David Smith's *Cubi* series. Consisting of a loosely ordered set of geometric solids anchored to a simple pier and lintel construction, the *Cubi* were explicitly architectural in their character, like a Doric column subjected to Cubist interrogation. They were also quite large, nearly 10 feet (3 meters) tall, and Smith placed them outdoors at his studio in Bolton Landing, New York, where their large-boned forms were more than adequate to hold their own against the backdrop of the Hudson River landscape.

246 **George Segal**, *Cinema*, 1963. This ghostly work is a sculptural memory sketch. Driving late at night, Segal saw a worker leaning over to change the letters on an illuminated marquee, and was struck by the way the gesture was caught against the harsh glare of the light. Working from memory, he re-created the scene with a metal and plaster figure, set against an illuminated wall, preserving something of the dreamlike quality of the nocturnal encounter.

"The Art of Assemblage" caused a whole generation of young sculptors to lurch from formalism. Even before the exhibition came down, George Segal (1924–2000), from the unlikely outpost of his New Jersey chicken farm, began to make plaster casts of his wife and friends. These he placed in bland everyday settings, such as a service station or a storefront [246]. Stripped of their specifics of personality or identity, his phantom figures became ciphers, with the disturbing arrested character of the plaster casts made from the victims of Pompeii. The anonymity of his effigies had a curious effect. By making them less real than the tangible objects around them, Segal perturbed and unsettled the intervening space—much as a pointing sculpture or directed light source can energize the space within a Baroque church.

At first glance Segal's sculptural environments seem far removed from the other anti-formalist tendencies of the day, the additive cacophony of the Happening and the reductive clarity of Minimalism. And yet all three shared the same tendency to recruit the dynamic space of the studio into the piece. The viewer of a Happening was not the detached spectator of a theatrical performance, but was a participant, willingly or not, as with Yoko Ono's 1965 *Cut Piece*, where viewers were invited to take a pair of shears and cut away part of her clothing. Likewise the radical paring down of Minimalist form also forced the viewer to become intensely aware of the space of the gallery, quite often to a disconcerting extent.

It is not surprising, then, that the same figures participated in all these genres. Robert Morris was both a Minimalist sculptor and a performer of Happenings. And the first Happening by Allan Kaprow (born 1927), who gave the art form its name, took place at Segal's chicken farm. Kaprow studied painting under Hans Hofmann, music under John Cage, and wrote an art history thesis under Meyer Schapiro on Mondrian, and his work—not surprisingly—showed a strongly conceptual and intellectual quality from the beginning. As formalized by Kaprow, the Happening was a critique and a parody of the regimented activity of the modern world, and it offered a healing dose of anarchy [247]. Almost differing widely in their specifics, most had much the same tone: one of organized, repetitive, and purposeful activity—performed with ritualistic solemnity of a rite—but directed toward a nonsensical end. Kaprow's *18 Happenings in 6 Parts* (1959) was typical; in one of the events, a young woman methodically squeezed orange juice into a dozen glasses, and drank them one at a time.

In the early 1960s, the Happening received an extraordinary amount of media attention, titillating a public that was more bemused than scandalized. It became a central component of the movement known as Fluxus, which was established by George Maciunas in 1962. Maciunas held that all aspects of the universe were interconnected and in a state of constant change, or flux; to celebrate that flux demanded an art that abolished boundaries, such as those between theater and sculpture, or between performer and observer. The philosophy was not terribly rigorous—Maciunas essentially grafted the artistic tradition of Dada on to the Transcendentalism of Emerson—but at the time it seemed like a profound revelation. Fluxus enjoyed an international vogue, particularly in Germany and Japan (where Yoko Ono was an early adherent), and from its circles emerged some of the decade's best-known performance artists, including Nam June Paik. Fluxus was ultimately more important overseas than in the United States, where public skepticism to theory remained the rule. Only one seed fell on fertile soil, and this was the insight that anyone at all, regardless of training or certification, might be an artist. This idea appealed greatly to American democratic sensibility, and it enjoyed a great vogue during the decade and beyond.

247 **Robert Morris**, *Untitled (Standing Box)*, 1961. Robert Morris was among the most important creators of Happenings.

248 Installation view of "Primary Structures" exhibition, Jewish Museum, New York, 1966. This exhibition introduced the American public to the mute geometry of Minimalism. Virtually all of the leading figures of the movement were represented, including Robert Morris, Donald Judd, Dan Flavin, and Sol LeWitt. It was perhaps the most strenuously formalistic exhibition of art ever held, even as it helped mark the end of formalism.

Kaprow's antic Happenings were provocative in the early 1960s but they gradually lost their revolutionary cachet as they became a well-established genre of art. After about 1970, the Happening was reclassified as Performance Art, and its tone shifted subtly. Instead of sprawling absurdist tableaux that conjured an anarchic universe, they tended to concentrate on a figure or two, engaged in a confrontational, often explicitly political act. This has remained true for more than a generation. Carolee Schneemann's *Interior Scroll* (1975), in which she slowly unfurled a scroll from within her body, is of this sensibility.

Robert Morris bridged the gap between the Happening and Minimalism. Even as he was performing with Schneemann, he was making sculpture of great geometric simplicity. His *Box With The Sound of its own Making* (1961) was a simple wooden box from which a tape recorder played three hours of hammering and sawing. It is easy to see that this was not the formalism of Greenberg, for the addition of sound violated his rule that genres should pursue their inherent properties. Having studied philosophy, Morris subjected Greenberg's formalism to an exhaustive and systematic critique, and discovered the paradoxes to which a continuous process of formalist refinement might lead. "Could a work exist which has only one property?" This was impossible, he concluded, since form always had color; and flatness always had texture. But the closest one might come to the purity of a single property was with the "simpler polyhedrons ... which do not present clearly separated parts."

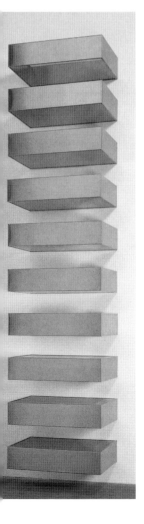

249 **Donald Judd**, *Untitled*, 1968. "I don't like any dramatic quality or incident or anything archaic," proclaimed Judd, and his *Untitled* lives up to his demand. Purged of all incident, it consists of ten precisely spaced boxes made of stainless steel. The bottoms and tops, however, are of transparent colored plexiglass, letting light filter through and making it a column of iridescent color.

Morris's essays and manifestoes, which began to appear in 1966, laid out the theoretical program for Minimalism. In the same year, the new tendency was dramatically presented to the American public at the major exhibition "Primary Structures." This took place at the Jewish Museum in New York, an important venue for introducing new art in those days [248]. Morris and most other significant Minimalists participated, including Carl Andre, whose forte was the geometrical arrangement of brick or metal panels on the gallery floor. The most startling sculpture, however, was that of Donald Judd (1928–94).

For some time, American sculpture had been collectively moving in the direction of simpler shapes and larger sizes. But there still persisted that lingering artifact of Abstract Expressionism, the gesture. In 1961, for example, Tony Smith made a piece called *Cigarette*, a 15-foot- (4.5-meter-) high rectangular solid that turned in four knucklelike bends. The piece anticipated Minimalism in its absolute emotional reserve, and only its sharp angles were vaguely suggestive of a gesture. But for Judd, even this was too much action. On the eve of the "Primary Structures" exhibition, he developed a form he called a "stack," which removed all sense of gesture and torque as completely as Louis's stain paintings eliminated drawing. Judd's stacks were a vertical arrangement of ten boxes, mounted on a wall and spaced so that the interval between them was exactly equal to the boxes themselves. This made the empty space as important as the alternating boxes, and drained them of almost all physical interest—either of texture, shape, or mass—so that the strongest note was that of a disembodied mechanical pulse [249].

Over the course of the next few years, Minimalism became even more minimal. Dan Flavin adopted Judd's deadpan pulse but he eliminated the solid boxes that produced it. Instead, he used arrays of fluorescent light that created an optical rhythm of color and shape, but drained of all corporeal substance. But Minimalism's last word came from Morris. In 1968, still brooding about making an art that had only one property, he seized upon a material that had neither color, nor weight, nor texture: steam. With a camera on hand to record the results, he released a steam vent outdoors and let the escaping jet melt away into the air. Here he realized his dream of a work of art "with only one property," in this case, volume. With *Steam*, after thirty years of development and systematic reduction of each art genre to its formal essence, formalism now reached its perfect fulfillment—and evaporated.

Chapter 10   Art and Agenda

Minimalism peaked in 1968. In that year, the twin towers of the World Trade Center were designed, a spare composition of two parallel prisms that Donald Judd might have authored. A Minimalist monolith was also the principal form in that year's science fiction film *2001: A Space Odyssey*. Even the Beatles' so-called *White Album* (1968) was Minimalist, its cover a vacant field of white. Thus the Minimalist aesthetic dominated both high art and popular culture—even as the boundary between the two was falling.

The year 1968 was also stamped by churning social turbulence throughout the world. In April, Czechoslovakia began to liberalize its Communist regime and to introduce political freedoms—only to be invaded by the Soviet Union four months later. In May, a student uprising in Paris brought the government almost to the point of collapse. Both events inspired student unrest in the United States, which reached its crescendo along with the war in Vietnam.

All this had momentous ramifications for American art. Formalism had originally arisen in order to keep art free of the distractions of war and social upheaval; now these same forces were used to discredit formalism itself. To a world that seemed on the brink of either nuclear devastation or social revolution, an aesthetic stance seemed akin to burying one's head in the sand. Art for art's sake was now seen at best as a quaint doctrine, and at worst reactionary. Many a young artist would now agree with a scurrilous item of graffiti found on a wall in Paris in 1968: "The most beautiful sculpture is a paving stone thrown at a cop's head."

Politics now surged back into the art world, massively and irresistibly, to a degree not seen since the 1930s. At first it was expressed as protest art against the Vietnam War, but after 1972 the suspension of the draft robbed the movement of its urgency. The war would drag on for three more years but artists soon shifted to other political causes, especially environmentalism and feminism, two social movements that arose in the late 1960s.

250 **Judy Chicago**, *The Dinner Party*, 1974–79. The thirty-nine guests of *The Dinner Party* are present only in surrogate form: in their explicitly gynecological place settings. The rigid formal geometry and the suggestion of altar cloths and ecclesiastical embroidery lends the piece a distinct sacramental quality, which clashes wildly with the uninhibited sexual content—a tension found in much feminist art.

As had happened so often before, moral instruction, rather than aesthetic pleasure, became the orienting principle of art after formalism. And as with other episodes of agenda art, from the Hudson River School to Social Realism, the artist had the advantage that comes with a sense of personal virtue. This impulse to provide lessons rather than pleasure affected American culture as a whole, not only the art world. Even Hollywood embraced the didactic agenda, and the 1970s witnessed a proliferation of issue movies, reflected by its annual Academy Award winners, dealing with Vietnam (1978), divorce (1979), and dysfunctional families (1980).

In 1976 art critic Rosalind Krauss and others founded the journal *October* to serve as a rallying point for post-formalist art. Its explicitly political orientation was reflected in its title, a reference to the Soviet Revolution of October 1917. For *October*, "Greenbergian formalism" was a distasteful epithet. Instead the journal promoted those who might be called agenda artists, whose works pursued a social or political agenda, or any agenda so long as it was not a formalist one. It especially championed the work of post-Minimalist and Environmental artists during its early years, including Robert Smithson, Alice Aycock, Dennis Oppenheim, and Nancy Holt.

One way of challenging formalist purity was with impurity, barraging the viewer with a welter of forms; another way was to present no form at all. This was the approach of Conceptual Art, which became the hallmark of the influential CalArts program, headed by John Baldessari and including on its faculty Chicago, Joseph Kosuth, and others. With Conceptualists, feminists, and activist artists of various stripes, CalArts had no ideological uniformity, other than an implacable consensus against formalism.

With Conceptual Art, the intellectual component, rather than the formal or aesthetic, was seen as the irreducible essence of art. Works of Conceptual Art might involve a text, as in the works of Joseph Kosuth, or a performance, or a combination of both [251]. But art of arresting visual character "distinctive in shape or line, or expressive in its swell and bulge of volume" was regarded as fundamentally unserious. Even a page of printed words might have unintended aesthetic

251 **Joseph Kosuth**, *White and Black*, from the *Art as Idea* series, 1966. In this series, Kosuth took the dictionary definitions of the words "white" and "black" and enlarged them on to 4 by 4-foot (13 by 13-meter) panels. The verbose work belonged to the famously laconic Andy Warhol, who donated it to Oberlin College.

properties, which might be ruthlessly expunged: in December 1968, the art dealer Seth Siegelaub—an important promoter of Conceptual Art—organized an exhibition in New York for which artists were told to photocopy their texts, ensuring that there would be no reverence for the actual physical pages. At CalArts, the worst criticism that might be leveled at a work of art was that it was "*retinal,*" in other words, that it addressed the eye rather than the mind. "Actual works of art are little more than historical curiosities," as Kosuth himself insisted in his influential essay "Art After Philosophy" (1969).

Nonetheless, Conceptual artists continued to make objects, and though they rejected formalism, they still made forms. A good example is *Hang Up* (1966) by Eva Hesse (1936–70), a modernist painter who was increasingly drawn to Conceptualism [252]. Here the concept is of an empty picture frame against the white wall of a museum. The actual form of the frame was incidental; it could just as easily have been a gilded rococo prodigy and the concept would have remained the same. This was precisely the point, as the punning title made that clear. On the one hand, the frame could literally be hung up; on the other hand, in the slang of the 1960s, as now, a hang-up meant an inhibition or a neurosis. For Hesse, the belief that there actually needed to be a painted piece of canvas within that frame was nothing more than a hang-up.

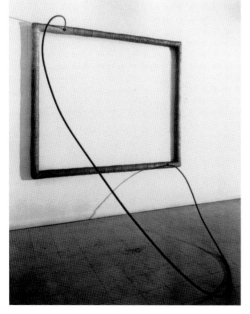

252 **Eva Hesse**, *Hang Up*, 1966. Eva Hesse (1936–70) studied at Yale with Josef Albers, a painter whose color studies and formal studies of the square always had a strong conceptual content. *Hang Up*, her first major work, pays its own radical homage to Albers's *Homage to the Square* series.

To describe the specific character of this art, with its ideological quarrel with formalism, Robert Morris coined the term "Anti-Form," the title of a 1968 essay. Unlike Greenberg, who would banish all properties from art except form, Anti-Form would tolerate everything, except form. Morris now abandoned his Minimalism to make objects that were impossible to view as closed and resolved forms, and shifted to materials that were almost practically impossible to view as discrete forms, such as felt.

A genre that was particularly congenial to the Anti-Form mood of the late 1960s was the artist's book—i.e., a work of art in the form of a book. Some of the earliest were made by Ed Ruscha (born 1937). His *Royal Road Test* (1967) resembles a Happening in that a pointless undertaking is subjected to a seemingly rational process: a manual typewriter was driven into the desert and flung from the window of a speeding Buick, and photographed during every step of the process [253]. Ruscha published an artist's book of the event, thereby solving the fundamental dilemma of Conceptual and Happening Art, the lack of a permanent object.

Permanence and impermanence was similarly the central concern of Earth Art (also known as Land Art, Earthworks, or Environmental Art), which first emerged as a coherent movement in 1968. Given the year, it is hardly surprising its aesthetic sense would be strongly Minimalist, especially in its love of large simple gestures and laconic expression. Walter De Maria's *Lightning Field* (1977), for example, placed a grid of 400 steel poles in the New Mexico desert, where they act as lightning rods; Holt's *Sun Tunnels* (1973–76) arranged four concrete tubes in the Utah desert so that the solstice could be viewed, as at Stonehenge. Occasionally the profundity was leavened with a dollop of absurdity, and made into a Happening: in 1969 Dennis Oppenheim seeded a wheat field in Holland with a giant X pattern, to make what was literally a *Canceled Crop*.

The context for Earth Art was not religion but science, yet its underlying cultural assumptions were close to those of the Hudson River School. Both believed that nature offers edifying lessons, that it represented a primal goodness in which man is an intruder, and that the confrontation with nature is the primal crisis of civilization. But the wistful sense of tragedy that haunted the

253 **Ed Ruscha**, *Royal Road Test*, 1967. Like many California artists and architects, Ed Ruscha preferred deadpan humor to intellectual posturing. He first came to public awareness with his Pop Art paintings of gas stations and the roadside architecture of Sunset Strip drawn in exaggerated perspective and with sharp Precisionist edges. His *Royal Road Test*, an artist's book that meticulously documents the destruction of a manual typewriter during the course of a road trip, is typical of his playful approach.

254 **Robert Smithson**, *Spiral Jetty*, Great Salt Lake, Utah, 1970. The symbolism of *Spiral Jetty* is deliberately obscure, a massive spiral built up out of truckloads of gravel and visible only from the air. Its antecedents are the giant earthworks of the Mound builder Indians, the most ancient and cryptic of American monuments.

earlier movement collapsed into despair and resignation in Earth Art. In 1968 Paul Ehrlich published his influential *The Population Bomb*, persuading many that overpopulation and pollution would make the earth uninhabitable in a few decades. This apocalyptic sense marks much Earth Art; in fact, some of it does not even seem to require human viewers at all, but is more in the sense of poignant graffiti left behind by fleeting visitors. Such is the aura of Robert Smithson's *Spiral Jetty*, a vast earthen spiral curling into Utah's Great Salt Lake, slowly vanishing beneath the rising lake [254].

Earth Art, if given sufficient room to stretch, can achieve genuine monumentality, but this was seldom possible and most large works are remote and inaccessible. The great exception is the Vietnam Veterans Memorial on the Mall in Washington, D. C., which cleverly drew on both Earth Art and Minimalism (although at maximum scale). Maya Lin made the design in 1981 while still an undergraduate at Yale University, winning a national competition in which 1,421 entries were submitted. The terms of the contest

255 Maya Lin, Vietnam Veterans Memorial, Washington, D.C., 1981–84. The public was initially skeptical of Maya Lin's design for this memorial. In rejecting the conventional classicism of the Mall—by showing a black form in a void rather than a white form in space—it seemed to disparage those killed in the war. But the completed structure had an unexpected therapeutic character that instantly swept away all criticism. Among Lin's subtle refinements were the use of polished black granite panels, so that the faces of visitors are reflected against the names, and the decision to list the names in order of their death. She began the list at the center of the wall, where it also ended, so the names of the first and the last killed almost touch one another, giving a tragic cyclical sense to the whole, rather than merely a bald timeline.

were few, mandating only that there be no explicit political content and that the memorial contain the names of all 58,000 Americans who died in the war. Lin's solution was a simple scheme of a wall and a void: those who approached to seek the name of a soldier would gently descend into in the earth, feeling a palpable sense of absence and void [255]. At a time when much agenda art tended toward the preachy and excessively literal, its spare abstraction stood out. It was instantly popular at the time of its dedication in 1982 and it has produced a national wave of local imitations.

Just as the environmental movement gave rise to Earth Art, so feminist art arose out of the women's liberation movement. In 1969 the activist group WAR (Women Artists in Revolution) was formed in New York to promote the cause of feminist art; it soon began to demonstrate for the equal representation of male and female artists in museums. But its focus eventually shifted from elevating the status of women in the existing art world to creating a new one, with different subject matter, modes of expression and entirely different criteria for the judging of art.

A certain tension ran through this. On the one hand, feminist art protested against the traditional sex roles that had subordinated women to the kitchen and sewing room; on the other hand, it recognized that women's crafts, such as quilting or ceramics, represented a long and proud legacy. Building on this, feminist artists made much of their collaborative working methods and their avoidance of heroic posturing, aggressive monumentality, or anything else that might suggest a male attitude. Above all, there was a stress on the depiction of women's bodies and their rhythms, shown either representationally or symbolically. Each of these elements is present in the work of Judy Chicago, who in 1971 helped establish the Feminist Arts Program at the California Institute of the Arts, the first of its kind.

Chicago's key work was *The Dinner Party* (1976), a triangular table elaborately set for thirty-nine guests chosen from the feminist heroes of history, from Sacagawea to Georgia O'Keeffe. Her point of departure was the Last Supper: "I became amused by the notion of doing a sort of reinterpretation of that all-male event from the point of view of those who had been expected to prepare the food, then silently disappear from the picture…" The absent guests are invoked only by their place settings, which present themselves as female sexual parts, with a brazen explicitness that was both shocking and funny [250]. Chicago deliberately stressed women's domestic crafts, including the fine needlework of the tablecloth and napkins, the ceramic plates and the china-painting. The resulting visual density and splendor was as far from the austerity of 1968 as possible, using the excess of Late Victorian interiors as a calculated offense to formalist sensibilities.

With the collapse of formalism, the stature of photography rose. Photographers had always struggled with the formalist requirement that content be subordinated in favor of form, since it was nearly impossible to banish subject matter and narrative content from a photographic image. One approach was to isolate bits of nature or architecture from their context, stressing their texture and geometric order. Aaron Siskind (1903–91) used a large format camera to record tufts of seaweed on a beach or paint flaking from a wood plank, trying to create a photographic counterpart to Abstract Expressionism. Still, as rich as his images were, they were essentially derivative, justifying themselves by their fortuitous resemblance to the work of Pollock and Calder.

But the camera lent itself readily to the spur-of-the-moment and the ephemeral, for which reason the new era of Happenings, Pop, and Conceptual Art proved quite congenial to photography. Diane Arbus (1923–71) perhaps best captured the new sensibility, finding her subjects among the bizarre or the alienated: transvestites, nudists, giants, midgets, and interracial couples (a shocking sight for many in the 1960s). She might show a grimacing child, mugging grotesquely for the camera while clutching a toy hand grenade. As with a Happening, the essence of her work is her avid and rather disconcerting way of toppling conventional barriers, in this instance that between war and play.

The photographs of Arbus, jarring though they might be, were always fully resolved in formal terms; their uncomfortable juxtapositions and melancholy outsiders invariably presented a complete situation and a complete world, no less self-sufficient in their way than a medieval altarpiece. But by the 1970s, photography was falling under the pull of the Anti-Form movement and formal completeness was no longer a virtue. The work of Cindy Sherman (born 1954) now won attention for her images that stubbornly refused to be resolved. Beginning in the mid-1970s, she took to photographing herself in enigmatic situations, producing images that imitated the conventions of film stills, the films themselves being spurious [256]. Although their refined composition and vague sadness called to mind Arbus, her images were never complete unto themselves but always implied a larger whole from which they had been dislodged, and which would never yield their secrets until that larger whole was recovered—an impossible hope, of course. This purposeful ambiguity, presented in terms of high stylishness, was the right note at the right time, and by the end of the decade Sherman achieved the status of international art celebrity.

256 **Cindy Sherman**, *Untitled Film Still no. 7*, 1968. Cindy Sherman's earliest photographs, such as this one, evoke the glamorous locales of the foreign films of her childhood. Over the course of the 1980s, her work relinquished glamor to concentrate on grotesque and maimed figures, which she fashioned from makeup and prosthetic body parts.

As the status of photography rose, that of painting declined. It is difficult to think of any single painting of the last generation that had nearly the effect of Frankenthaler's *Mountains and Sea* in 1952. Besides photography, painting now competed with even newer genres of art—Performance and Assemblage in the 1950s; video art in the 1960s—to which ambitious young artists, anxious to distinguish themselves from the pack, were increasingly drawn. In part it was because painting was simply not as good a medium for agenda art. As the language of formalism, abstract painting was not easily susceptible to political content. It was difficult to assign political content to painting, without descending into explicit representation, which was still frowned upon (although less so since the liberation brought about by Pop).

257 **Bill Viola**, *The Crossing* (detail), 1996. Bill Viola's video art is free of traditional narrative to a surprising extent, and instead produces effects that are closer to what medieval stained-glass windows would be if they were able to move: dignified and mystic devotional images. Here, two video monitors are placed back to back; one shows a man in the process of being consumed by fire, the other by water.

Video art—which only became technologically feasible at the end of the 1960s—helped to depose the classical triumvirate of painting, sculpture, and architecture. At first, the camera and video monitor were integrated into existing genres. In 1969, for example, Nam June Paik and Charlotte Moorman collaborated in the performance *TV Bra for Living Sculpture*, in which Moorman played the cello while wearing only two small video monitors across her chest. But as technology improved in quality during the ensuing decades, artists began to explore the aesthetic nature of the video image. This was formalist thinking, of course, but it was only natural to speculate what the peculiar properties and limitations were in a new genre of art. In particular, they sought to distinguish video art from commercial television and cinema, resisting traditional narratives that might cause the viewer to suspend disbelief.

Bill Viola (born 1951) achieved prominence as the first major artist to use videos neither as a prop in a performance nor as a component of an installation, but on its own terms: as a maker of flickering, moving images of often murky and indistinct character. Like Inness in the 1870s, he recognized the mystic quality of blurred objects that emit light. He also recognized that video, as a photographic medium, found its natural language in realism. In his characteristic work, stately figures move slowly and with a kind of ritualistic purposefulness [257].

The video image, because of the limitations of scale, does not lend itself to panoramic subjects, for it tends to diminish them; likewise, because of its pixelated graininess, it is not suited for the precise examination of small things. It is at its best somewhere in between, and its scale is particularly well suited for showing the human form, either the head or the whole figure. This was a common theme in the art of the 1970s, which looked with renewed interest and curiosity at the human form. This should not be mistaken for Renaissance humanism, which viewed the body in idealized terms, as God's handiwork. The new realism was likely to show slack unidealized bodies in states of boredom or torpor. In the paintings of Philip Pearlstein, heads and feet are cut off as awkwardly as in badly cropped photographs. In consequence, it is impossible to see the body as something whole and complete, and beautiful [258]. Instead, it appears as an arresting and dynamic shape in space, owing just as much to Franz Kline as Thomas Eakins [218 and 128].

The new realism also sported a *trompe l'oeil* wing. Duane Hanson and John De Andrea, two sculptors working independently but on parallel tracks, each devised an uncanny verisimilitude in the making of life-size replicas of the human body out of fiberglass and polyvinyl. Complete even to the tiny hairs glued on their arms, these figures were wonderfully unsettling, especially when one turned to the museum guard at an exhibition to discover that he too was a sculpture—or not. For Hanson, this

258 **Philip Pearlstein**, *Male and Female Nudes with Red and Purple Drape*, 1968. Philip Pearlstein painted his models from life, standing so close that they fill the whole field of vision, sprawling across the picture plane. This painting is typical in the way the strong lighting tends to flatten out the form and make the flesh look sallow and pale, the very antithesis of an idealized nude, such as Vanderlyn's *Ariadne* [55].

259 **Neil Welliver**, *Shadow*, 1977. The realists of the 1970s were indelibly stamped by the aesthetic lessons of modern art and abstraction. *Shadow* is an inviting and intimate landscape but its surface forms a flat decorative pattern—so that the viewer who tries to think himself into the landscape always bumps up against the intermediate photograph.

was the only critical success that mattered, as it was for Charles Willson Peale, when he boasted that George Washington once bowed respectfully to his *trompe l'oeil* painting of his children. But, like Pearlstein's nudes, these realistic sculptures were not idealized, and they were likely to represent bored housewives shopping or overweight sunbathers. As with the billboard classicism and Las Vegas imagery of postmodern architecture, the overall tone was snide and knowing.

One branch of realism was free of irony, or indeed of any emotional commentary whatsoever. This was the hard-edged photorealism practiced by Robert Bechtle, Richard Estes, and Neil Welliver, which achieved remarkable success during the 1970s. Innovative artistic movements are rarely new in every one of their traits, and photorealism retained much of the aloof impersonality of Minimalism. Even in their most lyrical subject matter, tranquil landscapes of the sort that Ansel Adams might have photographed, emotion was tamped down tightly; a kind of impervious detachment prevailed, remote and icy [259].

260 **Barbara Kruger**, *"Untitled"* (*I shop therefore I am*), 1987. At first Barbara Kruger applied her wry epigrams to photographs but by 1987 the epigram stood alone, as here. But even when her aesthetic decisions were limited to the choice of words and of type font, such works were more like Happenings than graphic art in that they were not complete without the public stir they caused when placed on buses and billboards.

In the pursuit of fashionable impersonality, artists devised various working methods that stressed process and method rather than personal effusion. Most mechanical of all was that of the photorealist Chuck Close (born 1940), who ruled each canvas into a precise grid of identical squares, and then painted them one after another, filling in a predetermined number each day. Strong intense feeling was literally screened out. If there was any urgent emotion in the art of this era, it was likely to be political emotion, which reached its climax during the 1980s. At the beginning of the 1980s, political art was more likely to be wry than strident.

Barbara Kruger (born 1945), for example, practiced political commentary with the low-key irony of Pop Art. Like Warhol, Kruger came from a background in commercial art. An art director for several magazines, including *Mademoiselle* and *House and Garden*, she brought to her art the approach of a photo editor—which consisted primarily in the provocative pairing of an image with a caption. These captions were often cryptic, and had a certain Warhol blandness about them, as in her *We Don't Need Another Hero*, for example, which took on explicit political meaning, which shows a young boy flexing his muscles to impress a girl; the viewer is left to draw out the political ramifications. In her subsequent work she experimented with leaving out the photograph entirely [260].

Over the course of the 1980s, agenda art shifted away from international to domestic politics, especially to questions of group identity. The key event was the crisis of AIDS. Between 1983, when it first came to public attention, and 1987, the number of AIDS deaths in the United States increased from about 1,500 to well over ten times that amount. While the numbers would continue to rise for a time, this was the period of the greatest uncertainty and fear. The disease disproportionately affected the gay community, and the artistic community as well.

In the mid-1980s, when the nature of the disease and its future was still terrifyingly mysterious, it was unclear precisely how one might address it in artistic terms. The slow and visible wasting process of the disease naturally served to focus increased attention on the human body, which had already become a subject of national contention in the battle over legalized abortion. The body now became a principal focus of art, but the ravaged body rather than the beautiful one. There was already precedent for this. In 1974, the artist Hannah Wilke (1940–93) had herself photographed seminude in provocative poses that suggested pinup art. But at the same time she covered herself with small pieces of chewed gum, which suggested sores or the patterns of ritual scarring [261]. This was not the human body as temple, in the classical sense of Powers' *Greek Slave* [62]. Instead, by pairing beauty and disease, it suggests the ambivalent body, both temple and sewer, and tragically sullied. Francesca Woodman worked in a similar vein, and before her 1981 suicide she repeatedly photographed her nude body in settings of squalor and with a tone of regret and ruefulness. In each instance, the subsequent spread of AIDS made their disquieting ambivalent work prophetic.

261 **Hannah Wilke**, *S.O.S.-Scarification Object Series*, 1974. Hannah Wilke covered herself with tiny pieces of chewed gum in this series. The pieces were shaped to suggest sexual organs, making the photographs more explicitly sexual even as the suggestion of disease stripped them totally of any pornographic charge.

As it turned out, most work avoided the gruesome specifics of the disease. On the few occasions where it did not, it was attacked for stigmatizing its victims. It was more likely to present issues in the neutral terms of allegory, as in the work of Robert Gober (born 1954), which pondered the theme of filth and cleanliness. In one, a sink was suspended in space, inverted and eerily bent in half; in another, the back of a sink reared up to split in two [262].

Others approached AIDS obliquely, either allegorically or in the terms of performance art. Felix Gonzalez-Torres scattered billboard-sized photographs of an unmade double bed across New York City. Andres Serrano photographed bodily fluids, such as blood, in richly colored cibachrome (a photographic process in which a print is made directly from a transparency, giving a particularly lush image). A few artists opted for confrontation rather than metaphor: in *Four Scenes from a Harsh Life* (1994), Ron Athey sliced the back of another performer and wiped the blood away with a cloth that he then hoisted over the uncomfortable audience. The general preoccupation with the despoiled body also influenced artists who were not gay. After 1985, Cindy Sherman began to use prosthetic body parts and, later, sexual prosthetics to make misshapen and monstrous bodies. At the same moment Paul McCarthy, the Los Angeles performance artist, was beginning to use mechanical surrogates, often with malformed appendages, in his stead. Both were featured at a 1993 exhibition at the Whitney Museum, which assigned the name Abject Art to this mode.

It was only a matter of time before this highly political art would come into conflict with large segments of the public. Many artists deliberately sought such a confrontation, as when Serrano photographed a plastic crucifix immersed in a jar of his own urine. But while much of the public was indeed provoked when it came across such work, it seldom was. And when it did, there was little recourse. The only direct attempt to suppress provocative art came in Cincinnati in 1989, with an exhibition of the photographs of Robert Mapplethorpe, who had died of AIDS that year. Some of these were

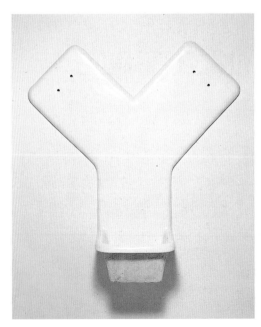

262 **Robert Gober**, *The Subconscious Sink*, 1985. Gober adapted the laconic aesthetic of Minimalism to the theme of AIDS, making plaster and metal allegories of hygiene and the impossibility of cleanliness. *The Subconscious Sink*, fractured unhappily in the middle, is an oblique expression of a despair that would be difficult to confront directly.

classical nudes [263] while others blatantly depicted subjects *in flagrante*. The exhibition was closed as a violation of public decency, and became the centerpiece of the Culture Wars, as the battles over public art came to be called.

Although the specter of censorship was raised throughout the Culture Wars, the Cincinnati affair is the only one that fits the definition, the suppression of art or literature by direct state action. Most of the incidents that comprised the Culture Wars hinged not on freedom of expression but on public funding of art and artists. At issue was the subsidizing of art, not its suppression. It could be argued (and so it was) that refusing a subsidy was in fact suppression, and so it was; but there were also arguments on the other side. The question became critical in 1989, when National Endowment for the Arts (NEA) grants were retroactively withdrawn from four artists. The most famous was Karen Finley, whose performance piece *We Keep our Victims Ready* involved her smearing her naked body with chocolate, a surrogate for excrement that referred to a charge of police brutality that had just been exposed as a hoax. In the political debate that ensued, Finley's piece came to represent in the mind of the public all that had gone bad with contemporary art.

263 **Robert Mapplethorpe**, *Thomas*, 1987. Robert Mapplethorpe was an odd combination, an elegant formalist who made crisply memorable photographs, but who also took an unabashed delight in the explicitly sexual and scatological. This photograph shows his tamer side, a study of elegance and force in strong silhouette.

264 Richard Serra, *Tilted Arc*, Federal Plaza, New York, 1981. *Tilted Arc* asked if there could be public art without a public. A slab of corten steel, it slashed across the Federal Plaza in New York, bisecting the space in an aggressive gesture that was as unfriendly as the Berlin Wall—and so Serra intended. Visitors to the federal immigration office were treated to a physical reminder of how difficult it can be to come into the United States. When the sculpture was removed, Serra's defenders charged censorship. The battle proved the complexity of the arts disputes of the 1980s, which did not always fall into the convenient model of a progressive vanguard fighting a rigid and highhanded establishment. In this case, it was the vanguard which seemed contemptuous of the public workers who used the space.

When the NEA was established in 1965, no one foresaw conflict between the government and the art world. Formalism was still in full vigor, and still insulated artists from political entanglements. Indeed, the first roster of grant recipients, including such artists as Tony Smith, Ed Ruscha, and Dan Flavin, was completely apolitical. With the rise of agenda art, however, art and politics soon overlapped. Once artists began to express explicitly political sentiments, it was inevitable that some segment of the population would take umbrage at subsidizing—in effect—political views for which they had no sympathy. Of course, it was not surprising that if art was to be used as politics, it could not claim the immunities of art while exercizing the prerogatives of politics. An artist could not expect to show photographs of Ronald Reagan with captions like "You're killing us," and not be judged as political—and therefore ineligible for government support. (Of course, not all attempts to suppress art came from the right. When Nicholas Nixon exhibited photographs of dying AIDS patients in 1988, members of the activist group ACT-UP intervened at MoMA, criticizing it for stigmatizing the victims of the disease.)

Throughout 1989, the NEA went through contortions to avoid political conflict, and even bad publicity. Often a simple verbal description of a grant was enough to generate a mountain of ridicule (e.g., to "drip ink from Hayley, Idaho, to Cody, Wyoming"). Beleaguered administrators took to coaching applicants to describe their projects in more vague terms. After 1977, "no project description necessary" was stamped on the application form for grants. Even then some artists seemed to miss the point, and by 1983 the space for the "Description of Proposed Activity" was dropped from the application entirely.

The battle over the NEA ran from 1989 to 1993, during which time there was considerable clamor for abolishing the agency outright, particularly during the presidential primaries and campaign of 1992. In the end, the agency eliminated the

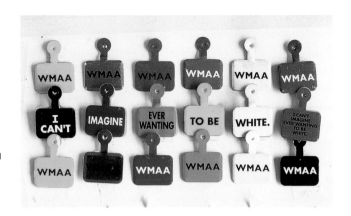

265 Daniel Joseph Martinez,
Museum Tags: Second Movement (Overture), 1993. Martinez designed his metal museum entrance tags for the 1993 Whitney Biennial. Only a few selected visitors received the entire phrase.

direct giving of grants to artists, which implied official endorsement; instead, grants would pass through institutions. The NEA Four, as they came to be called, sued to have their grants reinstated and in 1993 won their case.

The Culture Wars revealed that American art had two constituencies, an active one of schools, museums, and galleries, and a passive one that comprised the public as a whole. If the public had been quiescent during the 1950s and 1960s, this did not mean that it endorsed such innovations as Happenings or Conceptual Art, but rather that it watched from a distance, variously bemused and befuddled. But when it came to public art—art in the public sphere—a posture of detachment was not possible. In those cases, the public spoke out, vociferously and sometimes angrily. The was the case with Richard Serra's *Tilted Arc*, an abstract piece of outdoor sculpture designed for Federal Plaza in New York [264]. The work was deeply disliked by the people who used the building it adorned, and was dismantled by popular request.

The Culture Wars did not reach a resolution but gradually faded out in the 1990s. The election of a liberal Democrat as president in 1992 shifted the focus of much of the political protest art of the previous twelve years. The speed with which attitudes changed is shown by the critical failure of the 1993 Whitney Biennial. Nicknamed the "Identity Biennial," this was perhaps the most wide-ranging exhibition of identity and agenda art of the entire period, and its preoccupation with race and identity was made clear at the very door to the museum. There visitors would be given a metal button to wear, which bore an obscure phrase such as *to be* or *imagine*. In fact, these were fragments of an entire statement, which appeared on the occasional button that read "I Can't Imagine Ever Wanting To Be White" [265]. Much of this work was roundly criticized for its heavy-handedness. As in the art of Abolition of the 1850s or Social Realist art of the 1930s, good politics was not necessarily a guarantee of good art. In the words of one reviewer, the exhibition was "A Fiesta of Whining."

In general, the artistic initiatives of the past generation have lacked the sense of being connected with issues and developments larger than themselves, as the art of the 1950s or 1960s did. The emergence of media art (using computers and the Internet) in the 1990s has occurred without any of the revolutionary jolt that Rauschenberg and Kaprow's innovations had once administered. In an odd way, the Happening has inured the public to artistic shocks. Any new genres might be considered as either a Happening or an Installation—two genres with infinitely pliable boundaries, and would have the comfortable frisson of a predictable event.

It was not only the lay public that was "theory-weary," as Irving Sandler put it. A growing number of artists now began to make work that was deliberately frivolous or playful. During the mid-1980s a counter-current emerged that was soon known as "commodity art," a kind of neo-Pop, purged of all politics and theory. For example, one of its most celebrated works was *Rabbit*, an enormous glistening rabbit so bulbous and featureless that it might have been an inflatable beach toy; in fact, it was made from stainless steel. *Rabbit* was by Jeff Koons (born 1955), the most prominent of the commodity artists. A kind of talkative Andy Warhol, Koons intimately knew the world of commerce and capitalism, having worked for a time on Wall Street. Like Warhol, he insisted on a complete emotional and even physical detachment from even the making of his art: "I'm basically the idea person," he told interviewers. "I'm not physically involved in the production."

Another sign of growing frustration with politics and theory was the growing acceptance of Outsider Art—art produced by individuals without formal training, often made under straitened circumstances. Many, in fact, were inhabitants of prisons or asylums, such as Henry Darger (1892–1972), whose disturbing epic of nude androgynous children battling monsters began life in an oppressive Victorian asylum designed by Frank Furness. The vogue for Outsider Art capitalized on the durable American belief that anyone can be an artist—or anything else, for that matter—by dint of effort and practice. It also appealed to the twentieth-century interest in psychology and primal states of mind. To a certain extent, Outsider Art revived the psychological, even

266 **Fred Wilson**, *Mining the Museum*, 1992. Wilson believed that "normally there is one museum for the beautiful things of one's culture and perhaps a separate room or a separate museum for the horrific things. Life, however, does not occur in neat categories." His *Mining the Museum* installation uncomfortably inserted the horrific into the beautiful, turning the entire museum and its collections into a vast extended installation piece.

surrealist content that had largely vanished from art with the fall of Abstract Expressionism. The most important sign of the respectability of Outsider Art was the building of the American Visionary Art Museum in Baltimore in 1995.

Outsider Art was one way of shaking up an art world that had grown complacent and self-absorbed. Another was to take existing art and force it to be seen in a new way. The most striking instance of this came in Baltimore as well. In 1992 the artist Fred Wilson created a provocative installation at the Maryland Historical Society called *Mining the Museum*, which consisted entirely of unexpected and unnerving juxtapositions [266]. One case, for example, labeled "Metalwork 1793–1880," showed an elegant array of silver teapots among which were placed a set of iron slave shackles. In another, a Victorian dollhouse at first looks charming and cheerful, until one notices the white figures lay prone on the floor while the black dolls sit comfortably on the furniture—a depiction of a violent slave revolt made all the more incendiary by being placed in the context of an innocent child's toy.

Architecture, even during the politicized 1980s, remained largely free of agenda art. To the extent that political views were at play at all, it was only in the public's association of postmodern architecture with capitalism. Postmodern architecture had seemed a vanguard movement in the 1970s but after about 1982, critical opinion quickly turned against it. After all, its most conspicuous monuments were the vivid commercial towers erected during the building boom of the 1980s and characterized by their compulsory granite cladding and oversize plywood columns. As the style came to be seen as a physical manifestation of an alleged "decade of greed," tainted by its association with the crassness of commerce, postmodernism became something of a dirty word in schools of architecture. Commercially successful architects such as Michael Graves and Helmut Jahn were scorned for their frivolity and envied for their success. To the architecture critic of the *New York Times*, postmodernism was a "career strategy for reactionaries, opportunists, and their deeply uncultivated promoters."

To some extent, the charge was justified. Postmodern architecture may have begun as a humanist endeavor, with a vision of a humane and expressive architecture and a variegated liveable city. But in the absence of sustained patronage to give it those humanistic values, it simply became a fashionable mode of decoration, with an unfortunate addiction to red granite stripes.

267 Duany Plater-Zyberk, Seaside, Florida, begun 1978. This represented the best of the New Urbanism. The planned community looked carefully at the attractive and humane suburbs of nineteenth-century America, emulating their gregariousness, their scale, and their use of porches (a form that had vanished after the invention of television and air-conditioning, or been replaced by the antisocial rear deck).

268 Peter Bohlin (Bohlin Cywinski Jackson), Adirondack House, New York, 1987–92. In recent years, architecture has been increasingly dominated by a short list of celebrity architects—those architects who win international reputations, often by cultivating a distinctive visual signature. Such a system has tended to disadvantage those architects such as Peter Bohlin who do not have an office style but derive the character of their commissions from the site, the program, and the client. Adirondack House is characteristic of Bohlin's deferential approach, and helps explain why he was elected by Bill Gates to design his colossal private estate in Seattle.

One wing of the postmodern revolution had no hint of the snide or ironic about it, and this was its urbanist arm. Young architects such as Andres Duany and Elizabeth Plater-Zyberk did not merely ransack the past for clever graphic forms, but believed that the past could offer lessons in humane living. Their most famous was the resort community of Seaside, Florida [267]. Other regional architects continued to draw on local tradition and materials, especially in houses, where the lines of historic continuity remain strongest. There is little in Peter Bohlin's Adirondack House (1987–92) that A. J. Downing would have rejected. The integration of the house in the landscape, the sense of the goodness of nature, the informality of natural materials, and the sense of assertive individualism, expressed on that favorite American site, the neighborless wilderness: all are deeply rooted in the nineteenth century, and earlier [268].

As postmodernism fell from favor, especially in the academy, the prestige of architectural modernism rose once more. Most important were the Whites, as the faction of neo-modernists gathered around Richard Meier and Peter Eisenman came to be known. They emerged in the 1970s as an alternative to postmodernism and took their inspiration from Le Corbusier's purist white modernism of the 1920s. Firmly rejecting postmodernism's color and playful use of historical form, as well

269 **Richard Meier**, Getty
Center, Los Angeles, 1984–97.
The Getty Center in Los Angeles
is the principal work of American
late modernism—the cool white
palette of cubes is from Le
Corbusier but the self-conscious
geometric fragmentation derives
from Deconstruction. Meier
famously wanted a glaringly white
treatment for his walls, but strong
local opposition forced him to use
buff-colored travertine instead
(14,000 tons in all).

270 **Eric Owen Moss**, 3535
Hayden Avenue, Culver City,
1997–98. Just as the Greek Revival
moved in a matter of years from
major government buildings to
wooden houses on the frontier,
so Gehry's example moved into
commercial architecture. The
California architect Eric Owen
Moss (born 1943) is best known
for the "spatial ambiguity" of his
work, such as this office building
in Culver City.

as Venturi's rhetoric of the facade, they turned to geometry as
the root of architectural order. In particular, they took the cube as
their point of departure, subjecting it to analysis and manipulation.

The Whites flourished particularly in institutional settings,
which viewed postmodernism with disdain because of its
flamboyance and the taint of commercialism. Their greatest coup
was the Getty Center in Los Angeles, the single most lucrative
architectural commission in American history, building and site
together costing nearly one billion dollars. Meier won the
commission with a project that made the most of the dramatic
site, an intersection of two ridges high above Los Angeles [269].
The two ridges meet at an angle of 22.5 degrees, which Meier
made the geometric leitmotif of the entire design, repeating it
again and again in the orientation of various major and minor
features. At the intersection of the ridges he placed the museum
rotunda, presiding over two rows of pavilions in which the art is
displayed, a scheme that deliberately evokes Jefferson's University
of Virginia and its ordered array of pavilions dominated by a
library rotunda [46].

During the 1970s and 1980s, the neo-modernism of the Whites
became increasingly theoretical. At the same time, their geometry
grew more intricate, and their axial dissections more obsessive,
until their buildings came apart literally. Or perhaps *literarily*, for it
was the French philosophical school of deconstruction, with its
doctrine about the infinite elasticity of text, that designated the
new movement that emerged from the Whites. Here a metaphor
about architecture was borrowed by philosophy and then
returned to architecture, punning on the predilection of
Deconstructionist buildings to fragment and disintegrate visibly.
Perhaps the first to do so was Frank Gehry's own house in Santa
Monica, which conspicuously unpeeled itself in 1978. Within a
few years young architecture students, always a bellwether of
changing taste, had abandoned postmodernism and shifted to
Deconstruction. By the 1990s, Deconstruction had become so
popular its forms had entered the commercial vernacular [270].

Gehry's literal deconstruction of his house was not an
operation that one can perform on a serious architectural
commission but he found a way to achieve the same explosive
disruption of architectural order and make it palatable to
institutional clients. By the end of the 1980s, he had devised an
entirely new architectural language in which trapezoidal and
curving elements met in a turbulent writhing mass. Gehry's most

271 **Frank Gehry**, Guggenheim Museum, Bilbao, Spain, 1992–98. This is one of the first major buildings to show the new formal range made possible by computer technology. The writhing and fluttering forms were first studied as models, even crumpled tissue papers, that could then be scanned and measured—generating programs that not only made the working drawings but actually cut the titanium sheets to their precise dimensions. Here a change in the design process had powerful consequences for the kinds of forms being produced, just as the modernist rejection of the rendered drawing in favor of three-dimensional models had once focused attention on the abstract play of volumes.

celebrated work, and perhaps his most successful, was his Guggenheim Museum in Bilbao, a building of ecstatic energy, its titanium-clad elements billowing like sails in a tempest [271].

As spectacular as the style of the Guggenheim is, it is ultimately important for other reasons, which have to do with the changing relationship between the building and the public.

It is telling that America's most important work of architecture at the turn of the millennium was built in Europe. Clearly art and architecture, as much as commerce, have been shaped by the present trend toward globalization, and here Thomas Krens, director of the Guggenheim Museum in New York, proved to be a client of unusual vision. After becoming director in the late 1980s, he immediately embarked on a bold program of institutional expansion. For Krens the art museum was in crisis, both as institution and building type. It was an eighteenth-century idea ("the encyclopedia") thrust into a nineteenth-century building type ("the modified palace"). Most sat on constricted urban sites,

272 **Ann Hamilton**, *corpus* installation, MASS MoCA, 2004. Despite the vast scope of the piece it is characterized by odd humor: machines clatter above and dispense computer paper at odd intervals, falling in long fluttering arcs, like mechanical snow.

whose modest display and storage capacity had long since been outpaced by collection growth, forcing most of their holdings to be kept perpetually out of sight. The modern museum, Krens proclaimed, required both a new concept and a new form.

The solution lay in a profoundly twentieth-century institution, the corporate franchise. Krens envisioned a worldwide network of affiliated branch museums so that the Guggenheim might circulate its vast reservoir of art languishing unseen in storage. Similar projects were launched in Salzburg and in a rehabilitated factory complex in North Adams, Massachusetts, but these ran into delays, making the Bilbao building the first test case of his innovative concept.

The galleries of Krens's museums had the massive scale of an airplane hangar, a scale that invited a very different kind of art than that of most of American history. From the beginning, American art tended to be scaled to the parlor and not the palace. For grand Baroque gestures there was no place, and it took centuries for art to shed its small-scale and graphic character. The 10- and 12-foot (3- and 3.6-meter) canvases of Pollock were unusual in their day, but with Krens's museums, installation pieces sprawled to industrial scale. Ann Hamilton's enigmatic *corpus* dominated the principal gallery of MASS MoCA in North Adams, a room measuring over 300 by 75 feet by 40 feet (91.4 by 22 by 12 meters) [272]. Tim Hawkinson filled the same space with his bizarre *Uberorgan*, a gigantic pipe organ whose individuals pipes snaked their way informally around the gallery like wayward vines, periodically emitting flatulent tones from the lowest end of the bass register.

It is obvious that a museum predicated on the idea of art tourism and mass audiences will be reluctant to offend its visitors. Such museums are more likely to have the character of a festival market place than a temple of the arts. And large and diverting installations like Hamilton's are experienced in a quite different way than the solitary and existential encounter that Pollock and Rothko demanded. Instead, these museums have moved ever more toward an art of public spectacle, providing visual delight with oversize elements and moving parts. While there is occasionally a theoretical program, it is generally incidental to the work, which may be appreciated without it. And much of the work is simply funny, as in the work of Louise Lawler, perhaps the first artist to take the principle that things are progressively funnier the more we try to be serious about them, and to apply it to the solemnity of the art museum [273].

It is this changed nature of the museum experience—away from the sanctuary or temple and toward the circus or opera—which partially accounts for the *Cremaster Series* (1994–2001) by Matthew Barney, a work that has been both widely popular and

273 **Louise Lawler**, *Big*, 2002–3. The favorite theme of the photographer Louise Lawler is the strange resonance that artworks acquire when accidentally juxtaposed with other objects in a museum, Her *Big* shows a massive and rather terrifying head of Picasso, made by the Italian artist Maurizio Cattelan, swathed in plastic and sitting on the floor behind a disconnected body while in the distant photograph by German Thomas Struth, museum-goers admire a headless statue from antiquity.

274 Matthew Barney, *Cremaster Series*, 1994–2001. One does not need to follow the arcane narrative of the five films of Matthew Barney's *Cremaster Cycle*, an allegory of sexual differentiation, to appreciate his flair for arresting visual imagery. Consisting variously of a five-part film series and a museum installation, it also has an Internet component, one of the first major works of art to do so.

achieved critical success. *Cremaster*, named after an obscure scatological reference, is a comprehensive multi-media production, which recalls a Hollywood film franchise with its commercial tie-ins. And indeed Barney devised an integrated marketing operation on the order of Warhol. Its centerpiece was a series of five films, augmented by photographs and sculpture, and a complex written program. Each film presented an extravagant fantasy, the meaning of which was expounded in a synopsis that suggested an opera libretto [274]. For a moment, around the turn of the Millennium, Barney's dense, complex, and layered phantasmagoria seemed to point the way toward a new kind of art world, in which new technologies, new marketing strategies, and a new sense of dynamic interaction with the public played a decisive role. It was on this basis that the *New York Times* pronounced Barney "ultimately the most important American artist of his generation."

Great national traumas have, from time to time, served to reorient art and to throw new attitudes into a clear light. The Civil War ended the reign of sentimental and moralizing art; the stock market crash of 1929 turned American art inward. It is too early to tell how the events of September 11, 2001 will affect American art but it is certain that they will.

There are signs that it has already happened. In the aftermath of formalism, most artists came to share one of two distinct attitudes toward their work, which might be described as the ironic and the critical. The ironic attitude is the legacy of Pop Art and postmodernism, and its roots can be traced from Koons through Warhol and Venturi to Rauschenberg and Johns. Essentially apolitical, it prospered in commercial settings and, in the form of postmodern architecture, reshaped the contemporary city. The critical attitude, by contrast, is emphatically political, and derives from the agenda art of the late 1960s. Its stronghold was not the commercial street—where architectural patrons, for example, seldom paid to see themselves mocked—but rather the world of museums, schools, and journals.

Much could be said on behalf of each artistic temperament, and how their emergence was an inevitable reaction to the highhandedness of formalism. But in the event, neither attitude was up to the demand of responding to the calamity of September 11. The ironic and the critical stance are each a kind of negation, and in the wake of the attacks the national mood sought something more like an affirmation. But since the resignation of President Nixon in 1974 and the fall of Vietnam in 1975, emphatic and heroic statements had been deeply unfashionable, even suspect, and a full generation had come of age without experience in making confident assertions.

This was clear in the response of artists and architects to the attacks. In September 2002, a year after the attacks, the artist Eric Fischl placed a bronze entitled *Tumbling Woman* in the Rockefeller Center. A life-size piece, it depicted a nude woman falling headfirst through the air; since the piece rested on the ground, it seemed to suggest the actual moment of impact. The timing and the placement gave the work unusual visibility and it met with spontaneous and almost universal revulsion, prompting its premature removal. When asked why he had not made a heroic piece, Fischl replied that he did not know what that was, other than to say "I see heroism in victimization."

Whether or not American artists could view buildings like the World Trade Center and the Pentagon without irony, the terrorists who attacked them certainly took them sincerely, regarding them as straightforward projections of American identity and values. Any buildings that replaced the Twin Towers would likewise be judged as symbols of American identity, by the world and by the American public. This consideration enormously complicated the project to rebuild the towers and place a memorial on the site.

In early 2003 the commission to design the new World Trade Center complex was awarded to Daniel Libeskind, a Polish-American architect whose Jewish Museum in Berlin had recently been completed. That too was a tragic building in a tragic place, which was reflected in his typically splintered and psychologically disorienting geometry. To the jurors of the architectural competition in New York, it confirmed Libeskind's skill in giving dignity to grief and tragedy. In many ways, the World Trade Center design recapitulated the theme and formal language of the Berlin museum, especially the faceted prismatic form of its principal feature, a "Freedom Tower" 1,776 feet (541 meters) in height [275]. As with Fischl's *Tumbling Woman*, however, there was considerable public outcry, and for much the same reason. Libeskind's design

275 **Daniel Libeskind**, World Trade Center Competition, 2003–4. Daniel Libeskind won the 2003 competition to design the new World Trade Center complex with a bold essay in architectural Deconstruction. It was widely criticized as a kind of architectural theme park, with too many distractions to provide the single clear focus that the commission demanded. Particularly controversial was the Wedge of Light, which was to be aligned so that the sun would fall on it on the anniversary of the attacks precisely between the time of the first impact and the collapse of the second tower—a gesture that was felt to conflict with, and detract from, the memorial on the footprint of the towers.

seemed to perpetuate the disaster architecturally: it retained the ruins of the concrete retaining wall that kept out the Hudson River after the buildings' destruction, to which the broken forms of the tower also seemed to point.

As an architectural statement, Libeskind's design was too cluttered and diffuse to be as effective a place of commemoration as Maya Lin's Vietnam Veterans Memorial had been but it was also seen as too ambivalent to be a statement of national resolve and fortitude. In the end, Daniel Child of SOM was appointed project architect while Libeskind was relegated to the role of site planner.

The World Trade Center story, as of this writing, has dragged on for four years and has not yet been resolved. It is the most chaotic debut of a major American building since the U.S. Capitol, which also suffered from multiple constituencies, blurred chains of command, and competing architects. In that case the building was

276 **Vincent Desiderio**, *Pantocrator*, 2002. Desiderio trained at the Pennsylvania Academy of the Fine Arts, and his triptych *Pantocrator* contemplates some of the same themes that Eakins once taught there. It is an allegory of sight and seeing—from the first perspective painting of Brunelleschi at the Florence Baptistery to the automated camera of an orbiting satellite. And to the side, a voyeur's furtive view of a woman's body, the human displaced by the machine. For Desiderio, today's Pantocrator (the Byzantine term for the ruler of all) is no longer the head of God peering from the cathedral apse but perhaps the merciless eye of science.

saved by Jefferson and Latrobe; at Ground Zero it remains to be seen. It might reshape and redirect public events as great buildings discussed here have—as Richardson's Trinity Church did—or it might prove the end of an era, like Girard College. This depends on the extent to which the new World Trade Center complex suits the contemporary mood, a curious alloy of confidence and anxiety about national identity at the moment, which has the apprehensive sense of 1930s art.

As overwhelming as the events of September 11 were, they could not instantly transform something as complex as American art. Much remained as it was before the attacks, although already existing tendencies might take on new meanings and resonances. For example, morbid and ghoulish themes had long been prominent in the installations of Banks Violette and the videos of Sue de Beer, although now they were associated with the unfulfilled void at Ground Zero. But at the same time there has been a growing body of work distinguished by a certain elegiac or mournful quality, as is seen in those who have undergone a great sorrow. This was strongest among traditional figurative painters, such as Vincent Desiderio, Karen Kilimnik and Elizabeth Peyton, each of whom has drawn renewed public interest. In some ways, their recent work recalls the mood of post-Civil War art, even in the return to clear linear expression [276]. It is an intelligent art, unable for the moment to return to single-minded certainties, but squarely opposed to cynicism, irony, and intellectual cant. Even in an age of globalization and blurred national boundaries, it is still possible to see that there is such a thing as American art.

Glossary

Abject Art Art featuring degraded or morbid subject matter, usually treated with cool clinical detachment; briefly fashionable in the early 1990s.

Abstract Expressionism A school of painting that arose in New York during the 1940s, drawing on both the abstract legacy of Cubism and the Surrealist doctrine of the liberated unconscious.

Action Painting An alternative term for Abstract Expression, in which the physical act of painting is stressed as much as the canvas that it produced.

Aesthetic Movement Influential doctrine in the period c. 1870 to c. 1900, according to which the central purpose of art is to give visual pleasure rather than to tell a story or teach a lesson.

Anti-Form Art movement of the 1960s and 1970s, which was against carefully composed and finished objects; related to Conceptual Art.

Arcadian Dwelling in an idealized pastoral state.

Art Deco Originally derived from the French *arts décoratifs*, the term was applied to the fashionable commercial architecture of the 1920s and 1930s, with its stylized ornament, streamlined forms, and rich chromatic effects.

Art Union A commercial enterprise in New York, active 1844–1852, which gave its subscribers prints of American paintings as well as a chance to win the original at regular lottery drawings.

Ashcan School Originally a term of derision applied to the urban realist painters who assembled around Robert Henri, first in Philadelphia during the 1890s and subsequently in New York.

assemblage Form of sculpture composed of found objects and deliberately crude materials, often with jarring juxtapositions, popularized by Robert Rauschenberg in the 1950s.

automatism The notion that the unconscious mind can be made to express itself directly, e.g. through automatic writing; a central theme of Surrealism.

balloon frame A method of building in wood that dispensed with the traditional heavy frame and instead used the thin wall partitions themselves as a self-supporting structural system; introduced in the 1840s, after machine-made nails and industrially sawn boards became economical.

brownstone A dark form of sandstone, popular as a building material since the 1840s, when its warm brown tones made it a novel alternative to the white marbles of the Greek Revival.

Brutalism Also known as New Brutalism, a mode of architecture created during the 1950s in England and later imported to the United States, characterized by rough use of materials, especially concrete, and a blunt, matter-of-fact approach to composition.

bungalow A compact cottage-like house, often with Arts and Crafts details, popularized in California in the early twentieth century.

City Beautiful Movement School of urban planning that sought to beautify cities through the use of parks and a harmonious coordination of architecture, usually classical in character.

Colonial architecture Refers generally to architecture of the colonies before Independence; this groups together all styles before 1776, including Georgian, Palladian, and the late-medieval architecture of the seventeenth century.

commodity art Art movement of the 1980s that teetered between satire of capitalism and a surrender to it, known for its deliberately vapid and pleasing consumer objects, often with a distinct Pop Art sensibility.

Conceptual Art Art in which the intellectual idea is more important than its physical realization as an object.

Corinthian Richest of the three principal orders of classical Greek architecture, characterized by elaborate capitals adorned with carved acanthus leaves.

Culture Wars Collective term for the various battles over government funding for the arts, censorship, and political activism by artists in the 1980s.

Dada A literary and artistic movement that arose during World War I, absurdist in character, and hostile to aesthetic and formal values in art.

deconstruction Originally a school of literary criticism which, when applied to architecture in the 1970s, came to stand for visibly deconstructed form, Assemblage-like collages of unconventional building materials, and an intellectual commitment to indeterminate form.

dentil In Greek, *teeth*, referring to the small blocks that support a decorative cornice.

Doric The simplest of the classical orders of ancient Greece, consisting of a simple capital carrying an entablature.

Düsseldorf School A school of sentimental and highly finished painting, centered in the German city of Düsseldorf, which enjoyed great prestige in the United States in the 1840s and 1850s.

Earth Art/Land Art/Earthworks/Environmental Art Monumental outdoor sculpture of the 1960s and 1970s in which the landscape itself plays the determining role, often devoted to ecological themes.

entasis Term in Greek architecture that refers to the slight outward bowing of a Doric column, which gives it an expression of buoyant strength.

environmental sculpture Sculpture in which a room or place is manipulated to create a comprehensive aesthetic experience, in which the experience of space rather than the shaping of a sculptural object is the principal concern.

expressionism Art which is forceful or vigorous in treatment or form in order to convey heightened or exalted emotion.

Fauvism Style of French painting that emerged after 1900, using lurid yellows and greens and scratchy surface treatment to heighten pictorial tension.

Federal style American architecture from roughly 1776 and 1820, characterized by lighter and more graceful proportions than the earlier Georgian style, and increasing complexity and spatial inventiveness in the planning.

formalism The doctrine that a work of art is to be judged only by its formal properties—such as line, shape, and color—rather than its narrative content or didactic purpose.

Functionalism The modernist idea that building should be designed according to a rigorous analysis of its functional requirements, and that the composition of the exterior should follow logically and inevitably from its floor plan.

Futurism Early modernist movement in Italy, inspired by Filippo Tommaso Marinetti's 1909 *Futurist Manifesto*, and advocating the idea that machines and the experience of rapid movement would generate a new visual language.

General Grant style Ironic term for the Second Empire style, associating it with the presidency of Ulysses S. Grant (1869–77), under whom a great many federal courthouses and post offices were built in the style.

Georgian architecture Refers to the classical architecture built in England during the reign of the first three Hanoverian kings; in America, for the period 1714 to 1776, when Independence was declared.

Gilded Age Ironic term coined by Mark Twain to describe post-Civil War America, its new wealth and the vulgarity with which it displayed it.

Gothic The system of architecture based on the pointed arch and ribbed vault that arose in France in the twelfth century and was widely used throughout Europe into the sixteenth century.

Gothic Revival The revival of medieval Gothic architecture, first as a fashionable novelty, but later, from about 1840 to 1880, as a principled intellectual and moral movement.

Greek Revival The phase of the classical revival from about 1820 to about 1850, in which the forms of classical Greek architecture were used with scholarly accuracy

grid Pattern formed by lines intersecting at right angles, and making regular squares or rectangles; valued in American town planning for its regularity and efficiency of property division.

hall The principal room of a medieval house; after c. 1700 used to refer to the formal passage of a classically composed house.

Happening Art that consists of a planned or spontaneous performance on the part of the artist(s), often in interaction with the public, pioneered during the 1950s by Alan Kaprow and others.

High Victorian Gothic The climax of the Gothic Revival in the 1860s and 1870s, based on a high degree of energy in the massing and ornament, extravagant use of architectural color and an exotic use of architectural styles.

historicism The practice of basing architecture on the historical styles of the past, either singly or in eclectic combination.

Impressionism (French and American) School of French art from c. 1860s to c. 1880s, based on modern subjects, bright and high-keyed colors, and an interest in natural light, which made its adherents the first artists to paint systematically outdoors (en plein air); the American variant, although inspired by France, tends to be somewhat darker in its colors and lacks the social and theoretical program of its prototype.

Industrial Revolution The sudden increase in the scale and productivity of industry, brought about by new mechanical processes in the late eighteenth century, particularly the steam engine.

Installation Art A category of modern sculpture in which an architectural space is made into a work of art by placing objects in it and otherwise influencing the space.

insulae The multi-story apartment houses of ancient Rome.

International Style Term for modern architecture coined by Henry Russell Hitchcock and Philip Johnson in 1932, emphasizing its international extent and freedom from specific national or geographical content.

Ionic One of the three orders of classical Greek architecture, characterized by the elegant spiral volutes of its capitals.

Junk Art Form of modern sculpture in which discarded or cheap items are combined, often with deliberate awkwardness.

lintel the horizontal beam of wood, stone or metal, capping a door or window opening.

Luminism School of painting in the 1850s and 1860s especially concerned with the properties of light and air, often treated in coastal scenes with simple, lucid compositional schemes.

mansard A roof with high sloping sides, either concave or convex, named after the French seventeenth-century architect François Mansart.

metope(s) The rectangular decorative panels, often bearing carved sculpture, which in a Doric entablature alternate with triglyphs.

Minimalism Art of radically simplified form, laconic expression, and impersonal tone, popular during the 1960s and 1970s.

mobile (hanging) A type of moving sculpture devised by Alexander Calder in the early 1930s, in which abstract components are suspended from wires and allowed to spin and swing freely in space.

Modernism The principal school of twentieth-century art and architecture, characterized by use of new forms of expressionism and new materials, and the insistence that a fundamentally transformed modern society required a fundamentally new language of art.

Moorish style An exotic revival style, popular in the mid-nineteenth century, and drawn freely from elements across the Islamic world, from North Africa to Persia.

mortise and tenon joints Wood framing technique in which a beam end is cut down to form a tongue (or tenon) that fits into a matching hole (or mortise) cut into another beam; a wooden peg is often driven through the mortise to hold it in place.

Munich School German school of painting popular in the 1870s, characterized by romantic and exotic subject matter, dark interiors, and rich painterly technique.

Neoclassicism The new classicism of the period from c. 1760 to 1820, characterized by its love of simple geometric forms and a new preference for Greek severity over Roman splendor.

New Urbanism School of anti-modernist urban planning, inspired by the lessons of traditional urbanism, including a commitment to human scale, front porches, and walkable streets.

New York School Collective term for the abstract painters and sculptors of 1940s and 1950s New York.

octagonal house A type of dwelling advocated by Orson Squire Fowler and briefly popular in the 1840s.

oculus Deriving from the Latin word for "eye," a round window.

Orphism Term coined around 1912 by French poet Guillaume Apollinaire, referring to an abstract art of lyrical expression and sensuous color.

Outsider Art Art created by artists not professionally schooled, often (although not always) by patients suffering from mental illness and incarcerated prisoners.

Palladian revival Movement inspired by the Renaissance architect Andrea Palladio (1508–80), whose *Four Books of Architecture* were widely imitated in Britain and her colonies during the eighteenth century.

panopticon plan The radial arrangement of wings so that they can be supervised from a central hub, frequently used for prisons after the 1820s.

pediment In classical architecture, the triangle formed by the two sides of a gable roof and the horizontal entablature running below them.

pendill(s) The decorative boss that drops from the underside of the overhanging second story in a seventeenth-century wooden house.

Performance Art Since the 1970s, the preferred term for Happenings.

peristyle The continuous colonnade on all four sides of a Greek temple; literally, "all-around columns."

Photorealism Painting that aspires to the clarity and objectivity of the photographic image; widely popular during the 1970s and 1980s.

Photo-Secession Movement founded in 1902 by Alfred Stieglitz, committed to raising the status of photography to that of a fine art on a par with painting and sculpture.

picturesque (movement) Collective term for a set of artistic values—especially contrast, irregularity, and surprise—which in the eighteenth century emerged as an alternative to the classical values of refinement, symmetry, and repose.

pier A rectangular column or support.

pilaster In classical architecture, a column that is rectangular rather than round in plan, often set directly upon a wall.

Pop Art An art movement in Britain and the United States, dating from the late 1950s and making ironic use of such "low" sources as commercial imagery, advertisements, and product labels.

porch/verandah A raised platform under a roof at the front or sides of a house, a typical feature of American domestic architecture since the early nineteenth century.

portico A formal entrance consisting of a pediment carried on columns or pilasters.

Post-Impressionism A further development of Impressionism after c. 1890, distinguished by its interest in pictorial flatness and the geometric structure of composition.

Postmodernism As an architectural style, the witty use of flattened and stylized historical forms, often with a colorful Pop Art sensibility, popular from c. 1965 to c. 1985; as a philosophy of art, a movement hostile to the authoritarian claims of high modernism and interested in the indeterminacy of meaning in contemporary art.

Post-painterly Abstraction Term coined by Clement Greenberg to describe the delicate abstract painting of the late 1950s, which suppressed violent active line in favor of fields of veiled color, often stained into the canvas.

Prairie Style Style of domestic architecture created by Frank Lloyd Wright after 1900, in which low spreading roof forms and strong horizontal expression echo the topography of the American Midwest, and in which the clear division between rooms and between interior and exterior is abandoned in favor of flowing continuous space.

Precisionism Style of American painting and photography in the 1920s, characterized by sharp edges, linear expression and a crisp factuality in expression.

Pre-Raphaelite movement School of English painting in the mid-nineteenth century which admired the art of the early Italian Renaissance, up to the career of Raphael, when it lost its last vestiges of medieval linearity.

Queen Anne revival Architectural movement of the 1870s and 1880s, especially popular in houses, with animated play of turrets, gables, half-timbering, and bay windows.

Regionalists Painters of the 1930s, typically in the Midwest, who found their subject matter in the towns and farms of their own locale.

romanesque The round-arched architecture of twelfth-century Europe, valued as a model in nineteenth-century America for its simplicity, economy, and rugged expression.

Romanticism A broadly based cultural and aesthetic movement of the late eighteenth and early nineteenth centuries, rejecting classical values of repose and rationality in art and turning instead to personal expression and intense emotion.

Rundbogenstil Literally, "round-arched style," a synthetic architectural style created in Germany in the 1820s and derived in part from the Romanesque; after the European revolutions of 1848, it was carried to the United States by refugee architects and was popular for churches and public buildings.

saltbox house A colonial house type in which the gabled roof is carried closer to the ground on the north side of the building.

Second Empire style The fashion in the 1860s and 1870 for modern French neo-Renaissance architecture, characterized by the mansard roof, vigorous use of projecting pavilions, segmental pediments and paired columns, and a close integration of architecture and sculpture.

serliana Also known as a Palladian window, a form of symmetrical opening in which a central round-arched window is flanked by two flat-headed windows, frequently used as the principal motif on a classical house.

Shakers Influential religious sect, especially active in the first half of the nineteenth century, noted for its communal structure, celibacy, and functional architecture.

Shingle Style Domestic architectural style popular in the 1880s, drawing on Colonial and Queen Anne sources but characterized by its freedom of planning and the abstract composition of its shingled masses.

skyscraper/setback skyscraper A tall building that pulls in its walls as regular intervals as it rises, in compliance with New York's zoning law of 1916.

Social Realism Influential art movement of the 1930s which sought to depict modern life realistically, and found its subjects in modern factory dwellers, city dwellers, and farmers, and which viewed art as a means toward improving social conditions.

spandrel(s) The residual triangular spaces to either side of the curve of an arch; in metal frame construction, refers to the horizontal panels between rows of windows.

Spanish Colonial style Also known as the Mission Style, a historical revival of reproduced the provincial Baroque forms that were first introduced in the American Southwest in the Spanish missions of the seventeenth and eighteenth centuries.

stabile Abstract sculpture mounted on the ground, for Alexander Calder, the counterpart to the hanging mobile.

staff A cheap material for temporary buildings, composed of jute and hemp that could be sprayed on to a frame, popularized in the 1890s.

stoa A roofed but unwalled public enclosure, used in ancient Greece for commerce, conversation, and other aspects of public life

stripped classicism A severely simplified form of modern classicism, often using stone cladding over a steel frame; especially popular in the 1920s and 1930s for public buildings.

Surrealism Art movement created in the 1920s by André Breton and others using distorted and impossible imagery derived from dreams and the unconscious.

Symbolism A late nineteenth-century art and literary movement, antirealist in tendency, and finding its meaning in symbols, often of a mystical or cryptic sort.

Synchromists Early abstract school of painting, established in 1914 by Morgan Russell and Stanton McDonald-Wright, two Americans studying art in Europe.

The Eight Loosely organized group of anti-academic and Ashcan School painters, led by Robert Henri, which exhibited together at the Macbeth Gallery in New York in 1907.

Tonalism Type of Aesthetic Movement art, which tended to give a canvas a single predominant hue, varying the tone rather than the color to create a decorative unity.

Utilitarianism Early nineteenth–century philosophical movement created by Jeremy Bentham, in which acts are judged only in terms of their usefulness.

Venetian Gothic The architecture of medieval Venice, distinguished by its rich contrasts of red brick and white marble, which was advocated by John Ruskin in the 1850s as a model for modern architecture.

video art Visual art (often by not always with an audio component) that is presented on more or more video screens or computer monitors.

Zip paintings Type of abstract painting popularized by Barnett Newman and consisting of a single vertical stripe running the full height of the canvas.

Select bibliography

General accounts

Baigell, Matthew, *A Concise History of American Painting and Sculpture*, New York, 1996

Bjelajac, David, *American Art: A Cultural History*, New York, 2001

Brooklyn Museum, *The American Renaissance, 1876–1917*, New York, 1979

Brown, Milton W., ed., *American Art: Painting, Sculpture, Architecture, Decorative Arts, Photography*, New York, 1979

——————, *The Story of the Armory Show*, New York, 1988

Doezema, Marianne, and Elizabeth Milroy, *Reading American Art*, New Haven, 1998

Dunlap, William; Rita Weiss, ed., *A History of the Rise and Progress of the Arts of Design in the United States*, New York, 1969

Haskell, Barbara, *The American Century: Art & Culture 1900–1950*, New York, 1999

Hunter, Sam, *American Art of the 20th Century*, New York, 1972

——————, ed., *An American Renaissance: Painting and Sculpture since 1940*, New York, 1986

Lynes, Russell, *The Art-Makers: An Informal History of Painting,*

Sculpture and Architecture in Nineteenth-Century America, New York, 1982

McCoubrey, John W., *American Tradition in Painting*, Philadelphia, 2000

Phillips, Lisa, *The American Century: Art & Culture, 1950–2000*, New York, 1999

Rose, Barbara, *American Art Since 1900*, New York, 1975

Wilmerding, John, *American Art*, Harmondsworth, England, and New York, 1976

Painting and painters

Alloway, Lawrence, et al., *Modern Dreams: The Rise and Fall of Pop*, Cambridge, Mass., 1988

Burns, Sarah, *Inventing the Modern Artist: Art and Culture in Gilded Age America*, New Haven, 1996

Ferber, Linda S., and William H. Gerdts, *The New Path*, New York, 1985

Fink, Lois Marie, *American Art at the Nineteenth-Century Paris Salons*, New York, 1990

Gerdts, William H., *American Impression*, New York, 1984

Greenberg, Clement, *Art and Culture: Critical Essays*, Boston, 1961

Johns, Elizabeth, *American Genre Painting: The Politics of Everyday Life*, New Haven, 1991

Lippard, Lucy R., *Pop Art*, London, 1985

Madoff, Steven H., ed., *Pop Art: A Critical History*, Berkeley, 1997

Mahsun, Carol Anne, ed., *Pop Art: The Critical Dialogue*, Ann Arbor, 1989

Novak, Barbara, *American Painting of the Nineteenth Century: Realism, Idealism, and the American Experience*, New York, 1969

Quick, Michael, et al., *Munich and American Realism in the 19th Century*, Sacramento, 1978

Richardson, E. P., *Painting in America, from 1502 to the Present*, New York, 1965

Sandler, Irving, *American Art of the 1960s*, New York, 1988

_____, *The Triumph of American Painting: A History of Abstract Expressionism*, New York, 1970

_____, *Art of the Postmodern Era: From the late 1960s to the early 1990s*, New York, 1996

Seitz, William C., *Abstract Expressionist Painting in America*, Cambridge, Mass., 1983

Wilton, Andrew, and Tim Barringer, *American Sublime: Landscape Painting in the United States 1820–1880*, Princeton, N.J., 2001

Zurier, Rebecca, Robert W. Snyder and Virginia M. Mecklenburg, *Metropolitan Lives: The Ashcan Artists and their New York*, New York, 1995

WASHINGTON ALLSTON

Bjelajac, David, *Washington Allston, Secret Societies, and the Alchemy of Anglo-American Painting*, Cambridge and New York, 1997

Gerdts, William H., and Theodore E. Stebbins, Jr., "A Man of Genius": *The Art of Washington Allston*, Boston, 1979

Richardson, E. P., *Washington Allston: A Study of the Romantic Artist in America*, Chicago, 1948

ALBERT BIERSTADT

Anderson, Nancy K., and Linda S. Ferber, *Albert Bierstadt: Art & Enterprise*, New York, 1990

THOMAS HART BENTON

Adams, Henry, *Thomas Hart Benton: An American Original*, New York, 1989

Benton, Thomas Hart, *An Artist in America*, Columbia, Missouri, 1983

GEORGE CALEB BINGHAM

Bloch, E. Maurice, *George Caleb Bingham*, 2 vols., Berkeley, 1967

MARY CASSATT

Barter, Judith, *Mary Cassatt: Modern Woman*, New York, 1998

Mathews, Nancy M., *Mary Cassatt: A Life*, New Haven, 1998

WILLIAM MERRITT CHASE

Bryant, Keith L., Jr., *William Merritt Chase, a Genteel Bohemian*, Columbia, Missouri, 1991

Gallati, Barbara Dayer, *William Merritt Chase*, New York, 1995

FREDERIC EDWIN CHURCH

Howat, John K., *Frederic Church*, New Haven, 2005

Kelly, Franklin, *Frederic Edwin Church and the National Landscape*, Washington, D.C., 1988

THOMAS COLE

Noble, Louis Legrand, *The Life and Works of Thomas Cole*, Cambridge, Mass., 1964

Powell, Earl A., *Thomas Cole*, New York, 1990

Truettner, William H., and Alan Wallach, eds., *Thomas Cole: Landscape into History*, New Haven and Washington, D.C., 1994

JOHN SINGLETON COPLEY

Prown, Jules, *John Singleton Copley*, Cambridge, Mass., 1966

WILLEM DE KOONING

Rosenberg, Harold, *De Kooning*, New York, 1973

Stevens, Mark, and Annalyn Swan, *De Kooning: An American Master*, New York, 2004

STUART DAVIS

Hills, Patricia, *Stuart Davis*, New York, 1996

Wilkin, Karen, *Stuart Davis*, New York, 1987

Sim, Lowery Stokes, *Stuart Davis: American Painter*, New York, 1991

CHARLES DEMUTH

Farnham, Emily, *Charles Demuth: Behind a Laughing Mask*, Norman, Oklahoma, 1971

Haskell, Barbara, *Charles Demuth*, New York, 1987

ARTHUR DOVE

Haskell, Barbara, *Arthur Dove*, San Francisco, 1974

ASHER B. DURAND

Durand, John, *The Life and Times of A. B. Durand*, New York, 1970

THOMAS EAKINS

Homer, William Innes, *Thomas Eakins: His Life and Art*, New York, 1992

Johns, Elizabeth, *Thomas Eakins, the Heroism of Modern Life*, Princeton, N.J., 1983

Sewell, Darrel, ed., *Thomas Eakins*, New Haven, 2001

ROBERT FEKE

Mooz, Ralph Peter, "The Art of Robert Feke," diss., Univ. of Pennsylvania, 1970

HELEN FRANKENTHALER

Elderfield, John, *Frankenthaler*, New York, 1989

SANFORD GIFFORD

Avery, Kevin J., and Franklin Kelly, eds., *Hudson River School Visions: The Landscapes of Sanford R. Gifford*, New Haven, 2003

ARSHILE GORKY

Herrera, Hayden, *Arshile Gorky: His Life and Work*, New York, 2003

Jordan, Jim M., and Robert Goldwater, *The Paintings of Arshile Gorky: A Critical Catalogue*, New York, 1982

Spender, Matthew, *From a High Place: A Life of Arshile Gorky*, New York, 1999

ADOLPH GOTTLIEB

Doty, Robert, and Diane Waldman, *Adolph Gottlieb*, New York, 1968

WILLIAM HARNETT

Bolger, Doreen, Marc Simpson and John Wilmerding, *William M. Harnett*, New York, 1992

MARSDEN HARTLEY

Haskell, Barbara, *Marsden Hartley*, New York, 1980

Kornhauser, Elizabeth Mankin, ed., *Marsden Hartley*, New Haven, 2002

CHILDE HASSAM

Hoopes, Donelson F., *Childe Hassam*, New York, 1979

MARTIN JOHNSON HEADE

Stebbins, Theodore E., Jr., *The Life and Work of Martin Johnson Heade: A Critical Analysis and Catalogue Raisonné*, New Haven, 2000

ROBERT HENRI

Henri, Robert, *The Art Spirit*, Philadelphia, 1923

Perlman, Bennard B., *The Immortal Eight: American Painting from Eakins to the Armory Show (1870–1913)*, New York, 1962

EVA HESSE

Lippard, Lucy, *Eva Hesse*, New York, 1976

WINSLOW HOMER

Cikovsky, Nicolai, Jr., and Franklin Kelly, *Winslow Homer*, New Haven, 1995

Goodrich, Lloyd, *Winslow Homer*, New York, 1944

Hendricks, Gordon, *The Life and Work of Winslow Homer*, New York, 1979

EDWARD HOPPER

Goodrich, Lloyd, *Edward Hopper*, New York, 1971

Levin, Gail, *Edward Hopper: An Intimate Biography*, New York, 1995

_____, *The Complete Oil Paintings of Edward Hopper*, New York, 2001

WILLIAM MORRIS HUNT

Hunt, William Morris, *On Painting and Drawing*, New York, 1976

Webster, Sally, *William Morris Hunt, 1824–1879*, Cambridge and New York, 1991

GEORGE INNESS

Cikovsky, Nicolai, *George Inness*, New York, 1971

_____, and Michael Quick, *George Inness*, New York, 1985

JASPER JOHNS

Crichton, Michael, *Jasper Johns*, New York, 1977

Johnston, Jill, *Jasper Johns: Privileged Information*, New York, 1996

Varnedoe, Kirk, *Jasper Johns: A Retrospective*, New York, 1996

EASTMAN JOHNSON

Carbone, Teresa A., and Patricia Hills, *Eastman Johnson: Painting America*, New York, 1992

FRANZ KLINE
  Christov-Bakargiev, Carolyn,
  Franz Kline 1910–1962, Milan,
  2004
BARBARA KRUGER
  Goldstein, Ann, et al., Barbara
  Kruger, Cambridge, Mass., 1999
FITZ HUGH LANE
  Wilmerding, John, Fitz Hugh
  Lane, New York, 1971
JOHN LA FARGE
  Adams, Henry, et al., John La
  Farge, New York, 1987
  Cortissoz, Royal, John La Farge,
  a Memoir and a Study, Boston
  and New York, 1911
EMANUEL LEUTZE
  Groseclose, Barbara S.,
  Emanuel Leutze 1816–1868:
  Freedom is the Only King,
  Washington, D.C., 1975
ROY LICHTENSTEIN
  Waldman, Diane, Roy
  Lichtenstein, New York, 1993
MORRIS LOUIS
  Elderfield, John, Morris Louis,
  Boston, 1986
STANTON MCDONALD-
WRIGHT
  Levin, Gail, Synchromism and
  American Color Abstraction
  1910–1925, New York, 1978
  Colors, Myth and Music: Stanton
  MacDonald-Wright and
  Synchromism, Raleigh, North
  Carolina, 2001
MAN RAY
  Foresta, Merry, et al., Perpetual
  Motif: The Art of Man Ray, New
  York, 1988
  Penrose, Roland, Man Ray,
  New York, 1989
ROBERT MOTHERWELL
  Arnason, H. Harvard, Robert
  Motherwell, New York, 1977
  Flam, Jack, Motherwell, New
  York, 1991
  Terenzio, Stephanie, ed.,
  The Collected Writings of Robert
  Motherwell, New York, 1992
WILLIAM SIDNEY MOUNT
  Frankenstein, Alfred, William
  Sidney Mount, New York, 1975
JOHN NEAGLE
  Torchia, Robert W., John
  Neagle: Philadelphia Portrait
  Painter, Philadelphia, 1989
BARNETT NEWMAN
  Temkin, Ann, ed., Barnett
  Newman, Philadelphia, 2002
GEORGIA O'KEEFFE
  Drohojowska-Philp, Hunter,
  Full Bloom: The Art and Life of
  Georgia O'Keeffe, New York,
  2004

Lynes, Barbara Buhler, Georgia
  O'Keeffe: Catalogue Raisonné,
  2 vols., Cambridge, Mass., and
  Washington, D.C., 1999
CHARLES WILLSON PEALE
  Richardson, E. P., Brooke
  Hindle and Lillian B. Miller,
  Charles Willson Peale and his
  World, New York, 1983
  Sellers, Charles Coleman,
  Charles Willson Peale,
  Philadelphia, 1947
JACKSON POLLOCK
  Landau, Ellen G., Jackson
  Pollock, New York, 1989
  Solomon, Deborah, Jackson
  Pollock: A Biography, New York,
  1987
  Varnedoe, Kirk, with Pepe
  Karmel, Jackson Pollock, New
  York, 1998
MAURICE PRENDERGAST
  Matthews, Nancy Mowll,
  Maurice Prendergast, New York,
  1990
JAMES ROSENQUIST
  Hopps, Walter, and Sarah
  Bancroft, James Rosenquist: A
  Retrospective, New York, 2003
MARK ROTHKO
  Ashton, Dore, About Rothko,
  New York, 1983
  Breslin, James E. B., Mark
  Rothko: A Biography, Chicago,
  1993
  Waldman, Diane, Mark Rothko:
  A Retrospective, New York,
  1978
ALBERT PINKHAM RYDER
  Brown, Elizabeth, Albert Pinkham
  Ryder, Washington, D.C., 1989
JOHN SINGER SARGENT
  Kilmurray, Elaine, and Richard
  Ormond, John Singer Sargent,
  Princeton, N. J., 1998
  Simpson, Marc, with Richard
  Ormond and H. Barbara
  Weinberg, Uncanny Spectacle:
  The Public Career of the Young
  John Singer Sargent, New
  Haven, 1997
CHARLES SHEELER
  Troyen, Carol, and Erica E.
  Hirshler, Charles Sheeler,
  Paintings and Drawings, New
  York, 1987
SMIBERT, JOHN
  Saunders, Richard H.M., John
  Smibert: Colonial America's First
  Portrait Painter, New Haven, 1995
FRANK STELLA
  Rubin, William S., Frank Stella,
  New York, 1970
  _____, Frank Stella,
  1970–1987, Boston, 1987

JOSEPH STELLA
  Haskell, Barbara, Joseph Stella,
  New York, 1994
GILBERT STUART
  Barratt, Carrie Rebora, and
  Ellen G. Miles, Gilbert Stuart,
  New Haven, 2004
  Evans, Dorinda, The Genius
  of Gilbert Stuart, Princeton,
  N.J., 1999
  Mount, Charles Merrill,
  Gilbert Stuart: A Biography,
  New York, 1964
THOMAS SULLY
  Biddle, Edward, and Mantle
  Fielding, The Life and Works of
  Thomas Sully, New York, 1970
  Fabian, Monroe H., Mr. Sully,
  Portrait Painter: The Works of
  Thomas Sully (1783–1872),
  Washington, D.C., 1983
JOHN TRUMBULL
  Cooper, Helen A., John
  Trumbull: The Hand and Spirit of
  a Painter, New Haven, 1982
  Jaffe, Irma B., John Trumbull,
  Patriot-Artist of the American
  Revolution, Boston, 1975
  Trumbull, John, Autobiography,
  Reminiscences and Letters of
  John Trumbull, from 1756 to
  1841, New Haven, 1841
JOHN VANDERLYN
  Odell, William T., "John
  Vanderlyn: French
  Neoclassicism and the Search
  for an American Art," diss.,
  Univ. of Delaware, 1981
ANDY WARHOL
  Bockris, Victor, The Life and
  Death of Andy Warhol, New
  York, 1989
  McShine, Kynaston, ed., Andy
  Warhol: A Retrospective, New
  York, 1989
  Pratt, Alan R., ed., Critical
  Response to Andy Warhol,
  Westport, Conn., 1997
  Smith, Patrick S., Andy Warhol's
  Art and Films, Ann Arbor, 1986
MAX WEBER
  Goodrich, Lloyd, Max Weber,
  New York, 1949
  Weber, Max, Essays on Art,
  New York, 1916
BENJAMIN WEST
  Abrams, Ann Uhry, The Valiant
  Hero: Benjamin West and Grand-
  Style History Painting,
  Washington, D.C., 1985
  Alberts, Robert C., Benjamin
  West: A Biography, Boston, 1978
  Erffa, Helmut von, and Allen
  Staley, The Paintings of Benjamin
  West, New Haven, 1986

JAMES ABBOTT MCNEILL
WHISTLER
  Curry, David Park, James
  McNeill Whistler: Uneasy Pieces,
  Richmond, Virginia, 2004
  Weintraub, Stanley, Whistler:
  A Biography, New York, 1988
  Whistler, James McNeill, The
  Gentle Art of Making Enemies,
  London, 1994
GRANT WOOD
  Corn, Wanda, Grant Wood:
  The Regionalist Vision, New
  Haven, 1983
  Dennis, James M., Grant Wood:
  A Study in American Art and
  Culture, New York, 1975

Architecture and architects
  Cummings, Abbott Lowell,
  The Framed Houses of
  Massachusetts Bay, 1625–1725,
  Cambridge, Mass., 1979
  Curran, Kathleen, The
  Romanesque Revival: Religion,
  Politics, and Transnational
  Exchange, University Park, Pa.,
  2003
  Hamlin, Talbot, Greek Revival
  Architecture, New York, 1964
  Kelly, J. Frederick, Early Domestic
  Architecture of Connecticut, New
  York, 1963
  Maynard, W. Barksdale,
  Architecture in the United States
  1800–1850, New Haven, 2002
  Morrison, Hugh, Early American
  Architecture, from the First
  Colonial Settlements to the
  National Period, New York, 1952
  Pierson, William H., and William
  Jordy, American Buildings and
  their Architects, 4 vols., Garden
  City, N.Y., 1970–1978
  Roth, Leland, American
  Architecture: A History, Boulder,
  Colorado, 2001
  Scully, Vincent, American
  Architecture and Urbanism, New
  York, 1969
  _____, The Shingle Style and
  the Stick Style, New Haven, 1971
  Stanton, Phoebe, The Gothic
  Revival and American
  Architecture, an Episode in Taste,
  1840–1856, Baltimore, 1968
  Upton, Dell, Architecture in the
  United States, New York, 1998

JAMES BOGARDUS
  Gayle, Margot, and Carol
  Gayle, Cast Iron Architecture in
  America, New York, 1998
CHARLES BULFINCH
  Kirker, Harold, The Architecture

of Charles Bulfinch, Cambridge, Mass., 1969

BURNHAM & ROOT
Hoffman, Donald, The Architecture of John Wellborn Root, Baltimore, 1973

RALPH ADAMS CRAM
Shand-Tucci, Douglass, Ralph Adams Cram: Life and Architecture, 2 vols., Amherst, 1994/2005

A. J. DAVIS
Peck, Amelia, ed., Alexander Jackson Davis, American Architect, 1803–1892, New York, 1992

A. J. DOWNING
Schuyler, David, Apostle of Taste: Andrew Jackson Downing, 1815–1852, Baltimore, 1996

FRANK FURNESS
Lewis, Michael J., Frank Furness: Architecture and the Violent Mind, New York, 2001
O'Gorman, James F., The Architecture of Frank Furness, Philadelphia, 1973

FRANK GEHRY
Ragheb, J. Fiona, ed., Frank Gehry Architect, New York, 2001

CASS GILBERT
Christen, Barbara S., and Steven Flanders, eds., Cass Gilbert, Life and Work, New York, 2001

GREENE AND GREENE
Bosley, Edward R., Greene & Greene, London, 2000
Makinson, Randell L., Greene & Greene: The Passion and the Legacy, Salt Lake City, 1998

GEORGE HOWE
Stern, Robert A. M., George Howe: Toward a Modern American Architecture, New Haven, 1975

RICHARD MORRIS HUNT
Baker, Paul, Richard Morris Hunt, Cambridge, Mass., 1980
Stein, Susan R., ed., The Architecture of Richard Morris Hunt, Chicago, 1986

THOMAS JEFFERSON
Howard, Hugh, Thomas Jefferson, Architect, New York, 2003

PHILIP JOHNSON
Franz Schulze, Philip Johnson: Life and Work, New York, 1994

LOUIS I. KAHN
Brownlee, D. B., and D. DeLong, Louis I. Kahn: In the Realm of Architecture, New York, 1991
Twombly, Robert C., Louis Kahn: Essential Texts, New York, 2003

BENJAMIN LATROBE
Hamlin, Talbot, Benjamin Henry Latrobe, New York, 1955

MAYA LIN
Lin, Maya, Boundaries, New York, 2002

McKIM, MEAD & WHITE
Roth, Leland, McKim, Mead & White, Architects, New York, 1983
Wilson, Richard Guy, McKim, Mead & White, Architects, New York, 1983

RICHARD MEIER
Frampton, Kenneth, Richard Meier, Milan, 2003

LUDWIG MIES VAN DER ROHE
Lambert, Phyllis, ed., Mies in America, New York, 2001

ROBERT MILLS
Bryan, John M., America's First Architect: Robert Mills, New York, 2001
Liscombe, Rhodri Windsor, Altogether American: Robert Mills, Architect and Engineer, 1781–1855, New York, 1994

JOHN RUSSELL POPE
Bedford, Steven McLeod, John Russell Pope, Architect of Empire, New York, 1998

H. H. RICHARDSON
O'Gorman, James F., Living Architecture: A Biography of H. H. Richardson, New York, 1997
Van Rensellaer, Marianna Griswold, Henry Hobson Richardson and his Works, New York, 1969

EERO SAARINEN
Merkel, Jayne, Eero Saarinen, London and New York, 2005
Saarinen, Aline, ed., Eero Saarinen and His Work, New Haven, 1962

SKIDMORE OWINGS MERRILL
Krinsky, Carol Herselle, Gordon Bunshaft, New York and Cambridge, Mass., 1988

WILLIAM STRICKLAND
Gilchrist, Agnes Addison, William Strickland, Architect and Engineer, 1788–1854, Philadelphia, 1950

LOUIS SULLIVAN
Sullivan, Louis, The Autobiography of an Idea, New York, 1924
Twombly, Robert, Louis Sullivan: His Life and Work, New York, 1986
_____, and Narciso G. Menocal, Louis Sullivan: The Poetry of Architecture, New York, 2000

Van Zanten, David, Sullivan's City: The Meaning of Ornament for Louis Sullivan, New York, 2000

RICHARD UPJOHN
Upjohn, Everard M., Richard Upjohn, Architect and Churchman, New York, 1968

ROBERT VENTURI
Brownlee, David B., David G. DeLong and Kathryn B. Hiesinger, Out of the Ordinary: Robert Venturi, Denise Scott Brown & Associates, Philadelphia and New Haven, 2001

FRANK LLOYD WRIGHT
Brooks, H. Allen, The Prairie School: Frank Lloyd Wright and his Midwest Contemporaries, Toronto, 1972
Levine, Neil, The Architecture of Frank Lloyd Wright, Princeton, N.J., 1996
Riley, Terence, ed., Frank Lloyd Wright, Architect, New York, 1994
Secrest, Meryle, Frank Lloyd Wright, New York, 1992
Storrer, William Allin, The Architecture of Frank Lloyd Wright: A Complete Catalogue, Chicago, 2002
Wright, Frank Lloyd, An Autobiography, New York, 1977

Sculpture, installation, and performance
Armstrong, Tom, et al., 200 Years of American Sculpture, Boston, 1976
Craven, Wayne, Sculpture in America, New York, 1968
Henri, Adrian, Total Art: Environments, Happenings, and Performance, New York, 1974
Jones, Amelia, Body Art/Performing the Subject, Minneapolis, 1998
Kaprow, Allan, Assemblage, Environments & Happenings, New York, 1966
Robinette, Margaret A., Outdoor Sculpture: Object and Environment, New York, 1976
Sandford, Mariellen R., ed., Happenings and Other Acts, New York, 1995
Ludwig, Allan, Graven Images: New England Stonecarving and its Symbols, 1650–1815, Middletown, Conn., 1966
Seitz, William C., The Art of Assemblage, New York, 1961
Taft, Lorado, The History of American Sculpture, New York, 1924

ALEXANDER CALDER
Gimenez, Carmen, and Alexander S. C. Rower, Calder: Gravity and Grace, London and New York, 2004
National Gallery of Art, Alexander Calder, 1898–1976, Washington, D.C., 1998

JUDY CHICAGO
Sackler, Elizabeth A., ed., Judy Chicago, New York, 2002

JOHN B. FLANNAGAN
Forsyth, Robert Joseph, "John B. Flannagan, His Life and Works," diss., Univ. of Minnesota, 1965

ROBERT GOBER
Schimmel, Paul, et al., Robert Gober, Zurich, 1997

HORATIO GREENOUGH
Tuckerman, Henry T., A Memorial of Horatio Greenough, New York, 1968
Wright, Nathalia, Horatio Greenough, the First American Sculptor, Philadelphia, 1963

ANN HAMILTON
Simon, Joan, Ann Hamilton, New York, 2002

DONALD JUDD
Haskell, Barbara, Donald Judd, New York, 1988
Serota, Nicholas, Donald Judd, New York, 2004

GASTON LACHAISE
Hunter, Sam, Lachaise, New York, 1993
Nordland, Gerald, Gaston Lachaise, the Man and His Work, New York, 1974

ROBERT MORRIS
Morris, Robert, Robert Morris, The Mind/Body Problem, New York, 1994

ELIE NADELMAN
Haskell, Barbara, Elie Nadelman: Sculptor of Modern Life, New York, 2003

ISAMU NOGUCHI
Hunter, Sam, Isamu Noguchi, London, 1979
Isamu Noguchi: Sculptural Design, Weil am Rhein, Germany, 2001

CLAES OLDENBURG
Celant, Germano, Dieter Koepplin and Mark Rosenthal, Claes Oldenburg: An Anthology, New York and Washington, D.C., 1995
Rose, Barbara, Claes Oldenburg, New York, 1970

HIRAM POWERS
Wunder, Richard P., Hiram Powers: Vermont Sculptor,

1805–1873, 2 vols., Newark, Delaware, 1991

ROBERT RAUSCHENBERG
Hunter, Sam, *Robert Rauschenberg*, New York, 1999
Kotz, Mary Lynn, *Rauschenberg, Art and Life*, New York, 2004
Tomkins, Calvin, *Off the Wall: Robert Rauschenberg and the Art World of Our Time*, Garden City, N.Y., 1980

JOHN ROGERS
Wallace, David H., *John Rogers: The People's Sculptor*, Middletown, Conn., 1967

WILLIAM RUSH
Pennsylvania Academy of the Fine Arts, *William Rush, American Sculptor*, Philadelphia, 1982

AUGUSTUS SAINT-GAUDENS
Dryfhout, John H., *The Work of Augustus Saint-Gaudens*, Hanover, N.H., 1982
Wilkinson, Burke, *Uncommon Clay: The Life and Works of Augustus Saint-Gaudens*, San Diego, 1985

GEORGE SEGAL
Hunter, Sam, and Don Hawthorne, *George Segal*, New York, 1984

RICHARD SERRA
Güse, Ernst-Gerhard, *Richard Serra*, New York, 1987

DAVID SMITH
Fry, Edward F., and Miranda McClintic, *David Smith, Painter, Sculptor, Draftsman*, New York, 1982
Wilkin, Karen, *David Smith*, New York, 1984

ROBERT SMITHSON
Hobbs, Robert, *Robert Smithson: Sculpture*, Ithaca and London, 1981

Photography and video
Doty, Robert M., ed., *Photography in America*, New York, 1974
Green, Jonathan, *American Photography: A Critical History 1945 to the Present*, New York, 1984
Lovejoy, Margot, *Digital Currents: Art in the Electronic Age*, New York, 2004
Orvell, Miles, *American Photography*, New York, 2003
Sandweiss, Martha A., ed., *Photography in Nineteenth-Century America*, New York, 1991

Welling, William, *Photography in America: The Formative Years, 1839–1900*, New York, 1978

ANSEL ADAMS
Alinder, Mary Street, *Ansel Adams: A Biography*, New York, 1996
Szarkowski, John, *Ansel Adams at 100*, Boston, 2001

MATTHEW BARNEY
Spector, Nancy, *Matthew Barney: The Cremaster Cycle*, New York, 2002

MATHEW BRADY
Panzer, Mary, *Mathew Brady and the Image of History*, Washington, D.C., 1997

LEWIS HINE
Steinorth, Karl, ed., *Lewis Hine: Passionate Journey, Photographs 1905–1937*, Zurich, 1996

DOROTHEA LANGE
Meltzer, Milton, *Dorothea Lange: A Photographer's Life*, New York, 1978

ROBERT MAPPLETHORPE
Morrisroe, Patricia, *Mapplethorpe: A Biography*, New York, 1995

EADWEARD MUYBRIDGE
Haas, Robert Bartlett, *Muybridge: Man in Motion*,

Berkeley, Los Angeles and London, 1976

CINDY SHERMAN
Cruz, Amada, Elizabeth A.T. Smith and Amelia Jones, *Cindy Sherman: Retrospective*, New York, 1997
Krauss, Rosalind, *Cindy Sherman, 1975–1993*, New York, 1993

EDWARD STEICHEN
Dennis Longwell, *Steichen: The Master Prints 1895–1914*, Museum of Modern Art, 1978

ALFRED STIEGLITZ
Greenough, Sarah, ed., *Modern Art and America: Alfred Stieglitz and his New York Galleries*, Boston, 2000
Hoffman, Katherine, *Stieglitz: A Beginning Light*, New Haven and London, 2004
Whelan, Richard, *Alfred Stieglitz: A Biography*, Boston, 1995

BILL VIOLA
Townsend, Chris, ed., *The Art of Bill Viola*, London, 2004

EDWARD WESTON
Watts, Jennifer A., ed., *Edward Weston: A Legacy*, London, 2003

List of illustrations

Dimensions of works are given in centimeters then inches, height before width.

1 Matthew Pratt, *The American School* (detail), 1765. Oil on canvas, 91.4 x 127.6 (36 x 50¼). Metropolitan Museum of Art, New York. Gift of Samuel P. Avery, 1897 **2** Attributed to Nehemiah Partridge, *Ariaantje Coeymans Verplanck (Mrs. David Verplanck)*, 1718 or *c.* 1722–24. Oil on canvas, 180.3 x 99.1 (71 x 39). Albany Institute of History & Art. Bequest of Miss Gertrude Watson 1938.5 **3** Ariaantje Coeymans House, Coeymans, New York, *c.* 1700–49. Library of Congress, Washington, D.C. **4** Groot Constantia, Stellenbosch, South Africa. Photo John Russell/Network Aspen Worldwide **5** Edward Hicks, *Peaceable Kingdom, c.* 1834. Oil on canvas, 76.2 x 90.2 (30 x 35½). National Gallery of Art, Washington, D.C. Gift of Edgar William and Bernice Chrysler Garbisch. Photo Carnegie Arts of the United States Photographic Collection, University of Georgia **6** William Lyon, *A Plan of the Town of New Haven with all the Buildings in 1748*. William L. Clements Library, University of Michigan **7** Old Ship Meeting House, Hingham, Massachusetts, 1681. Photo Carnegie Arts of the United States Photographic Collection, University of Georgia **8** Anonymous, *Elizabeth Clarke Freake and Baby Mary, c.* 1671/74. Oil on canvas, 108 x 93.4 (42½ x 36¾). Worcester Art Museum, Worcester, Massachusetts **9** Thomas Smith, *Self-portrait, c.* 1690. Oil on canvas, 62.2 x 60.3 (24½ x 23¾). Worcester Art Museum, Worcester, Massachusetts **10** Parson Joseph Capen House, Topsfield, Massachusetts, 1683. Photo Carnegie Arts of the United States Photographic Collection, University of Georgia **11** Parlor at Parson Joseph Capen House, Topsfield, Massachusetts, 1683. Photo Carnegie Arts of the United States Photographic Collection, University of Georgia **12** Cross-section showing the lean-to addition of Harrison-Linsley House, Branford, Connecticut, 1690 **13** Stanley-Whitman House, Farmington, Connecticut, 1720. Library of Congress, Washington, D.C. **14** St. Luke's Church, Smithfield, Isle of Wight County, Virginia, *c.* 1632. Library of Congress, Washington, D.C. **15** The Bodleian Plate engraving showing the principal public buildings of Williamsburg, Virginia. Photo Library of Congress, Washington, D.C. **16** Thomas Lee House, Stratford, Westmoreland County, Virginia, 1725–30 **17** Peter Harrison, Redwood Library, Newport, Rhode Island, 1748–50. Photo Carnegie Arts of the United States Photographic Collection, University of Georgia **18** Gustav Hesselius, *Lapowinsa*, 1735. Oil on canvas, 83.8 x 63.5 (33 x 25). Historical Society of Pennsylvania, Philadelphia **19** Jeremiah Theus, *Elizabeth Rothmaler*, 1757. Oil on canvas, 75.9 x 63.5 (29⅞ x 25). The Brooklyn Museum, Carll H. DeSilver Fund **20** John Smibert, *The Bermuda Group: Dean George Berkeley and His Family*, 1729. Oil on canvas, 177 x 236 (69¹¹⁄₁₆ x 92¹⁵⁄₁₆). Yale University Art Gallery, New Haven, Connecticut **21** Isaac Royall House, Medford, Massachusetts, 1733–37 and 1747–50. Photo Carnegie Arts of the United States Photographic Collection, University of Georgia **22** Robert Feke, *Isaac Royall and His Family*, 1741. Oil on canvas, 142 x 198 (55⅞ x 17¹⁵⁄₁₆). Harvard Law School Art Collection, Cambridge, Massachusetts **23** Robert Feke, *Portrait of Mrs William Bowdoin (nee Phebe Murdock)*, 1748. Oil on canvas, 126.4 x 102.5 (49¾ x 40⅜). Bowdoin College Museum of Art, Brunswick, Maine. Bequest of Mrs. Sarah Bowdoin Dearborn **24** British Mezzotint of Anne Oldfield, 1705–40. Ink, paper-laid, 15.7 x 11.5 (6³⁄₁₆ x 4½). Courtesy Winterthur **25** Peter Harrison, Redwood Library, Newport, Rhode Island, 1748–50. Photo Library of Congress, Washington, D.C. **26** Edward Hoppus, plate from Andrea Palladio's *Architecture, Book IV*, 1735. Courtesy Winterthur **27** Old North Church, Boston, 1723. Library of Congress, Washington, D.C. **28** Congregational Meeting House, Farmington, Connecticut, 1771. Photo Carnegie

Arts of the United States Photographic Collection, University of Georgia **29** Peter Harrison, Brick Market, Newport, Rhode Island, 1761–62. Photo John T. Hopf/Preservation Society of Newport County, Newport, Rhode Island **30** Richard Munday, Old Colony House, Newport, Rhode Island, 1739. Photo Carnegie Arts of the United States Photographic Collection, University of Georgia **31** Mount Pleasant, Fairmount Park, Philadelphia, 1762–65. Photo Wayne Andrews **32** Interior of Mount Pleasant, Philadelphia, 1762–65. Photo Carnegie Arts of the United States Photographic Collection, University of Georgia **33** Joseph Blackburn, *Isaac Winslow and His Family*, 1755. Oil on canvas, 138 x 202 (54 5/16 x 79½). Museum of Fine Arts, Boston. Abraham Shuman Fund **34** John Wollaston, *Mrs John Dies*, *c.* 1750. Oil on canvas, 114.3 x 91.4 (45 x 36). Mead Art Museum, Amherst College, Amherst, Massachusetts **35** Benjamin West, *The Death of General Wolfe*, 1770. Oil on canvas, 151.1 x 213.4 (59½ x 84). National Gallery of Canada, Ottowa **36** Matthew Pratt, *The American School*, 1765. Oil on canvas, 91.4 x 127.6 (36 x 50¼). Metropolitan Museum of Art, New York. Gift of Samuel P. Avery, 1897 **37** John Singleton Copley, *Boy with a Squirrel (Henry Pelham)*, 1765. Oil on canvas, 76.8 x 63.5 (30¼ x 25). Museum of Fine Arts, Boston. Anonymous gift **38** John Singleton Copley, *Portrait of Paul Revere*, 1768. Oil on canvas, 88.9 x 72.4 (35 x 28½). Museum of Fine Arts, Boston. Gift of Joseph W., William B., and Edward H. R. Revere **39** John Singleton Copley, *Watson and the Shark*, 1778. Oil on canvas, 182.1 x 229.7 (71¾ x 90½). Museum of Fine Arts, Boston **40** Charles Willson Peale, *The Artist in His Museum*, 1822. Oil on canvas, 263.5 x 203 (103¾ x 79⅞). Pennsylvania Academy of the Fine Arts, Philadelphia **41** Samuel McIntire, Gardner-Pingree House, Salem, Massachusetts, 1804–5. Photo Carnegie Arts of the United States Photographic Collection, University of Georgia **42** Charles Bulfinch, Third Harrison Gray Otis House, Boston, facade, 1806. Photo Carnegie Arts of the United States Photographic Collection, University of Georgia **43** Charles Bulfinch, Massachusetts State House, Boston, 1795–98. Photo Carnegie Arts of the United States Photographic Collection, University of Georgia **44** Thomas Jefferson, Monticello, Charlottesville, Virginia, 1769–84 and 1796–1809. Photo Thomas Jefferson Memorial Foundation, Monticello, Virginia **45** Thomas Jefferson, with Benjamin Henry Latrobe, University of Virginia, Charlottesville, 1856. Lithograph, 45.1 x 67.3 (17¾ x 26⅝). Special Collections Library, University of Virginia **46** Thomas Jefferson, Southern Elevation of the Rotunda, before 1821. The Papers of Thomas Jefferson, Special Collections Library, University of Virginia **47** Andrew Ellicot, after Pierre Charles L'Enfant, *Plan of the City of Washington in the Territory of Columbia*, 1792. Photo Library of Congress, Washington, D.C. **48** Phillip Hart, Rejected Competition Design for U.S. Capitol, 1792. Ink and pencil drawing. Maryland Historical Society, Baltimore. **49** William Thornton, Design for the East Front, U.S. Capitol, *c.* 1793–95. Pencil, ink, and washes on paper 37.2 x 62.3 (14⅝ x 24½). Library of Congress, Washington, D.C. **50** Benjamin Henry Latrobe, *Perspective of Front and Side of Bank of Pennsylvania, Philadelphia* (detail), 1798–1801. Watercolor on paper, 26.7 x 45.7 (10½ x 18). Photo Carnegie Arts of the United States Photographic Collection, University of Georgia **51** John Plumbe, Jr., *United States Capitol*, 1846. Daguerreotype. Library of Congress, Washington, D.C. **52** John Trumbull, *The Death of General Montgomery in the Attack on Quebec*, 1786. Oil on canvas, 62.5 x 94 (24⅝ x 37). Yale University Art Gallery, New Haven, Connecticut **53** John Trumbull, *The Declaration of Independence, July 4th, 1776*, 1786–1820. Oil on canvas, 53.7 x 79.1 (21⅛ x 31⅛). Yale University Art Gallery, New Haven, Connecticut. Trumbull Collection **54** John Vanderlyn, *The Death of Jane McCrea*, 1804. Oil on canvas, 81.3 x 67.3 (32 x 26½). Wadsworth Atheneum Museum of Art, Hartford, Connecticut. Purchased by the Wadsworth Atheneum acc. no. 1855.4 **55** John Vanderlyn, *Ariadne Asleep on the Island of Naxos*, 1809–14. Oil on canvas, 174 x 221 (68½ x 87). Pennsylvania Academy of the Fine Arts, Philadelphia. Gift of Mrs. Sarah Harrison (The Joseph Harrison Jr. Collection) **56** Gilbert Stuart, *The Skater (Portrait of William Grant)*, 1782. Oil on canvas, 245.5 x 147.6 (96⅝ x 58⅛). National Gallery of Art, Washington, D.C., Andrew W. Mellon Collection **57** Gilbert Stuart, *George Washington*, 1796. Oil on canvas, 121.9 x 94 (48 x 37). Museum of Fine Arts, Boston. Jointly owned by the Museum of Fine Arts, Boston and The National Portait Gallery, Washington, D.C. **58** Charles Willson Peale, *The Peale Family*, *c.* 1770–73 and 1808. Oil on canvas, 143.5 x 227.3 (56½ x 89½). New York Historical Society **59** William Rush, *The Schuylkill Chained*, 1825. White-painted Spanish cedar, 100 x 221.6 x 67 (39⅜ x 87¼ x 26 7/16). Philadelphia Museum of Art, Philadelphia. Commissioners of Fairmount Park, Philadelphia **60** Washington Allston, *Moonlit Landscape*, 1819. Oil on canvas, 61 x 88.9 (24 x 35). Museum of Fine Arts, Boston. Gift of William Sturgis Bigelow **61** Thomas Sully, *Lady with a Harp: Eliza Ridgely*, 1818. Oil on canvas, 215 x 143 (84⅝ x 56 5/16). National Gallery of Art, Washington, D.C. **62** Hiram Powers, *The Greek Slave*, *c.* 1843. Marble 166.4 (65½) including integral base. Yale University Art Gallery, New Haven, Connecticut. Olive Louise Dann Fund **63** Horatio Greenough, *George Washington*, 1840. Marble, 345 x 259 x 21 (135 13/16 x 101 15/16 x 8¼). National Museum of American Art, Smithsonian Institution, Washington, D.C. **64** Thomas Sully, *Nicholas Biddle*, 1826. Oil on canvas, 63.5 x 76.2 (25 x 30). The Andalusia Foundation **65** William Strickland, Second Bank of the United States, 1818–24. Photo Wayne Andrews **66** Thomas U. Walter, *Comparative Plans, Temple of Minerva; Parthenon; Girard College; and Bank of the United States*, no date, Property of the Stephen Girard Collection. Photo Girard College History Collections, Philadelphia **67** John Neagle, *Portait of William Strickland*, 1829. Oil on canvas, 76.2 x 63.5 (30 x 25) Yale University Art Gallery, New Haven, Connecticut. Mabel Brady Garvan Collection **68** Robert Mills, Treasury Department, Washington, D.C., 1836–42. Library of Congress, Washington, D.C. **69** James C. Bucklin and Russell Warren, Providence Arcade, Rhode Island, 1828. Photograph *c.* 1865. Rhode Island Historical Society **70** Town and Davis, Design for the Astor Hotel, New York, *c.* 1830. Watercolor, ink, and graphite on paper, 51.6 x 80 (20 5/16 x 31½). Metropolitan Museum of Art, New York. Harris Brisbane Dick Fund, 1924. (24.66.30) **71** James Lamb, Wilcox-Cutts House, Orwell, Vermont, 1843. Photo Carnegie Arts of the United States Photographic Collection, University of Georgia **72** Thomas U. Walter, Girard College, Philadelphia, 1833–48. Photo Carnegie Arts of the United States Photographic Collection, University of Georgia **73** Francis William Edmonds, *The City and the Country Beaux*, *c.* 1839. Oil on canvas, 51.1 x 61.6 (20⅛ x 24¼). Sterling and Francine Clark Art Institute, Williamstown, Massachusetts. **74** James Renwick, North elevation of the Smithsonian Institute, Washington, D.C., 1848 **75** John Randel, Jr., cartographer, adapted and published by William Bridges, *This Map of the City of New York and Island of Manhattan as Laid Out by the Commissioners*, 1811. Hand-colored line engraving on copper. Library of Congress, Washington, D.C., Geography and Map Division **76** Thomas Cole, *Landscape with Tree Trunks*, 1828. Oil on canvas, 67.3 x 82.5 (26½ x 32½). Museum of Rhode Island School of Design, Providence. Walter H. Kimball Fund **77** Thomas Cole, *View from Mount Holyoke, Northampton, Massachusetts, after a Thunderstorm (The Ox-bow)*, 1836. Oil on canvas, 130.8 x 193 (51½ x 76). Metropolitan Museum of Art, New York. Gift of Mrs. Russell Sage, 1908 (08.228) **78** Thomas Cole, *The Voyage of Life: Youth*, 1842. Oil on canvas, 134 x 195 (52¾ x 72¾). National Gallery of Art, Washington, D.C. **79** Asher Brown Durand, *Kindred Spirits*, 1849. Oil on canvas, 116.8 x 91.4 (46 x 36). Crystal Bridges—Museum of American Art, Bentonville, Arkansas **80** Alexander Jackson Davis, Llewellyn Park, West Orange, New Jersey, 1853. From Andrew Jackson Downing, *A Treatise on the Theory and Practice of Landscape Gardening*, New York and London, 1840 **81** A Lake or River Villa in the Bracketed Style, from A. J. Downing, *The Architecture of Country Houses*, 1850, fig. 164 Design XXXII **82** Alexander Jackson Davis, Lyndhurst, Tarrytown, New York, 1838. Library of Congress, Washington, D.C. **83** Frederick Law Olmsted & Calvert Vaux, Central Park, New York. View in 1863. New York Historical Society **84** *Cast Iron Factory*, New York, 1849. From James Borgardus, *Cast Iron Buildings*. Courtesy Peabody Essex Museum, Salem, Massachusetts **85** Samuel Cowperthwaite, *The State Penitentiary for the Eastern District of Pennsylvania*, 1855. Lithograph by P. S. Duval & Co., 22.2 x 26.5 (8¾ x 10 7/16). The Library Company of Philadelphia **86** Orson Squire Fowler House, Fishkill, New York, 1848. Frontispiece from O. S. Fowler, *A Home for All*, revised edition, 1854 **87** Samuel Sloan, Longwood, Natchez, Mississippi, begun 1860. Photo Carnegie Arts of the United States Photographic Collection, University of Georgia **88** Richard Upjohn, Trinity Church, New York, 1839–46. Lithograph after the architect's drawing, 1847. The J. Clarence Davies Collection, Museum of the City of New York **89** Thomas Cole, *The Architect's Dream*, 1840. Oil on canvas, 134.6 x 213.5 (53 x 84 1/16). Toledo Museum of Art, purchased with funds from the Florence Scott Libbey Bequest in memory of her father, Maurice A. Scott **90** Frederick A. Peterson, Cooper Union Building (Foundation Building), New York, 1853–59. Watercolour by Frederick A. Peterson, *c.* 1855. Courtesy of The Cooper Union **91** Emanuel Leutze, *Washington Crossing the Delaware*, 1851. Oil on canvas, 378.5 x 647.7 (149 x 255). Metropolitan Museum of Art, New York. Gift of John S. Kennedy, 1897 97.34 **92** Richard Caton Woodville, *War News from Mexico*, 1848. Oil on canvas, 68.6 x 62.9 (27 x 24¾). National Academy of Design, New York **93** Albert Bierstadt, *Rocky Mountains, "Lander's Peak"*, 1863. Oil on linen, 110.8 x 90.1 (43⅝ x 35½). Fogg Art Museum, Harvard University Art Museums. Gift of Mrs. William Hayes Fogg **94** Martin Johnson Heade, *Approaching Thunder Storm*, 1859. Oil on canvas, 71.1 x 111.7 (28 x 44). Metropolitan Museum of Art, New York, Gift of Erving Wolf Foundation and Mr. and Mrs. Erving Wolf, 1975 **95** Fitz Hugh Lane,

"Starlight" in Fog, 1860. Oil on canvas, 76.2 x 127 (30 x 50). Collection of the Butler Institute of American Art, Youngstown, Ohio **96** *Distribution of the American Art Union Prizes, at the Tabernacle, Broadway, New York, 24th Dec, 1847*, 1848. Lithograph by Sarony & Major after D'Avignon. Library of Congress, Washington, D.C. **97** Sanford Robinson Gifford, *Kauterskill Clove*, 1862. Oil on canvas, 122 x 101 (48¹⁄₁₆ x 39¾). Metropolitan Museum of Art, New York **98** George Caleb Bingham, *Fur Traders Descending the Missouri*, 1845. Oil on canvas, 74.3 x 92.1 (29¼ x 36¼). Metropolitan Museum of Art, New York **99** William Sidney Mount, *The Power of Music*, 1847. Oil on canvas. Cleveland Museum of Art, Leonard C. Hanna, Jr. Fund 1991.IIO **100** Randolph Rogers, *Nydia, The Blind Girl of Pompeii*, 1853. Marble, height 140 (55⅛). Metropolitan Museum of Art, New York **101** John Rogers, *Slave Auction*, 1859. Plaster, height 33.7 (13¼). Courtesy New York Historical Society **102** Eastman Johnson, *Negro Life in the South (Old Kentucky Home)*, 1859. Oil on canvas, 91.4 x 114.3 (36 x 45). Courtesy New York Historical Society **103** John La Farge, *Magnolia Blossom*, *c.* 1870. Oil on board, 28 x 22 (11 x 8¹¹⁄₁₆). National Academy of Design, New York **104** William Trost Richards, *Corner of the Woods*, 1864. Pencil on buff paper, 59 x 44.5 (23¼ x 17½) . M. & M. Karolik Collection, Museum of Fine Arts, Boston **105** Peter Bonnet Wight, National Academy of Design, New York, 1862–63. Photograph *c.* 1888. New York Historical Society **106** Jasper Francis Cropsey, *Autumm—on the Hudson River*, 1860. Oil on canvas, 152.4 x 274.3 (60 x 108). National Gallery of Art, Washington, D.C. Gift of the Avalon Foundation 1963.9.1 **107** Frederic Edwin Church, *Twilight in the Wilderness*, 1860. Oil on canvas, 101.6 x 162.6 (40 x 64). Cleveland Museum of Art, Mr. and Mrs. William H. Marlatt Fund 1965.233 **108** Frederic Edwin Church, *Cotopaxi*, 1862. Oil on canvas, 121.9 x 215.9 (48 x 85). Detroit Institute of Arts, Founders' Society Purchase, Robert H. Tannahill Foundation Fund, Gibbs-Williams Fund, Dexter M. Ferry, Jr. Fund, Merrill Fund, Beatrice W. Rogers Fund, and Richard A. Manoogian Fund **109** Calvert Vaux and Frederic Edwin Church, Olana, Hudson, New York, 1870–72 and 1888–89. Photo Emily Lane **110** Alexander Gardner and Timothy O'Sullivan, *A Harvest of Death, Gettysburg, Pennsylvania*, 1863, from Gardner's *Photographic Sketchbook of the War*, 1865. Wet plate, albumen. New York Public Library **111** Thomas Nast, *A Group of Vultures Waiting for the Storm to "Blow Over": "Let Us Prey"*, from *Harper's Weekly* (23 September, 1871). Full-page woodcut, 36.8 x 24.1 (14½ x 9½). Library of Congress, Washington, D.C. **112** Winslow Homer, *The War for the Union, 1862—A Cavalry Charge.* Wood engraving, 34.9 x 52.4 (13¾ x 20⅝). *Harper's Weekly 6, no. 288* (5 July 1862). Fine Arts Museums of San Francisco, Achenbach Foundation for Graphic Arts. Gift of Dr. and Mrs. Robert A. Johnson **113** Winslow Homer, *Prisoners from the Front*, 1866. Oil on canvas, 61 x 96.5 (24 x 38). Metropolitan Museum of Art, New York. Gift of Mrs. Frank B. Porter, 1922 (22.207) **114** Winslow Homer, *Inside the Bar*, 1883. Watercolor on paper, 39.1 x 72.4 (15⅜ x 28½). Metropolitan Museum of Art, New York. Gift of Louise Ryals Arkell, in memory of her husband, Bartlett Arkell, 1954 **115** Alfred B. Mullet, Old Executive Office Building (formerly State, War, and Navy Building), Washington, D.C., 1871–88. Photo Abbie Rowe **116** Richard Morris Hunt, Studio Building, 57 West Tenth Street, New York, 1857. Drawings and Archives Department, Avery Architectural and Fine Arts Library, Columbia University, New York **117** William Ware and Henry Van Brunt, Memorial Hall, Harvard University, 1870–78. Courtesy Harvard University Press Office **118** William Morris Hunt, *The Belated Kid*, 1854–57. Oil on canvas, 137.8 x 98.4 (54¼ x 38¾). Museum of Fine Arts, Boston. Bequest of Miss Elizabeth Howes 07.135 **119** John La Farge, *Portrait of Henry James, the Novelist*, 1862. Oil on canvas, 52.1 x 34.3 (20½ x 13½) The Century Association, New York, P1862.3 **120** William Morris Hunt, *The Flight of Night*, 1877. Pennsylvania Academy of the Fine Arts, Philadelphia. Photo Carnegie Arts of the United States Photographic Collection, University of Georgia **121** Frank Furness and George W. Hewitt, Pennsylvania Academy of the Fine Arts, Philadelphia, 1871–76 **122** John Ferguson Weir, *Forging the Shaft: A Welding Heat*, 1877. Oil on canvas, 132.1 x 186.1 (52 x 73¼). Metropolitan Museum of Art, New York. Gift of Lyman G. Bloomingdale, 1901 **123** Lilly Martin Spencer, *Raspberries on a Leaf*, 1858. Oil on panel, 26.7 x 36.8 (10½ x 14½). Widener University, Alfred O. Deshong Collection, D.161 **124** William Michael Harnett, *The Old Violin*, 1886. Oil on canvas, 96.5 x 60 (38 x 23⅝). National Gallery of Art, Washington, Gift of Mr. and Mrs. Richard Mellon Scaife in honor of Paul Mellon 1993.15.1 **125** Frank Furness, Pennsylvania Academy of the Fine Arts, Philadelphia, 1871–76. Photo William H. Pierson, Jr. **126** Frank Furness, Provident Life and Trust Company Bank, Philadelphia, 1879. Library of Congress, Washington, D.C. **127** Thomas Eakins, *Miss Amelia van Buren*, *c.* 1891. Oil on canvas, 114.3 x 81.2 (45 x 32). Phillips Collection, Washington, D.C. **128** Thomas Eakins, *William Rush Carving His Allegorical Figure of the Schuylkill River*, 1876–77. Oil on canvas, 51.1 x 66.4 (20⅛ x 26⅛). Philadelphia Museum of Art. Gift of Mrs. Thomas Eakins and Miss Mary Adeline Williams, 1929 **129** Thomas Eakins, *The Gross Clinic*, 1875. Oil on canvas, 244 x 198 (96 x 78). Jefferson Medical College of Jefferson University, Philadelphia **130** Eadweard Muybridge, *Female Figure Hopping*, 1887. Sequence photography. Plate 185 from *Animal Locomotion*, Philadelphia, 1887. Cooper-Hewitt, National Design Museum, Smithsonian Institution, New York **131** James Abbott McNeill Whistler, *Symphony in White, No. I: The White Girl*, 1862. Oil on canvas, 213 x 107.9 (83⅞ x 42½). National Gallery of Art, Washington, D.C., Harris Whittemore Collection 1943.6.2 **132** Thomas Wilmer Dewing, *Summer*, *c.* 1890. Oil on canvas, 107 x 138 (42⅛ x 54⁵⁄₁₆). National Museum of American Art, Smithsonian Institution, Washington D.C. **133** James Abbott McNeill Whistler, *Nocturne in Black and Gold (The Falling Rocket)*, *c.* 1875. Oil on oak panel, 60 x 47 (23⅝ x 18½). Detroit Institute of Art, Dexter M. Ferry Jr. Fund **134** John Singer Sargent, *The Daughters of Edward D. Boit*, 1882. Oil on canvas, 221 x 221 (87 x 87). Museum of Fine Arts, Boston. Gift of Mary Louisa Boit, Florence D. Boit, Jane H. Boit, and Julia O. Boit, in memory of their father, Edward Darley Boit **135** John Singer Sargent, *Madame Pierre Gautreau (Madame X)*, 1884. Oil on canvas, 209.6 x 109.9 (82½ x 43¼). Metropolitan Museum of Art, New York. Arthur Hoppock Hearn Fund, 1916 **136** Mary Cassatt, *The Bath*, 1890–91. Drypoint and aquatint on cream laid paper, 36.8 x 26.3 (14½ x 10⅜). Art Institute of Chicago **137** Childe Hassam, *Rainy Day, Columbus Avenue, Boston*, 1885. Oil on canvas, 66.4 x 121.9 (26⅛ x 48). Toledo Museum of Art. Purchased with funds from the Florence Scott Libbey Bequest in memory of her father, Maurice A. Scott **138** Augustus Saint-Gaudens, Adams Memorial, Rock Creek Cemetery, Washington, D.C., 1886–91. Library of Congress, Washington, D.C. **139** Frank Duveneck, *He Lives By His Wits*, 1878. Oil on canvas, 113.7 x 71.1 (44¾ x 28). Private collection, Cincinnati, Ohio **140** William Merritt Chase, *In the Studio*, *c.* 1882. Oil on canvas, 71.2 x 101.9 (28¹⁄₁₆ x 40⅛). Brooklyn Museum of Art, New York. Gift of Mrs. Carll H. de Silver in memory of her husband **141** Henry Hobson Richardson, Trinity Church, Boston, 1872–77 **142** McKim, Mead & White, Low House, Bristol, Rhode Island, 1886–87. Photo Carnegie Arts of the United States Photographic Collection, University of Georgia **143** Bruce Price, Travis C. Van Buren Residence, Tuxedo Park, New York, 1886 **144** F. L. Ames Gate Lodge, North Easton, Massachusetts, 1880–81. From *Monographs on American Architecture, no. 3*, 1886 **145** Winslow Homer, *West Point, Prout's Neck*, 1900. Oil on canvas, 77.8 x 122.2 (30⁵⁄₁₆ x 48⅛). Sterling and Francine Clark Art Institute, Williamstown, Massachusetts **146** H. H. Richardson, Marshall Field Wholesale Store, Chicago, 1885–87. Photo Chicago Architectural Photographing Co. **147** Burnham & Root, Monadnock Building, Chicago, 1889–91. Photo Chicago Architectural Photographing Co. **148** Louis Sullivan, Wainwright Building, St. Louis, Missouri, 1890–91. Photo Hedrich Blessing **149** Louis Sullivan, Schlesinger & Mayer Store (now Carson Pirie Scott Store), Chicago, 1899–1904. Photo Chicago Architectural Photographing Co. **150** Louis Sullivan, detail of entrance of Schlesinger & Mayer Store (now Carson Pirie Scott Store), Chicago, 1899–1904. Photo Carnegie Arts of the United States Photographic Collection, University of Georgia **151** George Inness, *Home of the Heron*, 1893. Oil on canvas, 76.2 x 114.3 (30 x 45). Art Institute of Chicago. Edward B. Butler Collection **152** Albert Pinkham Ryder, *Jonah*, *c.* 1885–95. Canvas mounted on fiberboard, 69.2 x 87.3 (27¼ x 34⅜). National Museum of American Art, Smithsonian Institution, Washington, D.C., Gift of John Gellatly **153** Richard Morris Hunt, Biltmore, Asheville, North Carolina, 1889–95. Photo © The Biltmore Company 1991 **154** McKim, Mead & White, Boston Public Library, 1887–95. Photomechanical print, *c.* 1900. Library of Congress, Washington, D.C. **155** Court of Honor, The World's Columbian Exhibition, Chicago, 1893 **156** Louis Sullivan, "Golden Door," Transportation Building. The World's Columbian Exposition, Chicago, 1893. Chicago Historical Society **157** McKim, Mead & White, Plan of Pennsylvania Station, New York. From *Architectural Review*, May 1906 **158** McKim, Mead & White, Main Waiting Room at Pennsylvania Station, New York, 1906–10 **159** John Russell Pope, Jefferson Memorial, Washington, D.C., 1939–43. Library of Congress, Washington, D.C. **160** Stanton Macdonald-Wright, *Conception Synchromy*, 1914. Oil on canvas, 91.4 x 76.5 (36 x 30⅛). Hirshhorn Museum and Sculpture Garden, Smithsonian Institution, Gift of Joseph H. Hirshhorn, 1966. Courtesy Mrs. Stanton Macdonald-Wright **161** Frank Lloyd Wright, exterior of Larkin Building, Buffalo, New York, 1904. Frank Lloyd Wright Foundation. Photo Eileen Tweedy **162** Frank Lloyd Wright, interior of Larkin Building, Buffalo, New York, 1904. Photo Horizon Press, New York **163** Frank Lloyd Wright, Robie House, Chicago, 1908–10. Photo Carnegie Arts of the United States Photographic Collection, University of Georgia **164** Henry Mercer, interior of Mercer Museum, Doylestown, Pennsylvania, 1914. Library of Congress, Washington, D.C.

165 Greene and Greene, David B. Gamble House, Pasadena, California, 1908–9. Photo Richard Bryant/arcaid.co.uk **166** Robert Henri, *Eva Green*, 1907. Oil on canvas, 60.9 x 51.4 (24 x 20⅛). Wichita Art Museum, Wichita, Kansas. Roland P. Murdock Collection **167** Everett Shinn, *The Orchestra Pit, Old Proctor's Fifth Avenue Theater*, c. 1906–7. Oil on canvas, 43.8 x 49.5 (17¼ x 19½). Collection of Arthur G. Altschul **168** George Luks, *The Wrestlers*, 1905. Oil on canvas, 122.9 x 168.6 (48⅜ x 66⅜) Museum of Fine Arts, Boston. The Hayden Collection **169** John Sloan, *Sunday, Women Drying their Hair*, 1912. Oil on canvas, 66 x 81.3 (26 x 32). Addison Gallery of American Art, Phillips Academy, Andover, Massachusetts **170** Lewis W. Hine, *Untitled (Girl in a Cotton Mill)*, no date. Gelatin silver print, 19.1 x 24.1 (7½ x 9½). Collection of Susan Ehrens and Leland Rice **171** Maurice Prendergast, *The Promenade*, 1913. Oil on canvas, 76.2 x 86.4 (30 x 34). Whitney Museum of American Art, New York. Alexander M. Bing Bequest 60.10 **172** Arthur B. Davies, *Dream*, 1908. Oil on canvas, 45.7 x 76.2 (18 x 30). Metropolitan Museum of Art, New York. Gift of George A. Hearn, 1909 **173** William Glackens, *Chez Mouquin*, 1905. Oil on canvas, 121.9 x 99.1 (48 x 39). Art Institute of Chicago, Friends of American Art, 1925.295. Reproduced by John H. Surovek, Palm Beach, Florida. Representative of The William Glackens Estate **174** George Bellows, *Stag at Sharkey's*, 1909. Oil on canvas, 92 x 122.6 (36¼ x 48¼). Cleveland Museum of Art, 1995. Hinman B. Hurlbut Collection **175** Edward Hopper, *Morning in a City*, 1944. Oil on canvas, 111.8 x 152.4 (44 x 60). Williams College Museum of Art, Williamstown, Massachusetts **176** Edward Steichen, *The Flatiron*, 1904. Gumbichromate over gelatin silver print, 49.8 x 39.1 (19⅝ x 15⅜). Metropolitan Museum of Art, New York. Alfred Stieglitz Collection, 1933 33.43.44. Reprinted with permission of Joanna T. Steichen **177** Alfred Stieglitz, *The Steerage*, 1907. Library of Congress, Washington, D.C. © ARS, NY and DACS, London 2006 **178** Installation photograph of the Armory Show, New York National Guard's 69th Regiment, New York, 1913. Courtesy Museum of Modern Art, New York **179** Marcel Duchamp, *Nude Descending a Staircase, No. 2*, 1912. Oil on canvas, 147.3 x 88.9 (58 x 35). Philadelphia Museum of Art. Louise and Walter Arensberg Collection. © Succession Marcel Duchamp/ADAGP, Paris and DACS, London 2006 **180** Max Weber, *Rush Hour, New York*, 1915. Canvas, 92 x 76.9 (36¼ x 30¼). National Gallery of Art, Washington, D.C. Gift of the Avalon Foundation **181** Max Weber, *Chinese Restaurant*, 1915. Oil on canvas, 101.6 x 121.9 (40 x 48). Whitney Museum of American Art, New York, Purchase 31.382 **182** Marsden Hartley, *Portrait of a German Officer*, 1914. Oil on canvas, 173.4 x 105.1 (68¼ x 41⅜). Metropolitan Museum of Art, New York. Alfred Stieglitz Collection, 1949 (49.70.42) **183** Joseph Stella, *The Voice of the City of New York Interpreted: The Bridge*, 1920–22. Oil and tempera on canvas, 224.1 x 137.2 (88¼ x 54). Newark Museum. Purchase, 1937, Felix Fuld Bequest Fund. © ARS, NY and DACS, London 2006 **184** Charles Demuth, *Trees and Barns: Bermuda*, 1917. Watercolor over pencil on paper, 24.1 x 34.1 (9½ x 13 7/16). Williams College Museum of Art, Williamstown, Massachusetts. Bequest of Susan Watts Street **185** John Marin, *Maine Islands*, 1922. Watercolor on paper, 42.8 x 50.1 (16⅞ x 19¾). Phillips Collection, Washington, D.C. The artist through Alfred Stieglitz, The Intimate Gallery, New York, 1926. © ARS, NY and DACS, London 2006 **186** Arthur Dove, *Foghorns*, 1929. Oil on canvas, 45.7 x 66 (18 x 26). Colorado Springs Fine Arts Center. Anonymous gift **187** Man Ray, *Le Violin d'Ingres*, 1924. Retouched original photograph, 48.3 x 37.6 (19 1/16 x 14 13/16). Private collection. © Man Ray Trust/ADAGP, Paris and DACS, London 2006 **188** Charles Sheeler, *Classic Landscape*, 1931. Oil on canvas, 63.5 x 81.9 (25 x 32¼). National Gallery of Art, Washington, D.C. Collection of Barney A. Ebsworth 2000.39.2 **189** Charles Demuth, *The Figure 5 in Gold*, 1928. Oil on cardboard, 91.4 x 75.6 (36 x 29¾). Metropolitan Museum of Art, New York; Alfred Stieglitz Collection, 1949 **190** Edward Weston, *Tomato Field, Monterey Coast*, 1937. Collection Center for Creative Photography, © 1981 Arizona Board of Regents **191** Stuart Davis, *Egg Beater Number One*, 1927. Oil on canvas, 74 x 91.4 (29⅛ x 36). Whitney Museum of American Art, New York. Gift of Gertrude Vanderbilt Whitney. © Estate of Stuart Davis/VAGA, New York/DACS, London 2006 **192** Elie Nadelman, *Dancer*, 1920–24. Painted cherry wood, 71.8 high (28¼). Wadsworth Atheneum Museum of Art, Hartford, Connecticut. Gift of James L. Goodwin and Henry Sage Goodwin, 1958.2. Reproduced courtesy of the estate of Elie Nadelman **193** Gaston Lachaise, *Walking Woman*, 1922. Bronze, 47 high (18½), at base 16.5 x 13.7 (6½ x 5⅜). Museum of Modern Art. Gift of Abby Aldrich Rockefeller. 635.39 **194** Cass Gilbert, Woolworth Building, New York, 1910–13. Museum of the City of New York. Photo Irving Underhill, Underhill Collection **195** Hugh Ferris, *Studies for the Maximum Mass Permitted by the 1916 New York Zoning Law*, c. 1925. Stages 1 to 4. Carbon pencil, brush and black ink, stumped and varnished, 67 x 51 (26⅜ x 20 1/16). Cooper-Hewitt, National Design Museum, Smithsonian Institution, New York/Art Resource, New York. Gift of Mrs. Hugh Ferriss **196** Eliel Saarinen, Competition Entry for the Chicago Tribune Building, 1922. Library of Congress, Washington, D.C. **197** Walter Gropius and Adolf Meyer, Competition entry for the Chicago Tribune Building, 1922 **198** Georgia O'Keeffe, *Radiator Building—Night, New York, 1927*, 1927. Oil on canvas, 121.9 x 76.2 (48 x 30). Fisk University Galleries of Fine Arts, Nashville, Tennessee. Alfred Stieglitz Collection. © ARS, NY and DACS, London 2006 **199** Mark Rothko, *No. 9 (Dark over Light Earth/Violet and Yellow in Rose)*, 1954. 212.1 x 172.1 (83½ x 67¾). Museum of Contemporary Art, Los Angeles, Panza Collection. © 1998 Kate Rothko Prizel & Christopher Rothko/DACS 2006 **200** Paul Cret, Federal Reserve Bank, Washington, D.C., 1935. Photo Carnegie Arts of the United States Photographic Collection, University of Georgia **201** Public Works Administration, Williamsburg Houses, Brooklyn, New York, 1938. Library of Congress, Washington, D.C. **202** Howe & Lescaze, P.S.F.S. (Philadelphia Saving Fund Society) Building, Philadelphia, 1929–32. Library of Congress, Washington, D.C. **203** William van Alen, Chrysler Building, New York, 1928–30 **204** Queensbridge Houses Project, New York, 1939–40. Fairchild Aerial Surveys **205** John Steuart Curry, *Tornado over Kansas*, 1929. Oil on canvas, framed size 128.3 x 164.5 (50½ x 64¾). Hackley Picture Fund, Muskegon Museum of Art, Michigan. Accession 35.4 **206** Grant Wood, *American Gothic*, 1930. Oil on board, 74.3 x 62.4 (29⅞ x 24⅞). Art Institute of Chicago. Friends of American Art Collection. © Estate of Grant Wood/VAGA, New York/DACS, London 2006 **207** Thomas Hart Benton, *The Ballad of the Jealous Lover of Lone Green Valley*, 1934. Oil and tempera on canvas, transferred to aluminum panel, 107.3 x 135.2 (42½ x 53¼). Spencer Museum of Art, University of Kansas, Lawrence. Purchase, Elizabeth M. Watkins Fund. © T. H. Benton and R. P. Benton Testamentary Trusts/ VAGA, New York/DACS, London 2006 **208** Isaac Soyer, *Employment Agency*, 1937. Oil on canvas, 87 x 114.3 (34¼ x 45). Whitney Museum of American Art, New York. Purchase 37.44 **209** Ansel Adams, *Winter Sunrise, Sierra Nevada from Lone Pine, California*, 1944. Williams College Museum of Art, Williamstown, Massachusetts. © Ansel Adams Publishing Rights Trust/Corbis **210** John B. Flannagan, *Jonah and the Whale*, 1937. Cast stone, 76.2 x 27.9 x 12.7 (30 x 11 x 5). Virginia Museum of Fine Arts, Richmond. Gift of Curt Valentin **211** Adolph Gottlieb, *Pictogenic Fragments*, 1946. Oil on canvas, 91.8 x 76.5 (36⅛ x 30⅛). Hirshhorn Museum and Sculpture Garden, Smithsonian Institution. Gift of Joseph H. Hirshhorn, 1966. © Adolph and Esther Gottlieb Foundation/VAGA, New York/DACS, London 2006 **212** Isamu Noguchi, *Kouros*, 1945. Pink Georgia Marble, 304.8 (120). Metropolitan Museum of Art, New York. © 2006 The Isamu Noguchi Foundation and Garden Museum/Artists Rights Society (ARS), New York 2006 **213** Alexander Calder, *Yucca*, 1941. Sheet metal, wire, and paint, 186.7 x 58.4 x 50.8 (73½ x 23 x 20). Solomon R. Guggenheim Museum, Hilla Rebay Collection, 1971.71.1936. Photo Solomon R. Guggenheim Foundation, New York/Ellen Labenski. © ARS, NY and DACS, London 2006 **214** Arshile Gorky, *The Liver is the Cock's Comb*, 1944. Oil on canvas, 237.5 x 393.7 (93½ x 155). Albright-Knox Art Gallery, Buffalo, New York. Gift of Seymour H. Knox, 1952. © ADAGP, Paris and DACS, London 2006 **215** Jackson Pollock, *Untitled (Naked Man with Knife)*, c. 1938–40. Oil on canvas, 127 x 91.4 (50 x 36). Tate, London. © ARS, NY and DACS, London 2006 **216** Jackson Pollock, *Autumn Rhythm: No. 30, 1950*, 1950. Oil on canvas, 266.7 x 525.8 (105 x 207). Metropolitan Museum of Art, New York. © ARS, NY and DACS, London 2006 **217** Willem de Kooning, *Woman I*, 1950-52. Oil on canvas, 192.7 x 147.3 (75⅞ x 58). Museum of Modern Art, New York. Purchase, 1953. © The Willem de Kooning Foundation, New York/ARS, NY and DACS, London 2006 **218** Franz Kline, *New York, N.Y.*, 1953. Oil on canvas, 201 x 128.5 (79⅛ x 50 9/16). Albright-Knox Art Gallery, Buffalo, New York. Gift of Seymour H. Knox. © ARS, NY and DACS, London 2006 **219** David Smith, *Hudson River Landscape*, 1951. Welded painted steel and stainless steel, 126.8 x 187.3 x 42.1 (49 15/16 x 73¾ x 16 9/16). Whitney Museum of American Art, New York. Purchase 54.14. © Estate of David Smith/VAGA, New York/DACS, London 2006 **220** Robert Motherwell, *Elegy to the Spanish Republic LXX*, c. 1961. Oil on canvas, 175.3 x 289.6 (69 x 114). Metropolitan Museum of Art, New York. Anonymous gift, 1965. © Dedalus Foundation, Inc./VAGA, New York/DACS, London 2006 **221** Andrew Wyeth, *Christina's World*, 1948. Tempera on gessoed panel, 81.9 x 121.3 (32¼ x 47¾). Museum of Modern Art, New York. Purchase. © Andrew Wyeth **222** Frank Lloyd Wright, Solomon R. Guggenheim Museum, New York, 1956–59. Photo David Heald, The Solomon R. Guggenheim Foundation, New York **223** Gordon Bunshaft (Skidmore, Owings, & Merrill), Lever House, New York, 1950–52. Photo Carnegie Arts of the United States Photographic Collection, University of Georgia **224** Ludwig Mies van der Rohe and Philip Johnson, Seagram Building, New York, 1958. Photo Carnegie Arts of the United

States Photographic Collection, University of Georgia **225** Barnett Newman, *Vir Heroicus Sublimus*, 1950–51. Oil on canvas, 242.2 x 541.7 (95⅜ x 213¼). Museum of Modern Art, New York. © ARS, NY and DACS, London 2006 **226** Philip Johnson, Glass House, New Caanan, Connecticut, 1949. By permission of Philip Johnson/Alan Ritchie Architects **227** Frank Lloyd Wright, Fallingwater, Bear Run, Pennsylvania, 1935–39. Photo Scott Frances/Esto/arcaid.co.uk **228** Eero Saarinen, TWA Airline Terminal at JFK International Airport, New York, 1956. Erza Stoller **229** R. Buckminster Fuller, U. S. Pavilion, Montreal Expo, Montreal, Quebec, Canada, 1967. Photo Habegger Ltd, Thun **230** Louis Kahn, Richards Medical Research Laboratory, University of Pennsylvania, Philadelphia, 1957–64. © 1977 Louis I. Kahn Collection, University of Pennsylvania and Pensylvania Historical and Museum Commission **231** Louis Kahn, interior of Exeter Library, Philips Exeter Academy, Exeter, New Hampshire, 1965–71. Photo Grant Mudford **232** Robert Rauschenberg, *Factum I*, 1957. Combine painting, 156.2 x 90.8 (61½ x 35¾). Museum of Contemporary Art, Los Angeles. Panza Collection. © Robert Rauschenberg/VAGA, New York/DACS, London 2006; Robert Rauschenberg, *Factum II*, 1957. Combine Painting, 155.9 x 90.2 (61⅜ x 35½). Museum of Modern Art, New York. Purchase and an anonymous gift and Louise Reinhardt Smith Bequest. Courtesy Leo Castelli Gallery. © Robert Rauschenberg/VAGA, New York/DACS, London 2006 **233** Robert Rauschenberg, *Monogram*, 1955–59. Combine: oil and collage on canvas with objects, 106.7 x 160.6 x 163.8 (42 x 63¼ x 64½). Moderna Museet, Stockholm. © Robert Rauschenberg/VAGA, New York/DACS, London 2006 **234** Helen Frankenthaler, *Mountains and Sea*, 1952. Oil on canvas, 220 x 297.8 (86⅝ x 117¼). Collection of the artist (on loan to National Gallery of Art, Washington, D.C.). © 2006 Helen Frankenthaler **235** Morris Louis, *Tet*, 1958. Acrylic resin on canvas, 241.3 x 388.6 (95 x 153). Whitney Museum of American Art, New York. Purchase, with funds from the Friends of the Whitney Museum of American Art, 1965. © 1958 Morris Louis **236** Frank Stella, *Die Fahne Hoch*, 1959. Enamel on canvas, 308.6 x 185.4 (121½ x 73). Whitney Museum of American Art, New York. Gift of Mr. and Mrs. Eugene M. Schwartz. © ARS, NY and DACS, London 2006 **237** Jasper Johns, *Target with Four Faces*, 1955. Encaustic on newspaper and cloth over canvas surmounted by four tinted plaster faces in wood box with hinged front. Overall, with box open 85.3 x 66 x 7.6 (33⅝ x 26 x 3). Museum of Modern Art, New York. Gift of Mr. & Mrs. Robert C. Scull. © Jasper Johns/VAGA, New York/DACS, London 2006 **238** James Rosenquist, *President Elect*, 1960–61. Oil on masonite, 226.1 x 505.5 (84 x 144). Musée National d'Art Moderne, Centre Georges Pompidou, Paris. © James Rosenquist/VAGA, New York/DACS, London 2006 **239** Andy Warhol, *100 Cans*, 1962. Albright-Knox Art Gallery, Buffalo, New York. Gift of Seymour H. Knox, Jr., 1963. © The Andy Warhol Foundation for the Visual Arts, Inc./ARS, NY and DACS, London 2006 **240** Roy Lichtenstein, *Torpedo...Los!*, 1963. Oil on canvas, 173 x 203 (68 x 80). Private collection. © The Estate of Roy Lichtenstein/DACS 2006 **241** Claes Oldenburg, *Proposed Colossal Monument for Park Avenue, N.Y. C.— Good Humor Bar*, 1965. Crayon and watercolor, 60.3 x 45.7 (23¾ x 18). Collection of Carroll Janis, New York. Photo by Allan Finkelman, courtesy of Solomon R. Guggenheim Museum, New York **242** Norman Rockwell, *The Problem We All Live With*, 1964 (*Look*: 14 January 1964). Oil on canvas, 91.5 x 147.5 (36 x 58). Old Corner House Collection. Reproduced by permission of the Norman Rockwell Family Agency, Inc. **243** Robert Venturi, Vanna Venturi House, Chestnut Hill, Philadelphia, 1962. Venturi, Scott Brown and Associates, Inc. Photo Matt Wargo **244** Michael Graves, Portland Services Building, Portland, Oregon, 1980–82. Proto Acme photo **245** David Smith, *Cubi XVIII*, 1964. Stainless steel, 294 x 152 x 55 (115¾ x 59 13/16 x 21⅝). Museum of Fine Arts, Boston. Gift of Susan W. and Stephen D. Paine. © Estate of David Smith/VAGA, New York/DACS, London 2006 **246** George Segal, *Cinema*, 1963. Plaster, aluminated plexiglass and metal, 477.5 x 243.8 x 99 (188 x 96 x 39). Albright-Knox Art Gallery, Buffalo, New York. Gift of Seymour H. Knox, 1964. © The George and Helen Segal Foundation/DACS, London/VAGA, New York 2006 **247** Robert Morris, *Untitled (Standing Box)*, 1961. Solomon R. Guggenheim Museum, New York. © ARS, NY and DACS, London 2006 **248** Installation view of "Primary Structures" exhibition, Jewish Museum, New York, 1966. Left to right; Donald Judd, *Untitled*, 1966, and *Untitled*, 1966; Robert Morris, *Untitled (2 L-Beams)*, 1965; Robert Grosvenor, *Transoxiana*, 1965. Photo Jewish Museum, New York. Judd © Judd Foundation. Licensed by VAGA, New York/DACS, London 2006. Morris © ARS, NY and DACS, London 2006 **249** Donald Judd, *Untitled*, 1968. Plexiglass and high grade steel, 10 units, each 23 x 101.5 x 79 (9 1/16 x 39 15/16 x 31⅛), total height 437 (172 1/16). Froehlich Collection, Stuttgart. © Judd Foundation. Licensed by VAGA, New York/DACS, London 2006 **250** Judy Chicago, *The Dinner Party*, 1974–79, Painted porcelain and needlework, 1463 x 1463 x 91.4 (576 x 576 x 36). Collection of the artist. © ARS, NY and DACS, London 2006. **251** Joseph Kosuth, *White and Black*, 1966. Photostat on posterboard, each panel 1264.9 x 121.9 (498 x 48). AMAM 1974.39a-b. Allen Memorial Art Museum, Oberlin College, Oberlin, OH. Gift of Andy Warhol, 1974. © ARS, NY and DACS, London 2006 **252** Eva Hesse, *Hang Up*, 1966. Acrylic paint on cloth over wood, acrylic paint on cord over steel tube, 182.9 x 213.4 x 198.1 (72 x 84 x 78). Art Institute of Chicago, through prior gifts of Arthur Keating and Mr. and Mrs. Edward Morris. © The Estate of Eva Hesse. Hauser & Wirth, Zurich and London **253** Ed Ruscha, *Royal Road Test*, 1967. Book. Metropolitan Museum of Art. Stewart S. MacDermott Fund, 1970 (1970.590.5). © 1967 Edward Ruscha and Mason Williams. Photo Patrick Blackwell **254** Robert Smithson, *Spiral Jetty*, April 1970. Rocks, earth, and salt crystals. Great Salt Lake, Utah. Courtesy John Weber Gallery, New York **255** Maya Lin, Vietnam Veterans Memorial, Washington, D.C, 1981–84. Black polished granite wall. Each of two wings, 750 (295¼). Photo Washington Covention and Visitors Association **256** Cindy Sherman, *Untitled Film Still no. 7*, 1978. Courtesy of the Artist and Metro Pictures Gallery, New York **257** Bill Viola, *The Crossing*, 1996 (detail). Video/sound installation. Photo: Kira Perov. Photo courtesy Bill Viola Studio **258** Philip Pearlstein, *Male and Female Nudes with Red and Purple Drape*, 1968. Oil on canvas, 191.1 x 191.8 (75¼ x 75½). Hirshhorn Museum and Sculpture Garden, Smithsonian Institution, Washington, D.C., Gift of Joseph H. Hirshhorn, 1974. © Philip Pearlstein, Courtesy Betty Cunningham Gallery, New York **259** Neil Welliver, *Shadow*, 1977. Oil on canvas, 243.8 x 243.8 (96 x 96). Museum of Modern Art, New York, gift of Katherine Lustman-Findling, Jeffrey Lustman, Susan Lustman Katz, and William Ritman in memory of Dr. Seymour Lustman. Courtesy of Alexandre Gallery, New York **260** Barbara Kruger, *"Untitled" (I shop therefore I am)*, 1987. Private collection. Courtesy Mary Boone Gallery, New York **261** Hannah Wilke, *S.O.S.- Starification Object Series*, 1974. 28 b/w photographs; 12.7 x 17.8 (5 x 7) each. Performalist Self-Portraits with Les Wollam. Photo eeva-inkeri. © 2005 Marsie, Emanuelle, Damon, and Andrew Scharlatt. Courtesy Ronald Feldman Fine Arts, New York **262** Robert Gober, *The Subconscious Sink*, 1985. Plaster, wood, steel, wire lath, semi-gloss enamel paint, 228.6 x 210.8 x 66 (90 x 83 x 26). Walker Art Center, Minneapolis; Clinton and Della Walker Acquisition Fund and Jerome Foundation Purchase Fund for Emerging Artists, 1985.396. Courtesy of the artist **263** Robert Mapplethorpe, *Thomas*, 1987. © The Robert Mapplethorpe Foundation Courtesy Art + Commerce **264** Richard Serra, *Tilted Arc*, 1981. Weatherproof steel, 30.5 x 304.8 x 6.4 (12 x 120 x 2½). Installed Federal Plaza, New York City. Collection General Services Administration, Washington, D.C. Destroyed 1989 by U.S. Government. Photo Anne Chauvet **265** Daniel Joseph Martinez, *Museum Tags: Second Movement (Overture)*, 1993, Whitney Biennial, Whitney Museum of American Art, New York **266** Fred Wilson, *Mining the Museum*, 1992. Various media. Installation photograph of exhibition at Maryland Historical Society, Baltimore, 1992. © Fred Wilson, courtesy PaceWildenstein, New York **267** Duany Plater-Zyberk, Seaside, Florida, begun 1978. Resort Village. Photo Alex S. MacLean/Landslides **268** Bohlin Cywinski Jackson, Adirondack House, New York, 1987–92. Photo © Karl A. Backus, AIA. Courtesy Bohlin Cywinsky Jackson **269** Richard Meier, Getty Center, Los Angeles, 1984–97. Photo John Edward Linden/arcaid.co.uk **270** Eric Owen Moss, 3535 Hayden Avenue, Culver City, California 1997–98. Photo Tom Bonner **271** Frank Gehry, Guggenheim Museum, Bilbao, Spain, 1991–97. © FMGB Guggenheim Bilbao Museoa. Photograph by Erika Barahona-Ede. All rights reserved **272** Ann Hamilton, *corpus*, installation at MASS MoCA, December 13, 2003–October 17, 2004. Sound, paper, cloth, video, air, and electromechanical devices. Photograph by Thibault Jeanson. Courtesy Sean Kelly Gallery, New York **273** Louise Lawler, *Big*, 2002–03. Courtesy of the Artist and Metro Pictures Gallery, New York **274** Matthew Barney, *Cremaster Series* (detail), 1994–2001. Courtesy Gladstone Gallery, New York **275** Daniel Libeskind, World Trade Center Competition, 2003–04. © Archimation, sept-view. © studio Daniel Libeskind, skyline **276** Vincent Desiderio, *Pantocrator*, 2002. Oil on linen, triptych, overall, 210.5 x 492.8 (82⅞ x 194). Pennsylvania Academy of Fine Arts, Philadelphia. © Vincent Desiderio, courtesy Malborough Gallery, New York

Index